Prentice-Hall
Series in Automatic Computation
George Forsythe, editor

The SIMSCRIPT II Programming Language

P. J. Kiviat, R. Villanueva, and H. M. Markowitz

Prentice-Hall, Inc., Englewood Cliffs, New Jersey

Current printing (last digit):

10 9 8 7 6 5 4 3 2

13-810176-0
13-810168- X
Library of Congress Catalog Card Number: 76-85281
Printed in the United States of America

PRENTICE-HALL INTERNATIONAL, INC., *London*
PRENTICE-HALL OF AUSTRALIA, PTY. LTD., *Sydney*
PRENTICE-HALL OF CANADA LTD., *Toronto*
PRENTICE-HALL OF INDIA PRIVATE LTD., *New Delhi*
PRENTICE-HALL OF JAPAN, INC., *Tokyo*

Preface

SIMSCRIPT II is a rich and versatile computer programming language well suited to general programming problems, though designed originally for discrete-event simulation applications. This book, which describes the SIMSCRIPT II language, is divided into chapters corresponding to language "levels," which provide an organized path through the language:

Level 1: A simple teaching language designed to introduce programming concepts to nonprogrammers.

Level 2: A language roughly comparable in power with FORTRAN, but departing greatly from it in specific features.

Level 3: A language roughly comparable in power to ALGOL or PL/I, but again with many specific differences.

Level 4: That part of SIMSCRIPT II that contains the entity-attribute-set features of SIMSCRIPT. These features have been updated and augmented to provide a more powerful list-processing capability. This level also contains a number of new data types and programming features.

Level 5: The simulation-oriented part of SIMSCRIPT II, containing statements for time advance, event-processing, generation of statistical variates, and accumulation and analysis of simulation-generated data.

Except for some basic knowledge concerning what a computer is and what a programming language translator does, no prior computer education or programming knowledge on the reader's part has been assumed. As a result, the book will not have equal appeal to all readers. Professional programmers will find it slow reading at first; novices may wish it read more slowly. This is undoubtedly inevitable. To reduce the discomfort of either too slow or too rapid a pace, we suggest a selective path through the book. Sections that are unusually difficult or contain features of powerful but sophisticated use are marked with an asterisk, and should probably be skipped on first reading by all but the most professional of programmers—who will probably want to read these sections first to see what SIMSCRIPT II has to offer them.

Since SIMSCRIPT II is a "large" language, this is a lengthy volume. The authors hope its length is justified by the mode of presentation chosen, which meets the need for a teaching as well as a reference manual. Once the language has been mastered, the much shorter *The SIMSCRIPT II Programming Language: Reference Manual*, will be a useful guide.

RAND's principal interest in developing SIMSCRIPT II was to enhance the discrete-event simulation capability of both RAND and its clients. The language has been designed to facilitate the simulation of large, complex systems, and to reduce the total time spent in designing, programming, and testing simulation models. Since the simulation facilities are imbedded in a general-purpose programming language, all programs written in SIMSCRIPT II benefit in the same way.

Throughout design and development, user considerations were paramount. For this reason, the language is free-form and English-like. Also, its compiler is "forgiving," in the sense that it corrects a large percentage of user syntax errors and forces execution of every complete program that is submitted. The combination of a free-form, English-like language, a forgiving compiler, and forced program execution greatly reduces the number of times a program must be submitted to get it to perform properly. To make the process even more efficient, a number of debugging statements and newly designed program control features are also provided.

Design and development have been carried out in two stages: language design and compiler implementation. This book describes the SIMSCRIPT II language; RAND's IBM 360 implementation of the language is described in P. J. Kiviat, H. J. Shukiar, J. B. Urman, and R. Villanueva, *The SIMSCRIPT II Programming Language: IBM 360 Implementation*, The RAND Corporation, RM-5777-PR.

We owe a great deal to, and would like to acknowledge the contributions of, George Benedict and Bernard Hausner, who, as early members of the SIMSCRIPT II development project, did much of the basic compiler design and programming. Similarly, we are indebted to Joel Urman of the IBM Corporation, who, while programming all of the input/output and operating system interface routines for the IBM 360 compiler, influenced our language design.

We also wish to acknowledge the contributions of many friends—compiler writers, language designers, and programmers—who have interacted with us over the years. Some of their suggestions are reflected in the simulation-oriented sections of the language. Much of their influence is seen in the part of SIMSCRIPT II that can be called a "general programming language." We would like to thank Bob Balzer, John Buxton, John Laski, Howard Krasnow, John McNeley, Kristen Nygaard, and Paula Oldfather for their suggestions and criticisms. Should they, or any others, perceive glints of their own ideas in SIMSCRIPT II, they should not be surprised.

Thanks are also due to Herbert J. Shukiar for the many helpful suggestions he made while reviewing the manuscript and using early versions of the compiler, to Richard E. Stanton and Wayne Hamilton, who contributed to the programming of the SIMSCRIPT II system, and to Sally Anderson, who labored over the Index, for which we are truly grateful.

We are deeply indebted to our editor, Willard Harriss, to our patient and painstaking typists, Doris Corbin and Ruthlouise Acar, and to our illustrator, Doris Dong.

This project was sponsored by The RAND Corporation as part of the continuing program of research which it conducts for the United States Air Force.

PHILIP J. KIVIAT
RICHARD VILLANUEVA

Santa Monica, California
April 1969

Contents

3   SIMSCRIPT II: LEVEL 3   **131**

4   SIMSCRIPT II: LEVEL 4   **193**

Tables

Chapter 1

SIMSCRIPT II: LEVEL 1

1-00 INTRODUCTION

A *computer program* is a list of instructions that direct a computer to perform certain tasks. A *computer language* is a special set
of symbols that a *programmer* uses to write programs. A SIMSCRIPT II
program is a computer program written in the SIMSCRIPT II programming
language. Here is a simple example of a SIMSCRIPT II program:

```
READ X, Y AND Z
ADD X + Y TO Z
PRINT 1 LINE WITH Z AS FOLLOWS
  X + Y + Z = ****
STOP
```

This program consists of four SIMSCRIPT II *statements*. The statements
are instructions to (1) read the values of three *variables* called X,
Y, and Z from punched cards, (2) add these variables together, (3)
print the sum of the variables, along with the label X + Y + Z =, and
(4) stop. They illustrate the basic computer operations of input
(reading data), computation, and output (printing results).

1-01 VARIABLES

As shown in the above example, programs use names as identifiers
to refer to values of program variables. A program statement such as
ADD X TO Y means ADD the value of X TO the value of Y. Since computer
programs often require more than 26 variables (the letters A through
Z), SIMSCRIPT II uses combinations of letters and digits for variable
names.

A *name* is any combination of letters and digits — A through Z and 0 through 9 — that contains at least one letter. For example, X, COST, COSTOFX, SIZE, MAN3, PART1, ACCOUNTSRECEIVABLE, 5Y, and 1A are all legal names, whereas 27, 1, and 4.6 are not.

Variable names refer to numbers that are stored internally in the computer; variable values may be whole numbers (integers) or numbers with a fractional part (decimal numbers). The value of a variable X may be 0 or 125 or 16.72 or -0.00001 or whatever number we assign to it. From here on, whenever a variable name is used, it is with the understanding that it refers to the value of a variable (a number stored in the computer) and not to the name itself.

At the start of program execution, all variable values are set equal to zero. These variables are said to be "initialized to zero."

1-02 CONSTANTS

Program statements often use numbers directly, such as the "2" in ADD 2 TO SUM, or the number "3.14" in SUBTRACT 3.14 FROM VOLUME. These numbers are called *constants*. When used, they refer to their literal values; they do not represent other values.

Constants may take on the same numerical values as variables, and may be used interchangeably with them in all computations. Constants differ from variables in that their values cannot be changed. ADD 5 TO 4 is not a legal use of the constant 4, because it is tantamount to trying to change the value of 4 to 9; ADD 5 TO X is a legal use of the variable X and the constant 5.

Whole numbers and fractional numbers, signed or unsigned, are allowed as constants. Where equivalent representations of a number exist, they have the same value; 2.5, +2.5, and 002.500 all represent the same number. The statements ADD -1 TO COUNTER, ADD -1.00 TO COUNTER, and SUBTRACT 1 FROM COUNTER all have the same effect.

1-03 ARITHMETIC EXPRESSIONS

Arithmetic expressions are formed by combining variables and constants with *arithmetic operators*. The arithmetic operators are:

+ (add), – (subtract), * (multiply), / (divide), and ** (exponentiate).

Two of these operators, + and –, can be used as unary operators, that is, with a single variable or constant. The constants +1 and –1 are examples of the use of + and – as unary operators on the constant 1. All of the operators can be used as binary operators, that is, with two variables (or constants, or a variable and constant).

If we let A and B represent either a variable or a constant, then:

(1) + A and – A are uses of + and – as unary operators.

(2) A + B, A * B, A / B, A ** B are examples of arithmetic expressions that use binary operators.

The simplest expression consists of a single constant, or a single variable, perhaps preceded by a unary + or – operator. An expression, +A, may be written as A, with the unary plus implied. This is not possible, of course, with the unary minus operator.

All operators must be explicitly expressed, and no two operators can appear consecutively. For example, multiplication of the variables A and B must be written as A * B, and not AB. The latter would be interpreted as the value of a variable called AB. Addition of the expressions A and –B can be written as A + (–B) or A – B, but not A + –B.

This last example shows that parentheses must be used to separate unary and binary operators. Parentheses may also be used (1) to clarify the operations in an expression so as to make it more readable, or (2) specify the order in which the operations in an expression are to be performed. *Simple expressions* can be connected by any of the arithmetic operators (+, –, *, /, **) to form *compound expressions*. The "parentheses rule" states that expressions are evaluated from left to right, removing parentheses before applying operator hierarchy rules. Imbedded parentheses are evaluated from the inside out. Thus:

(1) a + (b*c) + d is evaluated by first computing (b*c) as the value of an intermediate expression e, and then by evaluating the expression a + e + d.

(2) a + (b/(c + (d*e))) is evaluated by first computing x = (d*e), then y = (c + x), then z = (b/y), then a + z.

Where parentheses are omitted, the hierarchy of operations is:

    a. Exponentiation   **

    b. Multiplication and division   * and /

    c. Addition and subtraction   + and -

This hierarchy specifies the order in which the different operations are performed relative to one another. Exponentiation is performed before multiplication or division, and either of these before addition or subtraction. For example, the expression A+B/C+D**E*F-G is taken to mean $A + (B/C) + (D^E * F) - G$. If precedence is not completely specified by these rules, the operator farthest to the left in the expression is performed first, as in A*B/C, which is computed as (A * B) / C.

    An expression is written as a string of variable names, constants, arithmetic operators, and parentheses. Any number of spaces from zero upward may be used to separate the parts of an expression, A+B, A+ B, A + B and A +B being treated identically. The exponentiation operator, **, is treated as a single unit and no spaces may appear between its two asterisks. Some example expressions are:

    (1)   PRICE   A variable is itself an expression.

    (2)   (PRICE)   Parentheses are optional.

    (3)   DUEIN-DUEOUT

    (4)   PRICE * QUANTITY

    (5)   PRICE * (ORDER-SALE)   Parentheses change precedence order.

    (6)   53   A constant is an expression.

    (7)   A + B + C + D

    (8)   X ** 2   In mathematical notation this is X^2.

    (9)   A + X ** 2 + X ** 4   Expressions (9) and (10) are identical.

  (10)   A + (X ** 2) + (X ** 4)

  (11)   X + Y/Z

  (12)   (X + Y) /Z   This is not the same as (11).

  (13)   -A**B   This means $-(A^B)$

1-04 LOGICAL EXPRESSIONS

Arithmetic expressions can be used with *relational operators* to form *logical expressions* that are either true or false. A logical expression is formed by joining two arithmetic expressions with a binary relational operator. The relational operators are:

=	equal
≠	not equal
<	less than
≤	less than or equal
>	greater than
≥	greater than or equal

When a logical expression is encountered during the execution of a program, current values of the variables in its arithmetic expressions are used to determine its truth or falsity. Thus, if X = 1 and Y = 0, the logical expression:

X = Y	is false
X ≥ Y	is true
X < Y	is false
X + Y = X * Y	is false

For readability in different contexts, SIMSCRIPT II provides alternate ways of writing logical expressions. Table 1-1 relates the mathematical symbol of each relational operator with keypunch symbols, English abbreviations, and "literary English" equivalents permitted in SIMSCRIPT II comparisons.

Unless the keypunch symbols (column 2) are used, each relational operator must be separated from the arithmetic expressions on either side by a parenthesis, or at least one blank column.

Typical logical expressions are:

```
a.  Y > 0
b.  AGE LESS THAN RETIREMENT
c.  CODE NOT EQUAL TO ZIP
d.  LEVEL LT THRESHOLD
e.  (FIXED + NUMBER * UNITS) GREATER THAN LOWBID
f.  A GE (B * X ** 2 + 3.57/C)
g.  (X ** 2 + Y ** 2) GREATER THAN Z ** 2
h.  X ** 2 + Y ** 2 > Z ** 2
```

Examples e and f demonstrate that arithmetic expressions may be enclosed in parentheses without changing their meaning. Examples g and h illustrate the use of equivalent forms of a relational operator.

Table 1-1

RELATIONAL OPERATORS

Mathematical Symbol	Keypunch Symbol	Permitted English Abbreviation	Permitted "Literary English" Equivalent
=	=	EQ	EQUAL TO EQUALS
$\neq$	$\neg$ =	NE	NOT EQUAL TO
<	<	LS LT	LESS THAN
>	>	GR GT	GREATER THAN
$\leq$	< =	LE	NO GREATER THAN NOT GREATER THAN
$\geq$	> =	GE	NO LESS THAN NOT LESS THAN

1-05 READING DATA FROM PUNCHED CARDS

Specific numerical values can be assigned to program variables by reading numbers (data) from punched cards. An example of the READ statement that does this is:

READ X, Y AND QUANTITY

X, Y, and QUANTITY are variable names. They are used in this state-ment in a *variable name list*.

In general a SIMSCRIPT II *list* consists of a string of quantities separated by either a comma, or the word AND, or a comma followed by the word AND. Some examples of lists as they might appear in READ statements are:

```
READ PRICE, QUANTITY, DISCOUNT
READ PLACE AND DISTANCE
READ NAME, DATE, PLACE AND TIME
READ NAME, AND DATE, PLACE AND TIME
```

The general form of a READ statement is

READ *variable name list*

When a READ statement is executed in a SIMSCRIPT II program, as many numbers are read from data cards as there are variable names listed in the statement. Successive numerical values are read and assigned to corresponding variables in the READ list. The numbers can be punched in the cards in integer or decimal form; e.g., the punched numbers 5, 5.0, and 5.000 are equivalent. Numbers must be separated from one another by at least one blank column. A number is also terminated at the end of a card.

Successive READ statements do not necessarily read new data cards, as SIMSCRIPT II programs treat input data as a continuous stream of numbers. The location of a number on a card is not considered.[†] The following example illustrates this "free form" concept.

READ X, Y, Z sets X = 3, Y = 2.1 and Z = 67.33 when each of these data card sets is read:

```
(1)  card 1    3.0 2.1  67.33
(2)  card 1    3.00
     card 2    2.1 67.33
(3)  card 1    3
     card 2                        2.1
     card 3            67.33
```

A READ statement is often the first statement encountered in a program, since it is typically used for assigning initial values to program variables. It is also used for reading in new values during the course of computation.

1-06 SKIPPING UNWANTED DATA

Data cards often contain more information than we want to use in a program, as, for example, when prepunched cards are obtained from someone else.

[†] The magnitude of a number is considered, however, since a digital computer can only store numbers that lie within a limited range and that have a limited precision. Numbers that exceed these limits cause SIMSCRIPT II programs to stop when an attempt is made to read them. These limits vary with the computer employed.

The SKIP statement simplifies the task of skipping unwanted data. A statement of the form

SKIP e FIELDS

passes over e data fields.[†] The arithmetic expression e is *rounded* to an integer if necessary. If it is negative it is treated as an error, causing the program to terminate. For example:

SKIP 2 FIELDS

skips the next two data fields, and

SKIP I/J FIELDS

skips no data fields if I/J is equal to 0, skips 3 fields if I/J = 2.7, or 4 fields if I/J = 4.13.

When a data field (value) is read, the SIMSCRIPT II system waits at the end of the data field in preparation for the next READ statement. Hence, when a field at the end of a data card is read, the card is retained until the next READ statement is executed.

The SKIP statement can also be used to skip the remainder of a current data card when it is written as

SKIP 1 CARD

An equivalent statement

START NEW CARD

or   START NEW INPUT[††] CARD

is somewhat more descriptive.

The SKIP card statement can be generalized to the form

SKIP e CARDS

or   SKIP e INPUT[††] CARDS

in which case the current data card and the following e - 1 cards are bypassed. If the expression (e) is zero, no cards are skipped; if it is negative, the program terminates with an error message.

[†]Data fields are contiguous strings of characters separated by at least one blank.

[††]The word INPUT is optional.

Example: SKIP 3 CARDS

ejects the current data card and skips over the next two data cards.

1-07 COMPUTING VARIABLE VALUES

One way of assigning a value to a variable is to use a READ statement. A second way is to use a LET statement. The general form of
this statement is:

LET *variable* = *arithmetic expression*

as in the statements

```
LET X = 0
LET X = (Y + 1)/15
LET PRICE = QUANTITY * SALESPRICE
LET BALANCE = STOCK - PURCHASE
LET UNITCOST = TOTALCOST/NUMBEROFUNITS
LET E = I*R
```

When a LET statement is executed, the current values of the
variables on the right of the equals symbol (=) are used to compute
the value of the arithmetic expression, and then this value is assigned
to the variable on the left of the equals symbol.

Used this way, the equals symbol is not a relational, but an
assignment operator. The statement LET X = Z + 1 says nothing about
the equality of the variable X and the expression Z + 1. It expresses
a command to evaluate Z + 1 and assign this quantity as the new value
of X. In the statement

LET X = Y*2

the value of the expression Y*2 is computed and assigned to the variable X. The previous value of X is replaced by the new value; and in

LET X = X + 1

a new value of X is computed by adding 1 to the current value of X
and assigning this new value to X.

1-08 SPECIALIZED COMPUTATION STATEMENTS

The ADD and SUBTRACT statements are used to add or subtract the

value of an arithmetic expression to or from a program variable.
Their action is like that of the LET statement, the difference being
that an arithmetic operator is incorporated in the statements themselves. The statement forms are:

ADD *arithmetic expression* TO *variable*
SUBTRACT *arithmetic expression* FROM *variable*

The statements are equivalent to the LET statements:

LET *variable* = *variable* + *arithmetic expression*
LET *variable* = *variable* - *arithmetic expression*

The ADD and SUBTRACT statements have the virtue of being easy to write
and straightforward in meaning. Some examples of these statements are:

ADD 1 TO COUNTER
ADD ITEM*COST TO BILL
SUBTRACT 3*X + 6*Y FROM Z
SUBTRACT COST FROM CASH

1-09 A PROGRAM ON CARDS AND THE FLOW OF COMPUTATION

SIMSCRIPT II programs are composed of sequences of conventionally
arranged symbols, some of which are standardized key words such as LET
and READ, others of which are programmer-constructed variable names
and numerical constants. The basic symbolic units that the SIMSCRIPT
II compiler recognizes in scanning program statements are names and
numbers, the special characters +, -, *, /, **, (,), ', ", >, <, |,
¢, ?, !, :, ;, %, ¬, &, $, @, #, =, _, and the punctuation marks
period, comma, and blank. Sections *1-01* and *1-02* described how names
and numbers are formed, and Secs. *1-03* and *1-04* illustrated the use
of some special characters. Except for passing mentions, the punc-
tuation marks period, comma, and blank have not been discussed.

SIMSCRIPT II ignores all periods written at the end of names and
numbers. While a programmer may wish to use terminal periods to
clarify or dress up a program, they are stripped from all names and
numbers during compilation. Thus the name JACK... is interpreted as
JACK, and the number 5. as 5; the names DOT, DOT., and DOT.., while
looking different, are all treated the same. Naturally, this does
not apply to periods used within numbers, as in 5.6 and 2457.856.

Commas are required in some places in SIMSCRIPT II statements and optional in others. In particular, they are required between items in a list of any sort, and optional after the logical condition of an IF statement.[†] Whenever a comma may or must be used in a particular statement, its use is made clear in the section of the text that defines the statement.

Since SIMSCRIPT II statements are not written in any specific format, but spaced across and between punched cards as a programmer wishes, blanks are needed to separate words (names, numbers, and key words) in statements. Two adjacent statement words must always be separated by at least one blank unless one of them is a special character. Thus, LET X = Y can be written as LET X=Y but not as LETX=Y, and IF (SIGN + 5) IS GREATER THAN DELTA can be written as IF(SIGN+5) IS GREATER THAN DELTA but not as IF(SIGN+5)ISGREATERTHANDELTA. Merely looking at a statement usually makes it clear whether a blank is needed or not. Since multiple blanks are treated as single blanks, blank characters can be freely used to improve the readability of statements, as many of the illustrations in this Report demonstrate.

Statements can be punched as desired on cards, with one slight restriction. A statement can be written on more than one card, or several statements can be written on the same card, but statement words (names, numbers, and key words) cannot be split between cards. The only effect of this is to restrict names and constants to 80 or fewer characters. (Remember that the exponentiation symbol ** is a single unit and cannot be split.)

Normally, computation proceeds from statement to statement in the order in which statements physically appear in a program deck. For example, in the four-statement example on p. 1, the program first executes the READ statement, then the ADD statement, then the PRINT statement, and halts when it reaches the STOP statement.

It is possible to alter the otherwise straightforward flow of computation by using a statement that directs a program to transfer

---

[†]This statement is discussed in Sec. 1-12.

to a *labeled statement* (Sec. *1-11*), or that specifies alternate program paths contingent on the truth of a logical expression (Sec. *1-12*).

A statement is labeled by putting a name before it, enclosed in
single quotation marks. This name is called the *label* of the statement, and reference to the label is understood as reference to the
statement. Thus in the program fragment

```
          'HERE' LET A = 0
               .
               .
               .
            GO TO HERE
               .
               .
               .
           GO TO THERE
               .
               .
               .
         'THERE' LET A = 0
```

the specified transfers are to the statements LET A=0.

A label name can be any combination of letters and/or digits.
Some possible label names are:

```
'READNEXTDATACARD'     'X'          '1'
'PARTI'                'SIMSCRIPT'  '12345'
'COMPUTE'              'A12345'
```

1-10 CLARIFYING COMMENTS IN A PROGRAM

Wherever it appears that a clarifying remark would be helpful to
the reader, a comment should be used. A *comment* is any string of
characters enclosed in double quotation marks ('') on the left, and
by either double quotation marks ('') or the end of a punched card on
the right. Comments can appear anywhere in a program except within
a word; they serve no function other than documentation. We strongly
recommend the liberal use of comments wherever the intent of a program
is not completely clear from its SIMSCRIPT II command description.

Some examples of comments are:

```
(a)   READ X, Y ''INDEPENDENT, DEPENDENT VARIABLES
(b)   READ DOLLARS ''CASH FLOW'', EQUITY ''PROPERTY VALUE
(c)   IF X EQUALS Y, ADD X TO SUM  GO TO SUCCESS
      OTHERWISE ''TAKE REMEDIAL ACTION'' GO TO ERROR
(d)   STOP ''NORMAL, NON-ERROR STOPPING POINT
```

1-11 CHANGING THE FLOW OF COMPUTATION BY DIRECT ORDER

If a label has been defined somewhere in a program, the flow of computation can be directed to the statement named by the label by using the GO TO statement. This statement is of the form

$$\text{GO TO 'label'} \quad \text{or} \quad \text{GO TO label}$$

Quotation marks are mandatory when a label is defined (i.e., when it appears in front of a referenced statement) but optional when used in a GO TO statement. The word TO is also optional. The ability to direct the flow of control within a computer program is often convenient and frequently essential. A simple example of a GO TO, based on the program of p. 1, reads a set of data cards instead of only one card:

```
'READ'   READ X, Y, Z
         ADD X + Y TO Z
         PRINT 1 LINE WITH Z AS FOLLOWS
            X + Y + Z = ****
         GO TO READ
```

The program returns to the statement labeled 'READ' after it has finished printing, and continues to do so until all the data cards are read, since an attempt to READ a card when there are no data automatically terminates a program.[†]

1-12 CHANGING THE FLOW OF COMPUTATION BY LOGICAL EXPRESSIONS

Additional power to transfer, namely "branching capability," is incorporated in a statement that enables a programmer to alter the flow of computation based on the current value of a logical expression. The IF statement tests the truth or falsity of a logical expression and branches (transfers) accordingly. The general form of the

---

[†]See Sec. 3-10; program termination on end-of-file.

IF statement is

   IF *logical expression   group of statements* REGARDLESS

as in

IF NUMBER > N**2   LET FLAG = 0 ADD NUMBER TO SUM REGARDLESS LET A = 5

If the logical expression is *true*, the statements between the logical
expression and the word REGARDLESS are executed, and then control is
passed to the statements following the word REGARDLESS. Of course,
a GO TO statement can be used to direct control to some other point
in the program if this is required. If the logical expression is
false, the expressions in this group are bypassed by control being
transferred to the statement following the word REGARDLESS. The
words ELSE, ALWAYS, and OTHERWISE may be used as equivalents for
REGARDLESS. Often the different shades of meaning effected by these
words aid in transmitting the intent of a program.

   A logical expression of the form *expression relational operator
expression* can be written as *expression* IS *relational operator expression*. Examples are:

        X IS EQUAL TO Y
        AGE IS GREATER THAN 27
        LIMIT IS NO LESS THAN LOW
        SPACE IS NOT EQUAL TO VOLUME

   The addition of the word IS improves the readability of IF statements. Some sample uses of IF statements are:

   (a) To read a set of 100 numbers and add together those
        numbers greater than 5.

```
'READ'      ADD 1 TO COUNT
            IF COUNT > 100 GO TO FINISH
            ELSE READ N
            IF N IS GREATER THAN 5   ADD N TO SUM
            REGARDLESS GO TO READ.
'FINISH'    ''CONTINUE PROGRAM''
```

   (b) To read a set of 200 numbers and sum all those numbers
        greater than or equal to 5 in one group, and all the
        numbers less than 5 in a second group.

```
'READ'      ADD 1 TO COUNT
            IF COUNT > 200 GO TO FINISH
            ELSE READ N
            IF N IS NO LESS THAN 5    ADD N TO SUM1
            GO TO READ
            OTHERWISE
            ADD N TO SUM2    GO TO READ
'FINISH'    ''CONTINUE PROGRAM''
```

(c) To test for an "end of data" signal.

```
'READ'      READ N
            IF N EQUALS 0    GO TO FINISH
            OTHERWISE ADD N TO SUM
            GO TO READ
'FINISH'    PRINT 1 LINE WITH SUM AS FOLLOWS
            ***.** IS THE VALUE OF THE SUM.
            STOP
```

(d) A data processing test.

```
IF SUM IS LESS THAN SUMTOTAL
            IF X IS GREATER THAN HI GO TO H
            ELSE IF X IS LESS THAN LO GO TO L
                    OTHERWISE
OTHERWISE
ADD X TO SUM
```

This program is represented in flow chart form as:

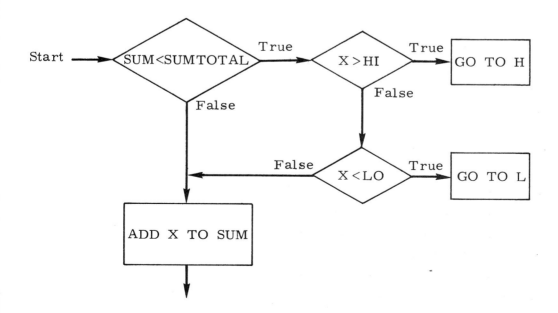

As shown, IF statements can be "nested" by putting IF statements within statement groups of other IF statements. When this is done, a simple indenting and alignment of statements is advised to make the flow of control clear. The following program illustrates this; notice how each IF is aligned in a card column with the OTHERWISE (or ELSE or ALWAYS or REGARDLESS) that matches it.

```
IF X IS LESS THAN A
    IF Y IS LESS THAN B
        LET Z = A + B
    REGARDLESS
            GO TO 'A1'
OTHERWISE
GO TO 'A2'
```

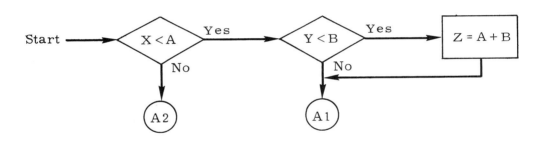

Grammatically, the IF statement often seems to ask for a comma as in: IF X = Y, GO TO 'READ' or IF AGE EXCEEDS LIMIT, STOP. For this reason, an *optional* comma is permitted in the IF statement after the logical expression.

The true branch of the IF statement, i.e., the statement group executed if the comparison is true, can contain any number of SIMSCRIPT II statements. The only qualification on this group is that it must be self-contained with respect to other IF statements that appear within it, since each IF is matched with a corresponding OTHERWISE, as left parentheses are matched with right parentheses in an expression. An unmatched, or out-of-place OTHERWISE can change the meaning of a program. In the above examples containing nested IF statements, note that each IF has a matching OTHERWISE.

1-13 DISPLAYING THE RESULTS OF COMPUTATION

The PRINT statement has been used in several examples to display titles and labeled computational results. This statement has two major forms, either

PRINT i LINES AS FOLLOWS

or

PRINT i LINES WITH *arithmetic expression list* AS FOLLOWS

followed by i lines of descriptive text and format information. The line count i is, of course, a positive integer constant. If i = 1 the word LINE can be used instead of LINES. Equivalents for the AS FOLLOWS portion of the statement are THUS, and LIKE THIS. Sample PRINT statements are:

```
PRINT 2 LINES AS FOLLOWS
PRINT 1 LINE THUS
PRINT 2 LINES WITH X AND Y LIKE THIS
PRINT 4 LINES WITH X, X**2, Y, Y**2, X*Y, N AS FOLLOWS
```

The i lines, called *format lines*, that follow the PRINT statement can contain as many as 80 columns of textual information and formats for arithmetic expressions whose values are to be printed. There can be either text, or formats, or both in any format line. The length of a format line is measured as the number of columns from column 1 to the last nonblank column in the line.

Textual information appearing in format lines is printed exactly as it appears; thus, the statement

```
PRINT 1 LINE AS FOLLOWS
......THIS IS A SAMPLE FORMAT LINE......
```

prints a single line of output containing the above message. The statement,

```
PRINT 2 LINES THUS
          SUMMARY REPORT
INCOME DATA                    EXPENSE DATA
```

expressed as ***|**, and six contiguous one-digit integer fields as
||||||.

Blank lines can be inserted between PRINT statements by the SKIP statement, or blank format lines can be used. If e is any arithmetic expression, then the statement

SKIP e OUTPUT[†] LINES

skips a number of lines equal to the value of e rounded to an integer, as in

```
SKIP 1 OUTPUT LINE
SKIP N LINES
SKIP X + 3*Y OUTPUT LINES
```

If e is negative, it is treated as zero. At most, one complete page will be skipped.

Pages can be ejected before printing, so that the next PRINT statement starts at the top of a new page, by using the statement

START NEW PAGE

The PRINT, SKIP, and START NEW PAGE statements can be used together to produce attractively labeled output reports.

As a final caution, note that whereas a PRINT statement can appear on a card with previous statements, each of its following format lines must appear on a separate card. This is illustrated in the following program:

```
'READ'   READ X    IF X IS LESS THAN 10, GO TO 'READ'
                    ELSE PRINT 1 LINE WITH X AS FOLLOWS
          THE VALUE OF X IS ***.**
                    IF X EQUALS 9999, STOP
                    OTHERWISE GO TO READ
```

1-14 THE LOGICAL END OF A PROGRAM

The STOP statement is used to terminate a program. Since there may be many STOP statements in a program, it need not appear physically

---

[†]The word OUTPUT is optional. In the SKIP and START NEW statements the following rules apply: (1) if INPUT or OUTPUT is specified the words CARDS and LINES are treated as synonyms, the input or output function stated is performed; (2) if neither INPUT nor OUTPUT is specified, direction is taken from the words CARDS and LINES; CARDS specifies input, LINES specifies OUTPUT.

at the end of a program deck. The following program illustrates the use of the STOP statement in conjunction with two IF statements:

```
'BACK' READ N
IF N EQUALS 0, STOP
OTHERWISE ADD N TO SUMOFN
ADD 1 TO TOTAL
PRINT 1 LINE WITH SUMOFN/TOTAL LIKE THIS
   AVERAGE N SO FAR = ***.***
IF TOTAL EQUALS 1000, STOP
ELSE GO 'BACK'
```

1-15   THE PHYSICAL END OF A PROGRAM

The last statement in every SIMSCRIPT II program must be END. It signals that the entire source program has been read. The example programs at the end of this section illustrate the use of the END statement.

1-16   SOME SAMPLE SIMSCRIPT II, LEVEL 1 PROGRAMS

The following programs illustrate the SIMSCRIPT II concepts and statements presented in this section. The programs are printed as they might appear on punched cards before being submitted to a computer for processing. Since the flexibility of the SIMSCRIPT II program statement format makes many card layouts possible, the formats used in these examples are only some of many possible choices.

1-16-1   Finding the Maximum and Minimum of a Set of Numbers

N numbers are on punched cards. The following program reads these numbers, and determines their minimum and maximum. When all the numbers have been processed, N, their average value, and their minimum and maximum values, are printed.

Notice that since the range of the numbers is unknown, the variable MAX is initialized to a large negative number and MIN to a large positive number to ensure that the largest and smallest data values are retained.

```
''THIS PROGRAM COMPUTES THE AVERAGE AND THE MINIMUM AND MAXIMUM OF
''A SET OF NUMBERS ON PUNCHED CARDS
    LET MAX=-99999.99999      LET MIN=-MAX
    READ N          '' THE NUMBER OF DATA OBSERVATIONS
'R' READ X          '' A DATA OBSERVATION
    ADD X TO SUM
    IF X IS GREATER THAN MAX, LET MAX=X  REGARDLESS
    IF X IS LESS THAN MIN, LET MIN=X  REGARDLESS
    ADD 1 TO COUNTER
    IF COUNTER IS LESS THAN N, GO TO R  ELSE
    START NEW PAGE
    PRINT 3 LINES WITH N,SUM/N,MAX,MIN AS FOLLOWS
        THE AVERAGE VALUE OF **** NUMBERS IS ****.****
        THE MAXIMUM VALUE IS *****.*****
        THE MINIMUM VALUE IS *****.*****

    STOP END
```

1-16-2 *A Simple Accounting System*

The following program processes sales and inventory receipt transactions in a prototype accounting system. Each transaction card contains a dollar amount, an account code for the debit account, and an account code for the credit account. A zero dollar amount signals the end of transactions.

At the statement labeled 'START', the 8 accounts and 2 totals are set to their last month's values by reading these values from punched cards. At the end of the program, updated values of these 10 variables are printed for use in next month's accounting run.

Each transaction is processed through one debit account; the sequence of IF statements after the label DEBIT direct the computation based on the debit code number (CODE1). Note the PRINT statement at ERR1, which catches a mispunched debit code, i.e., a code other than 1, 2, 3, 4, or 5. Each transaction is similarly processed through a credit account.

When all the transaction cards have been read, a balance sheet and the monthly balances are printed. Note the different uses of the PRINT statement: to print titles and headings, and to print labeled variable values.

```
''      THIS PROGRAM IS A SIMPLE ACCOUNTING SYSTEM
'START'    READ CASH,RECEIVABLES,INVENTORY,PLANT,EQUIPMENT,TOTALASSETS,PAYABLES,
              LOAN,EQUITY,TOTALLIABILITIES
'READ'     READ DOLLARS,CODE1,CODE2
'TEST'     IF DOLLARS EQUALS 0, GO TO 'FINISHED'
           OTHERWISE ADD 1 TO TRANSACTIONCOUNTER
'DEBIT'    IF CODE1 EQUALS 1, ADD DOLLARS TO CASH  GO TO TOTALD  ELSE
           IF CODE1 EQUALS 2, ADD DOLLARS TO RECEIVABLES  GO TO TOTALD  ELSE
           IF CODE1 EQUALS 3, ADD DOLLARS TO INVENTORY  GO TO TOTALD  ELSE
           IF CODE1 EQUALS 4, ADD DOLLARS TO PLANT  GO TO TOTALD  ELSE
           IF CODE1 EQUALS 5, ADD DOLLARS TO EQUIPMENT  GO TO TOTALD  ELSE
'ERR1'     PRINT 1 LINE WITH TRANSACTIONCOUNTER AND CODE1 AS FOLLOWS
                    TRANSACTION **** HAD CODE1 PUNCHED AS ***
           STOP
'TOTALD'   ADD DOLLARS TO TOTALASSETS
'CREDIT'   IF CODE2 EQUALS 1, SUBTRACT DOLLARS FROM PAYABLES  GO TO TOTALC  ELSE
           IF CODE2 EQUALS 2, SUBTRACT DOLLARS FROM LOAN  GO TO TOTALC  ELSE
           IF CODE2 EQUALS 3, SUBTRACT DOLLARS FROM EQUITY  GO TO TOTALC  ELSE
'ERR2'     PRINT 1 LINE WITH TRANSACTIONCOUNTER AND CODE2 AS FOLLOWS
                    TRANSACTION **** HAD CODE2 PUNCHED AS ***
           STOP
'TOTALC'   SUBTRACT DOLLARS FROM TOTALLIABILITIES
           GO TO 'READ'
'FINISHED' START NEW PAGE  PRINT 1 LINE WITH TRANSACTIONCOUNTER THUS
                ***** TRANSACTIONS WERE PROCESSED THIS MONTH
           SKIP 5 OUTPUT LINES
           PRINT 9 LINES CONTAINING CASH,PAYABLES,RECEIVABLES,LOAN,INVENTORY,
                          PLANT,EQUITY,EQUIPMENT,TOTALASSETS
                          AND TOTALLIABILITIES AS FOLLOWS
                    ASSETS            LIABILITIES
               CURRENT ASSETS       CURRENT LIABILITIES
                  CASH      $*****      ACCOUNTS PAYABLE $*****
                  RECEIVABLES  *****    LOAN              *****
                  INVENTORY    *****
               FIXED ASSETS         EQUITY
                  PLANT     $*****      EQUITY          $*****
                  EQUIPMENT    *****
                  TOTAL ASSETS $*****  TOTAL LIABILITIES $*****
           SKIP 3 OUTPUT LINES
           PRINT 2 LINES WITH CASH,RECEIVABLES,INVENTORY,PLANT,EQUIPMENT,
                          TOTALASSETS,PAYABLES,LOAN,EQUITY AND
                          TOTALLIABILITIES AS FOLLOWS
*****  *****  *****  *****  *****  *****
*****  *****  *****  *****
           STOP  END
```

1-16-3 Computing the Value of π

The number $\pi = \frac{22}{7} \simeq 3.14159$ recurs constantly in engineering and scientific computations. The following program uses an "infinite series" representation of π to compute its value to four-decimal-place accuracy. The specific formula used is

$$\frac{\pi}{4} = 1 - \frac{1}{3} + \frac{1}{5} - \frac{1}{7} + \frac{1}{9} - \ldots$$

The program starts by initializing the variables SIGN and DIVISOR to their starting value of 1. The variable PI is automatically initialized to 0 at the start of the program.

At the label TERM the value of the next term (1/DIVISOR) is computed. At the label TEST, a test is made to determine if enough terms have been computed to give sufficient accuracy, using the fact that any term with value less than 0.00025 will add, or subtract, less than 0.001 to, or from, the sum of the series when it is multiplied by 4 to evaluate π.

If the term is greater than or equal to 0.00025, the sign of the term, which alternates between +1 and -1, is computed and the value of the term is added to the variable PI. The program then returns to the label TERM to continue the summation of the series.

When the term is less than 0.00025, the program transfers to the label FINISHED, where the expression PI*4 is printed.

```
''      THIS PROGRAM COMPUTES THE VALUE OF PI TO AN ACCURACY OF 0.001
'INITIALIZATION'   LET SIGN=1     LET DIVISOR=1
'TERM'             LET TERM=1/DIVISOR
'TEST'             IF TERM IS LESS THAN 0.00025,PRINT 1 LINE WITH PI*4 LIKE THIS
                        THE VALUE OF PI IS *.*****
                   STOP
                   OTHERWISE  ADD SIGN*TERM TO PI
                              LET SIGN=-SIGN
                              ADD 2 TO DIVISOR
                              GO TO 'TERM'
                   END
```

1-16-4 Computing the Square Root of a Number

The square root of a number is a commonly needed value. A higher level of SIMSCRIPT II provides a facility for automatically computing square roots, but the following program ignores the facility and uses a mathematical formula to evaluate the square root of a number to a specified accuracy. The formula is an iterative one, with each succeeding value of the approximation to the square root generating a better approximation. The iterative formula is

$$x_{i+1} = \frac{1}{2}\left(x_i + \frac{N}{x_i}\right)$$

where i is the number of the iteration and x_i is the approximation to the square root of N.

The program is designed to be executed repeatedly for several values of N. It starts by printing a title for the table of square roots it is going to generate. At the label READ, the values of N and the required accuracy EPSILON are read from punched cards, and a test is made to see if this N, with a value of 0, is a signal that there are no more data cards.

If N is greater than 0, a first guess at the square root of N is made at the label GUESS. This guess sets x_i, here called SQRT1, equal to N/2. The iteration starts at the statement label 'LOOP', where $x_{i+1} = \frac{1}{2}$ (x_i + N/x_i) is computed; x_{i+1} is called SQRT.

If DELTA, the difference between SQRT1 and SQRT, is less than EPSILON, the required accuracy has been achieved. The values of N SQRT and EPSILON are then printed and control is transferred to 'READ' to get a new data card.

As long as DELTA remains greater than or equal to EPSILON, another iteration is required. For this, x_i is set equal to x_{i+1} by setting SQRT1 equal to SQRT and returning control to 'LOOP'. At 'LOOP' a new approximation to the square root is computed. The sequence of approximations converges to within EPSILON of the correct value of the square root of N.

A second program computes a square root in the same way, but uses a different procedure for obtaining successive values of N. This program illustrates the use of an iteration sequence, a series of numbers that are equally spaced between two values, to control the computation section of the program. This important concept is elaborated in Level 2.

```
'' THIS PROGRAM COMPUTES THE SQUARE ROOT OF N TO AN ACCURACY OF EPSILON
'' N IS A POSITIVE NUMBER,  EPSILON IS GREATER THAN 0 AND LESS THAN 0.00001

          PRINT 1 LINE AS FOLLOWS
                N      SQUARE ROOT OF N      EPSILON
'READ'    READ N,EPSILON
          IF N EQUALS 0, STOP    OTHERWISE
          LET SQRT1=N/2
'LOOP'    LET SQRT=(SQRT1 + N/SQRT1)/2
          LET DELTA=SQRT1-SQRT
          '' USE THE ABSOLUTE (+) VALUE OF DELTA IN THE TEST
          IF DELTA IS LESS THAN 0,LET DELTA=-DELTA
          REGARDLESS  IF DELTA IS LESS THAN EPSILON,
          GO TO 'PRINT'
          OTHERWISE  LET SQRT1=SQRT
          GO TO 'LOOP'
'PRINT'   PRINT 1 LINE WITH N,SQRT,EPSILON AS FOLLOWS
               ***        **.****        *.****
          GO TO 'READ'
          END

'' THIS PROGRAM COMPUTES THE SQUARE ROOT OF N TO AN ACCURACY OF EPSILON
'' THE DATA IS NOW IN THE FORM OF A LOWER AND UPPER VALUE OF N AND AN
'' INCREMENT BY WHICH THE LOWER VALUE IS ADVANCED TO THE UPPER VALUE.
'' THE VALUE OF EPSILON IS CONSTANT FOR ALL VALUES OF N

          READ N,NINCREMENT,NLAST,EPSILON
          PRINT 1 LINE CONTAINING EPSILON AS FOLLOWS
                  N      SQUARE ROOT OF N      ACCURACY=*.****
'NEXTN'   LET SQRT1=N/2
'LOOP'    LET SQRT=(SQRT1 + N/SQRT1)/2
          LET DELTA=SQRT1-SQRT
          '' USE THE ABSOLUTE (+) VALUE OF DELTA IN THE TEST
          IF DELTA IS LESS THAN 0,  LET DELTA=-DELTA
          REGARDLESS  IF DELTA IS LESS THAN EPSILON, GO TO 'PRINT'
          OTHERWISE  LET SQRT1=SQRT  GO TO 'LOOP'
'PRINT'   PRINT 1 LINE WITH N AND SQRT LIKE THIS
               ***           **.****
          IF N EQUALS NLAST, STOP
          OTHERWISE ADD NINCREMENT TO N  GO TO 'NEXTN'
          END
```

1-16-5 A Program for Regression Analysis

Computer programs are often used to analyze data by statistical techniques such as regression analysis. The following program determines the coefficients a_0 and a_1 of the regression equation

$$y_i = a_0 + a_1 x_i$$

using the formulae

$$a_1 = \frac{N\sum_{i=1}^{N}x_i y_i - \sum_{i=1}^{N}x_i \sum_{i=1}^{N}y_i}{N\sum_{i=1}^{N}x_i^2 - \left(\sum_{i=1}^{N}x_i\right)^2}$$

$$a_0 = \frac{\sum_{i=1}^{N}y_i - a_1\sum_{i=1}^{N}x_i}{N}$$

where

N is the number of observations of x_i and y_i

$\sum_{i=1}^{N}x_i$ represents the sum of all the x_i

$\sum_{i=1}^{N}x_i^2$ represents the sum of all the x_i^2

etc.

```
''  THIS PROGRAM COMPUTES THE COEFFICIENTS OF THE REGRESSION EQUATION
''  Y=AO + A1*X . OBSERVATIONS OF X AND Y ARE ON PUNCHED CARDS

'OBS'     READ N
'READ'    READ X,Y
          ADD X TO SUMX
          ADD X**2 TO SUMXX
          ADD Y TO SUMY
          ADD Y**2 TO SUMYY
          ADD X*Y TO SUMXY
          ADD 1 TO NUMBEROFOBSERVATIONS
'TEST'    IF NUMBEROFOBSERVATIONS IS LESS THAN N,  GO TO 'READ'
              OTHERWISE
          LET A1=(N*SUMXY-SUMX*SUMY)/(N*SUMXX-SUMX**2)
          LET AO=(SUMY-A1*SUMX)/N
          PRINT 1 LINE WITH AO AND A1 AS FOLLOWS
                    THE REGRESSION EQUATION IS Y=***.*** + ***.*** X
          STOP      END
```

Chapter 2

SIMSCRIPT II: LEVEL 2

2-00 *VARIABLE AND LABEL NAMES REVISITED*

Chapter 1 defines variable and label names separately; a variable
is any combination of letters and digits that contains at least one
letter, and a label is any combination of letters and digits without
the "at least one letter" constraint. Another way of stating this is
to define a *name* as a combination of letters and digits and an *integer*
as a combination of digits, and allow a *variable name* to look like a
name and a *label* like a name or an integer. It is easy to expand
these rules slightly to permit more readable programs by incorporating
periods into the definitions of names and labels.

Let a *name* be any combination of letters, digits, and periods that
contains at least one letter or two or more nonterminal periods. Let
a *constant* be any combination of digits, possibly containing one
period. Then a variable name must look like a name and a label can
look like a name or a constant. This allows variables to be distinguished from numbers while maintaining the widest latitude in
name formation.

Some examples of possible variable and label names are:

Variable names	Label names
PART.NUMBER	LABEL
NUMBER.OF.PARTS	SECTION.1
TOTAL	1
SECTION.....1	12345
.PAGE	12.345
3.7.6	PART.4
.....6	ERROR

While the fact has already been mentioned, it cannot hurt to emphasize once more that terminal periods cannot be used in forming names. The names X, X.., and X.... all represent the same variable value; the labels '5' and '5.' are identical.

While SIMSCRIPT II does not prohibit the use of any particular words[†] or names, it does define a number of special words that it recognizes in certain contexts. A SIMSCRIPT II programmer can guard against using any of these names incorrectly by remembering them or the special naming conventions used for them.[††] Each of these names either begins with a letter followed by a period (as in the name L.27) or ends with a period followed by a letter (as in the name SQRT.F). A programmer can regard these rules as defining prohibited word-forms or as guides that say, "Check with the Appendix whenever you want to use a name of this form."

2-01 *VARIABLE MODES*

So far no explicit restrictions have been placed on the magnitude or precision of the numbers represented by variable names.[†††] Complete freedom from concern over the expression of numerical quantities can be a good thing; however, programs can often be more efficiently written if a programmer places some restrictions on the type of numbers a program deals with.

A *variable definition statement* is a declarative message from a programmer to the SIMSCRIPT II compiler. Definition statements declare that variables have certain properties; the compiler uses this information to generate efficient codes.

[†]The one exception is the word AND, which should not be used as a name.

[††]These words are listed in the Appendix.

[†††]Particular implementations of SIMSCRIPT II on different computers will of necessity impose restrictions due to characteristics of the computer hardware used in the implementation. Thus you might be able to express some numbers (very large or very small) on some computers, but not on others. These limitations are seen by a programmer in the magnitude and precision of the numbers he can express, and in the results of his computations.

SIMSCRIPT II variables can be declared as INTEGER or REAL. Variables declared as INTEGER represent whole numbers; variables declared as REAL represent numbers that can have fractional values. The numbers 56, -6745, 91, -1, and 0 are INTEGER valued; the numbers 56.0, 35.7846, 0.999876, -27.45, and 0.0 are REAL valued. Note that a whole number such as 56 can be expressed either as INTEGER or REAL. It is the possibility of a fractional value, and not any particular value, that makes a variable require a REAL definition.

Every SIMSCRIPT II program has a *preamble* that contains variable definition information. Often this preamble is not written, but implied, as in Level 1, where all variables are treated as REAL. Whenever a variable has a property that differs from one that SIMSCRIPT II assumes, a definition statement must be used. Programs containing a preamble must begin with the one-word statement PREAMBLE. Following variable definition statements must be marked off from succeeding program statements by the word END. (See examples in Sec. *2-04.*)

As stated, the *mode* of a variable (whether it is INTEGER or REAL) is assumed REAL unless otherwise specified; the "normal form" of SIMSCRIPT II variables is decimal numbers.

The assumed REAL condition can be changed by using the statement

NORMALLY, MODE IS INTEGER

This statement resets the compiler's "background conditions" so that all following program variables are assumed INTEGER unless otherwise specified. The comma after the word NORMALLY is optional; the word IS can be replaced by the equals symbol (=). Thus, the above statement can be written as

NORMALLY MODE IS INTEGER
or   NORMALLY MODE = INTEGER

Individual variables that differ from the implied or NORMALLY defined mode can have their mode specified in a DEFINE statement. This statement lists one or more variable names and defines their common mode. The statement

DEFINE X, Y, Z, PARTNER.ONE AND ME AS INTEGER VARIABLES

illustrates the way in which the DEFINE statement is used to declare
that the five variables X, Y, Z, PARTNER.ONE, and ME are all INTEGER
valued. If the background conditions were INTEGER, the word REAL
could be used to define the variables as REAL.

The DEFINE statement has a number of alternative forms; the only
words that must appear in it are DEFINE, the variable names being
defined, AS, and the word VARIABLE or VARIABLES. The words A, AN,
INTEGER, and REAL are included when needed. Some examples of the
DEFINE statement are:

```
DEFINE X AS A REAL VARIABLE
DEFINE X AS AN INTEGER VARIABLE
DEFINE X AND Y AS INTEGER VARIABLES
DEFINE X, Y, Z AS VARIABLES
DEFINE X AS A VARIABLE
```

In later sections, the NORMALLY and DEFINE statements are expanded to include more than mode definition, as mode is but one of
several properties that can be used to describe variables. These
descriptors will be added to the mode specification; sometimes mixes
of NORMALLY and DEFINE statements will be used in a program's preamble.

When a variable is defined with a certain mode it can only be
used in ways that are consistent with its definition. One source of
error is reading data from punched cards that conflict with the form
in which variable values can be stored. Table 2-1 specifies the
actions taken when different combinations of data and variable definitions occur.

2-02 EXPRESSION MODES

While statements that combine INTEGER and REAL variables are
allowed, a programmer should be aware of the way in which computations
are carried out whenever "mixed mode" expressions are used.

(1) Arithmetic expressions of the form $A^{\dagger}$ op B, where op is

------

†A and B represent variables of specified mode, or constants of
that mode.

Table 2-1

REAL-INTEGER INPUT DATA CONVERSIONS

Data Punched as	Variable Defined as	Action
INTEGER	INTEGER	Data value stored in variable
INTEGER	REAL	Data value converted to decimal representation and then stored in variable; e.g., 55 stored as 55.0
REAL	REAL	Data value stored in variable
REAL	INTEGER	Program terminates with error message; not possible to store fractional value in integer representation

any of the arithmetic operations +, -, and *, are

INTEGER if both A and B are INTEGER

REAL if either A or B is REAL

(2) Expressions A/B are always REAL;[†]

(3) Expressions A**B are always REAL.

Compound expressions are evaluated from left to right as a sequence of simple expressions that are evaluated according to the above rules. In the following examples, if A, B, and C are INTEGER, then

A/B + C is REAL
A + B + C is INTEGER
A**B + C is REAL

When an expression appears on the right-hand side of a LET statement or in an ADD or SUBTRACT statement, and its mode differs from the mode of the variable on the left-hand side, the expression is converted to the mode of the variable before the value of the variable is changed. When the arithmetic expression constituents of logical expressions differ in mode, all INTEGER expressions are converted to

---

[†]Two INTEGER expressions can be divided to yield a truncated INTEGER result by a procedure described in Sec. 2-18.

REAL before evaluating the logical expression as true or false.

Conversions from INTEGER to REAL are straightforward. An INTEGER to REAL conversion takes the whole number that is the value of an INTEGER variable and converts it to a REAL number with the same value; 25 becomes 25.0, -11 becomes -11.0, and so forth.

REAL to INTEGER conversions are more complex. REAL values are rounded to whole numbers by adding +0.5 to the variable if its value is positive or -0.5 if it is negative, and truncating the result. If X is INTEGER and e is some REAL valued expression (formed according to the above rules), then

$$\text{LET } X = e \text{ sets } X = 0 \text{ if } e = 0.2 \text{ since}$$
$$0.2 + 0.5 = 0.7 \rightarrow 0$$

$$\text{LET } X = e \text{ sets } X = 1 \text{ if } e = 1.4999 \text{ since}$$
$$1.4999 + 0.5 = 1.9999 \rightarrow 1$$

$$\text{LET } X = e \text{ sets } X = 2 \text{ if } e = 1.50000 \text{ since}$$
$$1.50000 + 0.5 = 2.0000 \rightarrow 2$$

2-03 SUBSCRIPTED VARIABLES

Variable names can be used to identify more than one quantity. This feature is particularly useful in programs dealing with data that have a regular structure, e.g., data in the form of lists or tables. Lists and tables are examples of *arrays*. Individual data items in an array are called *elements* of the array. A simple list of items (Fig. 2-1) is called a one-dimensional array; a table of items (Fig. 2-2) is called a two-dimensional array; in general, a data collection that has n reference indices, as a position in a list, or a row and column location in a table, can be described by an *n-dimensional* array.

Fig. 2-1 -- A list structure; a one-dimensional array

	Column 1	Column 2	Column 3	Column 4	Column 5
Row 1					
Row 2					
Row 3					

Fig. 2-2 -- A table structure; a two-dimensional array

The elements of the array shown in Fig. 2-1 can be described by an identifying name, LIST for example, and an *index* number which can assume integer values from 1 to the total number of elements in the list. The array name is used to identify the collection of elements; the index number, called a *subscript*, enclosed in parentheses after the array name, is used to denote particular elements. Thus the first element in the array LIST is called LIST(1), the fifth element LIST(5), and the Ith element LIST(I).

Groups of variables that have a one-dimensional array structure can therefore be described by an identifier and a single subscript. Figure 2-3 shows the list of Fig. 2-1 with the individual element names inserted. Each element's subscript denotes its position in the structure of the list; the value of the third element in the array is in the variable LIST(3), the value of the seventh element in LIST(7), etc.

LIST(1)	LIST(2)	LIST(3)	LIST(4)	LIST(5)	LIST(6)	LIST(7)	LIST(8)	LIST(9)

Fig. 2-3 -- Elements of a one-dimensional array called LIST

Variables with a two-dimensional array structure can be described by an identifier and a pair of subscripts. The identifier (as always) is the name of the array; each subscript denotes an element location in a coordinate dimension. In Fig. 2-4, the first subscript is used as the element location in the row direction, and the second as the element location in the column direction. Array elements are specified

Column Number

		1	2	3	4	5
	1	TABLE(1, 1)	TABLE(1, 2)	TABLE(1, 3)	TABLE(1, 4)	TABLE(1, 5)
Row Number	2	TABLE(2, 1)	TABLE(2, 2)	TABLE(2, 3)	TABLE(2, 4)	TABLE(2, 5)
	3	TABLE(3, 1)	TABLE(3, 2)	TABLE(3, 3)	TABLE(3, 4)	TABLE(3, 5)

Fig. 2-4 -- Elements of a two-dimensional array called TABLE

by writing their respective subscripts, enclosed in parentheses and separated by a comma,[†] after the array name. Figure 2-4 shows the two-dimensional array of Fig. 2-2, here called TABLE, with the individual element names inserted. Note how the subscript values indicate each element's position in the structure of the table.

Arrays with more than two dimensions can be described in this notation. A three-dimensional array called CUBE might have elements CUBE(I, J, K), a seven-dimensional array called SEVEN.DIM might have elements SEVEN.DIM(A, B, C, D, E, F, G).

Subscripted variables (the elements of arrays) can be INTEGER or REAL valued. All elements of an array must have the same mode. If their mode differs from that of the compiler's background conditions it can be declared in a DEFINE statement in the same way as unsubscripted variables. For instance, if the assumed mode of all as yet undeclared variables has been set to REAL, then we might write the statement

DEFINE LIST AND TABLE AS INTEGER ARRAYS

The words VARIABLE, VARIABLES, ARRAY, and ARRAYS can be used interchangeably to improve the readability of declarations.

The *dimensionality of an array*, whether it has 0, 1, 2, 3 or more subscripts, must be defined in the preamble. A *dimensionality specification phrase* can be included in either NORMALLY or DEFINE statements, depending on whether it is to apply as a background

---

[†]Only a "," can be used; AND and ,AND are not allowed.

condition or as a local property declaration. The phrase is written somewhat differently in each case.

In a NORMALLY statement, a dimensionality specification phrase can appear by itself or can be separated from a mode specification phrase by a comma. An n-dimensional array background condition is declared by any of the phrases,

```
         DIMENSION = n       DIMENSION IS n
         DIM = n             DIM IS n
```

as in the statements

```
         NORMALLY, MODE IS INTEGER AND DIMENSION = 2
         NORMALLY, DIM = 3
         NORMALLY DIMENSION IS 1, MODE IS REAL
```

The mode and dimensionality phrases can appear in separate statements, or in any order in the same statement. As additional specification phrases are added in later sections, phrase choices will be increased but these rules will not change; the general form of the NORMALLY statement is

```
         NORMALLY, specification phrase list
```

In a DEFINE statement the same general rules apply. A dimensionality specification can be made for a list of subscripted variables with the dimensionality phrase n-DIMENSIONAL or n-DIM as in the statements

```
         DEFINE LIST AS AN INTEGER, 1-DIMENSIONAL ARRAY
         DEFINE LIST AND VECTOR AS REAL, 1-DIMENSIONAL ARRAYS
         DEFINE CUBE AS A 3-DIMENSIONAL, INTEGER ARRAY
```

Note that if a majority of program variables are arrays of a particular dimension they can be defined by a NORMALLY statement, and the DEFINE statement can be used to specify unsubscripted variables and subscripted variables of other dimensionality, as in

```
         PREAMBLE
         NORMALLY, MODE IS INTEGER, DIMENSION = 2
         DEFINE X, Y, Z AND Q AS REAL VARIABLES
         DEFINE VECTOR AS A 1-DIMENSIONAL ARRAY
         END
```

A variable must not, however, be used in more than one DEFINE statement. It is permissible to write

        NORMALLY, MODE IS REAL, DIMENSION = 1
        DEFINE X AS AN INTEGER, 0-DIMENSIONAL VARIABLE

It is not permissible to write

        NORMALLY, MODE IS REAL, DIMENSION IS 1
        DEFINE X AS AN INTEGER VARIABLE
                        .
                        .
                        .
        DEFINE X AS A 0-DIMENSIONAL VARIABLE

Each unsubscripted (0-dimensional) variable uses one computer
word to store its value; for each variable, e.g., MONEY, UNIT.COST,
there is a memory location that contains the value of MONEY, the
value of UNIT.COST. Similarly, each element of each array needs a
distinct computer word where its value can be stored. A one-dimensional array with 10 elements uses 10 memory locations, a two-dimensional array with 3 rows and 5 columns uses (3*5) = 15 memory locations,
and so forth.

A programmer does not have to make provisions for allocating
memory locations to unsubscripted variables; when the compiler en-
counters a new unsubscripted variable, e.g., X, it automatically
assigns a memory word to that name. This is not true for subscripted
variables, for an array can have any number of elements, and unless
the compiler is told exactly how many, memory space cannot be assigned.

The RESERVE statement allocates computer memory to arrays. The
dimensionality of each array is indicated by asterisks in subscript
positions; *subscript size expressions* declare the largest value that
each subscript position index can assume. The product of these expressions is the total number of memory cells allocated to each array.
Thus the statement

        RESERVE X(*) AS 25, TABLE(*,*) AS 5 BY 27, CARGO(*) AS 18
                AND CUBE(*,*,*) AS 3 BY 6 BY 10

allocates memory space for a one-dimensional array X with 25 elements
X(1), X(2), ..., X(25), a two-dimensional array TABLE with (5*27)=135

elements TABLE(1,1), TABLE(1,2), TABLE(1,3), ..., TABLE(1,27), TABLE
(2,1), ..., TABLE(2,27), TABLE(3,1), ..., TABLE(5,27), a one-dimensional
array CARGO with 18 elements, and a three-dimensional array CUBE with
(3*6*10)=180 elements.

Subscript size expressions need not be constants, as in the above
example, but can be arithmetic expressions containing variables, including other subscripted variables that have been previously defined
and whose value has been specified. If such expressions are REAL,
they are rounded to INTEGER before they are used as array dimension
specifiers. Thus the statement

```
    RESERVE X(*) AS N, TABLE(*,*) AS N BY 2*N, LIST(*) AS MAN.NUMBER
                    AND Y(*) AS S**T/2.5
```

defines the arrays X, TABLE, LIST and Y as long as the variables N,
MAN.NUMBER, S and T have previously been defined.

If a subscript expression in a RESERVE statement is 1, there is
only one element allocated to that dimension. The statement RESERVE
X(*) AS 1 defines an array X with one element X(1); the statement
RESERVE TABLE(*,*) AS 1 BY 3 defines a two-dimensional array with
three elements — TABLE(1,1), TABLE(1,2), and TABLE(1,3). For all
practical purposes, these one- and two-dimensional arrays are equivalent to the unsubscripted variable X and a one-dimensional array
TABLE(i), i=1, 2, 3, respectively.

A subscript size expression cannot be zero or negative. If an
attempt is made to reserve space with a zero- or negative-valued
expression, a program terminates with an error message.

A RESERVE statement can appear anywhere *but* in the preamble of
a SIMSCRIPT II program. It is an executable statement, and until a
RESERVE statement containing an array name has been executed, storage
is not allocated for that array and its element values are not defined.
RESERVE statements are normally found at the head of a program. Each
subscripted variable must be reserved before it can be used — a firm
rule to bear in mind. For example, the pair of statements

```
        RESERVE LIST(*) AS 10        LET LIST(1)=1
```

allocates memory space to the array LIST before it assigns a value to the element LIST(1). Each reserved array is initialized to zero after memory space is allocated to it. If, either inadvertently or deliberately, a RESERVE statement is executed more than once, the SIMSCRIPT II operating program recognizes that storage has already been allocated to the listed variables and ignores all but the first RESERVE statement.

When two or more arrays have the same dimensions, an abbreviated notation can be used. If A, B, and C are separate two-dimensional arrays, the following statement allocates an identical amount of memory space to each:

RESERVE A (*,*), B(*,*), C(*,*) AS 5 BY 10

Any RESERVE statement can contain a sublist of this form among its list of arrays, as in

```
RESERVE X(*) AS 5, FILE(*,*,*) AS 4 BY N+M BY 6, TABLE(*,*) AS 2 BY 3,
LIST1(*) AND LIST2(*) AS N+M, QUEUE(*,*) AS 3 BY Y,
A(*), B(*) AND C(*) AS 15
```

The dimensionality of an array is frozen when it is declared in a DEFINE statement. Dimensionalities declared in NORMALLY statements can be overridden by subsequent definitions in DEFINE statements, as in the statements

```
NORMALLY, DIMENSION = 2, MODE IS REAL
DEFINE X AS A 1-DIMENSIONAL ARRAY
```

Once a dimensionality has been frozen, however, it must be used consistently. In cases where there is disagreement between uses of an array, the SIMSCRIPT II compiler takes the following actions:

When a subscripted variable has too few subscripts, the missing subscripts are considered to be in the rightmost subscript position, a 1 is inserted in each empty position and a warning message is issued. For example, the incorrect LET statement in the following program segment

```
RESERVE TABLE(*,*) AS N BY M    LET TABLE(I) = 1
```

is interpreted and compiled as LET TABLE(I,1) = 1.

When a subscripted variable has too many subscripts, the extra subscripts are considered to be in the rightmost subscript positions,

each extra subscript is deleted from the element reference and a
warning message is issued. For example, the incorrect LET statement
in the program segment

RESERVE LIST(*) AS 10   LET LIST(I,J) = 1

is interpreted and compiled as LET LIST(I) = 1.

If an array name appears in a RESERVE statement without asterisks
to indicate its subscript positions, asterisks are filled in to make
the array agree with the dimensionality previously declared in a
DEFINE statement. If no dimensionality declaration has been made,
the number of subscript size expressions is assumed to be the dimensionality. Thus, if an array has been declared as two-dimensional
by the statement

DEFINE MATRIX AS A 2-DIMENSIONAL, INTEGER ARRAY

or if no dimensionality declaration has been made for the array the
statement

RESERVE MATRIX AS 5 BY 7

is compiled as

RESERVE MATRIX(*,*) AS 5 BY 7

without a warning message being issued. The form commonly used in
RESERVE statements is an array name without asterisks. It is shorter
to write, and, in the presence of DEFINE and NORMALLY declarations,
unambiguous. The long form is useful for program documentation.

2-04 *USING SUBSCRIPTED VARIABLES*

The following examples illustrate some uses of subscripted
variables:

(1) To read a number from a data card, and add together those
subscripted variables in a list that are greater than the number.

```
        PREAMBLE
        DEFINE NUMBER AS A 1-DIMENSIONAL ARRAY
        DEFINE INDEX AS AN INTEGER VARIABLE
        END
        RESERVE NUMBER(*) AS 500


            :  ⎰ program statements assign values to
            :  ⎱ the elements of the array NUMBER


        READ N         LET INDEX=1
'LOOP'  IF NUMBER(INDEX) IS GREATER THAN N, ADD NUMBER(INDEX) TO SUM
        REGARDLESS    ADD 1 TO INDEX
        IF INDEX IS LESS THAN 500, GO TO LOOP  ELSE
        PRINT 1 LINE WITH SUM AS FOLLOWS
                    SUM = *.**
        STOP         END
        '' NOTE THAT INDEX MUST BE INITIALIZED TO 1 IN THE PROGRAM
        '' SUM IS AUTOMATICALLY SET TO 0 AT THE START OF EXECUTION
        '' NUMBER AND N ARE BOTH REAL BY IMPLICATION
```

(2) To search through a list of numbers for all those that lie between a lower and an upper bound; to print such numbers.

```
        PREAMBLE
        NORMALLY, MODE IS INTEGER
        DEFINE LIST AS A 1-DIMENSIONAL ARRAY
        END
        READ N ''NUMBER IN LIST'', X ''LOWER BOUND'' AND Y ''UPPER BOUND
        RESERVE LIST(*) AS N        LET INDEX=1

            :  ⎰ somewhere in here program statements
            :  ⎱ assign values to each element of LIST


'LOOP'  IF LIST(INDEX) IS GREATER THAN X, ''AND''
        IF LIST(INDEX) IS LESS THAN Y,
        PRINT 1 LINE WITH INDEX AND LIST(INDEX) LIKE THIS
                    NUMBER *** = ***.***
        OTHERWISE
        REGARDLESS
        IF INDEX IS LESS THAN N, ADD 1 TO INDEX  GO TO LOOP
        ELSE    STOP    END
```

(3) To read a matrix (double-subscripted variable) of decimal numbers and pairs of subscript values; to print the corresponding matrix value and the matrix value whose subscripts are the reverse of the pair read in.

```
PREAMBLE
DEFINE MATRIX AS A 2-DIMENSIONAL ARRAY
DEFINE I, J AND N AS INTEGER VARIABLES
END
READ N ''THE DIMENSIONS OF THE ARRAY
RESERVE MATRIX AS N BY N    READ MATRIX†
'READ.LABEL'   READ I,J   ''THE SUBSCRIPT PAIR
PRINT 2 LINES WITH I,J,MATRIX(I,J) AND MATRIX(J,I) THUS
    I=*  J=*  MATRIX(I,J) = ***.**
              MATRIX(J,I) = ***.**
GO TO READ.LABEL     END
```

Note that there is no test to terminate the program; it continues reading cards and printing until there are no more data cards to be read.

(4) To illustrate the "parentheses rule" as it applies to the
evaluation of expressions containing subscripted variables.

> Rule: Expressions containing parentheses are processed
> from left to right and all parentheses are removed
> before an expression's final value is computed.
> In the parenthesis removal process, subscripted
> variables are fetched from storage and their
> values put in temporary unsubscripted variables.
> Compound expressions containing parentheses are
> simplified.

(4a) LET TEMP = X(I) + Y(J) is executed by, first, performing
the substitutions X(I) → x, Y(J) → z; second, by evaluating the expression x + z; and third, by storing the result in the variable TEMP.

(4b) LET TEMP = X(I+J) + Y(J) is executed by, first, evaluating
the expression I+J → i; second, using this value, by performing the
substitution X(i) → x; third, by performing the substitution Y(J) → z;
and fourth, by evaluating and storing the value of the expression x + z.

(4c) LET TEMP = X(I + X(I+J) + 5) + Y(J + X(I+J) + 3) is executed
by eliminating parentheses from left to right and simplifying nested
parentheses from the inside out. Computations and simplifications
are made in the following order:

---
†See Sec. 2-06 for a discussion of this statement. It reads the
N*N element values of MATRIX that were defined in the RESERVE state-
ment.

$$(1)\quad I+J \to i \qquad\qquad (5)\quad I+J \to i$$

$$(2)\quad X(i) \to x \qquad\qquad (6)\quad X(i) \to x$$

$$(3)\quad I+x+5 \to j \qquad\quad (7)\quad J+x+3 \to j$$

$$(4)\quad X(j) \to z \qquad\qquad (8)\quad Y(j) \to q$$

$$(9)\quad z+q \to TEMP$$

Since common subexpressions may not be recognized,[†] e.g., (1) and (5), efficiency can be achieved by computing them in separate statements.

(5) To illustrate the use of INTEGER and REAL arrays in the context of a realistic problem, the following program processes sales order cards for a department store generating shipment orders, notices of out-of-stock conditions, and final inventory reports. The program assumes that several stores, located in different places, sell the same items, that all merchandise is shipped from one central location, and that top management is interested in the stores' performance.

```
           PREAMBLE
           NORMALLY, MODE IS INTEGER
           DEFINE STOCK AS A 2-DIMENSIONAL ARRAY
           DEFINE STORE AND ITEM AS 1-DIMENSIONAL ARRAYS
           DEFINE PRICE, ITEM.INVENTORY AND STORE.INVENTORY AS
               REAL, 1-DIMENSIONAL ARRAYS
           END

           RESERVE STOCK AS 100 BY 10, STORE AND STORE.INVENTORY AS 10,
               ITEM, PRICE AND ITEM.INVENTORY AS 100
           READ STOCK AND PRICE ''LAST PERIODS FINAL STOCK
               ''BALANCE AND CURRENT PRICES
'SALE'     READ STORE.NUMBER, ITEM.NUMBER AND QUANTITY
           IF ITEM.NUMBER IS ZERO, GO TO SUMMARY    ELSE
           IF STOCK (ITEM.NUMBER, STORE.NUMBER) IS LESS THAN QUANTITY
           PRINT 3 LINES WITH STORE.NUMBER, ITEM.NUMBER, QUANTITY AND
           QUANTITY-STOCK(ITEM.NUMBER, STORE.NUMBER) THUS
           STORE ** IS LOW ON STOCK OF ITEM NUMBER ***
           ORDER OF **** UNITS CANNOT BE FILLED
           **** UNITS ARE BEING BACKORDERED
           LET QUANTITY= STOCK(ITEM.NUMBER,STORE.NUMBER)
           OTHERWISE   SUBTRACT QUANTITY FROM STOCK (ITEM.NUMBER,
               STORE.NUMBER) PRINT 1 LINE WITH QUANTITY, ITEM.NUMBER
               AND STORE.NUMBER AS FOLLOWS
                   SHIP **** UNITS OF ITEM *** TO STORE **
           GO TO SALE
```

[†]This is a function of the optimization procedures used in different implementations of the language.

```
'SUMMARY'    LET I = 0
'LOOP'       LET J = 0  ADD 1 TO I.   IF I = 11, GO TO PRINT   ELSE
'AGAIN'      ADD 1 TO J  IF J = 101, GO TO LOOP   ELSE
             ADD STOCK(J,I) TO STORE(I)  ''STORE SALES''
             ADD STOCK(J,I)  TO ITEM(J)  ''ITEM SALES''
             ADD STOCK(J,I)*PRICE(J) TO STORE.INVENTORY(I)
               ''SALES DOLLARS''
             GO TO AGAIN
'PRINT'      LET J = 0
'NEXT'       ADD 1 TO J. IF J = 101, GO TO OUTPUT   ELSE
             LET ITEM.INVENTORY(J) = ITEM(J)*PRICE(J)
               ''ITEM DOLLARS''
             GO TO NEXT
'OUTPUT'     START NEW PAGE
             PRINT 1 LINE AS FOLLOWS
               SUMMARY REPORT AT END OF CURRENT PERIOD
             SKIP 2 OUTPUT LINES
             LIST STORE, STORE.INVENTORY, ITEM, ITEM.INVENTORY
               AND STOCK†
             STOP
             END ''OF PROGRAM
```

2-05 CONTROL PHRASES

A SIMSCRIPT II statement can be executed more than once by appending a control phrase to it. This concept is illustrated by the example

$$FOR\ I = 1\ TO\ 10,\ LET\ X(I) = 5$$

The phrase FOR I = 1 TO 10 controls the execution of the LET statement following it, causing the statement to be repeated 10 times, first with I = 1, next with I = 2, then with I = 3, and so on, until it is executed for the last time with I = 10. The effect of the example is to set the first 10 elements of the array X equal to 5.

The general form of a *control phrase* is

FOR *variable* = *arith expression*$_1$ TO *arith expression*$_2$ BY *arith expression*$_3$

Any REAL or INTEGER *unsubscripted* variable can be used as the variable in the control phrase. The first time a *controlled statement* (like the LET statement above) is executed, the control phrase variable is set equal to the value of *expression*$_1$; a type conversion is made if

---

†See Sec. *2-11* for a discussion of this statement.

necessary. If the value of $expression_1$ is not greater than that of $expression_2$ (it usually is not), the controlled statement is executed. After execution, the value of $expression_3$ is added to the control phrase variable, and if this new value is again less than $expression_2$ the controlled statement is repeated. This process continues, with the control phrase variable taking on successively larger values until it exceeds the value of $expression_2$. A comma at the end of a control phrase is optional.

If the phrase "BY $expression_3$" is left out of the control phrase, as in the above example, a value of 1.0 is assumed for $expression_3$. This short form of the control phrase is convenient for executing a controlled statement over a range of successive subscript values. The longer form is useful for statements in which calculations involving the control variable are performed, as in the program segment

```
FOR N = LOW TO HIGH BY INCREMENT, ADD INCREMENT*N TO SUM
```

The foregoing statement does not operate on a subscripted variable, but uses the properties of the control phrase to perform a series of calculations that follow some prescribed order and accomplishes the same task as the statements

```
LET N = LOW
'LOOP'  ADD INCREMENT*N TO SUM
ADD INCREMENT TO N  IF N≤HIGH, GO TO LOOP  ELSE...
```

Arithmetic expressions in control phrases, which have so far been denoted as $expression_1$, $expression_2$, and $expression_3$, from here on will be labeled e_1, e_2, and e_3. Each one can be any legitimate arithmetic expression; they need not be of the same mode, since conversions will be made if necessary. If any of the expressions are REAL, all computations involved in computing the successive values of the control phrase variable, called v from here on, will be REAL.

Possible Subscript Control Phrases	Successive Values of v
FOR I = 1 TO 5,	1,2,3,4,5
FOR I = -5 TO 5,	-5,-4,-3,-2,-1,0,1,2,3,4,5,
FOR I = 0.0 TO 2.0 BY 0.5	0.0,0.5,1.0,1.5,2.0
FOR I = 10 TO N BY M,	if N is less than 10 the controlled statement will not be executed
	if N is at least equal to 10, the controlled statement will be executed with I=10, 10+M, 10+2*M, ..., 10+n*M until I exceeds N

The above illustration shows that it is impossible to step backward, as for example, I = 5, 4, 3, 2, 1, with this control phrase. A variant of the phrase is used for this purpose. The form is

$$\text{FOR } v \text{ BACK FROM } e_1 \text{ TO } e_2 \text{ BY } e_3$$

Everything applicable to the forward stepping control phrase applies to this phrase; the only difference is in the direction in which the control phrase variable changes value.

Control phrases can be *nested* together for dealing with arrays of more than one dimension, as in

$$\text{FOR I = 1 TO N, FOR J = 1 TO M, LET X(I,J)=VALUE}$$

Used this way, the control phrase on the left is said to be an outer phrase, and the phrase on the right an inner phrase. In computing successive values of I and J, the inner phrase is stepped through its entire range of values for each value of the outer control phrase variable. The controlled statement is executed each time. Thus, if N = 3 and M = 4, the above statement would be executed in the sequence

Step	I	J	Statement Executed
1	1	1	LET X(1,1) = VALUE
2	1	2	LET X(1,2) = VALUE
3	1	3	LET X(1,3) = VALUE
4	1	4	LET X(1,4) = VALUE
5	2	1	LET X(2,1) = VALUE
6	2	2	LET X(2,2) = VALUE
7	2	3	LET X(2,3) = VALUE
8	2	4	LET X(2,4) = VALUE
9	3	1	LET X(3,1) = VALUE
10	3	2	LET X(3,2) = VALUE
11	3	3	LET X(3,3) = VALUE
12	3	4	LET X(3,4) = VALUE

An indefinite number of phrases can be nested together in this way. Each successive phrase is an outer phrase to its right-hand phrase, and an inner phrase to its left-hand phrase. Control variables of outer phrases can be used in the expressions e_1, e_2, and e_3 of inner phrases, as their values are defined within these phrases. Thus we might have the nested phrases

FOR I = 1 TO N, FOR J = 1 TO I, LET X(I,J) = 0

If N = 3 this statement will be executed as

Step	I	J	Statement Executed
1	1	1	LET X(1,1) = 0
2	2	1	LET X(2,1) = 0
3	2	2	LET X(2,2) = 0
4	3	1	LET X(3,1) = 0
5	3	2	LET X(3,2) = 0
6	3	3	LET X(3,3) = 0

Table 2-2 contains a list of the SIMSCRIPT II statements described thus far that are controllable and uncontrollable by subscript control phrases.

Table 2-2

STATEMENTS

Controllable Statement Types	Uncontrollable Statement Types
LET ADD SUBTRACT READ PRINT START NEW SKIP RESERVE[a]	IF GO TO STOP NORMALLY DEFINE PREAMBLE END

[a]How this might usefully be done is explained in Sec. *2-08.*

For example:

(a) FOR I = 1 TO MAX, READ X(I)
        reads the successive values X(1), X(2), ..., X(MAX)

(b) FOR X = 1 TO N, ADD X**2 TO SUM

   computes $\sum_{X=1}^{N} X^2 = N*X**2$

(c) FOR I = 1 TO N, ADD X(I)**2 TO SUM

   computes $\sum_{I=1}^{N} X_I{}^2$

(d) PRINT 1 LINE AS FOLLOWS
        INDEX   VALUE
     FOR INDEX = 5 TO 10, PRINT 1 LINE WITH INDEX AND
     VALUE(INDEX) LIKE THIS
          **   **.**
        prints a labeled list of numbers stored in the
        one-dimensional array VALUE.

2-06 *READING SUBSCRIPTED VARIABLES*

Subscripted variable values can be read by the READ statement in several ways. The statement can be used to read individual elements of arrays, entire arrays, or elements of arrays under the control of one or more control phrases. In the following paragraphs let LIST

be a singly-subscripted variable defined by the statement RESERVE
LIST(*) AS 10.

Individual elements of arrays are read by listing their names
(the array identifier followed by the appropriate subscript expres-
sion(s) enclosed in parentheses) in the list of a READ statement.
Values of LIST(1), LIST(5), and LIST(9) are read by the statement

READ LIST(1), LIST(5), LIST(9)

A variable list can contain array elements whose subscript designators
are expressions, such as LIST(N*M+2/J) or LIST(I), as long as the
variables appearing in these expressions have had values assigned to
them. They are assigned if they appear in a READ statement before
their use in the same statement as subscripts,[†] as in

READ N,M, LIST(N), LIST(LIST(N)+M)

This example shows that both unsubscripted and subscripted variables
can appear in the same READ statement list.

Entire arrays can be read by using only their names in a READ
list. READ LIST reads the 10 elements of LIST, as defined by the
RESERVE statement; numbers are read and assigned to the elements of
LIST in increasing subscript order, the first data item is assigned
to LIST(1), the next to LIST(2) and so on. If LIST were a multidimensional array, the data would be assigned to successive elements
whose subscripts change in increasing order, with the last subscript
position varying most rapidly. A two-dimensional array is read in
row by row, as in LIST(1,1), LIST(1,2), LIST(1,3), ..., LIST(1,N),
LIST(2,1), LIST(2,2), ..., LIST(2,N), etc.

Mixtures of unsubscripted variables, elements of arrays, and
entire arrays can be read in one READ statement. If LIST and VECTOR
are one-dimensional arrays, TABLE a two-dimensional array, and X and
Y unsubscripted variables, the statement

READ X, LIST(7), VECTOR, TABLE, Y, LIST(Y)

reads a data item and assigns its value to X; reads another data item

---

[†]The statement's variable list is processed from left to right.

and assigns its value to LIST(7); reads as many data items as there are elements in the array VECTOR and assigns them to the elements of VECTOR; reads as many data items as there are in the array TABLE and assigns them to the elements of TABLE; reads a data item and assigns it to Y; and reads a data item and assigns it to the element of LIST indexed by the subscript Y.

A subscript control phase can also be used to control the selection of array elements in a READ statement. The statement

$$FOR\ INDEX = L\ TO\ N,\ READ\ LIST(INDEX)$$

reads N-L+1 data items and assigns their successive values to the elements LIST(L), ..., LIST(N).

Some examples illustrate a few of the many forms a READ statement can take. X, Y, and Z are subscripted variables defined by the statement

$$RESERVE\ X(*),Y(*)\ AS\ 4,\ Z(*,*)\ AS\ 4\ BY\ 4$$

while A, B, and C are unsubscripted variables.

(1) READ A,B,C,X(1),Y(3),Z(2,3) reads six numbers and assigns their values to A, B, C, and to the three subscripted variables X(1), Y(3), and Z(2,3).

(2) READ A, X, B reads six numbers and assigns their values to A, X(1), X(2), X(3), X(4), and B, respectively.

(3) READ A,B FOR I=1 TO 3, READ X(I) READ Y reads nine numbers and assigns their values to A, B, X(1), X(2), X(3), Y(1), Y(2), Y(3), and Y(4), respectively.

(4) FOR I = 1 TO 4, READ X(I) AND Y(I) reads eight numbers and assigns their values to X(1), Y(1), X(2), Y(2), X(3), Y(3), X(4), and Y(4), respectively.

(5) READ Z reads sixteen numbers and assigns them to

$$
\begin{array}{cccc}
Z(1,1) & Z(1,2) & Z(1,3) & Z(1,4) \\
Z(2,1) & Z(2,2) & Z(2,3) & Z(2,4) \\
Z(3,1) & Z(3,2) & Z(3,3) & Z(3,4) \\
Z(4,1) & Z(4,2) & Z(4,3) & Z(4,4)
\end{array}
$$

, respectively.

(6) FOR I = 1 TO 4, FOR J = 1 TO 4, READ Z(I,J) reads sixteen numbers and assigns them as in (5).

(7) FOR I = 1 TO 4, READ Z(2,I) reads four numbers and assigns them to the elements of the second row of Z: Z(2,1), Z(2,2), Z(2,3), Z(2,4), respectively.

The above examples show that a control phrase does not control the index of a variable within a READ statement, but controls the *entire* READ statement. Thus, each variable that appears in a controlled READ statement should contain the control variable as a subscript; if it does not, successive data values are assigned to this variable as the control phrase iterates over the range of the control phrase variable. This is seen in the statement below, which reads and assigns values to the unsubscripted variable A and the subscripted variables $X(1)$, $X(2)$ and $X(3)$. Naturally, all but the last value of A is lost, i.e., the first value read is replaced by the second, and the second is replaced by the third.

```
FOR I = 1 TO 3, READ A, X(I)
```

2-07 CONTROL PHRASES EXTENDED TO INCLUDE CONTROL OVER MORE THAN ONE STATEMENT

The concept of a control phrase (sometimes called a FOR phrase) can be expanded to permit the phrase to control not one, but an arbitrary number of statements. Statements to be controlled as a group are enclosed between the words DO and LOOP. A control phrase controls grouped statements in exactly the same way it controls a single statement. As an example, consider a program that reads data, examines each item to see if it has a certain property, and indicates by a coded reply whether or not each item passes the property test.

```
PREAMBLE
NORMALLY, MODE IS INTEGER  DEFINE X AND TEST.NUMBER AS REAL VARIABLES
DEFINE CODE AS A 1-DIMENSIONAL ARRAY
END
READ NUMBER.OF.SAMPLES AND TEST.NUMBER
RESERVE CODE AS NUMBER.OF.SAMPLES
FOR I = 1 TO NUMBER.OF.SAMPLES,
DO
    READ X
    IF X IS LESS THAN TEST.NUMBER, LET CODE(I) = 1
    REGARDLESS ADD CODE(I) TO SUM
LOOP
PRINT 1 LINE WITH 100*(SUM/NUMBER.OF.SAMPLES) THUS
    PER CENT ITEMS LESS THAN TEST NUMBER = **.**
STOP    END
```

In the foregoing example the statements READ, IF, LET, REGARDLESS, and ADD appear between the statements DO and LOOP. The logic of

these statements is exercised once for each iteration of the controlling FOR phrase.

A DO loop (as we shall call this expanded structure from here
on) can also be constructed from a backward iterating FOR phrase. Its
grammar can often be improved by the optional words THE FOLLOWING or
THIS after the word DO, and the substitution of the word REPEAT for
LOOP. Thus we can write

```
            FOR N = 1 TO 10, DO THE FOLLOWING...REPEAT
   or       FOR N = 1 TO 10, DO...LOOP
   and      FOR I BACK FROM 10 TO 1, DO THIS...LOOP
   or       FOR I BACK FROM 10 TO 1, DO...REPEAT
```

Normally, a DO loop is executed over the entire range of a FOR
phrase. The value of the control phrase variable upon normal exit
from a loop (through the LOOP statement, that is) is the first computed value of V that fails the continuance test. If the loop is
terminated at any other time, as by a GO TO statement within a loop
that transfers control to a statement outside the loop, the variable
retains its current value.

Since the variable V, and the control expressions e_2 and e_3 can
be variables or expressions containing variables, they can be recomputed within a loop. This can affect the sequence of values of
the control phrase variable, either shortening or extending it, and
it can affect the computations performed by the program. The following two examples illustrate the use of recomputed FOR phrase values
within a loop:

```
   (1)  RESERVE VALUE(*) AS N
        FOR V = I TO J BY K, DO THE FOLLOWING
        IF VALUE(V) < V, ADD 1 TO K  ALWAYS ADD VALUE(V) TO SUM
        LOOP

   (2)  FOR V = I TO J BY V*2, DO ... LOOP
```

In Example (2), if I = 1 initially, the variable V takes on successive values of 1, 3, 9, 27, 81, ..., until V is greater than J.

As implied above, labels can be used within a loop to transfer
control around statements in the loop, or to end the loop prematurely
by transferring to a statement outside it. It is possible to transfer
in and out of loops at will as long as each transfer recognizes the

organization of the FOR phrase mechanism and does not expect more from
the compiler than it is able to do. Each FOR phrase is compiled into
a series of program steps that work, roughly, as follows (the word
roughly is used since variations of the FOR statement require different treatments, e.g., the direction of the inequality will change in
the IF test when a BACK FROM phrase is used):

The program

$$\text{FOR } V = e_1 \text{ TO } e_2 \text{ BY } e_3$$
$$\text{DO}$$
$$\vdots$$
$$\text{Statement group}$$
$$\vdots$$
$$\text{LOOP}$$

is compiled into the program

```
        LET V=e₁
        GO TO L.2
'L.1'   ADD e₃ TO V
'L.2'   IF V > e₂, GO TO L.3
        OTHERWISE
           ⋮
        Statement group
           ⋮
        GO TO L.1
'L.3'   continue with program
```

L.1, L.2, and L.3 are local labels that the compiler constructs; they
cannot be used by a SIMSCRIPT II programmer.

DO loops can be nested within one another for control over subscripted variables with two or more subscripts. Recall that subscript
indexing takes place *within* the bounds of the DO and LOOP or REPEAT
statements. To print a matrix of numbers, we might write:

```
FOR I = 1 TO N, DO
FOR J = 1 TO M, DO†
PRINT 1 LINE WITH I, J, MATRIX(I,J) AS FOLLOWS
    MATRIX(*,*) = *.***
LOOP ''ON J, THE SECOND SUBSCRIPT†
REPEAT ''ON I, THE FIRST SUBSCRIPT
```

---

†The careful reader will note that this statement is not required,
as the preceding FOR only controls one statement. In fact, neither
the preceding DO nor the following REPEAT is required.

This example can be clarified by using indentation like that used with nested IF statements.

```
FOR I = 1 TO N, DO
    FOR J = 1 TO M, DO
        PRINT 1 LINE WITH I, J, MATRIX(I,J) AS FOLLOWS
        MATRIX(*,*) = *.***
    LOOP ''J''
    REPEAT  ''I''
```

If N = 2 and M = 3, this program prints:

```
MATRIX(1,1) = -.---
MATRIX(1,2) = -.---
MATRIX(1,3) = -.---
MATRIX(2,1) = -.---
MATRIX(2,2) = -.---
MATRIX(2,3) = -.---
```

* 2-08 PROGRAMMER-DEFINED ARRAY STRUCTURES—POINTER VARIABLES

It was previously stated that each array is assigned a number of computer words equal to the product of its subscript-size expressions. This is not quite correct. Each array has as many computer words as contain the values of its elements, plus additional words that point to these element values. This section describes how these *pointer words* are used to connect array storage, and how they can be used to a programmer's advantage.

Each array has a *base pointer* that points to the array as it is structured in memory. For a one-dimensional array X, the base pointer is named X(*), for a two-dimensional array Y, the base pointer is named Y(*,*), and so on. The base pointer is used in a RESERVE statement when memory space is allocated to an array. The function of the RESERVE statement is to allocate computer words to an array and assign the internal location of these words as the value of the base pointer.

In the following examples, one-, two-, and three-dimensional arrays are used to describe how pointer words are employed in structuring arrays. The structure of higher dimensional arrays follows directly.

The base pointer of a one-dimensional array points directly to data elements that are stored contiguously in whatever mode the array

has been declared. The base pointer, whose value is a computer location, is always in INTEGER mode. A one-dimensional array X, allocated
storage by the statement

RESERVE X(*) AS 10

is stored as:

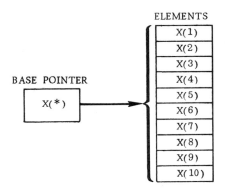

The base pointer is in a computer word that is separated from the
array elements. The actual locations assigned to the elements depend
upon the order in which RESERVE instructions have been executed in a
program.

The base pointer of a two-dimensional array points, not to its
doubly-subscripted data elements, but to an array of pointers that,
in turn, point to the elements of the *rows* of the array. The base
pointer and all the row pointers are in INTEGER mode; the data element
words are in whatever mode the array has been declared. A two-dimensional array X, which has been allocated storage by the statement

RESERVE X(*,*) AS 5 BY 3

is stored as:

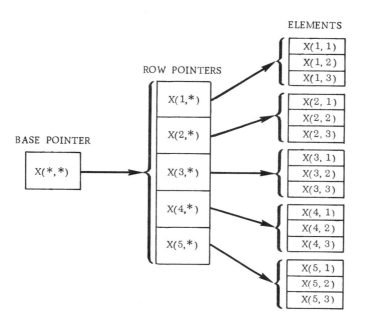

A three-dimensional array is treated similarly — the base pointer points to an array of row pointers, each of which points to an array of *column* pointers, of which each, in turn, points to an array of data elements. A three-dimensional array X, which has been allocated storage by the statement

RESERVE X(*,*,*) AS 5 BY 3 BY 2

is stored as:

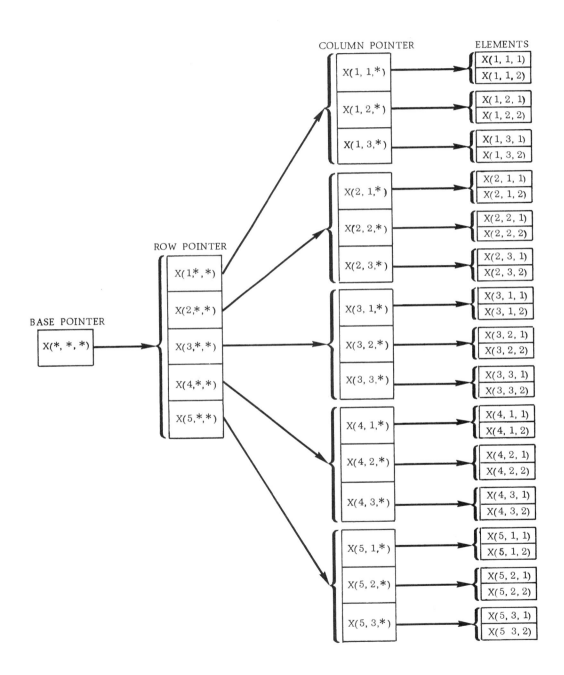

Every element reference with at least one asterisk in its subscript list is a pointer; every element reference without asterisks
in its subscript list is a data word. Pointers are cascaded from one
dimension to another, ending at a data word array.

All of this, while seemingly complicated, need not be bothersome
to a programmer. Arrays are allocated storage by the RESERVE statement, and elements (subscripted variables) are referenced by previously
described methods; pointer words need not be mentioned explicitly,
nor need the manner in which rows and columns of arrays are linked be
taken into consideration. A programmer has the advantage of a flexible
array mechanism without being penalized if he does not choose to use it.

The pointer mechanism provides two primary advantages. The first
and most apparent advantage is that the potential for fitting large
programs into core storage is increased because it is unnecessary to
locate an unused block of core capable of holding an entire array, it
being necessary only to find a number of smaller blocks that can be
linked together. The second, and potentially more useful, advantage
is the ability to manipulate pointers as though they were data values.
This permits the construction of arbitrary data structures to suit
the specific requirements of different problems, and is accomplished
by allowing the asterisk notation used above for pointers to appear
in all SIMSCRIPT II statements. The notation is meaningful only in
a small number of statements, of course. The utility and application
of this feature are best described in a series of examples.

(1) It is used to construct a "ragged table," a two-dimensional
array with a different number of elements in each row. The construction follows:

    (a) Set up a base pointer and an array of row pointers

        RESERVE TABLE(*,*) AS 5 BY *

This statement assigns an array of five elements, each of which contains an unassigned pointer, to the base pointer TABLE(*,*). The
asterisk in the array assignment clause 5 BY * indicates that only
pointers, not data values, are to be stored. After execution of this
statement, the following structure exists in memory:

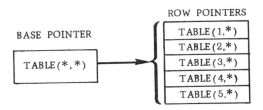

The base pointer points to the array of row pointers; the row pointers
do not point to anything since arrays have not yet been assigned to them.

   (b)   Set up a loop to assign data arrays to each of the row
pointers.   Since a dimension must be given for each row, read a value
for each row from a data card.

```
FOR I=1 TO 5,
   DO READ D
      RESERVE TABLE(I,*) AS D
   LOOP
```

The RESERVE statement assigns an array of D elements to each row
pointer TABLE(I,*), as I varies from 1 to 5. If the values of D
read are 4, 2, 6, 1, and 3, respectively, the final ragged table
structure looks as follows:

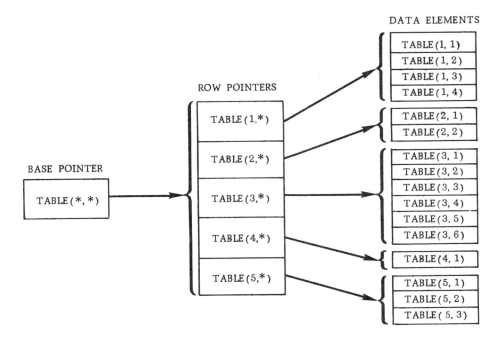

The ragged table TABLE(I,J) can be used the same as any rectangular array. The only care a programmer must exercise is to ensure that he does not ask for a nonexistent array element, as, for example, TABLE(4,3) in the above illustration.

(2)   Section *2-03* indicates that once an array has been reserved it cannot be reserved again. To prevent this from happening, the SIMSCRIPT II system ignores instructions to reserve an array when the pointer to the array has a value in it. When a program is first initialized, all array pointers are zero, making the first RESERVE possible. After this, the presence of a nonzero value in a pointer variable dictates whether or not a reserve will be executed.

At times it is useful to be able to perform multiple array reservations, keeping track of array pointers as they are replaced. This can be done by storing a pointer, setting it to zero, and executing a new RESERVE statement. Although the pointer variable will point to the latest array that is reserved, it is possible at any time to restore it to a previous value (which still points to an array of values in memory) and use those previously computed values. The example below illustrates how such a mechanism can be employed:

A program is to be developed that stores genealogical information in the form of a family tree. Such a tree has an individual at its apex, his parents at the next level, his parents' parents below that, and so on. Figure 2-5 illustrates a family tree containing four levels of genealogical information.

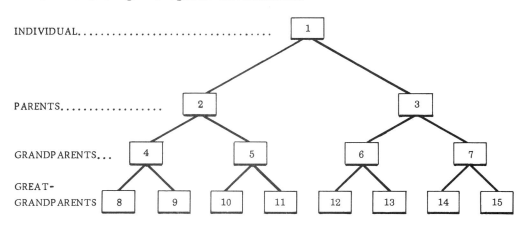

Fig. 2-5 -- Family tree

This information can be stored in a rectangular array, as depicted
in Fig. 2-6. While simple to do, it is wasteful of computer memory
because of all the empty cells.

1							
2	3						
4	5	6	7				
8	9	10	11	12	13	14	15

Fig. 2-6 -- Family tree stored in a rectangular array

A more memory-conserving storage scheme is shown in Fig. 2-7. It
allocates no more computer words than there are data to store. Our
task is to show how this scheme can be programmed and used utilizing
the technique of array pointers.

1							
2	3						
4	5	6	7				
8	9	10	11	12	13	14	15

Fig. 2-7 -- Family tree stored in a ragged table

In the following program, the data of each level is stored in an
array TREE. At level one, TREE has one element, at level two, two
elements, at level three four elements, ..., at level N, 2^{N-1} elements.
The array pointers for the N arrays are stored in a list called LEVEL.
It has N elements, one for each level of the genealogical tree.

Assume that we are given the number of levels in the tree and the names (coded as integer numbers) of the family members arranged in proper order on punched cards. We first construct a tree with the family data suitably arranged. The following program does this:

```
PREAMBLE NORMALLY, MODE IS INTEGER
DEFINE LEVEL AND TREE AS 1-DIMENSIONAL ARRAYS
END

READ N    RESERVE LEVEL(*) AS N
FOR I=1 TO N,
DO
    RESERVE TREE(*) AS 2**(I-1)    READ TREE
    LET LEVEL(I)=TREE(*) LET TREE(*)=0
LOOP
END
```

For N=4, the memory structure at the end of program execution looks as follows:

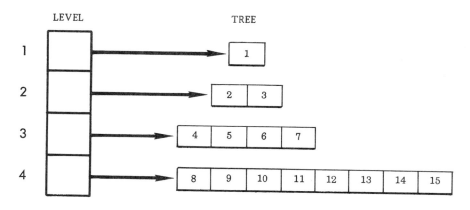

To print out a person's K^{th} level ancestors, one writes

```
READ K
LET TREE(*)=LEVEL(K)
LIST TREE†
```

To pick out specific ancestors, one can search through the tree until the correct code is found using the following program:

---

†This statement displays an entire array; see Sec. *2-11.*

```
                READ CODE
                FOR I=1 TO N,
                DO
                    LET TREE(*)=LEVEL(I)
                    FOR J=1 TO 2**(I-1),
                    DO
                        IF TREE(J) EQUALS CODE, GO TO PRINT
                        OTHERWISE
                    LOOP
                LOOP
                PRINT 1 LINE WITH CODE AS FOLLOWS
                UNABLE TO FIND AN ANCESTOR WITH THE CODE **
                STOP
      'PRINT'   PRINT 1 LINE WITH CODE, J AND I AS FOLLOWS
           ANCESTOR ** FOUND IN POSITION * OF LEVEL *
                STOP
                END
```

(3)   The pointer mechanism can be used to set up an array whereby some rows contain INTEGER numbers and some rows REAL numbers. Usually this cannot be done, since an array name has a single mode value, but it can be accomplished if all data items are stored in a single array and dummy arrays used to access the data rows for processing.

(a)   Declare three arrays as follows:

```
        DEFINE TABLE AS A 2-DIMENSIONAL, REAL ARRAY
        DEFINE WHOLE AS AN INTEGER,1-DIMENSIONAL ARRAY
        DEFINE DECIMAL AS A REAL,1-DIMENSIONAL ARRAY
```

(b)   Allocate memory space to the array in which the data are to be stored.

```
        RESERVE TABLE(*,*) AS 10 BY 10
```

(c)   Read INTEGER values into the fourth row of the array by using the statements

```
        LET WHOLE(*)=TABLE(4,*)
        READ WHOLE
```

The first statement sets the base pointer of the one-dimensional array WHOLE equal to the row pointer of the fourth row of TABLE. This has the effect of assigning the 10 data element values of the fourth row of TABLE to WHOLE — both TABLE(4,*) and WHOLE(*) point to the same memory locations. The second statement reads 10 data values into the array WHOLE, which is also a row of TABLE. They are read as integers, since WHOLE has been declared an INTEGER array. The READ statement knows how many elements to read, since every pointer word—in this instance WHOLE(*) — knows the number of elements it points to, as well as pointing to the elements.

(d) Read REAL values into the seventh row of the array TABLE by using the statements

```
LET DECIMAL(*)=TABLE(7,*)
READ DECIMAL
```

or the statement
```
FOR I=1 TO 10, READ TABLE(7,I)
```

Both statements can be used, since TABLE has been defined as a REAL array.

(4) The pointer mechanism can be used to make the processing of a three-dimensional array more efficient by eliminating the necessity of recomputing two subscripts each time an element is accessed in a FOR loop. The program segment described in (a) can be made more efficient by rewriting it as shown in (b).

(a) FOR I=1 TO 10, READ CUBE(J+7,K+L,I)

(b) LET DUMMY(*)=CUBE(J+7,K+L,*)
     FOR I=1 TO 10, READ DUMMY(I)

where DUMMY has been defined as a one-dimensional array of the same mode as CUBE and has not had storage reserved for it.

The revised statement eliminates the need for recomputing the sub-scripts of CUBE that are not affected by the FOR loop every time a new element is accessed. Little additional memory space is taken, for the array DUMMY never has more words allocated than are needed for its base pointer.

The use of pointer words thus greatly enhances a programmer's ability to construct and use data structures, and its applications are manifold; for instance, rows of matrices can be interchanged by simply changing pointer values, and large matrices with many identical rows can be compressed by having several pointers point to the same array.

The most general form of the RESERVE statement illustrating the full power of the pointer system can now be stated as

RESERVE *pointer list* AS *array description*

where a pointer list consists of a list of subscripted variables
having at least one asterisk in their subscript list and an array
description describes the size and content of the array or arrays
being reserved and pointed to. If an array description does not contain any *notational asterisks*, as in the descriptions 5, 6 BY N,
3 BY M+7 BY 4, and N BY M BY X**2 BY 2, a data array is reserved and
pointed to by the pointer mentioned. If an array description contains
a notational asterisk, the asterisk indicates that pointer words are
being reserved and that subsequent RESERVE statements allocate data
arrays to them. It is only meaningful to have a single notational
asterisk in an array description, as this is sufficient to indicate
that pointers, not data, are being allocated. As noted in example (1)
of Sec. *2-08*, this asterisk must come after any constants and expressions that define the dimensions of prior subscript positions.   The
following RESERVE statements illustrate these concepts:

(1)   RESERVE ARRAY(*,*) AS 5 BY 7

    (Allocates a 5 by 7 data array.)

(2)   RESERVE ARRAY(*,*) AS 6 BY *

    (Allocates six pointer variables.)

(3)   RESERVE ARRAY(1,*) AS 12

    (Allocates twelve data elements to a pointer variable.)

(4)   RESERVE ARRAY(*,*) AS 5

    (Allocates a five-element array to a declared two-dimen-
    sional variable. Although this statement will compile,
    it should be used carefully for it will usually cause a
    programming error. The array elements cannot be accessed
    directly, as ARRAY is a two-dimensional variable. To be
    accessed, the pointer must be transferred to a one-dimen-
    sional array pointer.)

(5)   RESERVE ARRAY(*) AS 5 BY *

    (Similar to (4), but with the dimensionality problem re-
    versed if ARRAY has not been defined as two-dimensional.)

(6) RESERVE X(*),Y(*) AND Z(*) AS N+3

> (Illustrates that several pointers can be assigned storage
> space of the same dimension and function (pointers or
> data). Each pointer, of course, is assigned a separate
> block of storage.)

(7) RESERVE X(*) AS 5, TABLE(J,*) AS N+8

> (Illustrates that several array reservations can be made
> in the same RESERVE statement. In this example, the first
> one allocates a five-element data array to a base pointer
> X(*) and the second allocates an N+8 element data array
> to a row pointer TABLE(J,*).)

Two features are provided that make the use of pointers easier.
The first concerns the physical act of writing programs and the second,
the task of operating with arrays of unknown size.

(1) A base pointer can be written as X(*) regardless of the number of its dimensions. For instance, if X is defined as three-dimensional, X(*) is interpreted as X(*,*,*). While this makes the use of
pointers convenient, one should be aware that, to a person unfamiliar
with the structure of a program's data, it obscures the actual operations that are taking place, e.g., example (5) above.

(2) The function DIM.F,[†] when given a pointer as an argument,
returns as its value the number of words pointed to. This is extremely
useful in programs that compute the values of array dimensions, as it
makes it unnecessary to save such values for later use. For example,
the following FOR loop uses the DIM.F function to determine its bounds:

    FOR I=1 TO DIM.F(MATRIX(*,*)), FOR J=1 TO DIM.F(MATRIX(I,*)),
       LET MATRIX(I,J)= I**2 + J**2

Using the DIM.F function rather than constants or expressions permits
the above statement to process ragged tables as well as rectangular
arrays.

2-09 COMPUTED TRANSFERS TO ALTERNATIVE STATEMENT LABELS

The GO TO and IF statements provide a facility for specifying a

---

[†]The concept of a function is presented in Secs. 2-15 to 2-18.
For present purposes, DIM.F can be thought of, and used, as a one-
dimensional INTEGER variable.

direct transfer of program control to a particular statement, or to
select, according to the truth or falsity of a logical expression,
either of two alternate program branches.

These statements are frequently inadequate, however. For example,
there may be more than two alternative program paths to choose from,
or a program may have to be written to accommodate transfers to statements that have not yet been written. Two new GO TO statements cir-
cumvent these problems.

If we let LABEL1, LABEL2, LABEL3, ..., LABELN represent statement
labels, and e represent an arithmetic expression, then a statement of
the form

GO TO LABEL1 OR LABEL2 OR ... OR LABELN PER e

evaluates e (rounding if it is REAL valued) and transfers program
control to LABEL1 if e=1, to LABEL2 if e=2, ..., to LABELN if e=n.
That is, the statement transfers control to the label in the first
label position, or the second label position, or the nth label position, according to the computed value of the expression e. Most
illegal transfers, $e \leq 0$ or $e > n$, are caught and cause program termination.

Each of the names in the label list (other than the first) must
be preceded by the word OR, or by a comma.[†] The word TO is optional.
Typical computed GO TO statements are:

```
GO TO ACCOUNT.ONE OR ACCOUNT.TWO PER CUSTOMER
GO TO READ.AGAIN, WINDUP, CONTINUE OR HALT PER INSTRUCTION
GO TO L1, 27, 999, 12, 27, 13, 999 PER X**2 + COUNT/N
```

In this last example note that the same label name can appear in
more than one position in a label list, and that label names can be
written without alphabetic characters.

When two distinct label names are used to identify the same
program statement, they are called equivalent labels. In the following examples the labels ADD and PLUS are used as distinct labels in
(1), and as equivalent labels in (2):

[†]In this statement the word AND cannot be used as a synonym for
comma.

```
(1)  'ADD'  ADD X TO COUNTER  'PLUS'  LET X=X+1
(2)  'ADD'  'PLUS'  ADD X TO COUNTER
```

When used with (1), the following GO TO statement transfers either to the ADD or the LET statement; when used with (2), it transfers to the ADD statement regardless of the label selected:

GO TO ADD OR PLUS PER INDEX

Equivalent labels are useful when certain portions of a program have been identified logically, but have not yet been written, or when a program is written in such a manner that portions of it can be included or removed without destroying the general program logic. The following program segment illustrates the use of equivalent labels to indicate that subsequent additions to the program will incorporate certain changes that are not presently included:

```
READ STOCK.NUMBER, ITEMS
GO TO MEAT, POULTRY, GROCERY, SUNDRIES, DAIRY OR PRODUCE
    PER STOCK.NUMBER/FACTOR
'MEAT'
'POULTRY'
'GROCERY'
'SUNDRIES'
'DAIRY'
'PRODUCE'
SUBTRACT ITEMS FROM QUANTITY(STOCK.NUMBER)
```

As long as $1 \leq$ STOCK.NUMBER/FACTOR ≤ 6, the GO TO statement always transfers control to the SUBTRACT statement.

The following program illustrates another use of a computed GO TO statement:

```
'READ' READ X, Y, OPERATION
    GO TO ADD, SUBTRACT, MULTIPLY OR DIVIDE PER
        OPERATION
'ADD'  LET ANSWER=X+Y  GO TO PRINT
'SUBTRACT'  LET ANSWER=X-Y  GO TO PRINT
'MULTIPLY'  LET ANSWER=X*Y  GO TO PRINT
'DIVIDE'  LET ANSWER=X/Y
'PRINT'  PRINT 1 LINE WITH X, Y, AND ANSWER AS FOLLOWS
    ****.** OP ****.** = *****.**,WHAT IS OP?
        GO TO READ
```

Just as variables can be subscripted, so can labels. For example, it might be desirable to use the statement

READ I   GO TO A(I)

rather than list all the possible label names in an ordinary computed
GO TO statement. The subscripted label GO TO statement form can be
used whenever this seems desirable. It is particularly useful in
programs containing GO TO statements that direct control to various
parts of a program when the program is frequently updated or augmented.
Subscripted labels allow labels to be added or deleted without changing
the GO TO statements that (may) pass control to them. The general
form of a subscripted label GO TO statement is

GO TO *label* (*arithmetic expression*)

As in other forms of the GO TO statement, the word TO is optional.
When a subscripted GO TO statement is executed, control is transferred
to the statement labeled with the same name and subscript value equal
to the INTEGER value of the expression in the GO TO statement. If
this INTEGER value has not been defined by a statement label, an undefined transfer may occur. For example, a program containing the
subscripted labels A(1), A(2), and A(3), and the statement GO TO A(I)
may transfer control to some indeterminate place if I is not equal to
1, 2, or 3. Most of the time illegal transfers will be detected and
programs terminated.

A subscripted label is formed by adding a single subscript to a
label name. Thus, the labels A1 and A2 might be replaced by the labels
A(1) and A(2). Other possible subscripted labels are:

NAME(1)	SECTION.1(1)	PART(30)
THIS.IS.LABEL(1)	SECTION.2(1)	A34B(12)

While subscripted labels must be defined with integer constants
in their subscript positions, it is unnecessary for subscripts to
start with 1, or for them to be consecutive. LABEL(4) can be defined
without having LABEL(1), LABEL(2), or LABEL(3) appear in the program.
Control, however, can only be transferred to subscripted labels that
have been defined. The previous example can be written using subscripted labels:

```
'READ'  READ X, Y AND OPERATION
        GO TO OPERN(OPERATION)
'OPERN(1)' LET ANSWER=X+Y  GO TO PRINT
'OPERN(2)' LET ANSWER=X-Y  GO TO PRINT
'OPERN(3)' LET ANSWER=X*Y  GO TO PRINT
'OPERN(4)' LET ANSWER=X/Y
'PRINT'    PRINT 1 LINE WITH X, Y AND ANSWER AS FOLLOWS
       ****.** OP ****.** = *****.**, WHAT IS OP?
              GO TO READ
```

2-10 SOME LEVEL 1 PROBLEMS REVISITED

2-10-1 Problem 1-16-1—Finding the Average, Maximum, and Minimum of a Set of Numbers

```
LET MAX = -99999.99999  LET MIN = -MAX  READ N
FOR I = 1 TO N, DO  READ X  ADD X TO SUM
   IF X IS GREATER THAN MAX, LET MAX = X REGARDLESS
   IF X IS LESS THAN MIN, LET MIN = X REGARDLESS
LOOP
START NEW PAGE  PRINT 3 LINES WITH N, SUM/N, MAX, MIN THUS
      THE AVERAGE VALUE OF *** NUMBERS IS *****.**
      THE MAXIMUM VALUE IS ******.***
      THE MINIMUM VALUE IS ******.***
STOP    END
```

2-10-2 Problem 1-16-2—A Prototype Accounting System

```
PREAMBLE  DEFINE ACCOUNT AS A 1-DIMENSIONAL ARRAY  END

RESERVE ACCOUNT(*) AS 10  READ ACCOUNT
'READ'  READ DOLLARS, CODE1, CODE2  IF DOLLARS EQUALS 0,
     GO TO FINI
ELSE  ADD 1 TO TRANSACTION.COUNTER  ADD DOLLARS TO ACCOUNT(CODE1)
SUBTRACT DOLLARS FROM ACCOUNT(CODE2)  ADD DOLLARS TO ACCOUNT(6)
SUBTRACT DOLLARS FROM ACCOUNT(10)  GO READ
'FINI'  START NEW PAGE PRINT 1 LINE WITH TRANSACTION.COUNTER
     AS FOLLOWS
***** TRANSACTIONS WERE PROCESSED THIS MONTH.
SKIP 5 OUTPUT LINES  PRINT 9 LINES CONTAINING ACCOUNT(1), ACCOUNT(7),
          ACCOUNT(2), ACCOUNT(8), ACCOUNT(3), ACCOUNT(4),
          ACCOUNT(9), ACCOUNT(5), ACCOUNT(6), ACCOUNT(10) THUS
       ASSETS                     LIABILITIES
       CURRENT ASSETS             CURRENT LIABILITIES
          CASH      $*******         ACCOUNTS PAYABLE   $******
          RECEIVABLES      *         LOAN                    *
          INVENTORY        *
       FIXED ASSETS        *
          PLANT            *      EQUITY
          EQUIPMENT        *         EQUITY                  *
       TOTAL ASSETS $*********    TOTAL LIABILITIES   $*******
```

```
SKIP 2 OUTPUT LINES  PRINT 2 LINES WITH ACCOUNT(1), ACCOUNT(2), ACCOUNT(3),
     ACCOUNT(4), ACCOUNT(5), ACCOUNT(6), ACCOUNT(7),
     ACCOUNT(8), ACCOUNT(9), AND ACCOUNT(10) AS FOLLOWS
     *****  *****  *****  *****  *****  *****
     *****  *****  *****  *****
     STOP   END
```

2-10-3 *Problem 1-16-5—A Program for Regression Analysis*

```
"A PROGRAM FOR REGRESSION ANALYSIS
READ N
FOR I = 1 TO N,
DO
READ X,Y    ADD X TO SUMX    ADD Y TO SUMY    ADD X**2 TO SUMXX
            ADD Y**2 TO SUMYY    ADD X*Y TO SUMXY
LOOP
LET A1 = (N*SUMXY - SUMX*SUMY)/(N*SUMXX - SUMX**2)
LET A0 = (SUMY - A1 + SUMX)/N
PRINT 1 LINE WITH A0 AND A1 AS FOLLOWS
     THE REGRESSION EQUATION IS Y = *.*** + *.*** X
STOP   END
```

2-11 *A NEW OUTPUT STATEMENT*

Many programming applications do not require the facilities of
the PRINT statement. A programmer is often satisfied with an econom-
ical means of displaying labeled values of selected variables with a
minimum of programming effort; as long as output is displayed neatly
and is well labeled, he is willing to compromise specialized report
formats for programming ease. This is particularly the case while
checking for errors,[†] and in programs that are run for results and
not for formal management reports.

The LIST statement prints labeled values of expressions and
singly- and doubly-subscripted variables. The form of the statement is

> LIST *list of arithmetic expressions and array names*
>
> as in   LIST   X, MAN, DELTA + 3.5/C

Expression and array values are printed in standard formats.
Although they can be listed together in a single LIST statement, they
are printed separately; a LIST statement containing a mixture of

---

[†]Called "debugging" in the programming vernacular.

different output types results in a report printed as if a new LIST statement were written each time a type change is made. If X, Y, and Z represent expressions or unsubscripted variables, NAME, GAME, and PLACE singly-subscripted variables, and ROUTE, MATRIX, and TABLE doubly-subscripted variables, then the statement

    LIST X, Y, NAME, GAME, ROUTE, Z, TABLE, MATRIX, PLACE

has the same effect as the series of statements

    LIST X, Y   LIST NAME, GAME   LIST ROUTE   LIST Z
    LIST TABLE, MATRIX   LIST PLACE

As indicated in previous examples, individual subscripted variables can be displayed, as well as entire arrays, by using different notations, e.g., $X(5)$ and X.[†]

Expression values are printed in rows across a page with the "name" of each expression above its value. As many values are put in each row as fit, according to the spacing conventions. These conventions allow 14 print positions for each value, with names right-adjusted within the 14 positions. Values are right-adjusted beneath their names. REAL values have the decimal point centered within the value field with 6 positions before and 6 after, and with 1 position left for the sign. Two positions are always left between successive fields across a page.

As an example of the LIST statement format for expressions, let the following variables and their values be printed by the LIST statement that follows:

• INTEGER variables

        N=5   MAN=245   MOTORCAR=0   KEY=156733578
        NUMBER.OF.JOBS.IN.QUEUE=45

• REAL variables

        TIME=345.87   LONGITUDE=37.37   PRICE=100.00
        TEMP.FAHRENHEIT=267.66   RATE=-545.6667
        RATIO=0.0

[†]In this statement corrections are not made for missing subscripts (see Sec. *2-07*); X is treated as an array name and not as an improperly specified element $X(1)$.

• Program statement

```
LIST N/MAN,MOTORCAR,TIME,LONGITUDE,NUMBER.OF.JOBS.IN.QUEUE,
     TEMP.FAHRENHEIT,PRICE+RATE,KEY,RATIO
```

• Program output

N/MAN	MOTORCAR	TIME	LONGITUDE
0.024081	0	345.870000	37.370000

NUMBER.OF.JOBS	TEMP.FAHRENHEI	PRICE+RATE	KEY
45	267.660000	-445.666700	156733578

RATIO
0.000000

These values, of course, are printed out differently on a printer with a wider width of paper.

Singly-subscripted variables are printed in columns following the same heading and spacing conventions as expressions. The length of each column is determined by the number of elements in the array, the longest array determining the maximum number of rows printed. Variables with fewer elements than the maximum show blanks in the positions where no elements appear. For example, if a RESERVE statement reads

    RESERVE N AS 10, MAN AS 5, MOTORCAR AS 7 AND TIME AS 4

and a LIST statement is written

    LIST N, MAN, MOTORCAR AND TIME

the following columns are printed (note that the left-hand margin is numbered to identify the element values):

	N	MAN	MOTORCAR	TIME
1	5	245	0	267.660000
2	4	18	1	268.870000
3	3	99	1	288.000000
4	2	8894	0	302.473215
5	1	4	1	
6	0		0	
7	-1		1	
8	-2			
9	-3			
10	-4			

Doubly-subscripted variables, both rectangular and ragged, are printed in rows and columns across and down a page, with the rows and columns numbered the same as the columns of the singly-subscripted variables. The heading convention places the array name above the

first column of element values; the spacing conventions are the same.
If more than one array is mentioned in a LIST statement, they are
printed successively in the order in which they are listed.   For
example, if TABLE is an array defined by the statement

RESERVE TABLE AS 5 BY 4

it is printed as follows if it is INTEGER:

TABLE			
1	2	3	4
0	556	90	78
24	88	8	5555
5	0	777	89
337	7	0	98
0	55	54	0

or as follows if it is REAL:

TABLE			
1	2	3	4
0.000000	556.000000	90.000000	78.000000
24.000000	88.000000	8.000000	5555.000000
5.000000	0.000000	777.000000	89.000000
337.000000	7.000000	0.000000	98.000000
0.000000	55.000000	54.000000	0.000000

Arrays with more columns than a page can contain are continued
on successive pages. For example, if TABLE had been reserved as
5 BY 7, an additional page would be printed as follows:

TABLE		
5	6	7
12	28	1000
301	-100	27
0	0	0
16	0	-16
-3	3	4

As the spacing conventions allow only six figures before and
after a decimal point, an output of very large and very small numbers
cannot be executed through the standard LIST format.   Numbers greater
than 999999.999999 or smaller than 0.000001 are printed in a scaled

scientific notation format instead.† As an example, assume that the variables X, MAN, and AVERAGE are to be printed by the statement LIST X, MAN AND AVERAGE, and that the value of MAN is 13,700,000,000. The following line will be printed:

X	MAN	AVERAGE
23.111100	1.370000E+10	9.252525

The LIST statement, unfortunately, can be misleading in one respect — that of significant figures. As a digital computer is a finite-word-length calculating machine, it can retain only a limited number of figures in its internal calculations; generally, the precision of computations is limited to eight or nine significant figures. Computations are subject to error, therefore, as when two 10-decimal-place fractions are added. Thus, there can be some danger in interpreting the twelve allowable decimal figures printed by the LIST statement as "true values." The same rules of careful error analysis that apply to other output to determine the significance of printed values should apply to LIST output.

2-12 MORE ON LOGICAL EXPRESSIONS

Thus far, logical expressions have been used to compare arithmetic quantities: a logical expression is true if the relationship it expresses is true, false if the relationship does not hold. Often, however, there is a need for logical expressions employing nonarithmetic comparisons. This section describes two applications of a logical expression using "property" relationships.

(1) As each arithmetic expression has a numerical value that is either positive, negative, or zero, an arithmetic expression can be compared with one of the property names POSITIVE, NEGATIVE, or ZERO, and a true or false condition set. This condition can then be used

---

†Scientific notation prints a number in the form of a decimal number between zero and ten scaled by a power of ten; 10.6 is printed as 1.06(10**+1), 0.00123 as 1.23(10**-3), 546372.3 as 5.463723(10**+5), etc. The power of ten, e.g., +1, -3, +5, indicates the direction and distance in which the decimal point must be moved to convert the fraction to the true number.

to direct the flow of program logic. The form of the logical expression is

> *arithmetic expression* IS *property name*
> or *arithmetic expression* IS NOT *property name*

The following program statements are permissible:

```
IF VALUE(ITEM) IS ZERO, GO TO NEW.ITEM    OTHERWISE
IF Y**2+X**2 IS POSITIVE, GO TO ROOT    ELSE
IF SUM IS NOT ZERO, GO TO NEW.STEP    OTHERWISE
```

The words POSITIVE, NEGATIVE, and ZERO are recognized in their correct context as property names when they follow the word IS or words IS NOT in a logical expression. Therefore, they can be used without reservation as variable names or labels. In fact, if POSITIVE is declared as a variable, the SIMSCRIPT II compiler has no difficulty with the statement

```
IF POSITIVE IS NEGATIVE, .......... ELSE
```

(2) Properties of certain special names can be used in logical tests. These names are automatically defined and their values changed during the course of computation. Section *2-13* describes these words, their property names, and how they are used.

2-13 SYSTEM-DEFINED VALUES

Programmers often use input data to control the flow of information within a program. Such statements as

```
READ N    GO TO LABELA OR LABELB OR LABELC PER N
and  READ N    IF N EQUALS 0, GO TO FINISH    OTHERWISE ....
```

are typical and have been used in several example problems.

SIMSCRIPT II offers a programmer several system-defined names that allow him to look at a number of properties of input data *before* they are read from cards by a free-form READ statement. When a programmer uses any of these names, the SIMSCRIPT II system automatically determines a property based upon the current input data status. The programmer is then free to use this property value as he wishes. The system-defined names are:

Name	Value
SFIELD.F	Starting column number of the next data field
EFIELD.F	Ending column number of the next data field
MODE	Mode of the next data field: either INTEGER or REAL
CARD	First data field on card indicator; either NEW card or NOT NEW
DATA	No data items in data deck indicator; either ENDED or NOT ENDED

Some examples illustrate the use of these system variables.

(1) The use of SFIELD.F: A deck of punched cards contains data punched in two different formats. Some of the cards have data punched beginning in column 1, while other cards are punched starting in column 25. A group of statements labeled '1' processes the cards with their data beginning in column 1, and a group of statements labeled '25' processes the other data cards. A value for SFIELD.F is determined before each new value is read, but the data item itself is not read until a READ statement is executed.

```
'LOOK'   IF SFIELD.F EQUALS 25, GO TO '25'   ELSE
'1'      READ X   ADD X TO SUMX   GO TO LOOK
'25'     READ Y   ADD Y TO SUMY   GO TO LOOK
```

(2) The use of EFIELD.F: N integers are punched on data cards when we want to count the number of one-digit numbers, the number of two-digit numbers, ..., or the number of ten-digit numbers in the data deck.

```
PREAMBLE
DEFINE COUNT AS AN INTEGER, 1-DIMENSIONAL ARRAY
END
RESERVE COUNT(*) AS 10
FOR I = 1 TO N, DO THE FOLLOWING
ADD 1 TO COUNT(EFIELD.F-SFIELD.F+1)   SKIP 1 FIELD '' TO THE
        '' NEXT NUMBER
REPEAT
```

A three-digit number, such as 274, in columns 32, 33, and 34 will have EFIELD.F = 34, SFIELD.F = 32, and will cause COUNT(34-32+1) = COUNT(3) to be incremented.

(3) The use of MODE: To search through a series of numbers on

cards and add together all the integers (not whole numbers, but numbers without decimal points).

```
                  FOR I = 1 TO N, DO    IF MODE IS INTEGER, READ NUMBER
                                        ADD NUMBER TO SUM
                                        GO TO LOOP
                                        OTHERWISE    SKIP 1 FIELD
          'LOOP'  LOOP
```

(4) The use of CARD: Although SIMSCRIPT II ignores card columns or card numbers when reading data, a programmer may want to know if he is at the beginning of a data card. Perhaps he wants to print a count of the number of data cards read at different stages of a program.

```
          'LOOP' IF CARD IS NEW, ADD 1 TO COUNT ''ADD ONLY ON A NEW CARD
                 OTHERWISE
```

(5) The use of DATA: A programmer may want to know if he is out of data without the necessity of adding a dummy data card and testing for 0 or some other value. He can do this by testing to see if the next data item to be read exists.

```
          'READ'    READ X
                 .
                 . } perform computations in here
                 .
                    IF DATA IS ENDED, STOP
                    ELSE GO READ
```

When there are no data, e.g., all data have been read and look-ahead is impossible, the system variables have these values:

Name	Value
SFIELD.F	0
EFIELD.F	0
MODE	ALPHA
CARD	NEW
DATA	ENDED

2-14 *SYSTEM-DEFINED CONSTANTS*

Scientific and engineering calculations often involve standard scientific constants; mathematical computations often require values of numerical constants. Numbers such as π = 3.14159........, and e = 2.718........ are two well-known and often-used constants.

SIMSCRIPT II maintains a library of standard values. When the name of a library constant is used in a SIMSCRIPT II program, the correct numerical value of the constant is inserted in its place. These constants may be used wherever a "regular" numerical constant can be used.

Library constants have names that look like variable names except that they end in .C. This is another reason why variable names should not end with a letter preceded by a decimal point.

The library constants and their values are listed in Table 2-3.

Table 2-3

SYSTEM-DEFINED CONSTANTS

Name	Standard Symbol	Value	Units	Mode
PI.C	π	3.14159265	--	REAL
EXP.C	e	2.718281828	--	REAL
INF.C	∞	{ largest value	--	INTEGER
RINF.C	∞	{ computer can store	--	REAL
RADIAN.C	-	57.29577	degrees/radian	REAL

2-15 THE STRUCTURE OF A SIMSCRIPT II PROGRAM

Problem solutions often require sequences of similar or identical statements to appear at different places in a program. Although these statements can be rewritten each time they are needed, it is far more convenient to combine them into groups and call on them by symbolic names.

Labeled groups of statements that can be called on by name are called *subprograms*. They are distinguished as programs because they do some specific task; they are called subprograms because they do not have an independent existence, but are controlled by other programs. A subprogram is *called* rather than executed in sequence as are the statements READ, LET, and RESERVE. When a subprogram is called, control passes from a *calling* program to the subprogram, along with instructions for returning control to the calling program. A subprogram can call upon other subprograms; it can be both a called and a calling program coincidentally.

Since subprograms cannot be executed directly but must be called, at least one nonsubprogram is required in every program deck. Every SIMSCRIPT II program *must* contain such a program, called a *main program*, and *may* contain one or more subprograms. When a program deck is compiled and loaded into memory for execution, the execution begins at the first instruction in the main program and proceeds from there, as the logic of the main program-subprogram package commands. All of the example programs used thus far have been main programs. In succeeding sections we will describe the structure and use of subprograms, and transcribe some of the main program examples into a subprogram framework.

Figure 2-8 shows three examples of main program-subprogram organizations. The examples in Fig. 2-8 consist of a main program and one or more subprograms, with arrows indicating the direction of program flow. An arrow pointing to a subprogram indicates a call on that subprogram, and an arrow pointing oppositely means a return to a calling program.

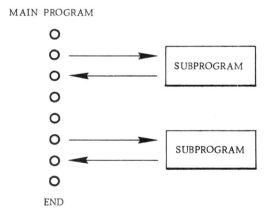

Fig. 2-8a -- Program consisting of a subprogram
called by a main program

In Fig. 2-8a the main program calls on the subprogram in two places. In each instance, after executing its statements, the subprogram returns control to the main program at the statement following the one that called it.

-81-

MAIN PROGRAM

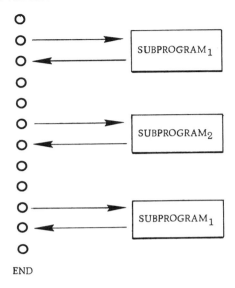

Fig. 2-8b -- Program consisting of two subprograms
called by a main program

MAIN PROGRAM

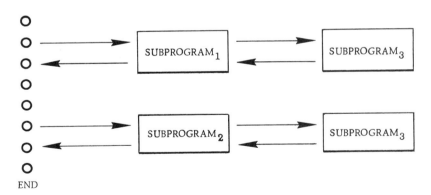

Fig. 2-8c -- Program consisting of three subprograms
and a main program

Figure 2-8b shows a slightly more complicated program composed
of a main program and two subprograms. The main program calls on
each of the subprograms; they are independent of each other.

Figure 2-8c illustrates a more complex situation in which a

main program and three subprograms interact. Subprograms 1 and 2 are
both called and calling programs — they are called by the main program and, in turn, they call on Subprogram 3. The call of Subprogram
1 or 2 by the main program is the first *level* of calling; the call of
Subprogram 3 by Subprograms 1 and 2 while under the control of the
main program is a second level. In general, there can be any level
of calling in effect within a program at any time. The calling rules
do not change from level to level — control always passes from a
calling to a called program and back again. Whether there are many
intermediate calls and returns between an original call on a subprogram
and a return to its calling program is insignificant. If A calls B
and B calls C, then C must return control to B before B can return
to A. A subprogram cannot return control to any routine other than
the one that called it, e.g., C cannot return directly to A.

Subprograms are like obedient servants. They can be called upon
to do a job, and they always report back when they are finished. The
fact that the servants may in turn have servants in no way complicates
the rules.

2-16 *SUBPROGRAM DEFINITION*

As a SIMSCRIPT II program can be composed of a main program and
a number of more or less independent subprograms, statements are needed
to inform the compiler of the overall program structure and enclose
the statements belonging to individual subprograms.

The main program in a program deck should be preceded by the
statement

MAIN

although this is not always necessary. Since all other sections of
a program deck must have a heading, it is possible to make MAIN
optional and assume a program is a main program if it is not otherwise labeled. Nevertheless, it is good programming practice to label
programs fully. From now on, we shall do so.

A *subprogram definition statement* precedes each subprogram and
(1) declares that the statements following are part of a subprogram;

(2) bestows a name to the subprogram; and (3) sets up a communication mechanism for transmitting data between the subprogram and programs calling it.

Each subprogram has a name that is used to call it. This name is declared in the subprogram definition statement that precedes the statements composing the *body of the subprogram*. Subprograms follow the same naming conventions as variables (see Sec. *2-00*). Each variable and subprogram name must be unique.

A subprogram definition statement has the form

ROUTINE *name*

The optional words TO and FOR are allowed after the word ROUTINE to make statements more grammatical. Thus, a program that extracts square roots might be called SQUARE.ROOT and could be defined by the statement

ROUTINE SQUARE.ROOT

or it might be called TAKE.SQUARE.ROOT, and be defined by the statement

ROUTINE TO TAKE.SQUARE.ROOT

or the original name might be preferred and be used in the statement

ROUTINE FOR SQUARE.ROOT

As the words TO and FOR are optional, care must be exercised to avoid using the short form of the statement when defining a subprogram named FOR or TO. If this is done, the compiler will continue to look for a subprogram name after it sees the words TO or FOR, and mistakenly use the next word it sees. For example, if a subprogram named FOR is defined by the statements

```
ROUTINE FOR
LET X = 1
END
```

the compiler assumes that the subprogram definition statement is ROUTINE FOR LET, misnames the routine, and leaves an incomplete statement X=1 to deal with next. The proper use of a subprogram definition statement with subprograms named FOR or TO should include the following optional, although ungrammatical, words:

```
ROUTINE FOR FOR        ROUTINE TO FOR
ROUTINE FOR TO         ROUTINE TO TO
```

Each subprogram is bracketed by a ROUTINE statement and an END statement. The statements between them constitute the body of the subprogram and are executed when the subprogram is called. The word *routine* will be used from here on to refer to subprograms.

Routines are generally used to process data. In a square root routine, a number is an *input* to the routine, and the value of the square root of the number is an *output* of the routine. Data are passed from calling to called programs and back again in two ways: implicitly, as values of global variables, and explicitly, through *arguments* in an *argument list.*[†]

A *global variable* is a variable whose name has a common meaning throughout a program; every use of the name of a global variable references the same memory location (and hence, the same data value) regardless of the routine in which it appears. *A variable is only defined as global when it appears in a* DEFINE *statement in the preamble.* Therefore, certain variable names must be put in DEFINE statements in order to declare them as global even though their properties are fully described by preceding NORMALLY statements. In such cases the DEFINE statement can be used without any properties, as in

DEFINE MAN, X, TIGER AND VECTOR.SUM AS VARIABLES

A *local variable*, on the other hand, has its value defined only within a particular routine. The same name can be used for a local variable in many routines; when it is so used it refers to a different quantity in each routine, as if a different variable name were being used in each place. Local variables can be used mnemonically in different routines without the various applications interfering with one another. When a name is defined within a routine, it is unique to that routine and does not conflict with other uses of the same name. Thus, it is possible to have many different elements with the same

---

[†]See p. 90.

name — variables and labels — in a program. Furthermore, local
variables are not always present in memory, as are global variables,
but pass in and out of existence as the routines in which they appear
are called. This dynamic quality conserves memory space, and it is
important in programs having a large number of local variables and
routine calls.

The preamble is used to define global variables. Any variable
not named in a program's preamble is local to whatever subprograms
it is used in. Names declared as global can be temporarily defined
as local within particular subprograms by using their names in DEFINE
statements within the routines. Local variables have the properties
of the background (NORMALLY) conditions in effect at the time they
are first encountered, unless they are otherwise defined through
DEFINE statements.

The following program implicitly specifies that X and Y, which
are not mentioned in the preamble but which do appear in the routines
RTN1 and RTN2, are INTEGER , unsubscripted local variables. The
names X and Y refer to different quantities in RTN1 and RTN2.

```
PREAMBLE
NORMALLY, MODE IS INTEGER, DIMENSION=2        )
DEFINE GHOST AND SPECTER AS REAL ARRAYS        }   Program Preamble
DEFINE VALUE AS A REAL, 1-DIMENSIONAL ARRAY    }
NORMALLY, DIMENSION= 0                          )
END
MAIN

    { This section is the main routine.  It can contain
    { references to both global and local variables.

END
ROUTINE RTN1

    { This section contains statements that use the
    { variables X and Y.

END
ROUTINE RTN2

    { This section contains statements that use the
    { variables X and Y.

END
```

All variables that do not appear in a program preamble are local.
Local variables can be used both in routines and in main programs.

Local variables that have different properties from those of the current NORMALLY conditions are declared by DEFINE statements in their respective routines. NORMALLY statements can be used in routines to set background conditions for local variables, but these conditions do not carry over from one routine to another. Only the last defined NORMALLY conditions in the preamble carry over from routine to routine. A main program can have local variables declared in DEFINE statements that follow the statement MAIN. The example below illustrates how NORMALLY and DEFINE statements are used to specify properties of local and global variables.

```
PREAMBLE
NORMALLY, MODE IS INTEGER                                    ⎫
DEFINE V1 AND V2 AS REAL, 1-DIMENSIONAL ARRAYS              ⎬  Program
DEFINE V3, V4 AND V5 AS 2-DIMENSIONAL ARRAYS                ⎬  Preamble
NORMALLY, MODE= REAL                                         ⎭
END

     MAIN READ N RESERVE V1,V2 AS N, V3,V4,V5 AS N BY N
     READ V1 AND V2    LET V3(1,1)=V1(V2(1))

          and other statements that make up a main program,
          including call statements for the following routines
                              .
                              .
                              .
     END  ''OF MAIN ROUTINE''


     ROUTINE TO PROCESS.DATA
     NORMALLY, DIMENSION= 1, MODE IS REAL
     DEFINE Z AS AN INTEGER ARRAY
     DEFINE L, M AND N AS INTEGER VARIABLES
     RESERVE Z AS 10
     'START'          .
                      .
                      .
     GO TO START

          and other statements that make up a routine
                              .
                              .
                              .

     END ''OF ROUTINE PROCESS.DATA
```

```
ROUTINE FOR PRINTING
DEFINE Z AS A 2-DIMENSIONAL VARIABLE
RESERVE Z AS 10 BY 5
'START'
        •
        •
        •
END ''OF ROUTINE PRINTING
```

Some points to observe from this example are:

(1) A preamble can have more than one NORMALLY statement. Each successive NORMALLY statement sets background conditions that hold until they are overridden. The last NORMALLY conditions hold for all undefined local variables in routines. Local variables in routines can have their properties defined by NORMALLY and DEFINE statements in the routines.

(2) The order of NORMALLY and DEFINE statements is always important. In the above routine PROCESS.DATA the variable Z is defined as an INTEGER, 1-DIMENSIONAL array by the NORMALLY and DEFINE statements. If these statements are reversed, the NORMALLY conditions of the program preamble will apply to Z and it will be defined as an unsubscripted variable, a definition that subsequently will be contradicted by the RESERVE statement, although this need not always be true. The order of definition statements is always important.

(3) Unsubscripted local variables (L, M, and N in PROCESS.DATA) are automatically assigned storage locations and initialized to zero when a routine is called. They are returned to "free storage" when control passes back from a routine to a calling program. Subscripted local variables are not automatically assigned storage locations, and must be RESERVED before they can be used. When an array is RESERVED, its elements are automatically initialized to zero.

(4) Local variables can have conflicting definitions in different routines without any difficulty, as Z is a 1-DIMENSIONAL,INTEGER local array in routine PROCESS.DATA and a 2-DIMENSIONAL,REAL array in routine PRINTING. If Z were used in the main program, it would be local to it, defined as unsubscripted, and REAL.

(5) Labels are always local. When a name is used as a label it references a program statement in the routine containing the label.

Label names can be duplicated in different routines without conflict.
Labels appearing in one routine are not defined within other routines,
and transfers cannot be made between routines by means of GO TO
statements.

(6) A subscripted local variable that does not appear in a
DEFINE statement within a routine has its dimensionality defined by
its first use, i.e., even if a routine's NORMALLY condition is 0-
dimensional, the statement LET X(I)=0 defines X as 1-dimensional.

(7) The concept of a routine preamble is a convenient fiction.
Definitional statements placed at the head of a routine are not preceded by PREAMBLE and followed by END, as are similar statements in
a program preamble. NORMALLY and DEFINE statements can be used anywhere within a routine.

2-17 ROUTINES USED AS FUNCTIONS

A function is a routine that yields a single value when applied
to a set of data. The value given is known as the result of the
function. The familiar symbols sin (y) and $\sqrt{x}$ represent the mathematical functions sine and square root, i.e., they represent procedures
for computing the value of the sine of y and the square root of x.

When a function is used in an expression, there is no intent to
substitute the literal symbol of the function in the expression but
only the number that results from applying the function to its
arguments (input values). The function symbol represents a procedure
for converting the value of an argument or arguments to a new value,
called the value of the function. We pretend that this value is
assigned to the function symbol and use it in subsequent calculations.
Thus y ← $\sqrt{x}$ means "compute the value of the square root of x and
assign it to the variable y."

Functions are so basic to computing that they must be incorporated into the rules for evaluating arithmetic expressions:

- Arithmetic expressions are composed of variables, constants, functions, arithmetic operators, and parentheses.

- Expressions are evaluated according to the parentheses
  and operator hierarchy precedence rules; functions are

evaluated by application of the parentheses rule (see
Sec. *1-03*, p. 2, and Sec. *2-04*, p. 40).

The following two examples illustrate the rules for evaluating
expressions that contain functions:

Expression: X*Y+SQRT.F(P+Q**2/M); SQRT.F is a function that
takes the square root of a single argument enclosed
in parentheses.

Evaluation: (1) Application of the parentheses rule evaluates,
from left to right, all terms containing parentheses.
A value is first computed for the expression P+Q**2/M.
In this intermediate computation, Q**2 is evaluated,
the result divided by M, and this result added to P.
This value is then used as the argument of the square
root function, which is called, and produces the
result s.

(2) The expression X*Y+s is evaluated by applying
the operator precedence rules; X and Y are multiplied,
and S is added to their product.

Expression: SQRT.F((X(I+1)**2+Y(J)**2)+(5.5*Z(2*I+J)-1)).

Evaluation: Application of the parentheses and operator precedence rules evaluate, in turn, the sub-expressions:

    (a)   I+1 → a   (b)   J → d   (c)   b**2 → c
          X(a) → b   Y(d) → e   e**2 → f
                                               c+f → g

    (d)   2*I → h   (e)   g+m → n   (f)   SQRT.F(n) → p
          h+J → i
          Z(i) → j
       5.5*j → k
        k-1 → m

An important rule to remember is that expressions are evaluated
term by term, with the parentheses rule being invoked within terms
whenever parentheses are used. In the event of consecutive parentheses, the most deeply imbedded parentheses are evaluated first.
Whenever an expression enclosed within parentheses consists of more
than one term, the operator precedence rules are applied to determine
the order of evaluation. Functions with argument lists and subscripted
variables are always evaluated under the parentheses rule. The following example illustrates the invocation of the parentheses rule to
evaluate a complicated expression containing a function call and consecutive parentheses:

Expression: 5.0 + (SQRT.F(I) + ((A+B)/C) + D)

Evaluation: (1) SQRT.F(I) → a

(2) A+B → b
    b/C → c

(3) a+c+D → e

(4) result= 5.0+e

Arguments are values that are transmitted from a calling to a called program. They represent variables that are local to a routine and that receive initial values when a routine is called. When a routine is written (described in Sec. *2-19*), local variables that are arguments of the routine are *formal* place-holders; they serve as receptacles into which values are dropped when a routine is called. When a routine is called (also described in Sec. *2-19*), actual values are put in the positions in which the formal arguments appear in the routine definition and these values are transmitted to the routine and used to initialize the routine arguments.

2-18 LIBRARY FUNCTIONS

Some functions are used so frequently that they are incorporated in the SIMSCRIPT II system. These functions are described in Table 2.4.

Each library function, with the exception of MAX.F and MIN.F, has a fixed number of arguments. The library functions can be used freely in all computations, although values, of course, cannot be assigned to them. Function arguments can be arithmetic expressions of any complexity (including function names) as long as they are of the correct mode and their values do not exceed any restrictions they may have (see Table 2-4). Some examples of the use of library functions are:

Statement	Action
(a) LET DECIMAL=FRAC.F(X)	fractional part of X
(b) IF SIGN.F(X/Y)=1,GO PLUS ELSE	branches if ratio is positive
(c) IF SFIELD.F>10,READ X ELSE	controls the input of data

Table 2-4

SIMSCRIPT II LIBRARY FUNCTIONS

Name	Arguments	Operation	Function Mode	Restrictions
ABS.F[†]	e	$\|e\| = \begin{array}{l} e \text{ if } e \geq 0 \\ -e \text{ if } e < 0 \end{array}$	mode of argument	none
MAX.F[†]	$e_1, e_2, \ldots, e_n$	value of largest argument	INTEGER if all arguments INTEGER REAL if one argument REAL	none
MIN.F[†]	$e_1, e_2, \ldots, e_n$	value of smallest argument	INTEGER if all arguments INTEGER REAL if one argument REAL	none
MOD.F[†]	e_1, e_2	$e_1 - TRUNC.F(e_1/e_2)*e_2$	INTEGER if all arguments INTEGER REAL if one argument REAL	$e_2 \neq 0$
DIV.F[†]	e_1, e_2	$TRUNC.F(e_1/e_2)$	INTEGER	e_1 and e_2 INTEGER; $e_2 \neq 0$
INT.F[†]	e	value of e rounded to an integer	INTEGER	none
REAL.F[†]	e	value of e expressed as a decimal number	REAL	none
FRAC.F	e	fractional part of e; $e-TRUNC.F(e)$	REAL	e must be REAL
TRUNC.F	e	integer part of e; $e-FRAC.F(e)$	INTEGER	e must be REAL
SIGN.F	e	1 if e > 0 0 if e = 0 -1 if e < 0	INTEGER	none
SFIELD.F	none	see Sec. 2-13	INTEGER	free-form input only
EFIELD.F	none	see Sec. 2-13	INTEGER	free-form input only
DIM.F	v	number of elements in array pointed to	INTEGER	v a pointer
SQRT.F	e	$\sqrt{e}$	REAL	$e \geq 0$ and REAL
EXP.F	e	$\exp(e) = EXP.C**e$	REAL	e must be REAL
LOG.E.F	e	$\log_e(e)$	REAL	$e > 0$ and REAL
LOG.10.F	e	$\log_{10}(e)$	REAL	$e > 0$ and REAL
SIN.F	e	$\sin(e)$	REAL	e REAL and expressed in radians
COS.F	e	$\cos(e)$	REAL	e REAL and expressed in radians
TAN.F	e	$\tan(e)$	REAL	e REAL and expressed in radians
ARCSIN.F	e	$\arcsin(e)$	REAL	$-1 \leq e \leq 1$ and REAL
ARCCOS.F	e	$\arccos(e)$	REAL	$-1 \leq e \leq 1$ and REAL
ARCTAN.F	e_1, e_2	$\arctan(e_1/e_2)$	REAL	$(e_1, e_2) \neq (0,0)$ and REAL

[†]Denotes a function compiled in-line rather than called as a routine.

Statement	Action
(d) LET Z=SQRT.F(X**2+Y**2)	$\sqrt{X^2 + Y^2}$
(e) ADD SQRT.F(SQRT.F(N)) TO SUM	$SUM + N^{\frac{1}{4}}$

(f) LET MAX=ABS.F(X(1))
     FOR I= 2 TO N,
      LET MAX=MAX.F(ABS.F(X(I)),MAX)
	finds $MAX\|X_i\|$

(g) LET VAR=MEAN*LOG.E.F(RANDOM)	mean [ln(random)]
(h) LET DECIMAL=MOD.F(X,1)	same as (a)
(i) FOR I=1 TO ABS.F(N-K), LET X(I)=1	initializes array X
(j) FOR J=1 TO DIM.F(TABLE(*)),LET TABLE(J)=0	zeroes array TABLE

2-19 PROGRAM-DEFINED FUNCTIONS

Routines that perform as functions can be defined. Computations are programmed in the routine, and the routine name is used to represent the function. Library and program defined functions are used in exactly the same way.

Routines used as functions can be defined with or without arguments. Alternate forms of the ROUTINE statement are indicated below.

(a) ROUTINE *name*
(b) ROUTINE *name* (*argument list*)
(c) ROUTINE *name* GIVEN *argument list*

Routines can be defined without arguments, as in (a), when all input values are transmitted to the routine through global variables. When arguments are used, they are names of local variables in the body of a routine. When a function is called, the values of expressions used in the argument list are transferred to the routine. In the routine SQRT, for example, defined by the statement ROUTINE FOR SQRT(N), N is a local variable appearing in the computational procedure for computing a square root. When the function SQRT is used in a program, it can be written as SQRT(4), or SQRT(VALUE*SUM-1) or SQRT(SQRT(Z**3)), with an arithmetic expression replacing the identifier of the argument list.

As illustrated in Sec. *2-16*, the optional words TO and FOR can be used between the word ROUTINE and a subprogram name. In the long form of the ROUTINE statement with arguments, the word GIVEN can be

replaced by the words GIVING, THE, or THIS to make declarations more
readable. These options make a large number of ROUTINE statement
forms possible. For example:

```
ROUTINE ALLOCATE
ROUTINE TO ADD(X AND Y)
ROUTINE FOR ADDING  GIVEN X AND Y
ROUTINE LOG(X,Y)
ROUTINE FOR ALLOCATING THIS MAN
```

When a routine with arguments is called as a function, however, it
can only be called as

name (arithmetic expression list)

Only a ",", not an AND or ,AND can be used to separate expressions in
a function call.

A routine used as a function returns a value to the calling program when it executes a RETURN statement. This statement is written as

RETURN WITH arithmetic expression

or   RETURN (arithmetic expression)

The value of the expression is computed before the routine returns to
the calling program. The computed value is returned in the mode of
the function, specified in the program preamble in a function mode
definition statement.

The DEFINE statement used to declare the mode of a function in a
program preamble is of the form:

DEFINE name AS mode FUNCTION

where the words AN INTEGER or A REAL are optional and can be substituted for the mode when appropriate. More than one function can be
declared in a single DEFINE statement, as, for example, in the statement

DEFINE ROOT, ALLOCATE AND COMPLEX.ADD AS REAL FUNCTIONS

Each function must be defined in the program preamble in order to
distinguish it from a variable in subsequent subprograms.

There can be more than one RETURN statement in a routine, for a
routine may be used for multiple purposes and have multiple exit
points, each of which returns a different value. All function values

are returned in the same mode, of course. The program shown below
illustrates the use of arguments and the ROUTINE and RETURN statements. The routine computes the 2^n-th root of an input value, where
n can take on the values 1, 2, or 3.

In the program preamble:

> DEFINE ROOT AS A REAL FUNCTION

Routine definition:

```
ROUTINE FOR ROOT (N,X)
IF N = 1, RETURN WITH SQRT.F(X)  ELSE
IF N = 2, RETURN WITH SQRT.F(SQRT.F(X))  ELSE
IF N = 3, RETURN WITH SQRT.F(SQRT.F(SQRT.F(X))) ELSE
RETURN WITH -1 ''WHICH IS AN ERROR MESSAGE CODE
END ''ROOT ROUTINE''
```

Routine used in other programs:

```
LET Y =ROOT(2, LIST(ROW,COLUMN))
ADD ROOT(M,X**2+V*WEIGHT/MASS) TO VAR
LET I=MAX.F(0,ROOT(K,Q))
```

In the last example, I is set equal to 0 if K is not 1, 2, or 3;
otherwise, it is set equal to the appropriate root of Q.

Notice that the arguments of ROOT are used in its body as decision
or computing variables. When the routine ROOT is called, the expressions that appear in the *positions* of N and X are evaluated and set
as the initial values of N and X in this call. Thus, unlike other
variables that are initialized to zero when a routine is called,
routine arguments are initialized to values specified in the statements that call them.

Routine arguments, unless defined, have their mode implied by
the background conditions in effect when the routine is compiled.

In a large program with several routines, it is likely that many
routine arguments will have different mode specifications. Most of
these will be made through DEFINE statements, as they will not agree
with the NORMALLY conditions. The properties of the remainder will
be specified by implication. The routines that contain DEFINE statements will be definitionally self-contained; the others will be defined in the context of the program preamble.

Consider the following routine:

```
ROUTINE FOR ILLUSTRATION(X,Y,Z,I)
DEFINE X, Y AND Z AS REAL VARIABLES
DEFINE I AS AN INTEGER VARIABLE
                    .
                    .
                    .
```

        END

This routine can be written without one of the DEFINE statements, depending on the NORMALLY conditions of the program preamble. It is written as shown above to ensure that the routine will not be altered no matter how the preamble is changed.

Arguments in statements that call a routine must match the arguments of the defined routine in mode. Routine ILLUSTRATION above can be called as ILLUSTRATION(1.0,2.0,0.5,1), but not as ILLUSTRATION-(1,2.0,0.5,1). Mode conversions are not made automatically as they are in "mixed mode" expressions.

The number of arguments in a routine, like the number of subscripts in a subscripted variable, is fixed. If a routine appears in different places in a program with a varying number of arguments, standard corrective rules are applied.

The "correct" number of arguments for a routine can be declared in the DEFINE statement that defines its mode. For this use the DEFINE statement has either of the phrases

    GIVEN i ARGUMENTS   or   GIVEN 1 ARGUMENT

added to it, as in the declarations

    DEFINE SQRT AS A REAL FUNCTION GIVEN 1 ARGUMENT

and

    DEFINE VALUE AS AN INTEGER FUNCTION WITH 3 ARGUMENTS

The words WITH or GIVING can be substituted for GIVEN as desired. The words ARGUMENT and its synonym, VALUE, are optional. Usually there is no difference between the number of arguments defined and the number used, and the correct number is the number found in all statements. But if, either inadvertently or by design, the number of arguments varies, the following rules are applied:

(a) If fewer arguments are listed than are correct, the missing arguments are assumed to be zero and a warning message issued. Thus, a routine that has been defined as

```
PREAMBLE
DEFINE SUM AS A REAL FUNCTION WITH 1 ARGUMENT
END
ROUTINE TO SUM(N)
DEFINE N AS AN INTEGER VARIABLE
FOR I = 1 TO N, ADD 1/I TO X
RETURN(X)
END
```

when used in a subsequent statement as

```
LET ANSWER=COUNT+TOTAL+SUM
```

will be compiled as though it were written

```
LET ANSWER=COUNT+TOTAL+SUM(0)
```

and a warning message will be generated. This is clearly an incorrect program, as SUM can never be anything but 0.

(b) If more arguments are listed than are correct, the extra arguments are ignored and a warning message issued. This could happen if the above example had its calling statement written incorrectly as

```
LET ANSWER=COUNT+TOTAL+SUM(N,M)
```

Such a statement will be compiled as though it were written

```
LET ANSWER=COUNT+TOTAL+SUM(N)
```

and a warning message will be generated.

If a function does not have its number of arguments defined, no check is made to determine if the correct number is used. The program is compiled as written, with responsibility for ensuring internal consistency left to the programmer.

It is now possible to illustrate the definition and use of some routines used as functions.

(1) A routine to evaluate the series

$$\sum_{i=1}^{N} \frac{1}{x^i} = \frac{1}{x^1} + \frac{1}{x^2} + \frac{1}{x^3} + \ldots + \frac{1}{x^N}$$

The routine has two arguments: the number of terms in the series that are to be summed, and the value to be substituted for x.

In the program preamble:

DEFINE SUM.SERIES AS A REAL FUNCTION WITH 2 ARGUMENTS

Routine definition:

```
ROUTINE TO SUM.SERIES GIVEN N AND X
DEFINE X AND SUM AS REAL VARIABLES
DEFINE I AND N AS INTEGER VARIABLES
FOR I = 1 TO N, ADD 1/(X**I) TO SUM
RETURN WITH SUM
END
```

Routine used as a function:

LET VALUE=SUM.SERIES(10,2) sets VALUE equal to the sum

$$\sum_{i=1}^{10} \frac{1}{2^i} = \frac{1}{2^1} + \frac{1}{2^2} + \frac{1}{2^3} + \dots + \frac{1}{2^{10}} \cong 0.999$$

LET VALUE=SUM.SERIES(N,X+Y) sets VALUE equal to the sum

$$\sum_{i=1}^{N} \frac{1}{(X+Y)^i} \; ; \text{ if } X=1, \; Y=4 \text{ and } N=3, \; VALUE= 0.248$$

LET VALUE= SUM.SERIES(40,SIN.F(THETA)) sets VALUE equal to

$$\sum_{i=1}^{40} \frac{1}{\sin(\theta)^i}$$

(2) A routine to compute a square root (see Sec. *1-16-4*).

In the program preamble:

DEFINE SQRT AS A REAL FUNCTION WITH 1 ARGUMENT

Routine definition:

```
ROUTINE FOR SQRT(V)
NORMALLY, MODE IS REAL
LET V=ABS.F(V) ''IF V IS NEGATIVE, TAKE ROOT OF +V
'GUESS'  LET S1=V/2
'LOOP'   LET S2=(S1+V/S1)/2
IF ABS.F(S1-S2) IS LESS THAN 0.0001,
     RETURN WITH S2
OTHERWISE  LET S1=S2    GO TO 'LOOP'
END
```

Routine used as a function:

same as library function SQRT.F, e.g., LET X=SQRT(Z)
note: SQRT(X) is accurate to 0.0001
        SQRT(-X)=SQRT(X)

(3)   An example to illustrate the definition and use of a routine
with a varying number of arguments. The routine has three arguments
X, Y, and Z; it has the value X if Z=0, X^2 if Z > 0 and X+Y if Z < 0.
In the program preamble:

    DEFINE VALUE AS A REAL FUNCTION

Routine definition:

    ROUTINE VALUE GIVEN Z, X AND Y
    DEFINE X, Y AND Z AS REAL VARIABLES
    IF Z EQUALS 0 RETURN(X)   ELSE
    IF Z IS GREATER THAN 0   RETURN WITH X**2   ELSE
    RETURN WITH X+Y   END

Routine used as a function:

(a)   LET VAL=VALUE(2.0,10.0)[†] compiles as LET VAL=VALUE(2.0,10.0,0.0)
      and sets VAL=100. — used this way if Z known to be ≥ 0.

(b)   LET VAL=VALUE(-1.0,16.0,Z) sets VAL=16 +Z

(c)   LET VAL=VALUE(N,Y,X+SQRT.F(N**2)) sets:

      VAL= Y if N=0

      VAL= Y^2 if N>0

      VAL= Y+X+SQRT.F(N**2) if N<0

In example (3c) some of the variables present in the routine
argument list when the routine is called have the same names as variables appearing in the function definition. They are not the same
variables. The variables X and Y used inside the routine are local
variables and are defined only within the routine. The variables in
the calling statement may be global, or they may be local to the calling routine. This is the only way that local variable values can be
passed out of a routine. Let the calling routine be

_____

[†]Since VALUE has REAL arguments, 2.0 and 10.0 rather than 2 and
10 must be used.

```
ROUTINE TO EVALUATE(N,Q,R)
DEFINE X,Y,Z,N,Q,R AS REAL VARIABLES
LET X=N**2*Q**2   LET Y=X+Q   LET Z=X+R
RETURN WITH VALUE(N,Y,Z+SQRT.F(N**2))
END
```

The local variable Y in EVALUATE is assigned a value and used as an
argument in the call on the routine VALUE. The values of N,Y and
Z+SQRT.F(N**2) in the routine EVALUATE are assigned as the initial
values of the local variables Z, X, and Y in the routine VALUE, in
that order. The names in the different routines, although identical,
do not refer to the same memory locations.

2-20 *ROUTINES USED AS MORE GENERAL COMPUTATIONAL PROCEDURES*

A routine used as a function returns a single result, but it may
also effect other changes by altering values of global variables.

Generally, a routine can be used as a *procedure*. A routine used
as a procedure is called on, not to return a single value, but to
perform a task. The task may be to compute one or more values and
return them to a calling program, to modify values of global variables,
or to perform some noncomputational act, such as executing a RESERVE
statement. A routine used as a procedure need not be declared in the
program preamble. There are two ways of examining a routine to determine whether it can be used as a procedure:

(a) Routines that are used as procedures can have arguments in
an output argument list. These arguments are unsubscripted local
variables that receive values computed within the routine. They are
initialized to zero each time the routine is called. The subsequently
computed values are assigned to named variables in a calling program
when the routine returns control to it.

(b) Routines that are used as procedures return control to a
calling program with a special RETURN statement. Because no single
value is returned as the value of a procedure, there is no need for,
nor any possibility of, executing a statement such as RETURN WITH
arithmetic expression.

A routine can, in general, have both input and output arguments.
Input arguments were discussed in Sec. *2-19*; they can be specified

in routines that are used either as functions or procedures. Output
arguments can only be used in routines that are used as procedures.
They are not always necessary, however, as a procedure can transmit
outputs through global variables. When this is done, the only way
to distinguish a routine used as a procedure from one used as a function is by the different RETURN statement and by the lack of a definition in the preamble.

Output arguments are specified by appending the phrase

YIELDING *argument list*

to a ROUTINE statement. An output argument list contains the names
of local variables, as in the statement

ROUTINE TO ANALYZE.CIRCLE GIVEN RADIUS YIELDING AREA AND CIRCUMFERENCE

In this statement, the local variable RADIUS is used to transmit an
input value from the calling to the called program. The local variables AREA and CIRCUMFERENCE are used to transmit output values from
the routine to calling programs.

Routines that are used as procedures are called by the statements

CALL *routine name*
PERFORM *routine name*
NOW *routine name*

If argument lists are used, they are written after the routine name.
Various forms of argument list structures can be used. The statements
below are equivalent:

CALL TARGET GIVEN RANGE YIELDING ELEVATION AND CHARGE
CALL TARGET (RANGE) YIELDING ELEVATION, CHARGE
NOW TARGET THE RANGE YIELDING ELEVATION AND CHARGE
PERFORM TARGET (RANGE) YIELDING ELEVATION, CHARGE

The following example shows how a routine used as a procedure is
defined and how it can be used:

Routine definition:

ROUTINE FOR CIRCLE GIVEN RADIUS YIELDING AREA AND CIRCUMFERENCE
DEFINE RADIUS, AREA AND CIRCUMFERENCE AS REAL VARIABLES
LET CIRCUMFERENCE= 2*PI.C*RADIUS
LET AREA= PI.C*RADIUS**2
RETURN
END

Routine used in a program:

    (a)   READ R CALL CIRCLE GIVEN R YIELDING P AND C

    (b)   IF A+B < 0 PERFORM CIRCLE(A) YIELDING A,B

    (c)   CALL CIRCLE(X+Y**2+Z**2+(P/Q)) YIELDING AREA AND CIRCUM

In (a) the routine CIRCLE is given the value R as an input argument. Using this value for the local variable RADIUS, it computes
the values AREA and CIRCUMFERENCE and assigns them to the output arguments P and C, respectively. The variables P and C are not used
within the routine CIRCLE; they receive new values when the routine
returns to the calling program.

In (b) the variable A appears in both the input and the output
argument list. When this is done there is no conflict, as there is
a clear order in which input and output arguments are communicated.
First, the initial value of A is transferred to the local variable
RADIUS. Next, the computations of the routine are performed. Finally,
new values of A and B are set when the routine returns to the calling
program.

In (c) an expression is used in the input argument list to transmit a value to RADIUS, the typical use of an input argument. Output
arguments, however, can only be variables (which may be subscripted)
as they do not denote values, but memory locations in which values
are stored.

The "correct" number of arguments for a routine used as a procedure can be declared in a program preamble by a statement of the
form

    DEFINE *name* AS A ROUTINE GIVEN i ARGUMENTS YIELDING i VALUES

As usual, some variations are allowed: *name* may be a list of routine
names and the word ROUTINES used; the word A is optional; WITH and
GIVING are synonyms for GIVEN; ARGUMENTS is a synonym for VALUES; both
the GIVEN and YIELDING phrases are optional. Examples of each of
these variations are given in later sections.

If a greater or smaller number of arguments appears in a CALL or
a ROUTINE statement than were defined as correct in a program preamble,

the same rules that apply to functions are observed. Missing arguments in input lists having less than the "standard" number of arguments are assumed to be zero and additional arguments are ignored. Additional arguments in output lists are ignored, and missing arguments, because they are needed to receive output variables, are created by the compiler. The values transmitted to them are not accessible to the calling program. Warning messages are issued.

If a routine is defined with only GIVING arguments, it is assumed to have no YIELDING values; if it is defined with only YIELDING values, it is assumed to have no GIVING arguments.

2-21 ROUTINES USED AS FUNCTIONS AND AS PROCEDURES

Often there is a possibility of using a routine as both a function and a procedure. The choice depends upon the number of output values the routine returns and the manner in which the routine is used. A routine can be used as a function and as a procedure by using both types of RETURN statements. When the routine returns from a RETURN WITH statement, it returns a value to a calling program; when it returns from a RETURN statement, it makes output assignments, if there are any, and returns to the statement following the CALL.

The routine CIRCLE of the previous section can be used as an example of how a routine can be written and used as both a function and a procedure.

In the program preamble:

```
DEFINE CIRCLE AS A REAL FUNCTION
```

Routine definition:

```
ROUTINE FOR CIRCLE GIVEN R AND N YIELDING A AND C
DEFINE R, A AND C AS REAL VARIABLES
DEFINE N AS AN INTEGER VARIABLE
LET A=PI.C*R**2  LET C=2*PI.C*R
IF N=0 RETURN  ELSE RETURN WITH A
END
```

Routine used:

```
(a)  LET COST=DOLLARS.PER.SQUARE.FOOT*CIRCLE(RADIUS,1)

(b)  READ R CALL CIRCLE(R,0) YIELDING AREA AND CIRC
     LET COST=DOLLARS.PER.SQUARE.FOOT*AREA
     LET LENGTH=NUMBER.OF.STRANDS*CIRC
```

Notice the added input argument that determines how the routine is used so that a proper return is effected. A code may be provided either this way or as a global variable.

2-22 *ARRAY POINTERS AS ROUTINE ARGUMENTS*

Thus far, all routine arguments were either arithmetic expressions or variables. They were expressions in input lists because, as was indicated, such lists transmit values from calling to called programs. They were variables in output lists because values computed in routines are assigned to them. The transmission of entire arrays was not mentioned.

Array pointers can be used as arguments of routines. When an array pointer is used in an argument list, the pointer to the array is passed to the routine. This pointer is used in place of a local variable pointer that appears in the routine. An array pointer can be used in an input or output argument list. There is no transfer of values of an array before or after a routine is executed as there is when unsubscripted variables or expressions are used as arguments; retrieval and assignment of array values during execution are accomplished through array pointers.

When an array is used as an argument of a routine, its dimensionality must be specified in a DEFINE statement in the routine. Each use (call) of a routine that has array arguments must have arrays of the same dimension in its argument lists. The following program illustrates the use of an array name in a routine used as a function:

```
ROUTINE FOR VECTOR.PRODUCT(X,Y)
DEFINE X AND Y AS REAL, 1-DIMENSIONAL ARRAYS
DEFINE SUM AS A REAL VARIABLE DEFINE I AS AN INTEGER VARIABLE
FOR I = 1 TO DIM.F(X(*)), ADD X(I)*Y(I) TO SUM
RETURN WITH SUM
END
```

In the above routine X and Y are local arrays. When the routine is called, pointer values are given to them. If the routine is called as VECTOR.PRODUCT(COST(*),UNIT(*)), the statement FOR I = 1 TO DIM.F(X(*)), ADD X(I)*Y(I) TO SUM is interpreted as FOR I = 1 TO DIM.F(COST(*)), ADD COST(I)*UNIT(I) TO SUM.

If a program has the arrays LIST and VECTOR defined and the following values:

LIST(1)	=	2	VECTOR(1) =	4
LIST(2)	=	3	VECTOR(2) =	6
LIST(3)	=	7	VECTOR(3) =	0
LIST(4)	=	-1	VECTOR(4) =	15
LIST(5)	=	0	VECTOR(5) =	-5

the statement LET VALUE=VECTOR.PRODUCT(LIST(*),VECTOR(*)) sets VALUE=11.

Arrays used as arguments need not be RESERVED in a routine unless they have not been RESERVED previously. If they are reserved within a routine, they must appear as both input and output arguments so that the location of the newly allocated memory can be passed back to the calling program. In this respect, array arguments are unlike subscripted local variables that must be RESERVED at the beginning of a routine.

The important features to remember about arrays used as arguments are (1) the pointer to an array is transmitted, rather than the individual element values, and (2) the dimensionality of the array must be declared in the routine. Some sample programs illustrate these points.

(1) A routine to compute the trace of a matrix. The trace of a matrix is defined as the sum of its diagonal elements

$$tr(A) = \sum_{i=1}^{N} A(i,i)$$

The array A must have both dimensions equal; it must be defined by a statement such as RESERVE A(*,*) AS N BY N. The following routine uses an array name as one of its arguments and the size of its dimensions as another.

In the program preamble:

DEFINE TRACE AS A REAL FUNCTION WITH 2 ARGUMENTS

Routine definition:

```
ROUTINE TRACE(N,MATRIX)
DEFINE SUM AS A REAL VARIABLE
DEFINE MATRIX AS A REAL, 2-DIMENSIONAL ARRAY  DEFINE I AND N AS
     INTEGER VARIABLES
FOR I = 1 TO N, ADD MATRIX(I,I) TO SUM
RETURN WITH SUM  END
```

Routine used in a program:

   (a)   To evaluate the trace of a matrix called TABLE
        LET VALUE=TRACE(DIM.F(TABLE(1,*)),TABLE(*,*))

   (b)   To sum the first 5 diagonal elements of TABLE
        LET VALUE=TRACE(5,TABLE(*,*))

Notice that a routine of the form of SUM.SERIES (see p. 97) cannot be used for this purpose, as it transmits the value of an argument to be summed and not a pointer. A function such as TRACE can be used several times in the same expression with different arguments, as:

```
LET SUM=TRACE(10,TABLE(*,*)) + TRACE(Y,ROSTER(*,*)) +
     TRACE(DIM.F(X(1,*)),X(*,*))
```

   (2)   A routine using array arguments and defined as a function, but doing more than merely returning a computed value to a program calling it.

In the program preamble:

```
DEFINE PROCESS.DATA AS A REAL FUNCTION
```

Routine definition:

```
ROUTINE TO PROCESS.DATA GIVEN CODE, LIST1 AND LIST2
NORMALLY, MODE= INTEGER
DEFINE LIST1 AND LIST2 AS 1-DIMENSIONAL ARRAYS
IF CODE IS GREATER THAN 0   GO TO PRODUCT
OTHERWISE FOR I = 1 TO DIM.F(LIST1(*)),
     DO LET LIST1(I)=SQRT.F(LIST1(I))
        LET LIST2(I)=SQRT.F(LIST2(I))
     REPEAT
'PRODUCT'   RETURN WITH VECTOR.PRODUCT(LIST1(*),LIST2(*))
END ''OF ROUTINE PROCESS.DATA
```

Routine used in program:

If PROCESS.DATA is called with CODE > 0, it returns the value of VECTOR.PRODUCT (see p. 103) to the calling routine; it does not alter the values of the arrays in the argument list. If called with CODE $\leq$ 0, the routine replaces the elements of LIST1 and LIST2 (or, more precisely, the elements indicated by the

array pointers used in the calling program) with their square
roots and returns with the VECTOR.PRODUCT of the altered arrays.

(3) A routine adding two two-dimensional arrays together and
storing their sum in a third array.

In the program preamble:

Nothing needed since routine is used as a procedure.

Routine definition [note use of comments in the ROUTINE statement]:

```
ROUTINE TO ADD.MATRICES GIVEN ''INPUTS'' A,B AND ''OUTPUT'' C
DEFINE A, B AND C AS REAL, 2-DIMENSIONAL ARRAYS
NORMALLY, MODE=INTEGER
FOR I = 1 TO DIM.F(A(*,*)), FOR J = 1 TO DIM.F(A(1,*)),
    LET C(I,J)=A(I,J)+B(I,J)
RETURN   END
```

Routine used in program:

(a) PERFORM ADD.MATRICES GIVEN COST.TO.MAKE(*,*),
        COST.TO.SHIP(*,*), AND TOTAL.COST(*,*)
(b) IF DIM.F(A(1,*)) EQUALS DIM.F(B(1,*))
        NOW ADD.MATRICES (A(*,*),B(*,*),APLUSB(*,*))
     OTHERWISE   CALL ERROR(1)

(4) A routine illustrating the use of local subscripted variables in a routine. It uses the routine TRACE (see p. 104) and a
local array TEMP to compute a function of an input array without
changing any values of the input array itself.

In the program preamble:

DEFINE QUANTITY AS AN INTEGER FUNCTION

Routine definition:

```
ROUTINE QUANTITY GIVEN N AND MATRIX
DEFINE MATRIX AND TEMP AS REAL, 2-DIMENSIONAL ARRAYS
DEFINE N AS AN INTEGER VARIABLE
RESERVE TEMP(*,*) AS N BY N
FOR I = 1 TO N, FOR J = 1 TO N,
    LET TEMP(I,J)=MATRIX(I,J)**2
RETURN WITH TRACE(N,TEMP(*,*))   END
```

The local variables I, J, and TEMP are "created" when the routine
is called, as when a calling program contains the statement

LET Q=QUANTITY(NO.SEGS, DISTANCE.TABLE(*,*))

The variables I and J have the NORMALLY conditions of the program preamble, as they are not mentioned in the routine preamble. The array TEMP is defined as REAL and two-dimensional in the routine preamble. Once TEMP has been reserved, it can be used in calls on other routines; this is done in the call on the routine TRACE.

Notice that QUANTITY has been defined as an INTEGER function. Because all the variables and the function TRACE are REAL, a conversion is made at the RETURN statement to assign an INTEGER value to QUANTITY before it returns to the program that called it.

(5) A routine illustrating the use of an array pointer in an output argument list. It is used as a monitor routine within a program to record array reservations for REAL, one-dimensional arrays. The array pointer appears in the output list so that the location of the allocated space can be returned to the array pointer in the calling program.

In the program preamble:

Nothing needed since the routine is used as a procedure.

Routine definition:

```
ROUTINE MONITOR GIVEN CODE, N YIELDING NAME
DEFINE CODE AND N AS INTEGER VARIABLES
DEFINE NAME AS A REAL, 1-DIMENSIONAL ARRAY
PRINT 1 LINE WITH CODE AND N AS FOLLOWS
     RESERVE EXECUTED FOR ARRAY ***, LENGTH ***
RESERVE NAME(*) AS N
RETURN
END
```

Routine used in program:

    (a)   CALL MONITOR (1,10) YIELDING VECTOR(*)
    (b)   CALL MONITOR GIVEN 4 AND I*J YIELDING LIST(*)

(6) A program illustrating a routine used as a procedure. Note the use of global variables and arguments in transmitting data from the main program to the routines and back again.

```
PREAMBLE
NORMALLY, MODE IS INTEGER
DEFINE COSTS AS A 2-DIMENSIONAL ARRAY
DEFINE MODE.FACTORS AND CLASS.FACTORS AS 1-DIMENSIONAL ARRAYS
DEFINE CAPACITY AS A 4-DIMENSIONAL ARRAY
DEFINE FROM, TO,MODE AND CLASS AS ''GLOBAL'' VARIABLES
END


MAIN
READ NFROM, NTO, NMODE,NCLASS    ''READ MAXIMUM DIMENSIONS
RESERVE COSTS(*,*) AS NFROM BY NTO, MODE.FACTORS(*) AS NMODE,
      CLASS.FACTORS(*) AS NCLASS,CAPACITY(*,*,*,*) AS NFROM
      BY NTO BY NCLASS BY NMODE
READ COSTS, CLASS.FACTORS,MODE.FACTORS    ''READ INITIAL DATA
'REQUEST'    READ FROM,TO,MODE,CLASS
'INQUIRE'    CALL RESERVATION YIELDING ANSWER
      IF ANSWER EQUALS 1
            NOW FIND.COST YIELDING PRICE
            PRINT 1 LINE WITH MODE,CLASS,FROM,TO,PRICE THUS
MODE * CLASS * RESERVATION FROM ** TO ** IS AVAILABLE FOR *** DOLLARS
            GO TO ''NEXT CUSTOMER'' REQUEST
      OTHERWISE ''FIND OTHER SPACE
            SUBTRACT 1 FROM CLASS
            IF CLASS IS GREATER THAN 0    GO TO INQUIRE
            OTHERWISE    LET CLASS=NCLASS
            SUBTRACT 1 FROM MODE
            IF MODE IS GREATER THAN 0    GO TO INQUIRE
            OTHERWISE PRINT 1 LINE WITH FROM AND TO LIKE THIS
THERE IS NO TRANSPORTATION AVAILABLE FROM ** TO ** TODAY
            GO TO REQUEST
            END ''OF MAIN ROUTINE''


ROUTINE FOR RESERVATION YIELDING ANSWER
IF CAPACITY(FROM,TO,CLASS,MODE) IS GREATER THAN 0
            SUBTRACT 1 FROM CAPACITY(FROM,TO,CLASS,MODE)
            LET ANSWER=1    RETURN
ELSE    LET ANSWER=0    RETURN
END


ROUTINE TO FIND.COST YIELDING SUM
LET SUM=COSTS(FROM,TO)*CLASS.FACTORS(CLASS)*MODE.FACTORS(MODE)
RETURN    END
```

The above program processes requests for transportation reservations. It reads customer requests for reservations on certain modes
of transportation (train, bus, airplane), in seats of a certain type
(first class, economy, tourist), from specified locations to specified

destinations. A reservation is made if there is unused capacity in
the category requested. When a reservation is made, a space is
assigned and the reservation is costed and reported. Costs are based
on distance and type of accommodation. If a space is not available
in the category requested, a search is made through successively lower
classes and modes until either a space is available, or all spaces
have been examined and determined unavailable. This program assumes
there is another routine that returns spaces to the system when they
are vacated.

The points to note in this program are:

(a) The program preamble sets the NORMALLY condition to INTEGER,
thereby declaring all variables throughout the program as integers
unless otherwise specified, and declares that a list of variables are
global. All other variables are local.

(b) The first READ statement sets initial values for four variables local to the main routine. If NFROM and NTO are set to 4 and
3 respectively, the program will accommodate requests for travel from
four locations to three locations.

(c) The RESERVE statement allocates storage to the arrays of the
program according to the specifications of the preceding data. These
arrays represent the basic costs of travel between two cities (COSTS),
the class and mode adjustment factors that modify the basic costs
(CLASS.FACTORS and MODE.FACTORS), and the number of spaces initially
available in each class and mode category between two such cities.

(d) The next READ statement initializes the program to the particular data values that are used in the run of the program.

(e) The next statements handle specific customer requests. Of
particular interest is the use of the global variables FROM and TO,
and CLASS and MODE, to transmit information from the main program to
the routines RESERVATION and FIND.COST. The local variables ANSWER
and PRICE have been used to show how local variables are used; there
is no particular reason for not making them global, or for not making
all variables local and communicating all information through argument lists.

(f) The local variable ANSWER in the routine RESERVATION has been given the same name as a local variable in the main routine to show that this can be done without conflict. A corresponding variable in the routine FIND.COST has been given a different name to show that the actual name is of no importance; only its location in the argument list is important. It also illustrates that the value computed as SUM in the routine FIND.COST is stored in the local variable PRICE in the main routine when FIND.COST returns to that program.

(g) FIND.COST can also be defined as a function. This is done by modifying the routine to:

```
ROUTINE TO FIND.COST
RETURN WITH COSTS(FROM,TO)*CLASS.FACTORS(CLASS)*MODE.FACTORS(MODE)
END
```

and using the routine name in place of the variable PRICE in the PRINT statement:

PRINT 1 LINE WITH TYPE,CLASS,FROM,TO AND FIND.COST AS FOLLOWS

The preamble will then be modified to include the statement:

DEFINE FIND.COST AS AN INTEGER FUNCTION

and the NOW statement in the main routine calling on FIND.COST as a procedure would be removed.

2-23 *RETURNING RESERVED ARRAYS TO FREE STORAGE*

When a RESERVE statement is executed it allocates a fixed number of memory cells to arrays named in the statement. The statement

RESERVE TABLE(*,*) AS 10 BY 50

assigns 500 memory words to the array TABLE when it is executed. Every array having memory space allocated to it can have this space returned to the free storage pool of the SIMSCRIPT II system by executing a statement such as

RELEASE TABLE(*,*)

This statement, which in its general form is

RELEASE *array-pointer list*

returns all elements of TABLE to free storage and causes the array
TABLE to be undefined until it is once more reserved. A statement
such as LET TABLE(1,1) = 1 cannot be executed after TABLE has been
released, since, for all practical purposes, the array TABLE does not
exist.

This feature is useful in programs that can be structured so
that all of their arrays need not be in storage at the same time.
The RESERVE-RELEASE feature can be used to define one or more arrays
that fit within memory capacity, operate on these arrays, release
them, define new arrays, operate on them, and so forth. The feature
is useful for executing programs that exceed computer capacity.

Because local arrays are not automatically released when a
RETURN statement is executed in routines in which they appear, a
RELEASE statement should be executed before returning. Should the
programmer forget to RELEASE a local array before returning from a
routine, the space allocated to the array will be forever inaccessible,
its pointer having been destroyed during the return operation. It is
not possible for SIMSCRIPT II to RELEASE all local arrays automatically,
since some of them may contain pointers to sections of global arrays.

The following routine illustrates the dynamic reservation and
release of a local array within a subprogram:

```
ROUTINE FOR ANALYSIS GIVEN ARRAY
DEFINE ARRAY AS A REAL, 2-DIMENSIONAL ARRAY
DEFINE TEMP AS A REAL, 2-DIMENSIONAL ARRAY
RESERVE TEMP(*,*) AS DIM.F(ARRAY(*,*)) BY DIM.F(ARRAY(1,*))
FOR I=1 TO DIM.F(ARRAY(*,*)), FOR J=1 TO DIM=F(ARRAY(1,*)),
   LET TEMP(I,J)=ARRAY(I,J)
PERFORM ROW.PERMUTATION GIVEN TEMP(*,*)
LET X= DETERMINANT(TEMP(*,*))
RELEASE TEMP(*,*)
RETURN WITH X
END


ROUTINE ROW.PERMUTATION GIVEN MATRIX
 ''  GENERATES A RANDOM PERMUTATION
 ''  AND EXCHANGES ROWS OF THE INPUT
 ''  ARRAY
END
```

```
ROUTINE FOR DETERMINANT GIVEN MATRIX
  '' COMPUTES THE DETERMINANT OF
  '' THE INPUT MATRIX
END
```

2-24 *GLOBAL VARIABLES, ROUTINES, AND SIDE EFFECTS*

When global variables are used in routines that interact with
one another, great care must be exercised to prevent unwanted side
effects. An *expected change* in a program is a change in value of one
or more variables that is obvious, or at least expected, from the
form of a statement. A *side effect* is a change that is not apparent
from the form of a statement alone. Side effects are important, as
they can cause unexpected and unwanted results if they are not taken
into account. The following routine illustrates a way in which a
side effect can enter into a program:

Routine definition:

```
ROUTINE VALUE(X)
LET A=SQRT.F(X)
RETURN WITH 4*A+A**3
END
```

Routine used in a program:

In the preamble:

```
DEFINE A,B AND C AS REAL VARIABLES
DEFINE VALUE AS A REAL FUNCTION
```

In the main program:

```
READ X AND A   LET Z=A+(VALUE(X)*C)
```

Since X is not defined in the program preamble, it is a REAL local
variable. If A=2, C=1, and X=9, Z is evaluated as follows: (1)
application of the parentheses rule evaluates (VALUE(X)*C) first,
setting A=3 and VALUE=39, and (2) application of the operator precedence rule adds the terms A and VALUE together, setting Z=42. The
side effect is the alteration of the value of A within the routine
VALUE.

If the above computation had been programmed differently, the
computed value of Z might not have been the same. The above LET

statement and the ones shown below look alike on the surface but produce different results in the context of the program.

In the main program:

READ X AND A LET B=A LET Z=B+(VALUE(X)*C)

If we again let A=2, C=1, and X=9, the two LET statements are evaluated as follows: (1) B=2; (2) the parentheses rule evaluates (VALUE(X)*C) setting A=3 and VALUE=39; and (3) the operator precedence rule adds the terms B and (VALUE(X)*C), setting Z=41. This differs from previous results.

Side effects are commonly introduced by using functions in FOR phrase control expressions that are evaluated before each iteration, and in complex logical expressions that may not always be evaluated completely (see p. 137). These side effects can be eliminated by (1) being aware of their existence, and (2) using local variables. The following program segment shows how a local variable can be used to inhibit a side effect that the routine FN is assumed to produce:

```
Write:     LET V=FN(K)
           FOR I=1 TO V,LET A(I)=0

Instead
of:        FOR I=1 TO FN(K),LET A(I)=0
```

Use of the local variable V also makes the program more efficient, as it eliminates the evaluation of FN(K) before each iteration of the loop.

* 2-25 RECURSIVE ROUTINES

All SIMSCRIPT II routines are recursive, meaning that they can call upon themselves. The concept of recursion is illustrated in the following routine, which computes the value of the factorial of n, where factorial (n)=n*(n-1)*(n-2)*...*(2)*(1).

```
           ROUTINE FOR FACTORIAL(N)
           IF N=1, RETURN WITH 1
           ELSE RETURN WITH N*FACTORIAL(N-1)
           END
```

The routine calls on itself repeatedly until it has reduced its argument to 1. If this function were called with N=4, it would be evaluated in the following steps:

```
FACTORIAL(4)=4*FACTORIAL(3)
            =4*(3*FACTORIAL(2))
            =4*(3*(2*FACTORIAL(1)))
            =4*(3*(2*(1)))
            =24
```

This is not an efficient way to compute a factorial, but it does illustrate the concept of a recursive call.

While recursively defined routines are not common, they are extremely useful in some computing areas — theorem-proving and language translation, for example.

Recursive routines are important because their local variables are unique to each routine call; each call has a separate "memory" that shares nothing with previous calls except their common routine structure. Global variables are, of course, defined across all levels of recursion, as their names represent the same values at all points in a program.[†] Global variables and values passed in argument lists are two ways that recursive routines can communicate at different levels.

Program efficiency and communication are two reasons why one might want to have nonrecursive routines. The mechanism for isolating variables from a program and making them local, not to a routine but to each call of a routine, is complicated. Computer time can be saved if this isolation is eliminated. Isolating local variables of routines between routine calls also makes it impossible for a routine to transmit information from one call to another through a local variable. In recursive routines this can only be accomplished by global variables or arguments.

All the local variables of a program, or selected local variables in individual routines, can be defined as SAVED or RECURSIVE. If a variable is SAVED it is stored in a memory location within a routine it is local to, and all references to it access this same location.

[†]Unless, of course, a global variable name has been locally defined in some routines.

A SAVED variable is not released when control returns to a calling program. If a variable is RECURSIVE it is stored in a memory location separate from the routine it is local to — there is one location for each recursive call on the routine and each call accesses a different location. RECURSIVE variables are released when control returns to a calling program. There are three different kinds of local variables: arguments, SAVED variables, and RECURSIVE variables. Arguments need not be defined, as this is done when they appear in input and output argument lists in ROUTINE statements. Arguments are always stored as RECURSIVE variables.

All local variables in a program, except arguments, can be declared as SAVED or RECURSIVE by using the phrase

TYPE IS SAVED   or   TYPE IS RECURSIVE

in the last NORMALLY statement of a program preamble, as in

NORMALLY, MODE IS REAL, TYPE IS SAVED

Since the last NORMALLY statement in the program preamble applies to all local variables unless they are otherwise qualified, this state-ment sets a background condition that is binding on all unqualified variables. If a TYPE phrase is not used, all local variables are treated as RECURSIVE.

Within routines, local variables can be declared as SAVED or RECURSIVE in a NORMALLY statement or in DEFINE statements. In DEFINE statements, use of the words SAVED or RECURSIVE is similar to use of the property words that define mode. A routine might contain the statements:

```
DEFINE VALUE AS A REAL,RECURSIVE VARIABLE
DEFINE X,Y AND Z AS RECURSIVE,INTEGER VARIABLES
DEFINE QUANTITY AS A SAVED VARIABLE
```

Local arrays can be treated as SAVED or RECURSIVE by making their base pointers SAVED or RECURSIVE. Thus, one might write

DEFINE TABLE AS A REAL,SAVED,2-DIMENSIONAL ARRAY

An important difference between SAVED and RECURSIVE local vari-ables lies in their initialized value when a routine is called. A

RECURSIVE local variable has an initial value of zero each time the routine in which it appears is called. Recursive variables are often used for this property alone. A SAVED local variable retains the value left in its storage location when the routine was last used. Thus, routines can use SAVED variables to pass messages from call to call concerning their operations. The first time a routine is called, all its local variables, both SAVED and RECURSIVE, are zero.

Recursion can best be understood by showing an example. The program below uses Horner's method for evaluation of polynomials. This method has the computational advantage of requiring only 2(K-1) arithmetic operations to evaluate a polynomial, fewer than are required by straightforward evaluation, and it expresses a polynomial of form A(K)=A(K-1)*X+...+A(1)*X**(K-1) as the recursive form A(K)+X*(A(K-1)+...+A(1)*X**(K-2)). The following brief SIMSCRIPT II routine demonstrates a program for evaluating this form:

In the program preamble:

DEFINE POLYNOMIAL AS A REAL FUNCTION

Routine definition:

```
ROUTINE FOR POLYNOMIAL GIVEN A,X AND K
DEFINE A AS A 1-DIMENSIONAL,REAL ARRAY
DEFINE X AS A REAL VARIABLE
DEFINE K AS AN INTEGER VARIABLE
IF K=0, RETURN WITH 0 ELSE
RETURN WITH A(K)+X* POLYNOMIAL(A(*),X,K-1)
END
```

To illustrate how the routine works, we describe the evaluation of the polynomial $9.2 + 2.1X + 3.3X^2$. The coefficients 9.2, 2.1, and 3.3 are stored in an array COEF as COEF(3), COEF(2), and COEF(1), respectively. The polynomial is to be evaluated with X=0.5.

The routine is called by using it as a function in the statement

```
LET VALUE=POLYNOMIAL(COEF(*),0.5,3)
```

The polynomial is evaluated as

```
POLYNOMIAL(COEF(*),0.5,3)=9.2 + 0.5*POLYNOMIAL(COEF(*),0.5,2)
                         =9.2 + 0.5*(2.1 + 0.5*POLYNOMIAL(COEF(*),0.5,1))
                         =9.2 + 0.5*(2.1 + 0.5*(3.3
                               + 0.5*POLYNOMIAL(COEF(*),0.5,0)))
                         =9.2 + 0.5*(2.1 + 0.5*(3.3 + 0.5*0.0))
                         =9.2 + 0.5*(2.1 + 0.5*3.3)
                         =9.2 + 0.5*3.75
                         =9.2 + 1.875
                         =11.075
```

An example of a recursively called routine for destroying a binary "tree" is shown below. The tree is constructed of two-element, one-dimensional, arrays that point to each other. To illustrate the tree-building process, the following program segment forms the apex of a binary tree named TREE:

```
        NORMALLY MODE IS INTEGER
        DEFINE NOD AND NODE AS 1-DIMENSIONAL ARRAYS
        RESERVE NODE(*) AS 2
        LET TREE=NODE(*)   LET NODE(*)=0
        RESERVE NODE(*) AS 2
        LET NOD(*)=TREE   LET NOD(1)=NODE(*)   LET NODE(*)=0
        RESERVE NODE(*) AS 2
        LET NOD(2)=NODE(*)   LET NODE(*)=0
                .
                .
                .
        END
```

NOD is used as a dummy array name to which a previous NODE pointer is assigned to allow nodes to connect to the nodes above them in the tree. The tree constructed by the program above is exemplified below:

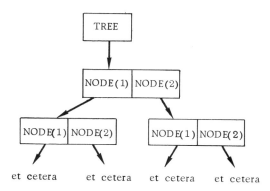

A routine to destroy such a tree is shown below. Given the pointer to the tree, the routine follows all paths in the tree and destroys the nodes on them.

```
ROUTINE DESTROY(NODE)
NORMALLY MODE IS INTEGER
DEFINE NODE AS A 1-DIM ARRAY
IF NODE(*) IS NOT ZERO,
    FOR I=1 TO 2, CALL DESTROY(NODE(I))
    RELEASE NODE(*)
REGARDLESS
RETURN END
```

This routine, when called by a statement such as NOW DESTROY(TREE), calls upon itself as each node destroys the nodes below it. Since each node either points to a successor node or is zero, the routine can tell whether it has to follow a downward path to destroy successor nodes, or whether it can destroy the node it is working on by releasing it. Perhaps the easiest way to understand this routine is to construct a typical tree, such as that shown in Fig. 2-9, and follow the logic through.

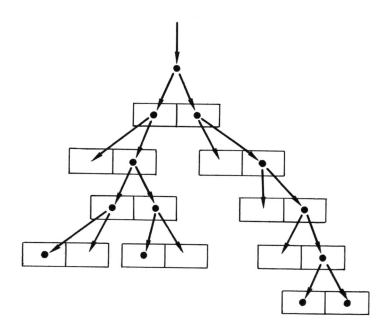

Fig. 2-9 -- A binary tree

By changing one statement, as shown below, the routine can easily be expanded to destroy not only binary trees, but those containing limitless branches as well.

```
ROUTINE TO DESTROY(NODE)
NORMALLY MODE IS INTEGER
DEFINE NODE AS A 1-DIMENSIONAL ARRAY
IF NODE(*) IS NOT ZERO,
   FOR I=1 TO DIM.F(NODE(*)), CALL DESTROY(NODE(I))
   RELEASE NODE(*)
REGARDLESS
RETURN    END
```

The DIM.F function allows each node to have several branches, rather than only two. Such a tree might look like Fig. 2-10.

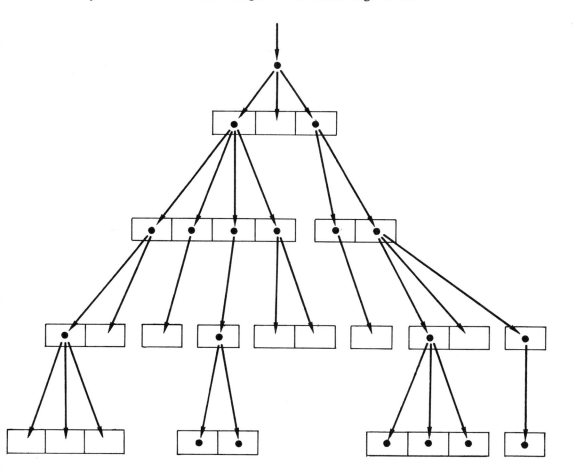

Fig. 2-10 -- A complex tree

2-26 *DEFINITION OF SYNONYMOUS NAMES AND OPEN ROUTINES*

It is not at all unusual to have large programs written by more than one person. Problems are often segmented into parts and the parts coded separately as subprograms. Later, the subprograms are combined, either manually or automatically by an executive program.

This approach presents a difficulty because great administrative care must be exercised to ensure that all programmers use the same names for global and local variables and that they define things consistently. The primary purpose of the two statements in this section is to simplify this task.

The statement

DEFINE X TO MEAN Z

means that whenever the word[†] X appears in a program it is replaced by the word Z; the compiler automatically substitutes Z for X before interpretation. It will not extract an embedded X, as in the name XRAY, and generate the name ZRAY.

The general form of the DEFINE TO MEAN statement is

DEFINE word TO MEAN string of words

where "string of words" represents the information punched after the word MEAN (separated from it by one blank) that extends to the end of the statement card. A "string" cannot be composed entirely of blanks or be a comment.

The rule for DEFINE TO MEAN substitution is simple: whenever the specified word is seen, the string is substituted for it and the statement compiled with the substitution. Thus, words can be defined

---

[†] A *word* is a name, number, or special character. It is possible to redefine variable, label, and routine names, statement keywords, special characters such as + and /, and numbers, as

```
DEFINE + TO MEAN *
DEFINE CONS TO MEAN 7.56
DEFINE < TO MEAN (
DEFINE > TO MEAN )
```

as synonyms, they can be replaced by complete statements, and so forth.

The scope of the DEFINE TO MEAN statement is similar to that of the NORMALLY statement. When used in a program preamble, it extends throughout an entire program until overridden; when used in a routine, it holds (until overridden) for that routine only. The effect of DEFINE TO MEAN statements can be withdrawn by the statement SUPPRESS SUBSTITUTION and reinstated by the statement RESUME SUBSTITUTION. The SUPPRESS SUBSTITUTION and RESUME SUBSTITUTION statements should be placed alone on cards, since substitution takes place for an entire card as it is read and before the contents are interpreted. If other statements appear on the same card as a SUPPRESS SUBSTITUTION statement, substitutions are made for such statements (if called for) before the SUPPRESS command is recognized. To suppress substitution for a particular word, the word itself is defined, as in the following example:

```
SUPPRESS SUBSTITUTION
DEFINE X TO MEAN X
RESUME SUBSTITUTION
```

If the SUPPRESS statement is not used, the current substitution will be made for X before the DEFINE statement is recognized, and X will never be redefined. For example, if X has previously been mentioned in the statement

```
DEFINE X TO MEAN QUANTITY
```

and the SUPPRESS SUBSTITUTION statement is omitted, the redefinition will be

```
DEFINE QUANTITY TO MEAN QUANTITY
```

which is not the desired definition.

DEFINE TO MEAN statements are not limited to preambles, but can be used anywhere in a program. They can be used to make short, local substitutions or extensive changes in vocabulary. The following examples illustrate some uses of the DEFINE TO MEAN statement:

(a)   Use of the statement to change a word in a routine to the
same word used in other routines in a large program.   The word represents a global variable in this illustration.

```
ROUTINE SAMPLE(X) YIELDING Y
DEFINE TABLE TO MEAN LIST [This statement inserted
DEFINE X AND Y AS REAL VARIABLES          in existing program.]
FOR I = 1 TO DIM.F(TABLE(*,*)),
FOR J FROM 1 TO DIM.F(TABLE(1,*)),
ADD TABLE (I,J) TO Y
IF Y IS LESS THAN X  RETURN
OTHERWISE LET Y=-1
RETURN END
```

(b)   Use of the statement to change vocabulary.   Assume you do
not like the words LET, ROUTINE, and END, and you prefer to use the
words SET, PROCEDURE, and FINISH instead.   If you precede programs
written with these words by the statements

```
DEFINE SET TO MEAN LET
DEFINE PROCEDURE TO MEAN ROUTINE
DEFINE FINISH TO MEAN END
```

the programs will be translated into SIMSCRIPT II vocabulary before
compilation.   For example, the program

```
PROCEDURE TO FIND.MAX(X)
DEFINE X AS A 1-DIMENSIONAL INTEGER ARRAY
SET MAX=X(1)    ADD 1 TO SET
FOR I = 2 TO DIM.F(X(*)), SET MAX=MAX.F(MAX,X(I))
RETURN WITH MAX
FINISH
```

when submitted for compilation preceded by the three DEFINE TO MEAN
statements will be compiled as

```
ROUTINE TO FIND.MAX(X)
DEFINE X AS A 1-DIMENSIONAL INTEGER ARRAY
LET MAX=X(1)    ADD 1 TO LET
FOR I = 2 TO DIM.F(X(*)), LET MAX=MAX.F(MAX,X(I))
RETURN WITH MAX
END
```

Notice the use of the word LET as both a variable and a key word.

(c)   Use of the statement to define macro-instructions.   A macro-
instruction is a compound instruction that is generated from one key
word.   The statement

DEFINE LOCAL TO MEAN DEFINE I,J,K,L AND M AS INTEGER VARIABLES

inserts a definition card for the variables I,J,K,L, and M wherever
the word LOCAL is used. This is useful when a number of routines use
the same local variables. A routine can be written as

```
ROUTINE EXAMPLE(X)
LOCAL
DEFINE X AS A REAL VARIABLE
        .
        .
        .
END
```

and, if it is preceded by the above DEFINE TO MEAN statement, it will
be compiled as

```
ROUTINE EXAMPLE(X)
DEFINE I,J,K,L AND M AS INTEGER VARIABLES
DEFINE X AS A REAL VARIABLE
        .
        .
        .
END
```

Entire sequences of statements can be generated directly into a
program by an extended form of the DEFINE TO MEAN statement. This
statement allows more than one line of statements to be substituted
for a particular key word, and it offers greater possibilities for
macro-instruction generation. The statement can be written in two ways:

> SUBSTITUTE THIS LINE FOR *word*
and   SUBSTITUTE THESE i LINES FOR *word*

In the first statement, the contents of the line *following* the statement is substituted for the key word wherever it appears; in the
second statement, the contents of the following i lines are substituted. As with the DEFINE TO MEAN statement, totally blank cards and
comments cannot be substituted.

DEFINE TO MEAN and SUBSTITUTE statements can be used freely in
a program with few restrictions. They can "call on" one another at
different levels of substitution. The following statements show how
a series of DEFINE TO MEAN and SUBSTITUTE statements can be applied
to a program statement and used to translate the words of the statement into legal SIMSCRIPT II code:

```
SUBSTITUTE THESE 2 LINES FOR ZZ
    SET VALUE=B
    GO TO START
DEFINE SET TO MEAN LET
DEFINE B TO MEAN X(I)*Y(I)+1
```

Program statement:

```
IF VALUE IS GREATER THAN 0 ZZ ELSE
```

Translated as:

```
ZZ is translated to SET VALUE=B
                    GO TO START
SET VALUE=B is translated to LET VALUE=B and then to
                             LET VALUE=X(I)*Y(I)+1
```

Compiled as:

```
IF VALUE IS GREATER THAN 0
  LET VALUE=X(I)*Y(I)+1
  GO TO START
ELSE
```

Certain words, such as statement key words, should be redefined with extreme caution. If, for example, the word A is defined, as in the statement

```
DEFINE A TO MEAN X
```

and a DEFINE statement such as DEFINE LIST AS A REAL ARRAY processed, X will be substituted for A, and will create the incorrect statement DEFINE LIST AS X REAL ARRAY.

2-27 SAMPLE SIMSCRIPT II, LEVEL 2 PROGRAMS

2-27-1 A Data Analysis Program

This program reads N data items $x_1, x_2, \ldots, x_n$ into a list. It then goes through the list computing the average of successive overlapping sequences of observations $x_i, x_{i+1}, \ldots, x_{i+M}$ for $M=1,2,3,\ldots,N-1$. These moving averages are compared with an input tolerance value, and if they are less than this value, the values of $i, i+M$, and the average are printed.

The following problem illustrates the use of the RESERVE statement,

the READ statement with a subscripted variable, and the use of FOR
loops to control the indexing of subscripted variables:

```
PREAMBLE  DEFINE LIST AS A 1-DIMENSIONAL ARRAY
DEFINE I,J,M AND N AS INTEGER VARIABLES
END
MAIN READ N
RESERVE LIST(*) AS N     READ LIST
READ TOLERANCE.VALUE
FOR M=1 TO N-1
     FOR I=1 TO N-M
          DO
              LET SUM=0
              FOR J=0 TO M, ADD LIST(I+J) TO SUM
              LET AVERAGE=SUM/(M+1)
              IF AVERAGE IS LESS THAN TOLERANCE.VALUE
                  PRINT 1 LINE WITH I, I+M AND AVERAGE AS FOLLOWS
                  ITEMS *** THROUGH *** HAVE AN AVERAGE OF **.***
              REGARDLESS
          LOOP
STOP    END
```

2-27-2 A Data Analysis Program

This program repeats the computations of the previous problem,
but instead of computing the average of the items $x_i, \ldots x_{i+M}$ it computes the average of a function of the items $f(x_i), \ldots f(x_{i+M})$. As
the function can vary for different problems, the program for computing its value is called as a routine and is not incorporated directly
into the data analysis program.

The program below illustrates how to write and use a routine
subprogram as a function.

```
PREAMBLE    DEFINE LIST AS A 1-DIMENSIONAL ARRAY
DEFINE I,J,M AND N AS INTEGER VARIABLES
DEFINE VALUE AS A REAL FUNCTION
END
MAIN READ N
RESERVE LIST(*) AS N    READ LIST
READ TOLERANCE.VALUE
```

```
FOR M=1 TO N-1,
    FOR I=1 TO N-M,
        DO
            LET SUM=0
            FOR J=0 TO M, ADD VALUE(LIST(I+J)) TO SUM
            LET AVERAGE=SUM/(M+1)
            IF AVERAGE IS LESS THAN TOLERANCE.VALUE
                PRINT 1 LINE WITH I,I+M AND AVERAGE LIKE THIS
                ITEMS *** THROUGH *** HAVE AN AVERAGE OF **.***
            REGARDLESS
        LOOP
STOP    END
ROUTINE FOR VALUE GIVEN VARIABLE
IF VARIABLE IS LESS THAN -1000    RETURN WITH -1
OTHERWISE IF VARIABLE IS GREATER THAN 1000    RETURN WITH 1
        OTHERWISE RETURN WITH VARIABLE/1000
END
```

2-27-3 A Matrix Multiplication Program

Two matrices (double-subscripted variables) are punched on data cards. Matrix A appears in the order $A(1,1)$, $A(1,2)$,...,$A(1,M)$, $A(2,1)$,...,$A(2,M)$,$A(3,1)$,...,$A(N,M)$. Matrix B appears in the order $B(1,1)$,$B(2,1)$,...,$B(S,1)$,$B(1,2)$,...,$B(S,2)$,$B(1,3)$,...,$B(R,S)$. A is punched row by row, and B, column by column. The values of the matrix dimensions N,M,R, and S precede the element data.

This program reads the data and, if possible, multiplies the matrices A and B together to form matrix C.

For matrix multiplication to be effected, M must equal R. The rules for computation are

if A has dimensions N, M and

B has dimensions M, S then

C has dimensions N, S and the elements of C are computed as

$$C(I,K) = \sum_{j=1}^{M} A(I,J)*B(J,K)$$

The program below illustrates the use of the RESERVE statement with variable dimensions executed in the body of a program, two forms of READ statement formats for inputting subscripted variables, nested FOR loops, and the use of the LIST statement.

```
MAIN
DEFINE I,J,K,M,N,R AND S AS INTEGER VARIABLES
READ N, M, R AND S   IF M IS NOT EQUAL TO R, PRINT 1 LINE THUS
MATRIX DIMENSIONS ARE NOT EQUAL, MULTIPLICATION IMPOSSIBLE
STOP   ELSE RESERVE A(*,*) AS N BY M,B(*,*) AS R BY S,C(*,*) AS N BY S
READ A   FOR J=1 TO S, FOR I=1 TO R, READ B(I,J)
FOR I=1 TO N, FOR K=1 TO S, FOR J=1 TO M
ADD A(I,J)*B(J,K) TO C(I,K)
LIST A, B AND C
STOP   END
```

2-27-4 A Matrix Multiplication Routine

This program presents the previous program written as a routine.
It returns a coded message if multiplication is not possible. Unlike
the foregoing program, this one does not assume that the matrix C contains all zeros, and an initialization statement is incorporated into
the routine.

The problem below illustrates how a routine is written and used
as a procedure. It demonstrates the use of input and output arguments in such routines.

```
ROUTINE TO MATRIX.MULTIPLY GIVEN A,B AND C, N,M,R AND S
     YIELDING CODE
DEFINE A, B AND C AS 2-DIMENSIONAL REAL ARRAYS
DEFINE N,M,R,S,I,J,K AND CODE AS INTEGER VARIABLES
IF M IS NOT EQUAL TO R LET CODE=0   RETURN
OTHERWISE LET CODE=1
FOR I=1 TO N, FOR K=1 TO S
     DO LET C(I,K)=0
        FOR J=1 TO M, ADD A(I,J)*B(J,K) TO C(I,K)
     REPEAT
RETURN   END
```

This routine might be used in a program by calling on it as

```
NOW MATRIX.MULTIPLY(TABLE1(*,*),TABLE2(*,*),TABLE3(*,*), N1, N2, N3, N4)
     YIELDING FLAG
IF FLAG EQUALS 0, GO TO ACTION.1
OTHERWISE LIST TABLE3
             .
             .
             .
```

2-27-5 *Definition and Use of a Routine as a Function*

Here, the program defines a routine to compute the quantity M defined as

$$M = \frac{\pi^2}{864} \, dL^3 \left(1-\frac{2x}{3L}\right)\left(3.080 \, \sin \frac{\pi x}{L} -0.7100 \, \sin \frac{2\pi x}{L} + 0.349 \, \sin \frac{3\pi x}{L}\right)$$

For values d=62.4, L=10, and x=4 the routine is used to compute and print the quantities

$$Q1 = \sqrt{M^2 - (M-1)^2}$$

$$Q2 = \begin{cases} 0 & \text{if } M < m \\ 1 & \text{if } M = m \\ 2 & \text{if } M > m \end{cases}$$

$$Q3 = \frac{\pi^2}{864} \left(1-q\right)^2 A^3 \left(1-\frac{2a^2}{3A}\right)\left(3.080 \, \sin \frac{\pi a^2}{A} - 0.7100 \, \sin \frac{2\pi a^2}{A}\right.$$

$$\left. + 0.349 \, \sin \frac{3\pi a^2}{A}\right)$$

```
MAIN
LET VALUE=M(62.4,10.0,4.0)
PRINT 1 LINE WITH SQRT.F(VALUE**2 - (VALUE-1)**2) LIKE THIS
    THE VALUE OF Q1 IS *.******
LET Q2=0    READ SMALL.EM
IF VALUE EQUALS SMALL.EM, LET Q2=1 ELSE
IF VALUE IS GREATER THAN SMALL.EM, LET Q2=2 REGARDLESS
PRINT 1 LINE WITH Q2 AS FOLLOWS
    THE VALUE OF Q2 IS *
READ Q,A AND LITTLE.EH
PRINT 1 LINE WITH M((1-Q)**2,A, LITTLE.EH**2) THUS
    THE VALUE OF Q3 IS ***.******
STOP    END


ROUTINE FOR M GIVEN D, L AND X
LET TEMP=(PI.C * X)/L
RETURN WITH (PI.C**2/864)*(D*L**3)*(1-(2*X)/(3*L))*(3.08*
    SIN.F(TEMP) - 0.71*SIN.F(2*TEMP) + 0.349*SIN.F(3*TEMP))
END
```

The routine and main program illustrate the use of a system-defined constant (PI.C), system-defined functions (SIN.F, SQRT.F), and the transmission of argument values to routines, and shows some methods by which temporary variables can be used to make computations

more efficient. Notice that, as there is no preamble, all variables
are implicitly REAL, and all are local to their respective routines —
the variables VALUE, SMALL.EM, Q1, Q2, Q,A and LITTLE.EH are local to
the main routine, and the variable TEMP is local to the routine M.

2-28 *MORE ON PROGRAM FORMATS*

As described in Sec. *1-09*, all 80 card columns can be used for
program statements. As blanks are ignored between words, a programmer
can design his own program formats by standardizing the number of
blank columns put before and after statements.

Since the SIMSCRIPT II compiler reads all 80 columns, a control
statement limiting the number of columns containing valid program
statements is needed if program cards are to be sequence numbered or
otherwise identified. If a program cannot be restricted to the first
70 columns, say, of a card, error messages will be produced each time
a sequence number is read. Of course, comment cards can be used to
delimit sequence numbers, as in the following example, but this is
inefficient in large programs.

```
ROUTINE FOR ANALYSIS GIVEN X YIELDING Y          ''ANAL 0001
DEFINE X AND Y AS REAL VARIABLES                 ''ANAL 0002
             .
             .
             .
   END
```

The preamble statement

LAST COLUMN IS *integer constant*

specifies that columns to the right of the indicated column do not
contain program statements. These columns appear on all program
listings produced during compilation, but do not enter into the compilation process. The symbol "=" is a synonym for the word "IS".
Each time a LAST COLUMN card is used in a preamble, the number of
program statement columns may change. The last LAST COLUMN statement
used in a preamble applies to all subprograms that follow.

The simplest preamble used to specify sequence number columns is:

```
PREAMBLE
LAST COLUMN IS 72
END
```

This specifies that in all succeeding cards only columns 1 through 72 contain program statements. Columns 73 through 80 are listed but ignored during compilation.

Chapter 3

SIMSCRIPT II: LEVEL 3

3-00 *A STATEMENT FOR SIMPLIFYING NESTED IF STATEMENTS*

A unique feature of one particular nested IF statement structure
is that a transfer is made out of the nest upon the failure of any
nested test. This is illustrated below.

```
IF VALUE(ITEM) EQUALS HI,LET PRIORITY(ITEM)=1
    IF TIME.DUE(ITEM) < NOW+7,ADD 1 TO PRIORITY(ITEM)
        IF WORK.TO.DO(ITEM) > LIMIT, ADD 1 TO PRIORITY(ITEM)
        ELSE
    ELSE
ELSE
```

The failure of any test causes a transfer to a matched ELSE statement that branches out of the nest. The essence of the logic of the
nest lies in the word THEN. If a condition is true, computation continues with the next statement, THEN IF ..., but if any condition is
false, control passes to its matching ELSE and out of the nest. The
THEN IF statement improves the readability of nested IF statements by
eliminating consecutive ELSE statements. In programs containing
sequences of IF statements, if one or more IF is preceded by the word
THEN, some ELSE statements can be eliminated, for when a logical test
associated with a THEN IF phrase fails, control passes to the ELSE
associated with the previous IF. To illustrate, the above program is
rewritten using THEN IF statements.

```
IF VALUE(ITEM) EQUALS HI, LET PRIORITY(ITEM)=1
    THEN IF TIME.DUE(ITEM) < NOW+7, ADD 1 TO PRIORITY(ITEM)
        THEN IF WORK.DUE(ITEM) > LIMIT, ADD 1 TO PRIORITY(ITEM)
    ELSE
```

The THEN IF statement is only applicable to nested logical tests
in which the false condition for each test is the same and where failure of any test automatically transfers out of the nest. The logic
of a sequence of nested THEN IF statements is shown in the following
flow diagram:

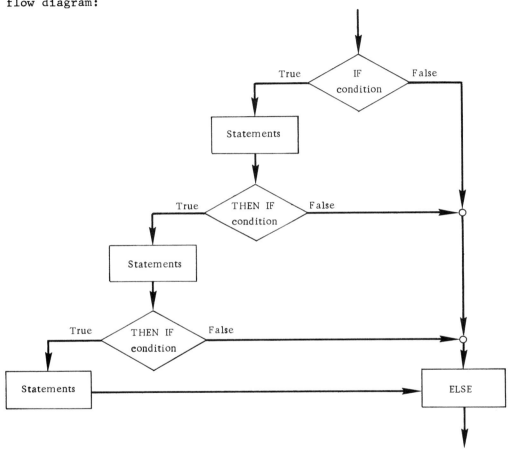

3-01 A STATEMENT FOR SIMPLIFYING NESTED DO LOOPS

FOR phrases, with their attached DO and REPEAT loops, can also
be nested. Often two or more FOR phrases end on the same program
statement, and a series of LOOP or REPEAT statements are needed to
close all the "open" DO's, as, for example, in

```
FOR I=1 TO N, FOR K=1 TO N,
     DO
          LET C(I,K)=0    LET D(I,K)=0
          FOR J=1 TO N,
               DO
                    ADD A(I,J)*B(J,K) TO C(I,K)
                    ADD A(I,J)**2*B(J,K)**2 TO D(I,K)
               LOOP
     LOOP
```

Consecutive LOOP or REPEAT statements can be eliminated by using the statement ALSO FOR whenever consecutive FOR loops terminate on the same statement. When an ALSO FOR is used, SIMSCRIPT II automatically pairs the DO that follows, with the LOOP that matches the DO of the preceding FOR statement. Using this statement, the above example can be written as

```
FOR I=1 TO N, FOR K=1 TO N,
     DO LET C(I,K), D(I,K)=0
     ALSO FOR J=1 TO N,
          DO ADD A(I,J)*B(J,K) TO C(I,K)
          ADD A(I,J)**2*B(J,K)**2 TO D(I,K)
     LOOP
```

The following sequence of FOR and ALSO FOR loops illustrates how DOs and LOOPs are matched when these phrases are interspersed:

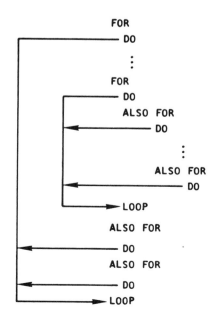

3-02 *SPECIFYING COMPLEX LOGICAL EXPRESSIONS*

Sections *1-04* and *2-12* discussed two types of logical expressions: expressions that use relational operators to compare two arithmetic expressions, and expressions that use the operators IS and IS NOT to compare a single arithmetic expression or a special name with a specified property. Logical expressions formed according to either of these rules are *simple* logical expressions in that they express a single logical relationship.

Section *1-04* also showed that a logical expression can be enclosed in parentheses without changing its meaning. Parentheses bind an expression as a unit and have no effect on its evaluation. All logical expressions can be enclosed within parentheses without any change in meaning.

	VALUE < LIMIT	is equivalent to	(VALUE < LIMIT)
and	SUM IS POSITIVE	is equivalent to	(SUM IS POSITIVE)

A logical expression can be negated by following it with the phrase IS FALSE, as in the logical expression

VALUE < LIMIT IS FALSE

The IS FALSE phrase serves a wider purpose than the mere improvement of readability — it can be used to state a desired condition without forcing an unnatural transposition of logic. For example, a test can be written as

	IF QUANTITY > INVENTORY GO TO ORDER ELSE
or	IF QUANTITY ≤ INVENTORY IS FALSE GO TO ORDER ELSE

with equal effect. For symmetry, the phrase IS TRUE is permitted. The form selected depends on how a programmer wants a logical expression to appear to a reader.

Simple logical expressions containing arithmetic expressions and relational operators can be assembled together to form *compound logical expressions*. Using e to represent an arithmetic expression and R to represent a relational operator, a compound logical expression can be written as

Form	Example
e R e	1 < X
e R e R e	1 < X < N
e R e R e R e	1 < X < N = SUM
e R e R e R e R e	1 < X < N = SUM IS GREATER THAN 5

In each of these cases all of the expressed logical relationships must be true in order that the compound expression be true. For example, in the second illustration, X must be greater than 1 and less than N. The notation used is actually a shorthand method of writing 1 < X and X < N.

Simple logical expressions can also be combined to form compound logical expressions by explicitly using the *logical operators* AND[+] or OR. If e_1 and e_2 are logical expressions, then

e_1 AND e_2 is true if *both* e_1 and e_2 are true

e_1 OR e_2 is true if *either* e_1 or e_2 or *both* e_1 and e_2 are true

Compound logical expressions can contain more than two simple logical expressions, as in the logical expression

e_1 AND e_2 OR e_3 AND e_4

When more than two simple logical expressions appear in an unparenthesized compound logical expression with the operators AND and OR, the operator AND is evaluated first. Parentheses can be used, however, to indicate a specific order of evaluation. In the absence of parentheses, the above expression is evaluated by convention as though it had been written

(a) (e_1 AND e_2) OR (e_3 AND e_4)

If a program requires some other logic, the statement can be written as

(b) e_1 AND (e_2 OR e_3) AND e_4

which means something quite different. Version (a) is true *either* if both e_1 and e_2 are true *or* if both e_3 and e_4 are true. Version (b) is true if e_1 is true *and* e_4 is true, *and either* e_2 *or* e_3 is true.

[+]In this context, a comma cannot be substituted for the word AND.

Compound logical expressions can be used with IS FALSE and IS TRUE phrases. An IS FALSE or IS TRUE phrase always applies to the logical expression preceding it. If this logical expression is compound, it must be enclosed in parentheses, e.g., the logical expression

$$e_1 \text{ IS FALSE AND } (e_2 \text{ OR } e_3) \text{ IS TRUE}$$

A few simple rules that govern the writing and evaluation of logical expressions are given below:

(a) A logical expression enclosed in parentheses remains a logical expression.

(b) In the absence of parentheses, AND is evaluated before OR, that is, from left to right across an expression, successive logical expressions are used as operands of AND operators, and these evaluated expressions are then used as operands of OR operators. Parentheses can always be used to indicate specific operator hierarchies.

(c) IS TRUE and IS FALSE phrases apply to logical expressions preceding them. If such a logical expression is compound, it must be enclosed in parentheses; otherwise the phrase only applies to the expression adjacent to it.

Some examples that illustrate the writing and evaluation of complex logical expressions are given below. In these examples, the variables I,J,K,L,M, and N are positive numbers, the variables Q,R,S, and T are negative numbers, and the variable Z is zero.

(a)	I EQUALS J	is true or false depending on the values I,J
(b)	I EQUALS Q	is always false
(c)	M+N IS POSITIVE	is always true
(d)	M+T IS POSITIVE	is true or false depending on the values M,T
(e)	I > 0 AND J > 0	is always true
(f)	I > 0 OR R > 0	is always true
(g)	I = J AND Z = 0	is true if I equals J, is false otherwise
(h)	I = J OR Z = 0	is always true
(i)	I = J AND K > N AND R = S	is true if all three conditions are true and false otherwise; it is evaluated as $((I = J) \text{AND} (K > N) \text{ AND } (R = S))$
(j)	I = J OR K > N OR R = S	is true if any one of the three conditions is true; it is false only if all are false

(k) I = J AND K > N OR R = S   is true if either of the two conditions
                                   around the OR is true; it is evaluated
                                   as (I = J AND K > N) OR (R = S)

(1) Z IS ZERO AND (I < 0 OR S < 0) AND Q = T   is true only if Q = T

(m) Z IS ZERO AND (I > 0 OR S < 0) AND Q = T   is true if Q = T

(n) J < K AND (I = Q OR S < 0) AND J + K < I   is true if J < K and
                                                  J + K < I

When a statement containing a compound logical expression is executed, it does not always follow that all logical conditions in the
statement are examined. For example, in the statement

            IF X > Y**2 AND COUNT > N, ADD ... ELSE

both logical expressions have to be true for the ADD statement to be
executed. If the first logical expression (X > Y**2) is false, there
is no need to evaluate the second (COUNT > N), as the compound logical
expression X > Y**2 AND COUNT > N can never be true regardless of the
values of COUNT and N. In normal circumstances, the fact that all
parts of a compound logical expression may not be evaluated each time
will cause no undue difficulty. It can cause problems if a programmer
uses a function in a logical expression and expects an evaluation
each time. As this evaluation may not always be performed, it is a good
rule not to use functions in the above manner if they have side effects.

3-03 LOGICAL CONTROL PHRASES

A *logical control phrase* contains a logical expression and a
logical control operator, and is ordinarily used in connection with
a FOR statement. The logical control phrases are

                WITH *logical expression*
                UNLESS *logical expression*
                WHILE *logical expression*
        and   UNTIL *logical expression*

A WITH phrase modifies the sequence of values that pass from a
FOR phrase to the statements that it controls. Its logical expression
is tested each time a new value of the FOR phrase control variable is
generated, and if the expression is false the control variable value
is skipped. This effectively passes control around these statements

for a selected set of control variable values. The phrase is useful
for screening values before they pass into FOR-phrase-controlled statements. An example of the use of a WITH phrase is

```
FOR I = 1 TO N, WITH X(I) LESS THAN CUT.OFF
    DO LET BID(I) = PRICE + PROPORTION(PRICE)
       ADD 1 TO NUMBER.OF.BIDS
    LOOP
```

In this example the WITH phrase screens out those values of I between
1 and N for which the logical expression X(I) < CUT.OFF is false. The
program performs as if it had been written as

```
FOR I = 1 TO N, DO
    IF X(I) ≥ CUT.OFF  GO TO LOOP
    ELSE   LET BID(I) = PRICE + PROPORTION (PRICE)
    ADD 1 TO NUMBER.OF.BIDS
'LOOP'     LOOP
```

The word WHEN can be used as a synonym for WITH. The word UNLESS
and the phrase EXCEPT WHEN can be used to show that the items passing
the indicated test are screened from the loop, rather than accepted,
as in the program

```
FOR I = 1 TO N, EXCEPT WHEN X(I) < CUT.OFF
    DO LET BID(I) = PRICE + PROPORTION (PRICE)
       ADD 1 TO NUMBER.OF.BIDS
    LOOP
```

A WHILE phrase allows a FOR to direct the sequence of program
control as long as a certain logical expression is true. Its logical
expression is reevaluated each time the FOR phrase changes the value
of its control variable. Thus, the program

```
FOR I = 1 TO N, WHILE X(I) LESS THAN CUT.OFF
    DO   LET BID(I) = PRICE + PROPORTION (PRICE)
         ADD 1 TO NUMBER.OF.BIDS
    LOOP
```

terminates the loop as soon as a value of X(I) is greater than or
equal to CUT.OFF. The program performs as if it had been written as

```
FOR I = 1 TO N,
    DO   IF X(I) ≥ CUT.OFF  GO TO NEXT
         ELSE   LET BID(I) = PRICE + PROPORTION (PRICE)
         ADD 1 TO NUMBER.OF.BIDS
    LOOP
'NEXT'
```

An UNTIL phrase allows a FOR to direct the sequence of program
control as long as a certain logical expression is not true. It has
the same effect as a WHILE phrase that has an IS FALSE phrase put
after its logical control expression. The program

```
FOR I = 1 TO N, UNTIL X(I) ≥ CUT.OFF
        DO   LET BID(I) = PRICE + PROPORTION (PRICE)
            ADD 1 TO NUMBER.OF.BIDS
        LOOP
```

performs exactly like the previous program.

WITH, UNLESS, WHILE, and UNTIL phrases can be attached to nested
FOR statements. When this is done, each WITH or UNLESS phrase applies
to the FOR statement immediately preceding it, and each WHILE or UNTIL
phrase applies to *all preceding* FOR phrases. The following program
illustrates this:

```
FOR DELTA= 1 TO 100 BY 0.5,
FOR Q = DT(1) TO DT(2) BY DELTA,
    WHILE(FN(Q) - FN(DT(1)))/(Q - DT(1)) > 0,
FOR V = -Q TO Q BY STEP, WITH GN(V) > MIN
DO
        ADD GN(V) TO SUM
        ADD 1 TO NUMBER.OF.SEGMENTS
LOOP
'NEXT'
```

The outer FOR phrases step the variables DELTA and Q through a sequence
of values as long as the logical expression in the WHILE phrase is
true. A false condition ends the FOR phrase control by transferring
to 'NEXT'. Each time the variables are stepped and the logical expression is true, the inner FOR steps the variable V through a sequence
of values. Only those values in the sequence, however, for which the
logical expression in the WITH phrase is true are passed on to the
statements in the DO loop.

Sequences of WITH, UNLESS, WHILE, and UNTIL phrases can be attached
to FOR phrases in any combination. More than one of each type of phrase
is permitted.

UNTIL and WHILE statements can also be used independently. When
used this way, the variables appearing within their logical expressions
do not come from a FOR phrase iteration, but from computations performed

within their range. The range of an independent logical control
phrase, like the range of a FOR phrase, is delimited by DO and LOOP
or REPEAT statements. The following example illustrates the use of
an independent WHILE statement in a program:

```
WHILE NUMBER.OF.SEATS IS NOT ZERO,
    DO  READ PASSENGER
        PERFORM TICKETING(PASSENGER)
        ADD FARE TO SUM
    LOOP
```

In this example, the value of the global variable NUMBER.OF.SEATS is
assumed to be changed in the routine TICKETING. As long as NUMBER.OF.
SEATS is positive, control is passed to the READ statement after the
LOOP statement has transferred back to the WHILE in expectation of
another iteration. When NUMBER.OF.SEATS becomes zero, the WHILE statement transfers to the statement following LOOP.

WHILE and UNTIL statements can be modified by WITH and UNLESS
phrases, and may be nested with other independent WHILE and UNTIL
statements and with FOR phrases. When nested WHILE and UNTIL statements end on the same LOOP statement, the phrases ALSO WHILE and ALSO
UNTIL can be used to eliminate the redundant LOOP.

Since there is no automatic termination of an independent WHILE
or UNTIL phrase as there is with a FOR phrase, a programmer must be
careful not to program a nonterminating loop, as in the following
program segment:

```
WHILE I IS GREATER THAN J,
    DO  READ X
        ADD X TO SUM
    LOOP
```

This loop is not terminal, as the values of I and J are not affected
by the loop.

3-04 *RETURNING ROUTINES TO FREE STORAGE*

The RELEASE statement can also be used to return space occupied
by routines to free storage. Used in conjunction with the release of
arrays, this provides a powerful facility for fitting large programs
into core. A routine is released by using its name in a RELEASE statement, as in

RELEASE START, INTERRUPT, AND ALLOCATE

Routine[†] and array names can be used in the same RELEASE statement. The general form of the RELEASE statement is

RELEASE *array pointer and routine name list*

Any variable or function whose value is a pointer can appear in a RELEASE list. If the first appearance of an array name is in a RELEASE statement the background dimensionality is assumed for the array.

Each routine must be declared as RELEASABLE[††] to be eligible for use in a RELEASE statement. This is done in the preamble, and must be done individually for routines by prefacing the word ROUTINE or ROUTINES in a DEFINE statement with the word RELEASABLE, as in the statements

```
DEFINE START AND MONITOR AS RELEASABLE ROUTINES
DEFINE INITIALIZE AS A RELEASABLE ROUTINE   and
DEFINE RTN AS A RELEASABLE ROUTINE WITH 3 ARGUMENTS, YIELDING 1 VALUE
```

As an example of the use of the RELEASE statement, consider the program below. The routine START is called to initialize global variables; after this is done it returns to the main program and is never called again. As the program is very large, the scheme described is employed in order to use the space taken by the routine START for an array called MATRIX.

program preamble	PREAMBLE DEFINE START AS A RELEASABLE ROUTINE NORMALLY, MODE IS REAL et cetera END
main routine	MAIN PERFORM START RELEASE START RESERVE MATRIX(*,*) AS N BY N other computations END

other routines	ROUTINE START
	    computations
	RETURN END
	       .
	    other routines of the program
	       .

[†]Except for in-line functions (see Table 2-4).

[††]This may not be necessary in some SIMSCRIPT II implementations.

3-05 EXTERNAL STORAGE AND RETRIEVAL OF ROUTINES

Programs that exceed computer capacity can be run if there is a facility for storing parts of programs on external storage devices such as drums, disks, and magnetic tapes, and reading them back into core storage when they are needed. For various reasons, it is impossible to design statements that provide such facilities independent of computer operating systems, i.e., as part of a machine-independent programming language. The task of this section is not to specify statements for the storage and retrieval of routines, but to describe ways in which this can be done; to discuss the effect of different schemes on SIMSCRIPT II programs; to suggest what seem to be useful statement forms; and to provide guidelines for particular implementations of storage and retrieval statements on a variety of computers.

Two general methods are available for executing large programs: program overlay and dynamic program relocation.

3-05-1 Program Overlay

The easier of the two program storage and retrieval schemes presented involves the partitioning of a program into *overlay sections*, with each section containing one or more routines. If the partitioning is done well (and if a program permits it to be done well), a program can be executed by sequentially bringing overlay sections into core on top of one another. If routines within particular sections only call on routines in the same section or on routines permanently located in core, this method is efficient. On the other hand, if routines call upon routines in other sections, time is spent replacing these sections in core so that the routines may be loaded and executed. Overlay is an efficient technique for sequentially designed programs; its efficiency decreases as the interaction between overlay sections increases.

There are several ways in which overlay can be implemented. All involve keeping a copy of each overlay section on an external medium and loading it into a *fixed overlay area* when the section is needed. Since the same copy is loaded each time a section is overlayed, it is impossible to transmit values of SAVED local variables between overlays.

When a section is overlaid, all the SAVED local variables in the section's routines are reset to zero. Care must be exercised in using SAVED local variables with an overlay feature.

The overlay of an overlay section can be invoked by a special statement such as

LOAD *overlay section name*

or it can be invoked automatically, by the use of a routine name within an overlay section somewhere in a program. Operating systems having an automatic overlay feature keep track of the location of all routines at all times, and bring overlay sections into core if routines within them but not in core are called. Routines are generally located within named overlay sections by *control cards* placed in a program card deck. In some implementations, however, program preamble statements may have to explicitly make such correspondences, such as the statement form

OVERLAY SECTION *name* CONTAINS ROUTINES *routine name list*

3-05-2 *Dynamic Program Relocation*

A more general program storage and retrieval scheme allows individual routines to be removed from core and restored at a later time, perhaps in a different place. While providing a greater amount of flexibility than does program overlay, such a scheme involves more effort to make it efficacious. Some computers, because of their internal design, may not even be able to implement the feature. As with overlay, two implementation methods are available: automatic relocation control, and explicit dynamic program control.

As pointed out above, with automatic overlay the mention of a routine in a program causes it to be loaded into core if it is not already there. Automatic relocation control differs from this procedure in that a relocatable routine need not always be placed in the same core locations.

Under explicit dynamic program relocation, a program is removed from core and saved on some external medium by a statement of the form

SAVE *routine name*

Execution of this statement both copies a routine and releases its memory space. Loading of the routine at a later time can be done in either of two ways: automatically, when the routine is called, or through a special statement. If loading is done automatically, several things are needed: the routine must be declared as dynamic in the program preamble by a statement such as

DEFINE *routine name* AS A DYNAMIC ROUTINE

so that appropriate flags and loading routines can be created; a special version of the CALL statement must be provided to load a missing routine before calling it if it is not in core; and an out-of-room error routine must be written to take care of situations where there is insufficient room to load a routine. Since there is no special program loading area as there is with overlay, it is possible that conflicts for core space may occur. Unless the system has instructions as to which routines it should save when such conflicts occur, it can do nothing but terminate a program.

If loading is done by programmer instruction, things are simpler. Statements of the form

IF *routine name* IS LOADED

and   IF *routine name* IS NOT LOADED

can test to see if a routine must be loaded before it is called, and can be used to release other routines, thus allowing room for a new routine. A statement such as

LOAD *routine name*

can then be used to load the routine into core so that it can be executed.

If dynamic program relocation facilities are available, they greatly enhance a programmer's capabilities by providing unlimited memory capacity for program storage. As with program overlay, SIM-SCRIPT II implementation manuals must be examined to see what particular features specific computer implementations provide.

3-06 A SEARCH STATEMENT

In certain types of programs a great deal of effort is devoted to finding sets of variables that satisfy stated conditions and computing functions of these variables. The FIND statement is used to search for the first of a set of variable values that satisfies some logical conditions. The statement

```
FOR I = 1 TO N, WITH X(I)*Y(I) > LIMIT, FIND FIRST.PAIR=THE FIRST I
   IF NONE   GO TO NO.PAIRS   ELSE ...
```

is a compound statement composed of a qualified FOR phrase and a FIND statement. The FOR phrase steps the variable I through the sequence of values 1,2,...,N, looking for values for which X(I)*Y(I) is greater than LIMIT. The FIND statement selects the first value of I in this sequence. The FIND statement further specifies that if no I satisfies the "WITH test," the program branches to the label NO.PAIRS; otherwise, it continues in sequence after the ELSE statement with the variable FIRST.PAIR equal to the first value of I for which the test is true.

The above compound statement is equivalent to the program

```
FOR I = 1 TO N,
DO
   IF X(I)*Y(I) IS GREATER THAN LIMIT,LET FIRST.PAIR=I   GO OUT
   OTHERWISE
LOOP
GO TO NO.PAIRS
'OUT'
```

A FIND statement is always controlled by a FOR phrase, and can optionally have an IF clause following it to direct the flow of control based on the outcome of the "find." This clause can be either

```
         IF NONE  statements  ELSE
   or    IF FOUND  statements  ELSE
```

If an IF NONE clause is used, the statements following it are executed if the find is unsuccessful; if an IF FOUND clause is used, the statements are executed if the find is successful. In both cases control passes to the ELSE statement if the IF condition is not met, i.e., FOUND or not FOUND.

The words THE and FIRST are optional after the equals sign at the head of the FIND statement, e.g., the statements

```
FIND MAXI = THE FIRST I
FIND MAXI = FIRST I
FIND MAXI = I
```

are equivalent and illustrate alternate forms of the basic FIND statement

FIND *variable = arithmetic expression*

If a variable named FIRST is used in a FIND statement, the optional word FIRST must also be used to make the statement unambiguous. Usually, the control variable in the FOR phrase will appear in the expression.[†] When the first index value is found for which the logical expression in the FOR phrase is true, the arithmetic expression is evaluated and its value assigned to the FIND statement variable, which may be subscripted. Thus, in the above example, the value of the expression I is assigned to the variable FIRST.PAIR when a value of I is found for which $X(I)*Y(I)$ is greater than LIMIT.

If the last, rather than the first, value must be found, a backward iterating FOR phrase is used. To find the last value of I for which $X(I)*Y(I)$ is greater than LIMIT, write

```
FOR I BACK FROM N TO 1, WITH X(I)*Y(I) GREATER THAN LIMIT,
     FIND LAST.PAIR = I   IF NONE, GO TO NO.PAIRS   ELSE
```

This statement is equivalent to the program

```
FOR I BACK FROM N TO 1,
DO
  IF X(I)*Y(I) IS GREATER THAN LIMIT,
       LET LAST.PAIR = I    GO OUT
  OTHERWISE
LOOP    GO TO NO.PAIRS
'OUT'
```

More than one FOR phrase can be used to control a FIND statement. When this is done, the FIND statement is usually written with a list of *variable = arithmetic expression* phrases, as in:

[†]It might not appear if the arithmetic expression contains a function whose implied arguments are global variables.

```
FOR I = 1 TO N, FOR J = 1 TO M WITH FN(I) < FN(J)
FIND FS(1) = THE FIRST I AND FS(2) = THE FIRST J
IF FOUND    GO TO LABEL(I)    OTHERWISE ...
```

In cases where there is no expression to compute, a special form of the FIND statement can be used. This form — FIND THE FIRST CASE — inhibits the generation of a LET statement to assign the value of the "found expression" to the "FIND variable." Both of the following two statements terminate with the same value of I:

```
(a)  FOR I=1 TO MAX, WITH V(I)<QQ(I) , FIND THE FIRST CASE
(b)  FOR I=1 TO MAX, WITH V(I)<QQ(I) , FIND I=THE FIRST I
```

3-07 *A STATEMENT FOR COMPUTING SOME STANDARD FUNCTIONS OF VARIABLES*

Computer outputs often take the form of statistics summarizing the behavior of a program. The number of sales made in a particular week is a statistic that describes the activity in a store, while another statistic is the value of the average sale. When information, such as sales receipts or item invoices, is stored in arrays, or can be computed by iterating through expressions, the COMPUTE statement simplifies the task of compiling descriptive statistics.

An example of the use of a COMPUTE statement is:

```
FOR I = 1 TO N, UNTIL X(I) > 17
COMPUTE MEANX = MEAN,AND MAXIMUMX = MAXIMUM OF X(I)
```

Like the FIND statement, the COMPUTE statement contains a list of variables that are set to a computed value after iteration. In this case the values are specified by statistical names, such as MEAN and MAXIMUM. In the above example the logical control phrase could have selected the individual elements accessed by the loop if the statement were written as

```
FOR I = 1 TO N, WITH X(I) > O COMPUTE MEANX = MEAN,MAXIMUMX = MAXIMUM
    OF X(I)
```

A COMPUTE statement has the general form:

COMPUTE *compute list* OF *arithmetic expression*

where *compute list* is a list of variable and statistical names of the

form "*variable = statistic name*." The optional word THE can be put
before each statistic name, and the word AS can be used in lieu of
the equal sign. A COMPUTE statement can be controlled by more than
one FOR phrase, as in the statement

FOR A = 1 TO N, FOR B = 1 TO M, COMPUTE MN AS THE MEAN OF TABLE(A,B)*LIST(B)

An optional logical control phrase appended to a FOR statement
controls the iteration sequence or the selection of individual variables,
as shown in the above examples.

When a COMPUTE statement appears within a DO loop with other statements, calculation of computed statistics, such as MEAN, takes place
at the first LOOP encountered. If, for some reason, control is transferred out of the loop, the statistics are undefined.

In the following example, computation of the indicated statistics
is executed at the close of the first DO loop. Within the "J" loop
the values of $X(J)$ are summed, and a count accumulated of the number
of $X(J)$ that go into the sum. Before statement$_4$ is executed, these
two values are used to compute MEANX.

```
FOR I = 1 TO N, DO
    statement₁
FOR J = 1 TO M, DO
    statement₂
COMPUTE MEANX AS THE MEAN OF X(J)
    statement₃
LOOP
    statement₄
LOOP
```

MEANX is undefined within the J loop.

To have a COMPUTE statement controlled by several control phrases,
a program is written with ALSO phrases, as:

```
FOR I = 1 TO N, DO
    statement₁
ALSO FOR J = 1 TO M, DO
    statement₂
COMPUTE SUMX AS THE SUM AND MAXX AS THE MAXIMUM OF X(I,J)
    statement₃
LOOP
```

The names that may appear in the statistical list, and their computations, are shown in Table 3-1.

Table 3-1

STATISTICAL NAMES USED IN THE COMPUTE STATEMENT

Statistic	Alternative or Abbreviation	Computation
NUMBER	NUM	Number of items selected in the iteration
SUM		Sum of the selected values of the expression
MEAN	AVERAGE, AVG	SUM/NUMBER
SUM.OF.SQUARES	SSQ	Sum of squares of the selected values of the expression
MEAN.SQUARE	MSQ	SUM.OF.SQUARES/NUMBER
VARIANCE	VAR	MEAN.SQUARE - MEAN**2
STD.DEV	STD	SQRT.F(VARIANCE)
MAXIMUM	MAX	Maximum value of the selected values of the expression
MINIMUM	MIN	Minimum value of the selected values of the expression
MAXIMUM(e)	MAX(e)	Value of computed e using the control variable values that produce the expression with the MAXIMUM value
MINIMUM(e)	MIN(e)	Same as MAX(e) but for minimum

The following example illustrates the use of each of these statistics (assume that an array X in a program has element values as shown):

N = 5
X(1) = 4.0   X(2) = 7.3   X(3) = 12.8   X(4) = 0.5   X(5) = 2.2   X(6) = 7.3

Let the program contain the statement:

```
FOR I = 1 TO 6, WITH (I < N AND X(I) < X(I + 1))   OR I = N,
COMPUTE NX = THE NUMBER, SUMX AS THE SUM, NM AS THE MEAN,
SSQX AS THE SUM.OF.SQUARES, MSQX AS THE MEAN.SQUARE, VARX AS
THE VARIANCE, SDVX AS THE STD.DEV, MINX AS THE MINIMUM,
MAXX AS THE MAXIMUM, MINI = THE MIN(I) OF X(I)
```

The above statement iterates the control variable I over the values
1,2,3,4,5, and 6, and selects only those values for inclusion in the
COMPUTE statement computations for which I < 5 and X(I) < X(I+1), or
for which I=5; thus, it selects X(1), X(2), and X(4) under condition
1 and X(5) under condition 2. For these index numbers, the statistical quantities are computed for the expression X(I). The computed
statistics are:

Computed Variable	Statistic	Computation
NX	NUMBER	4
SUMX	SUM	$4.0 + 7.3 + 0.5 + 2.2 = 14.0$
MX	MEAN	$14.0/4 = 3.5$
SSQX	SUM.OF.SQUARES	$(4.0)^2 + (7.3)^2 + (0.5)^2 + (2.2)^2 = 74.38$
MSQX	MEAN.SQUARE	$74.38/4 = 18.595$
VARX	VARIANCE	$18.595 - 3.5^2 = 6.345$
SDVX	STD.DEV	$SQRT.F = 2.52$
MINX	MINIMUM	0.5
MAXX	MAXIMUM	7.3
MINI	MIN(I)	4

3-08 ALPHA--A NEW MODE

Since computers can manipulate characters as well as numbers, the
manipulation of arbitrary symbols has become a feature of many programming languages. The ALPHA mode defines a variable as containing
alphanumeric characters rather than numbers, an alphanumeric character
being a letter, digit, or special symbol such as + or ?. A *character
string* is a sequence of ALPHA characters, such as appear in the following list:

```
LIST          PART.NUMBER     MY HOUSE      ****EUREKA****
---->         X + Y = Z       1,678,000     34.5
''''          <<<<<<<<<<      .........     23 SKIDOO
```

Any character that can be represented within a computer, including a
blank character, may appear in a character string. In the above

example, the string MY HOUSE is eight characters long and includes a
blank character.

The number of characters that can be stored in a computer word
varies, as does the number of digits that can be stored in an INTEGER
variable. The number for a specific SIMSCRIPT II implementation is
given in that implementation's instruction manual. In all implementations, however, ALPHA variables are stored in the same way — characters are left-adjusted within a computer word. If a single character
is read into an ALPHA word, it is put in the leftmost character position and followed by blanks.

ALPHA variables are declared by statements such as

        DEFINE V AS AN ALPHA VARIABLE
    and NORMALLY, MODE IS ALPHA

ALPHA variables can be dimensioned, and can be SAVED or RECURSIVE.
ALPHA functions are also possible. Defining a function as ALPHA means
that the "value" returned by the function is treated as a character
string, rather than as a numerical quantity.

ALPHA variables are treated as INTEGER variables in all computations except input/output. This means that the sum of two ALPHA
variables is the (normally meaningless) algebraic sum of their internal
character representations. If X and Y are ALPHA variables and X contains the character string ONE and Y the character string TWO, the
statement ADD X TO Y produces meaningless garble; it does not produce
the character string ONE TWO.

ALPHA variables are often used in IF tests to permit input data
to be readable rather than being mere arbitrary code numbers. If the
end of a deck of data is to be signaled by a flag, it is easier to
understand the organization of the deck if the flag is the character
string END than if it were, for instance, the number 999. An ALPHA
variable or function can be used in a logical expression in either of
two ways: (1) with another ALPHA variable or function in tests such as

        IF INPUT.CHARACTER EQUALS ALPHABET(I)
    and WITH VALUE NOT EQUAL SYMBOL

or (2) with a *literal* in tests such as

```
            IF INPUT.CHARACTER EQUALS "?"
    and     WITH VALUE NOT EQUAL "*END*"
```

A literal, as shown, is a character string enclosed in quotation marks.[†] A quotation mark within a character string is represented by an underscore (_). Literals are ALPHA constants. They are compiled directly into programs, cannot be altered, and can be used just like ALPHA variables. Of course there can be no more characters in a literal than in an ALPHA variable. Literals appear in examples throughout the remainder of this section; their utility should be apparent from their use.

The remainder of this section is concerned with the effect ALPHA variables have on previously described input/output statements. Their effect on all other statements has already been discussed, i.e., they are treated as INTEGER quantities.

In a free-form READ statement of the form READ V, where V has been declared as ALPHA, reading begins at the first nonblank character and terminates when the first blank appears or after reading as many characters into V as it can contain. Successive ALPHA values can be separated by blanks, as can numbers. Thus, blanks cannot be read into ALPHA variables by a free-form READ. A number to the right of a full ALPHA word of characters need not be separated from them by a blank, although one is certainly permissible. Assume that a computer word can hold four alphanumeric characters and that X is ALPHA and I is INTEGER. The READ statement

```
        READ X(1),X(2),X(3) AND I
```

reads the first four contiguous nonblank characters into X(1), the second four into X(2), and the third four into X(3), and then reads into I however many digits follow to the first blank. If the free-form "look ahead" feature is used (see Sec. 2-13), the mode of the next value to be read can be ascertained by the statement

```
            IF MODE IS ALPHA
```

If this value is an integer number, it is reported as INTEGER, even

---

[†]The single character " used to bracket a literal is different from the two characters '' used to bracket a comment.

though a string of digits is a legitimate character string. Since the
system does not know how characters are to be used but only their form,
the value has to be reported as INTEGER.

In a LIST statement of the form LIST V, where V has been declared
as ALPHA, the contents of V are displayed similarly to INTEGER values
except that character strings are left-adjusted. Additionally, leading zeroes are not suppressed, as they are legal alphanumeric characters. In ALPHA mode, zero and blank are distinct symbols.

In a PRINT statement where the format of an item must be described
by a "picture" of asterisks, single parallels, and decimal points, each
ALPHA character must be pictured. Unlike INTEGERS, where only the
position of the rightmost digit must be shown, all characters of an
ALPHA variable must be indicated either by * or |. If more characters
than are stored in an ALPHA word are indicated, only the leftmost
positions are used. This choice of rules, quite different from the
rules for INTEGER printing, is made to allow the greatest flexibility
in displaying alphanumeric information.

3-09 A FORMATTED INPUT/OUTPUT STATEMENT

The READ, PRINT, and LIST statements permit programs to (1) read
data in free-form from punched cards, (2) display computational results
in picture-like formats, and (3) generate labeled data displays without
consideration of specific formats or data arrangements. There is much
more to computer I/O than these facilities, however. For example,
there are other types of input/output units, such as magnetic tapes,
disks, and drums. In addition, there are recognized needs for facilities to read and write formatted data and to transmit information in
internal machine representation as well as decimal format.

This section presents a set of statements for performing input/
output functions with many types of I/O devices. Unfortunately, these
statements can only serve as guidelines for SIMSCRIPT II compiler
implementations, and cannot be taken as strict language specifications due to the variance in input/output device designs among computer systems, as well as to the special relationship between input/
output operations and computer operating systems. Specifications
that appear in single statements in our proposal may have to appear

in two separate statements in some computer systems. We can specify
the constituents of an I/O statement and demonstrate its capabilities,
but we cannot ensure that these specifications are compatible with
all computer systems. It will be the task of the individual SIMSCRIPT
II implementation reports to describe the way in which input/output
statements differ from those described here.

   In general, three things must be specified when an input/output
operation takes place: a physical device, an information list, and
a format. In the statements READ, PRINT, and LIST, a physical device
is implied (card reader or printer), an information list is stated
explicitly, and a format is, in the first instance, "free," in the
second, a "picture," and in the third, standardized. The statements
following provide flexible options for expressing each of these items.

Physical Device Specification

   Since data can be read from, or written on, a large number of
data devices of different types, the device to be used in any particular
instance must be specified. This is done by giving each distinct
device a name or code number. It is difficult to specify the form of
the code as this is an item that differs among computer systems. For
convenience we will assume that each device has a *device name* abbreviated as "d," and leave the precise specification of the form of "d"
to specific implementation manuals. If "d" refers to a number, any
arithmetic expression should be allowed. For example, assume that an
installation has as its input/output devices a line printer, a card
reader, a card punch, six magnetic tape drives, a magnetic drum, and
two disk units. By convention we number (name) these devices 1,2,...,12,
respectively. A particular device is selected as a *current input unit*
or *current output unit* by executable statements of the form

```
            USE d FOR INPUT      or    USE UNIT d FOR INPUT
    and     USE d FOR OUTPUT     or    USE UNIT d FOR OUTPUT
```

TAPE can be used in place of UNIT when applicable. Such statements
specify that the named devices are to be used in logically subsequent
input and output statements; that is, since they are executable

statements, the physical order in which they appear in a program need
not be important; GO TO statements can transfer from USE to READ and
WRITE statements that might physically precede them.

Each time a USE statement is executed, a global variable named
READ.V or WRITE.V is assigned the value of the designated unit "d."
These variables can be used freely in all SIMSCRIPT II statements, as
in   IF READ.V = 5, GO TO SWITCH.UNIT   ELSE

When a program does not contain any USE statements, as in Level 1
and 2 programs, SIMSCRIPT II assumes that a designated "standard"
card reader and "standard" line printer are used for its READ, PRINT,
and LIST operations. Among the items of information that must be
specified when a SIMSCRIPT II compiler is used in a specific environ-
ment are the device names of such standard units. READ.V and WRITE.V
are initially set to the values of these devices.

If the current input unit is specified as the current output unit,
the current input unit is changed to the "standard" card reader. If
the current output unit is specified as the current input unit, the
current output unit is changed to the "standard" line printer. Since
a device cannot be used for both input and output at the same time,
this ensures that error messages will be properly displayed and increases the chances of catching programming errors in unit assignments.

The READ, PRINT, and LIST statements can, of course, be used with
other units, as well as with the designated standard units. Free-
form data may be read from any one of a number of card readers or
magnetic tape units if they are designated as the current input unit,
whereas output can be written onto magnetic tape, as well as being
displayed on printers.

Input/Output Devices

A great many input/output devices are available to a computer
user today, but few computer installations have access to all of them.
The devices people are most familiar with and that are found in the
majority of installations are punched card readers and punches, line
printers, typewriters, magnetic tape transports, magnetic drums, and

varying forms of disk storage devices. Devices less common, although
also widely used, are paper tape readers and punches, cathode-ray tube
displays, light pens, and pressure-sensitive input tablets. Although
SIMSCRIPT II can provide commands for dealing with all of these devices
explicitly, it does not do so. Rather, it provides a mechanism for
dealing with all devices that read and write information sequentially.

Each device has certain characteristics, and is organized, or
can be organized, in specific ways. SIMSCRIPT II utilizes one particular mode of organization that is shared by all devices, but one
that is by no means inclusive for all possible organizations. Such
a mode is the sequential classification of a *data stream* into *fields*
and *records*.

A field is a logically defined group of consecutive *characters*
within a record; it does not necessarily correspond to any physically
distinguishable unit. A format (delineated later in this section)
describes a data field; data fields are defined by formats and delineated by blank characters in free-form data streams. A record is a
physically distinct sequence of data fields.

Within each SIMSCRIPT II program are input and output *buffers*.
Input buffers are filled, and output buffers emptied, by programmer
instructions in READ and WRITE statements, and by the SIMSCRIPT II
system when statements such as PRINT and LIST are used. Individual
READ and WRITE statements do not necessarily access an entire record,
but proceed sequentially through input and output buffers as data
elements are selected. Normally, a programmer need not concern himself with the functioning of input and output buffers except to empty
them by indicating that subsequent input or output operations are to
begin on a new line or card. Following subsections describe how this
is accomplished.

Because SIMSCRIPT II has facilities for operating on fields and
records and because its source language statements are independent of
particular devices, it has a set of conventions that define the concepts of field and record for different types of devices. These
devices are shown in Table 3-2. The distinctions shown in the table
will become clear, as the statements that employ them are described

Table 3-2

INPUT/OUTPUT UNIT CHARACTERISTICS

I/O Device	Maximum Field Width	Record
Punched card	80 columns	Card
Line printer	-b- columns	Line
Magnetic tape	none	-a-
Magnetic drum	none	-a-
Magnetic disk	none	-a-
Typewriter	-b- columns	Line
Paper tape	none	-a-

[a] Delimited by an internal, program-generated mark.

[b] Determined by peripheral equipment characteristics.

in the following pages. The statements will also be clarified by the examples shown at the end of the section.

The Formatted I/O Statements READ and WRITE

The READ statement used thus far has only been able to read free-form data. A READ statement that accepts formatted data has the form

READ *variable list* AS *format list*

in which each variable value to be read has its input data format described by a corresponding descriptor in a format list. These formats, which are codes telling how the input data are placed on data cards, are described in the next subsection.

The WRITE statement transfers values from within the computer to specified external media, such as line printers or magnetic tapes. Every WRITE statement is formatted. With the sole exception of the LIST statement, it is always the programmer's obligation to indicate the arrangement of output data. The WRITE statement looks like the READ statement; its form is

WRITE *arithmetic expression list* AS *format list*

In this statement the indicated expressions are evaluated and printed in the form described by their matching format descriptors.

Before these READ and WRITE statements can be described through examples, the format descriptors must be defined. There are ten of them; five are used for expressing numerical pictures and five are used for spacing, skipping lines, and similar actions. The five numerical descriptors, which define integer, decimal, scientific notation, alphanumeric, and internal computer representation data fields, will be described first.

I (Integer) Descriptor

A descriptor of the form n I w is used for converting numbers from their internal integer computer storage representation to an external format, and vice versa. The character I is always followed by an expression (W), specifying the maximum number of digits in the integer field, including the sign. The I can be preceded by a number (n), declaring that the descriptor defines n consecutive identical data fields. The formats 2 I 6 and 14 I 3 define 2 fields of 6 positions and 14 fields of 3 positions, respectively. *There must be at least one blank between the fields n, I, and w.*

When an I format is used for input, it specifies that the full contents of a field W digits wide are to be stored as the value of a corresponding variable in a READ statement. Blank field positions, leading, embedded, or trailing, are treated as zeroes. If a field is unsigned, it is interpreted as positive, although a plus sign can be punched. Excepting the sign character, only numbers can be punched in an I data field. If W is larger than the maximum number of digits that can be stored in a computer word, only the rightmost, storable digits are used. The additional digits are skipped over. If W is less than a "full word," the digits read are right-adjusted and the word filled out on the left with zeroes.

On output, an I format places a right-adjusted integer in a field of specified width. Numbers larger than the field width are converted to scientific notation.[†] Positive numbers are printed unsigned, while negative numbers have their sign printed to the left of the highest-order digit. Leading zeroes are suppressed.

D (Decimal) Descriptor

A descriptor of the form n D(a,b) is used for converting numbers from internal to external decimal representation, and vice versa. The a field specifies the number of characters in the data field, including the sign and decimal points, the b field specifies the number of digits to the right of the decimal point, and the optional n field specifies the number of consecutive values of the format.

When used for input, the D format accepts numbers punched with or without decimal points. If a decimal point is omitted, one is implied before the first digit in the b field. When a decimal point is present, it overrides the location specified by b. Very large and very small numbers can be input in scientific notation, for when used for input the D and E formats are equivalent.[†]

Used in output statements, D formats describe the precision in which decimal numbers are displayed. Numbers more precise than their output formats are rounded, as described in Table 1-2, Sec. *1-13*. Every number output by a D format is punched in a field of a columns: the first column is used for the sign, the next a-b-2 columns are for digits, the next column is for the decimal point, and the remaining b columns are for digits. The sign is printed if a number is negative, otherwise it remains blank. If the integer part of a negative decimal number does not fill up the a-b-2 positions allotted to it, the sign is shifted to the right, next to the high-order digit. Leading zeroes are suppressed. If a number has trailing zeroes, as in the number 10.0, which is whole-valued, the trailing zeroes are printed. The trailing zeroes are blank only if the value of a number is exactly zero, as opposed to a number that has a very small value in the computer's internal representation.

[†]See p. 161.

E (Scientific) Descriptor

Extremely large and extremely small numbers, and numbers that vary widely in scale, can be read and written in a constant field width by using an E format. This format is similar to the D format in that it specifies a field width and a decimal point position by the numbers a and b in the form n E(a,b), but it differs from the D format in having a scale factor field. The scale factor field appears to the right of a decimal number and indicates the necessary number of places right or left the decimal point must be moved to convert the scaled number to its proper form.

The E format is thus equivalent to the D format, plus a scale factor. Numbers read under E format control are of the general form

$$\pm xxx.xxxE\pm xx$$

although some latitude is allowed in writing the scale factor. A positive scale factor, such as E+02 or E 7 raises the value of a printed number — 24.795E+04 represents an internally stored value of $24.795 \times 10^4 = 247950$. A negative scale factor decreases the value of a printed number — 24.795E-04 represents an internally stored value of .0024795.

The E format can be used for both input and output. When used for output, it aligns numbers according to the format specification and prints a scale factor indicating the true value of the printed number. All E formatted numbers are a print positions wide, with the first a-4 positions used for the number, including its sign and decimal point, and the last four positions used for the scale factor E±xx. Positive scale factors print without the plus sign, as E 10, E 5, and E 1. Negative scale factors print the negative sign after the E, as E-10, E- 5 and E- 1.

E formatted input data can be punched in a variety of ways, as the scale factor may or may not contain a sign or the letter E. The numbers 1.0E+05, 1.0E05, +1.0E 5, and 1.0E+5 are equivalent input data representations of the number 100,000 under the input format E(7,1). As shown, either a sign or the letter E must be present to separate the number and scale factor fields.

Emphasis must again be directed to the fact that when values are too large to be printed in their indicated formats, data are displayed in scientific notation. The rules governing this are as follows:

Field Width	Characters Printed	Example: number=247.538
1	E	E
2	*sign of number* E	+E
3	*sign of number* E *sign of exponent*	+E+

4	*sign of number* E *sign of exponent* d
	  d= digit if $0 \leq$ exponent ≤ 9
	   = * if exponent ≥ 10
		+E+2

5	*sign of number* E *exponent*	+E+02
6	*sign of number* digit E *exponent*	+2E+02
7	*sign of number* digit.E *exponent*	+2.E+02
8	*sign of number* digit.digit E *exponent*	+2.4E+02
≥ 9	*sign of number* digit.*additional digits* E *exponent*	+2.47E+02 +2.475E+02 +2.4754E+02 +2.47538E+02

Numbers can be punched in scientific notation for free-form as well as for format-directed input. A number of the form *number exponent* is interpreted as a scientific notation input field in free-form input statements. No blanks are allowed between the *number* and *exponent* parts of the field. The forms of these parts are:

number a REAL or INTEGER constant

exponent E±xx E is optional
       + is not needed if exponent is positive

examples:

1.0067E+10	1.0067+10
9.46755+04	9.46755E4
4.0E1	4.0+1
9.999-6	9.999E-06
5E6	5+6

A (Alphanumeric) Descriptor

The alphanumeric descriptor n A w is similar to the I descriptor
in form and action. On input, the contents of a specified field are
stored as the value of a corresponding variable in a READ list. This
variable must have been declared as ALPHA. Since an ALPHA variable
can contain any legitimate characters that can be punched in a card,
including blanks, these punched characters are stored. If the number
of characters in the field is less than the number of characters in
an ALPHA computer word, the characters are stored in the leftmost
positions in the word, followed by blanks. If more characters are
specified than can be stored, the leftmost are stored and the remainder
skipped over.

When used in output statements, the A format extracts characters
from the leftmost part of an output variable or function. The format
A 1 displays the leftmost character, A 2 displays the two characters
farthest to the left, and so on.

C (Computer Representation) Descriptor

Few computers use decimal notation internally. Most use binary
coding schemes that represent decimal numbers as sequences of zeroes
and ones. Generally, a group of binary bits constituting a character
in a number system other than binary or decimal is used as an input/
output character. Because strings of such numbers are short, they are
easy to interpret. The unit on the IBM 7090 class computers that have
36 binary bits per computer word is the octal byte. Each 36-bit word
can be treated as twelve 3-bit bytes that take on the values 0,1,2,3,4,
5,6, and 7.

The format n C e interprets characters read or written in the
unit of the computer on which a particular SIMSCRIPT II compiler is
implemented. The format C 12 on an IBM 7090 means read or write 12
octal characters; the format C 4 on an IBM 360 means read or write 4
hexadecimal characters. The two, of course, are incompatible — no
more than 8 hexadecimal characters can be stored in a 360 word.
Nevertheless, there are times when internal representation must be
displayed and a machine-dependent format is required.

Forming Format Lists

Format lists are composed of sequences of format descriptors separated by commas. During the execution of READ and WRITE statements, format lists are scanned from left to right and individual format descriptors used as they are needed. With few exceptions, variables being read and expressions being written must agree in mode with their format descriptors. The exceptions are INTEGER and ALPHA modes that can be used interchangeably; when they are interchanged, the mode of the format descriptor governs. When a format descriptor is preceded by a repetition character n, n consecutive READ or WRITE quantities use the same format. Some examples of READ and WRITE statements that use formatted data follow:

(a) READ X, ANSWER AND Y AS I 3, I 2, I 2

If we assume that data are on punched cards, and the above statement — the first in a program — starts reading at column one, the value punched in columns 1-3 is assigned to X , the value punched in columns 4-5 is assigned to ANSWER, and the value punched in columns 6-7 is assigned to Y. The data card might appear as

```
column number
00000000011111...
12345678901234
160 3 8
```

in which case X=160, ANSWER=3, and Y=8, or, it may appear as

```
column number
0000000001111...
12345678901234
 -336-9
```

in which case X=-3, ANSWER=36, and Y=-9. The data are read sequentially. The information needed to locate a number and determine its form is contained in the format descriptors.

(b) READ X, ANSWER AND Y AS I 3, 2 I 2

Here, the format list is the same as (a) except that the second and third format descriptors have been combined.

(c)   WRITE X, ANSWER AND Y AS I 3, 2 I 2

In this example, the values of the expressions X, ANSWER, and Y, are output in the indicated format. We will assume that the output has been specified to appear on the standard line printer and that this statement is the first to be executed. If the values of X, ANSWER, and Y are 9, -3, and 0, respectively, the printed line appears as

```
column number
00000000011111...
12345678901234
  9-3 0
```

Notice that leading zeroes are left blank, but that the rightmost zero in a zero-valued integer is printed.

(d)   READ X,Y,Z AS 3 D(10,3)

Three decimal fields are specified, the first in columns 1-10, the second in columns 11-20, and the third in columns 21-30. Assume the data punched as

```
column number
00000000011111111112222222222 3333...
12345678901234567890123456789 0123...
   126.345  -18.62   768954346
```

The first data field is assigned to X and the decimal point is where it is expected, in column 7. The second data field is assigned to Y; here the decimal point is not where it is expected, in column 17. Therefore, the punched number overrides the stated format, and the value -18.62 is assigned to Y. A characteristic of the D format is that it allows itself to be overridden if a decimal point is punched within a field. If no decimal point is punched, as occurs in the third data field, its location is determined by the format. In this call, the value 768954.346 is assigned to Z.

(e)   READ X AS D(8,2)

Such a data item might be punched as

```
column number
00000000011111...
12345678901234
  16.5E 2
```

The punched decimal point overrides the format. The scale factor
multiplies the resulting number by 10**2 so that the value 1650 is
assigned to X. The flexibility of the decimal format is shown in the
following statement that defines a data card so that a large range of
numbers can be accommodated:

(f)   READ X(1), X(2), X(3), X(4), X(5) AS 5 D(10,2)

A data card may appear as

```
column number
00000000000000000002222222222333333333344444444445...
12345678901234567890123456789012345678901234567890...
    41.25 19.22E-03   4537992                -167.1
```

in which case X(1)=41.25, X(2)=0.01922, X(3)=45379.92, X(4)=0.00,
and X(5)=-167.1.

(g)   WRITE A,B,C,D,E AS 2 I 4, D(10,3), E(9,1), I 6

This statement defines output pictures for five expressions — A to
E. Assume that A and B are INTEGER variables with current values 9
and 132, C is a REAL variable with current value 19.2, D is a REAL
value with current value 8.25, and E is an INTEGER variable with
current value -1863976. The output will look like

```
column number
00000000011111111112222222222333333333344444444445...
12345678901234567890123456789012345678901234567890...
    9 132    19.200  8.3E+00-2E+06
```

The output of E illustrates the action taken when a value is too large
for its field. In this instance, a seven-digit integer could not be
printed in a six-digit field, and was converted to a six-character
scientific representation. The actual value -1.86397×10^6 was rounded
to a value that could be printed 2×10^6 and would retain the most
significance.

(h)   READ A(1),A(2),A(3) AS 3 A 4

If we assume that the array A has been defined as ALPHA, and that each computer word holds four characters, the following data will be read and stored in A(1), A(2), and A(3):

```
column number
000000000111111111
123456789012345678
INPUT DATA
```

A(1) contains the characters INPU, A(2) the characters T DA, and A(3) the characters TA_ _. The character _ denotes a blank.

(i)   The above string of characters can be printed by the statements

```
        FOR I=1 TO 3, WRITE A(I) AS A 4
  or    WRITE A(1), A(2), A(3) AS 3 A 4
```

which produce the identical output of

```
column number
0000000001111
1234567890123
INPUT DATA
```

(j)   The word INPUT alone can be printed by the statement

```
        WRITE A(1) AND A(2) AS A 4, A 1
```

which produces the output

```
column number
000000000111
123456789012
INPUT
```

(k)   Let I be an INTEGER variable and A an ALPHA variable. The statement WRITE I AS I 4 displays the value of I as an integer number. If I had been assigned the value 138 by a LET statement, the number 138 would be printed. The statement WRITE I AS A 4, however, displays the value of I as an alphanumeric string. Had A been assigned the value THIS by the statement READ A AS A 4, and then I assigned the value THIS by the statement LET I=A, the value THIS would be printed.

Thus far, the examples have pretended that each new READ or WRITE statement starts at the beginning of a new data card, line, or record. This does not always occur. It has been a convenient fiction for the exposition of format descriptors.

All READ and WRITE statements operate on a continuous string of characters and only skip to a new data card or output line when so instructed. Thus, the two statements

READ X AS I 5   READ Y AS D(10,2)

read successive fields from the same data card (record). Often, of course, data are split between data cards, or must be read from different, noncontiguous parts of the same data card. A method of positioning the *current input pointer* or *current output pointer* is needed to do this. Such pointers are variables that point to the last referenced columns in the various input and output data streams. They can be advanced by the statements START NEW INPUT CARD, START NEW OUTPUT CARD, and START NEW PAGE, which we have already seen, and by five nonnumerical formats. These formats can be interspersed among numerical formats, or they can appear alone in READ and WRITE statements. Examples of the use of these formats are given following their description.

B (Beginning Column) Descriptor

This format is used to specify the position in which the first character of an item of input or output data is found or displayed. The format B n positions the current input/output device at column n. When several B format descriptors are used within a format list, they do not have to appear in ascending numerical order; for instance, the format B 47, I 10, B 5, D(6,3), B 57, D(7,3), B 20, I 4 prints a line of the following form:

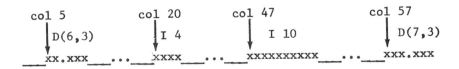

S (Skip Column) Descriptor

Spaces may be skipped between output items, or columns may be
skipped on input data cards by specifying, through the S n format,
that n spaces are to be skipped before reading or printing the next
item of data. Skipped positions are left blank on output, while data
punched in skipped positions are ignored on input.

/(Skip to New Record) Descriptor

Thus far, format descriptors have presented conventions for
locating and laying out data within input/output records. There is
an implicit understanding that each format list refers to a single
punched card of information or printed line of output; we are aware
that input/output records change only when a START NEW INPUT CARD or
START NEW OUTPUT LINE statement is executed. Unless this occurs,
statements continue to read from the same card or to print on the
same line. A record can be changed within a format list, however, by
using a / format descriptor. This descriptor may be used repeatedly
within a format list; each time it is encountered it skips a record
on the current input/output unit.

* (Skip to a New Page) Descriptor

This format descriptor is analogous to the / format; its sole
function is to eject a page on a line printer. If used in other circumstances, as when punching cards, it is ignored.

" " (Character String) Descriptor

Constant alphanumeric data can be included in output formats by
using a character string format descriptor. All characters included
between double quotation marks are printed as they appear except for
the underscore, which is printed as ". The spacing of the character
string can be specified by other format descriptors such as B, S,
and /, as well as by blanks within the character string. A character
string cannot exceed the length of a printed line. If a long string
is required, it must be split into two strings separated by a /. Some
examples follow.

(a) READ I AND J AS I 5,/,I 5

A value for I is read from the first five columns following the present location of the current input pointer for the current input unit. A value for J is read from columns 1-5 of the record following.

(b) READ I AND J AS B 1, I 5,/,I 5

The current input pointer is returned to the first column of the current record. If the pointer is greater than 1, a new record is not selected; instead, the pointer is moved back. Values for I and J are then read from the first five columns of this record and the one following.

(c) READ I, J, K AS 3 D(10,2),/

The above statement establishes a "record-oriented" input format. Each group of variable values is contained on a different card; after one group is read, a new card is read in preparation for the next group.

(d) WRITE A, B, C, D, E, F AS I 5,S 50,I 5,/,/,/,/,4 D(10,4)

The statement above writes two integer variables spaced 50 columns apart in an integer format, concludes this record, bringing the current output pointer to the head of the output buffer, skips three records, and writes four decimal values on a second record.

(e) WRITE N AND AVERAGE AS "OF",I 3," TO DATE, THE AVERAGE IS ",D(6,2)

Two values embedded in character strings are written from the above statement. If writing occurs on a line printer and the current output pointer is at the beginning of a line, the output looks as follows for N=97 and AVERAGE=53.287:

OF 97 TO DATE, THE AVERAGE IS 53.29

(f) READ A(1),B(2),A(3),A(4),A(5) AS B 5,I 10,D(7,3),/,B 20,3 I 5

This statement begins in column 5 of the current input unit and reads two values in integer and decimal formats, respectively, then starts a new record and reads three integer values starting in column 20.

(g) WRITE AS *,/,/,/,/

The above statement starts a new output page and skips four lines. No output values are transmitted.

Controlled READ and WRITE Statements

Occasionally, it is necessary or desirable to read an array of values under the control of a READ statement,[†] as in

FOR I=1 TO N, READ A(I)

Here, the free-form READ reads a sequence of values across the current input record. If, however, values are packed in a format with no blanks between them, the free-form READ cannot be used. One is tempted to write

FOR I=1 TO N, READ A(I) AS I 4

This would be feasible if the values of A(I) were spaced across an entire record or limited to one record. If, however, the data are arranged so that meaningful values are contained only in columns 1 through 60 of a data card, the above statement will read through column 60 and take values from columns 61-80. One wants to skip to a new card upon reaching column 61, but cannot write

FOR I=1 TO N, READ A(I) AS I 4,/

as this reads one value per input record. A new convention is needed.

An expression enclosed in parentheses placed before a format list repeats that format list the indicated number of times and then skips to a new record. If N=12 and four numbers are to be read per card from columns 1 through 24, the following statements read 12 values from 3 cards:

START NEW CARD
FOR I=1 TO N, READ A(I) AS (4)I 6

This form may also be used if groups of variables with different formats are in a record. The following statement reads 4 groups of data

---

[†]Input of an entire array by use of its name only is restricted to the free-form READ statement.

in the format I 6,D(6,2) from each data card until 2*N values have
been read.

FOR I=1 TO N, READ A(I),B(I) AS (4) I 6,D(6,2)

This repetition facility can be used with both READ and WRITE statements, but it can only be used in statements controlled by FOR phrases.
This particular form of the READ statement assumes that input starts
at the beginning of a data card (record). This is the reason for the
START NEW CARD statement in the foregoing example. The statement can
terminate, of course, with the current input pointer positioned in
the middle of a record. This is a function of the format used.

Similar rules apply to the PRINT and LIST statements, as well as
to all input/output operations performed by the SIMSCRIPT II system.
Output is printed wherever the current pointer points, assuming it is
at the head of a record. After output, the system positions the
pointer at the head of the next record.

Variable Formats

The use of format descriptors containing expressions as well as
constants is one feature available in READ and WRITE statements that
has not been discussed. Arithmetic expressions can be used to control
field widths in formats for data layout purposes. For instance, a
curve of the function $\log_e(i)$ using * as a graphical character is
generated by the statement shown below.

FOR I=1 TO 100, WRITE AS B LOG.E.F(I),"*",/

Table 3-3 indicates where expressions can be used in format descriptors and states their form. This feature allows formats to be constructed during program execution, freeing programs from particular
data forms. Constants defining a format can be read in, perhaps in
free-form, before a deck of data cards, to specify the form in which
the data appear. If a program reads in sets of data cards that are
grouped three items to a card with the first item being INTEGER and
the balance REAL, the initialization routine of the program could contain the free-form READ statement

Table 3-3

FORMAT DESCRIPTOR FORMS

Format Descriptor	General Form
Integer field	i I e
Decimal field	i D(e,e)
Scientific field	i E(e,e)
Starting column	B e
Space skip	S e
Alpha field	i A e
Computer rep-field	i C e

NOTE: i is an INTEGER constant;
       e is an arithmetic expression.

        READ C1, C2, C3, C4, C5

and the program could contain the formatted READ statement

        READ I, A, B AS B C1 , I C2 , S C3 ,2 D(C4,C5)

and the program's data deck might look like

    column number
    00000000000000000222222222233333333333...
    12345678901234567890123456789012345678...

      6 4 10   5 2
           342   16.25 1.5
           -10   0.5 73.4

Local Input/Output Unit Specifications

We have at this point examined all but one of the variations of
the READ and WRITE statements. The final feature is the ability to
locally override current input and current output unit specifications
declared in USE statements. This facility is provided by the phrase,
USING d, which may be attached to any READ or WRITE statement, as in
the statements

        READ I, J AND K AS I 6,/,2 I 3 USING N
        WRITE AS * USING 7 ''SKIPS TO A NEW PRINTER PAGE
        WRITE IDENTIFICATION AS *,I 7,/,/,/ USING M+2
        READ X USING TAPE 12

This phrase sets the current input or output unit to the indicated
unit during the statement's execution, and returns it to its previous
value on its completion. The optional words TAPE or UNIT can be
written before the unit number, if desired, as in the last example.

A Final Remark

As a final remark, we explain a programming convenience that can
shorten the number of symbols necessarily written when several statements contain identical format lists or sublists. The DEFINE TO MEAN
statement may be used to define format strings and to call upon them
"by name" in the following way:

```
DEFINE INTEGER.LIST TO MEAN I 2,2 I 3
READ A,B,C AS INTEGER.LIST
        .
        .
        .
WRITE I,J,K,L,M AS INTEGER.LIST, 2 I 10
```

The first statement is compiled as

```
READ A,B,C, AS I 2,2 I 3
```

and the second as

```
WRITE I,J,K,L,M AS I 2,2 I 3,2 I 10
```

This is but one of many uses of the DEFINE TO MEAN statement.

3-10 MISCELLANEOUS INPUT/OUTPUT STATEMENTS AND FACILITIES

3-10-1 End-of-File Conditions

As described in Sec. 3-09, data can be organized into fields and
into records. Files are often used in magnetic tape applications,
and features are present in SIMSCRIPT II to assist in their use. The
statement CLOSE d puts an *end-of-file marker* on the current output
unit. The statements

```
        ADVANCE e INPUT FILES      BACKSPACE e INPUT FILES
and     ADVANCE e OUTPUT FILES     BACKSPACE e OUTPUT FILES
```

move the current input or output units forward or backward the indicated number of files, i.e., past e end-of-file markers. The statement

ADVANCE 1 INPUT FILE

moves a unit to the beginning of the next file, in position to read the first record in the file. The statements

      ADVANCE e INPUT FILES USING d BACKSPACE e INPUT FILES USING d

and   ADVANCE e OUTPUT FILES USING d BACKSPACE e OUTPUT FILES USING d

are available.

The CLOSE, ADVANCE, and BACKSPACE statements also allow an optional word before the device specification, as in

CLOSE TAPE K
ADVANCE 2 INPUT FILES USING UNIT 7

Whenever a READ statement is executed, there is a possibility of running off the end of a data file. When dealing with cards, this is tantamount to running out of data; when dealing with tape it is equivalent to running into an end-of-file marker. The free-form READ statement, as previously noted, provides a check for an end-of-file condition through the statement IF DATA IS ENDED. A similar check is needed for formatted I/O, and this is provided through a global variable and a system action, rather than through a special statement.

The automatically defined global variable EOF.V is initialized to zero when a SIMSCRIPT II program is begun. A programmer can leave the variable alone or set it equal to 1 in a LET statement. When an end-of-file marker is encountered by a READ statement, the SIMSCRIPT II system refers to EOF.V for action direction. If EOF.V=0, reading the end-of-file marker is considered an error, and the program terminates with an error message. If EOF.V=1, the variables in the READ list are assigned values of zero, EOF.V is set to 2, and control returns to the statement following the READ. In other words, a value of EOF.V≠0 is considered a message to the SIMSCRIPT II system that says, in effect, "Do not terminate my program; return zero values and let me know that I have encountered an end-of-file marker." By testing EOF.V after a READ statement, a programmer can determine whether the statement read

true data values or encountered an end-of-file marker. This facility
can be used in the following ways:

(1) As an end of data signal:

```
'READ' READ X AS I 2 USING TAPE 6
       IF EOF.V = 2, GO TO FINISH
       ELSE  ADD X TO SUM  ADD 1 TO COUNTER
       GO TO READ
'FINISH' WRITE COUNTER, SUM/COUNTER AS "THE AVERAGE OF",
       I 4,"ITEMS PROCESSED IS",D(6,2)
       STOP  END
```

(2) To transfer to an error routine rather than terminate:

```
READ X AS D(10,3)
IF EOF.V = 2, GO TO ERROR.PRINTOUT  ELSE
```

3-10-2 *Positioning Tapes, Disks, and Drums*

A device that has been read from, or written on, is repositioned
at its starting point by the statement

REWIND d

The words TAPE and UNIT are optional after REWIND. After a unit has
been rewound, it must be "used" before it can be read from or written
on again. A REWIND command before a unit has been "used" is ignored.

3-10-3 *Input/Output of Nondecimal Information*

When information is used only for transmission between computers
or is saved for subsequent resubmission to a working program, it need
not be converted from its internal computer representation to "human-
readable" form. A much more efficient direct transfer of information
can be obtained without formatting through the statements

READ *variable list* AS BINARY

and WRITE *arithmetic expression list* AS BINARY

where a current unit is implied, or through the statements

READ *variable list* AS BINARY USING d

and WRITE *arithmetic expression list* AS BINARY USING d

where a unit is specified. These statements are especially useful
for storing intermediate results too voluminous to keep in core on

tape, or disk, and for reading them back when they are needed. Binary and formatted data cannot be written together on the same device. The following program shows how to save a computed array, release it for other use, and, at a later time, reuse the array values:

```
PREAMBLE  DEFINE ARRAY AS A 2-DIMENSIONAL ARRAY
NORMALLY, MODE IS INTEGER
END


MAIN
READ N ''FREE-FORM READ
     RESERVE ARRAY(*,*) AS N BY N
        .
        .
        .
     computations assigning values
     to the elements of ARRAY
        .
        .
        .
FOR I=1 TO N, FOR J=1 TO N, WRITE ARRAY(I,J) AS BINARY USING TAPE 1
REWIND TAPE 1
RELEASE ARRAY(*,*)
        .
        .
        .
     statements that use the released
     memory space and then give it up
        .
        .
        .
RESERVE ARRAY(*,*) AS N BY N
USE TAPE 1 FOR INPUT
FOR I=1 TO N, FOR J=1 TO N, READ ARRAY(I,J) AS BINARY
        .
        .
        .
     additional computations and output
        .
        .
        .
STOP    END
```

* 3-11 INTERNAL EDITING OF INFORMATION

The SIMSCRIPT II system has one buffer for each input/output device. The size of each buffer varies, depending upon the use of the unit (input or output, formatted, or free-form) and the medium

used (cards, tape, printer). All reading and writing occurs through
these buffers. Both the current input pointer (RCOLUMN.V) and current
output pointer (WCOLUMN.V) travel along the buffers, point to the last
accessed character, and read or write physically when a / format is
encountered or the end of a buffer is reached.

The current output buffer is called OUT.F, and can be accessed
as an ALPHA function. OUT.F(1) refers to the first character in the
buffer, OUT.F(10) to the tenth character, OUT.F(132) to the last
character.[†] As a computer word contains more than one alphanumeric
character and the OUT.F function returns only one character, the value
of OUT.F is a left-adjusted ALPHA word; e.g., if the first buffer
position contains the letter A and each word can hold four ALPHA
characters, the value of OUT.F(1) is A___.[††] It is possible to edit
output information by inserting alphanumeric or numeric data directly
into the buffer. When a new record is begun, by either a START NEW
statement or a / format descriptor, the buffer is emptied and filled
as the ensuing formats dictate. Thus, the statement

```
WRITE X AS /,"THE BUFFER CONTAINS",I 3," CHARACTERS"
```

empties the buffer (OUT.F(1) through OUT.F(132) now contain blanks)
and inserts the characters THE_BUFFER_CONTAINS in OUT.F(1) through
OUT.F(19), the value of X in OUT.F(20) through OUT.F(22), and the
characters _CHARACTERS in OUT.F(23) through OUT.F(33). To change the
buffer so that the string reads THE.BUFFER.CONTAINS.33.CHARACTERS
(assume X=33), one could write the program

```
      FOR I=1 TO 131, UNTIL OUT.F(I)="_" AND OUT.F(I+1)="_"
      DO   IF OUT.F(I)="_", LET OUT.F(I)="."
           ELSE
      LOOP
```

or, on realizing that WCOLUMN.V points to the last character written
into the buffer, one could write

[†]Assuming an output buffer of 132 characters.

[††]In this section a blank character is represented by an underscore.

```
      FOR I=1 TO WCOLUMN.V,
      DO IF OUT.F(I)="_", LET OUT.F(I)="."
         ELSE
      LOOP
```

If numbers representing dollar amounts are written, dollar signs ($) can be put before the first digit of each number in a similar way:

```
      FOR I=1 TO WCOLUMN.V,
      DO IF OUT.F(I)="_" AND OUT.F(I+1)¬="_",
         LET OUT.F(I)="$",
         ELSE
      LOOP
```

A special internal buffer called THE BUFFER can be used for data editing with READ and WRITE statements. The length of THE BUFFER is specified by the system global variable BUFFER.V. Space is allocated to THE BUFFER by the statements

USE THE BUFFER FOR INPUT   and   USE THE BUFFER FOR OUTPUT

or the statements

   WRITE *expression list* AS *format list* USING THE BUFFER
and READ *variable list* AS *format list* USING THE BUFFER

BUFFER.V has a default value of 132. It can be set to a different value before its first USE.

The examples below illustrate how mode conversion is executed in the internal buffer.

(1) In this procedure, X is an INTEGER variable and A is ALPHA, X=100, and each ALPHA word can hold four characters; the initial value of A is irrelevant.

WRITE X AS /, I 4 USING THE BUFFER

This statement sets the internal buffer to:

```
| _ | 1 | 0 | 0 | _ | _ | _ |        | _ | _ |
  1   2   3   4   5   .   .   .  ....... 131 132
```

Note that / clears THE BUFFER and sets the current output pointer to its first position. The statement

READ A USING THE BUFFER

executes a free-form read from the internal buffer, left-adjusting the
value read so that the stored value of A looks like

A $\boxed{1\ 0\ 0\ \_}$

(2) If the initial characters of four ALPHA variables are to be
merged to form a new ALPHA value, one can write

```
WRITE A(1),A(2),A(3),A(4) AS 4 A 1 USING THE BUFFER
READ NEW AS A 4 USING THE BUFFER
```

3-12 WRITING FORMATTED REPORTS

The PRINT statement that we have been using since Sec. *1-11* has
functioned as both a simple mechanism for displaying short error messages and as a more complex report layout statement (Sec. *1-16-1*).
This section adds two phrases to the PRINT statement and introduces
two control statements to provide a full-fledged report generator
capability.

These new features permit a programmer to specify the layout of
printed results, to control the printing of headings and titles, to
eject pages between various report sections, and to arrange "wide
reports" on standard-width paper. Figure 3-1 illustrates the kind of
complex report that can be generated.

The statement BEGIN REPORT marks the start of a *report section*
within which various kinds of control can be exercised. A report
section, like a routine, is terminated by an END statement. The
statements

```
BEGIN REPORT
FOR I=1 TO N, PRINT 1 LINE WITH I,X(I) THUS
     **        **.***
END
```

illustrate a simple report section that merely marks off a controlled
output statement. The report section prints N lines containing two
values each. If the output is to be labeled, the program can be
written as

PAGE 1

DEPOT TO BASE SHIPMENTS

DEPOT	1	2	....	24
BASE				
1	X	X	......	X
2	X	X	......	X
.				
.				
50	X	X	....	X

PAGE 2

DEPOT TO BASE SHIPMENTS

DEPOT	1	2	....	24
BASE				
51	X	X	......	X
52	X	X	......	X
.				
.				
100	X	X	....	X

PAGE 3

DEPOT TO BASE SHIPMENTS

DEPOT	1	2	....	24
BASE				
101	X	X	......	X
102	X	X	......	X
.				
.				
120	X	X	......	X
TOTAL	XX	XX	......	XX

PAGE 4

DEPOT TO BASE SHIPMENTS

DEPOT	25	26	....	48
BASE				
1	X	X	......	X
2	X	X	......	X
.				
.				
50	X	X	....	X

PAGE 5

DEPOT TO BASE SHIPMENTS

DEPOT	25	26	....	48
BASE				
51	X	X	......	X
52	X	X	......	X
.				
.				
100	X	X	....	X

PAGE 6

DEPOT TO BASE SHIPMENTS

DEPOT	25	26	....	48
BASE				
101	X	X	......	X
102	X	X	......	X
.				
.				
120	X	X	......	X
TOTAL	XX	XX	......	XX

PAGE 7

DEPOT TO BASE SHIPMENTS

DEPOT	49	50	.....	60	TOTAL
BASE					
1	X	X	......	X	XXX
2	X	X	......	X	XXX
.					
.					
50	X	X	......	X	XXX

PAGE 8

DEPOT TO BASE SHIPMENTS

DEPOT	49	50	.....	60	TOTAL
BASE					
51	X	X	......	X	XXX
52	X	X	......	X	XXX
.					
.					
100	X	X	......	X	XXX

PAGE 9

DEPOT TO BASE SHIPMENTS

DEPOT	49	50	.....	60	TOTAL
BASE					
101	X	X	......	X	XXX
102	X	X	......	X	XXX
.					
.					
120	X	X	......	X	XXX
TOTAL	XX	XX	......	XX	XXX

Fig. 3-1 -- An illustrative management report

```
BEGIN REPORT
PRINT 1 LINE AS FOLLOWS
     I        X(I)
FOR I=1 TO N, PRINT 1 LINE WITH I,X(I) THUS
     **       **.***
END
```

This prints a heading above the N lines of output that identify the
displayed values. If N is large and the output continues on more
than one page, only the results on the first page are labeled. All
other pages are untitled.

A *heading section* may be defined within a report section so that
titles are printed and any necessary computation performed whenever
a page is ejected. A heading section is started by the statement
BEGIN HEADING and ended by the statement END. All statements between
a BEGIN HEADING and its matching END are executed whenever a page is
ejected by an output statement within an *enclosing* report section,
but after the heading section itself.

To title all pages of output in the foregoing example, the program
can be written as

```
BEGIN REPORT
BEGIN HEADING
PRINT 1 LINE AS FOLLOWS
     I        X(I)
END '' HEADING SECTION
FOR I=1 TO N, PRINT 1 LINE WITH I, X(I) THUS
     **       **.***
END
```

The statements in a heading section are executed the first time
they are encountered and thereafter every time a page is changed.
Pages are changed whenever the current line count exceeds the number
of printed lines a page can contain. The system variables LINE.V
and LINES.V have the values of the current line count and the permitted
number of lines per page, respectively. LINE.V is initialized to 1
when an output device is first USED; it is stepped from 1 to the current value of LINES.V each time a new line is printed. A separate
count of LINE.V is kept for each output device. LINES.V may be changed
by a programmer at any time to vary the number of lines that appear
on each output page. The SIMSCRIPT II system automatically sets
LINES.V= 55 at the start of each program's execution.

Pages are numbered sequentially, beginning with 1, with the number of the page currently being written contained in the system variable PAGE.V. As with LINE.V, a separate count of PAGE.V is kept for each output device. PAGE.V may be reset at any time. When this is done, numbering continues in sequence from the new value. PAGE.V and LINE.V always refer to the current output unit.

Within a heading section, the statement

```
                   IF PAGE IS FIRST
```

may be used to select statements to be executed only on the first page of a report section's output. The following program illustrates one way of using the report facilities described thus far:

```
PREAMBLE
NORMALLY, MODE IS INTEGER
END

MAIN 'DATA' READ LINES.V, N, UNIT
IF LINES.V IS NOT ZERO, CALL DISPLAY(N,UNIT)
GO TO DATA
ELSE  STOP
END

ROUTINE TO DISPLAY (M,U)
USE U FOR OUTPUT
LET PAGE.V= 1
BEGIN REPORT '' SECTION
BEGIN HEADING '' SECTION
IF PAGE IS FIRST,
   PRINT 1 LINE AS FOLLOWS
   TABULATION OF MATHEMATICAL FUNCTIONS
     SKIP 3 OUTPUT LINES
REGARDLESS
   PRINT 1 LINE WITH PAGE.V AS FOLLOWS
                         PAGE NO. **
   SKIP 2 OUTPUT LINES
   PRINT 1 LINE AS FOLLOWS
   I SQRT(I)  I SQ  LOG(I)
   SKIP 1 OUTPUT LINE
END ''HEADING SECTION
FOR J= 1 TO M, PRINT 1 LINE WITH J,
  SQRT.F(J), J**2,LOG.10.F(J) THUS
 **  **.**   ****  *.***
END '' REPORT SECTION
RETURN
END '' ROUTINE DISPLAY
```

The above program (1) in its MAIN routine reads in control information and (2) in its DISPLAY routine uses a report section to prepare a labeled output display. The variable LINES.V is used both to control the number of lines printed per page in successive reports and to terminate the program.

Within the routine DISPLAY, an output unit is selected outside the report section and PAGE.V is set to 1. This enables each report to be printed on a separate device, if desired, and sets the number of the first page of each report to 1. Within the report section SKIP statements are used to separate heading information.

If the data read by this program are the sequence of values 50, 100, 5, 20, 40, 6, 0, 0, 0, two reports will be printed. The first will display the values of j, $\sqrt{j}$, j^2, and $\log(j)$ for $j=1,2,\ldots,100$ on three pages of output unit 5. If we assume that printing starts at the top of the first page, it will contain the heading TABULATION OF MATHEMATICAL FUNCTIONS, the page number, the heading I SQRT(I) I SQ LOG(I) and values for $j=1,2,\ldots,41$. The second page will contain the page number, the heading I SQRT(I) I SQ LOG(I) and values for $j= 42$, 44, ..., 86. The third page will resemble the second, except that it will contain values for $j = 87,89, \ldots, 100$.

The second report will be similar to the first, except that it will display values for $j = 1, 2, \ldots, 40$ on pages that contain only 20 lines. The heading TABULATION OF MATHEMATICAL FUNCTIONS will be printed on the current page, renumbered 1, of output unit 6.

Whenever it is necessary to begin each report section on a new page, as might be done in this example, the BEGIN REPORT statement can be written as

BEGIN REPORT ON A NEW PAGE

which ejects a page on the current output device unless the current page has not been written on (LINE.V= 1, WCOLUMN.V= 0). This prevents blank pages from being ejected between reports.

The form of a "typical" report using the statements described thus far is

```
        BEGIN REPORT ON A NEW PAGE
                      .
                      .
                      .
              program statements
                      .
                      .
                      .
        BEGIN HEADING
                      .
            IF PAGE IS FIRST, ... ELSE
                      .
                      .
                      .
            SKIP N LINES
                      .
                      .
        END''HEADING
                      .
                      .
                      .
              program statements
                      .
                      .
                      .
        END''REPORT
```

with the variables LINE.V and PAGE.V being used in computational,
decisionmaking, and output statements. PRINT statements appear in
heading and report sections, and usually are controlled by FOR or
WHILE statements in the part of the report section labeled "program
statements." The flow of control in a report section such as appears
on this page is as follows:

(1) Execute statements between BEGIN REPORT and BEGIN
     HEADING, if any;

(2) Execute statements in the heading section, if any;

(3) Execute statements between END''HEADING and END''
     REPORT if any, executing statements in the heading
     section every time a page is changed.

These statements are adequate for many reports. A report for
which they are not suited is one that must print more than 80 columns
of information per line. Adding the word DOUBLE to a PRINT statement
in the following way

PRINT i DOUBLE LINES WITH *expression list* THUS

specifies that 2i, rather than i, format lines follow that are to be
read in pairs and interpreted as one format line 160 columns long.
To fill an entire line on a printer 132 columns wide, one would write
a statement as

```
PRINT 1 DOUBLE LINE AS FOLLOWS
AAAAAAAAAAAAA..................................AAAAAA
AAAAAAAAA...............AAAAAAAAAA
```

The first format card has an A punched in each of its 80 columns; the
second format card has an A punched in its first 52 columns. "Double
width" PRINT statements are not restricted to report sections. Any
PRINT statement can be expanded to double width.

The inclusion of an optional clause in the BEGIN REPORT and
PRINT statements adds one more important report-generation feature.
Figure 3-2 shows the kind of report the clauses handle, reports that
have rows of data with more items in each row than a single page can
contain.

In preparing reports of this kind, a series of pages is printed
with different column indices. In Fig. 3-2, pages 1 and 2 are printed
with column indices ranging from 1 to 50, and pages 3 and 4 are printed
with column indices ranging from 51 to 100. This feature, specifying
an iteration sequence for column indices and having pages printed
that, when separated and put together side-by-side look like printing
on a wide page, is known as *column repetition*. It is specified by
an optional clause in the BEGIN REPORT statement

BEGIN REPORT PRINTING *for* IN GROUPS OF e PER PAGE

The word *for* represents a FOR, WHILE, or UNTIL statement, perhaps
qualified, that generates column indices. The arithmetic expression
e specifies the number of indices in this iteration sequence to be
used on each page. Thus, the statement

BEGIN REPORT PRINTING FOR I = 1 TO 50 IN GROUPS OF 10 PER PAGE

specifies that five sets of column indices will be used for five ex-
ecutions of a report section. The report section will be executed

```
+-----------------------------+   +-----------------------------+
|                    PAGE  1  |   |                    PAGE  3  |
|                             |   |                             |
|    1 2 3 4 .........50      |   |    51 52 ..........100      |
|  1                          |   |  1                          |
|  2                          |   |  2                          |
|  3                          |   |  3                          |
|  4                          |   |  4                          |
|  5                          |   |  5                          |
|  6                          |   |  6                          |
|  7                          |   |  7                          |
|                             |   |                             |
+-----------------------------+   +-----------------------------+


+-----------------------------+   +-----------------------------+
|                    PAGE  2  |   |                    PAGE  4  |
|                             |   |                             |
|    1 2 3 4 .........50      |   |    51 52 ..........100      |
|   8                         |   |   8                         |
|   9                         |   |   9                         |
|  10                         |   |  10                         |
|  11                         |   |  11                         |
|  12                         |   |  12                         |
|                             |   |                             |
+-----------------------------+   +-----------------------------+
```

Fig. 3-2 -- A report using row and column repetition

first with I= 1,2,3,4,5,6,7,8,9, and 10; second with I= 11,12,...,20;
...; and fifth with I= 41,42,...,50. The index values are not given
to the report section individually, but in groups that are used all
at once by a special version of the PRINT statement.

If a controlling *for* phrase in a BEGIN REPORT statement is empty,
i.e., produces no values, the entire report section headed by this
statement is skipped, e.g., FOR I=1 TO 4, WITH X(I) > 0, and no X(I)
is greater than 0.

The groups of iteration values are used in a PRINT statement by
a clause specifying that a group of values are to be printed using

the indices generated by a preceding BEGIN REPORT statement. The
following example illustrates one such use:

```
        BEGIN REPORT PRINTING FOR J= 1 TO 25 IN GROUPS OF 5
            PER PAGE
        BEGIN HEADING
            PRINT 1 LINE WITH A GROUP OF J FIELDS THUS
                *   *   *   *   *
            SKIP 1 OUTPUT LINE
        END HEADING
            FOR I= 1 TO 6, PRINT 1 LINE WITH A GROUP OF
            X(I,J) FIELDS THUS
                **  **  **  **  **
        END REPORT
```

This program generates five pages of output. Page 1 uses the first
five values of J. A heading displays the values of J, and a row
repetition statement prints the values of X(I,J) for those values of
J and I= 1,2,3,4,5,6. Figure 3-3 illustrates how such a page might
appear.

```
        1   2   3   4   5
        **  **  **  **  **
        **  **  **  **  **
        **  **  **  **  **
        **  **  **  **  **
        **  **  **  **  **
        **  **  **  **  **
```

Fig. 3-3 -- Column repetition,
page 1

Page 2, Fig. 3-4, looks exactly like page 1 in form, but uses
the second five values of J to select values for display.

Pages 3, 4, and 5 are similar, with page 3 using J=11,...,15,
and page 4 using J= 16,...,20, etc.

The phrase A GROUP OF _ FIELDS in a PRINT statement notifies the
compiler that a sequence of index values generated for the enclosing

```
 6   7   8   9  10

**  **  **  **  **
**  **  **  **  **
**  **  **  **  **
**  **  **  **  **
**  **  **  **  **
**  **  **  **  **
```

Fig. 3-4 -- Column repetition,
page 2

column repetition block is to be used in computing the output fields. As shown, one format must be provided for each of the fields in the column repetition group. If the BEGIN REPORT statement specifies groups of six, then six formats must be provided in each PRINT group.

Other, nonrepetition values may also be printed by a PRINT statement containing a A GROUP OF _ FIELDS clause. For example, the previous displays can be better labeled by using the statement

```
    FOR I= 1 TO 6, PRINT 1 LINE WITH I, AND A GROUP OF
        X(I,J) FIELDS THUS
        *  **  **  **  **  **
```

Several values can be alternated within a A GROUP OF _ FIELDS clause, each using the index values. For example, the previous program might want to display both X(I,J) and Y(I,J) as follows:

```
    FOR I= 1 TO 6, PRINT 1 LINE WITH I , AND A GROUP OF
        X(I,J),Y(I,J) FIELDS THUS
        *  **  *.*  **  *.*  **  *.*  **  *.*  **  *.*
```

A format must be given for each output value, of course. All repeated formats must agree in mode. It is not possible to write

```
    PRINT 1 LINE WITH A GROUP OF I FIELDS THUS
```

and have the format line be

```
    *  *.*  *  *.*  *
```

All repeated formats need not be identical, e.g., * and **, but they must be of the same mode.

If it is not necessary that each set of column repetition groups start on a new page, the PER PAGE clause may be omitted from the BEGIN REPORT statement. The following report section uses this feature to display a matrix containing more columns than can be put on one line:

```
FOR I=1 TO N, DO
PRINT 1 LINE WITH I AS FOLLOWS
    ROW **
BEGIN REPORT PRINTING FOR J= 1 TO M IN GROUPS OF 24
PRINT 1 LINE WITH A GROUP OF X(I,J) FIELDS THUS
* * * * * * * * * * * * * * * * * * * * * * * *
END''REPORT
SKIP 2 LINES
LOOP
```

Such a program produces a report that, for M= 50, looks like Fig. 3-5.

```
ROW 1

* * * * * * * * * * * * * * * * * * * * * * * *
* * * * * * * * * * * * * * * * * * * * * * * *
* *
ROW 2

* * * * * * * * * * * * * * * * * * * * * * * *
* * * * * * * * * * * * * * * * * * * * * * * *
* *
```

Fig. 3-5 -- An example of column repetition

Note that the total number of column indices generated need not be an even multiple of the group size, e.g., 50 and 24 above.

A final feature makes it possible to generate attractively labeled reports that have row, as well as column, summarizations, even if the reports use column repetition. This is done by adding a clause to the PRINT statement that suppresses some output until all column

repetition data have been printed. A typical statement using this
feature will look as follows:

```
BEGIN REPORT PRINTING
FOR J= 1 TO M IN GROUPS OF 10 PER PAGE
PRINT 1 LINE WITH A GROUP OF X(I,J) FIELDS,
    SUMX(I) SUPPRESSING FROM COLUMN 70 AS FOLLOWS
    *   *   *   *   *   *   *   *   *   *   ****
                                            ↑
                                         Column 70
```

If M=30, three sets of column indices will be generated; the above
format line will be repeated three times, on three separate pages.
Only on the last page, however, will the last format be used, and
the value SUMX(I) printed. The SUPPRESSING clause specifies that
all formats from column 70 on are to be inhibited until all column
index values have been used. This includes both data and textual
material. The three pages printed by the above statements are shown
in Fig. 3-6.

The program in Fig. 3-7 generates the report shown in Fig. 3-1
and illustrates the statements of this section. The program is shown
as it would appear on punched cards. When writing reports, wider
paper is recommended. Double-length formats can be written across
a page and cards punched from them.

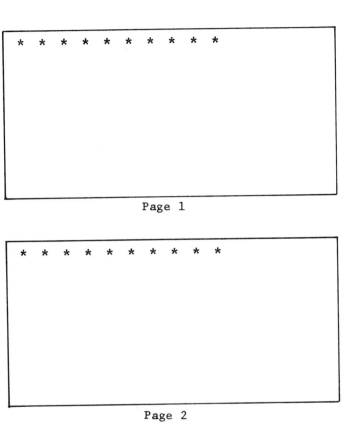

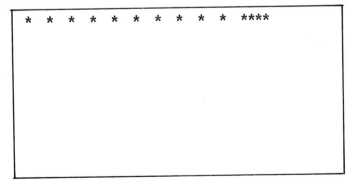

Fig. 3-6 -- An example of format suppression

```
0000000001111111111222222222233333333334444444444555555555566666666667777777778
12345678901234567890123456789012345678901234567890123456789012345678901234567890

LET PAGE.V=1
BEGIN REPORT ON A NEW PAGE PRINTING FOR DEPOT=1 TO 60 IN GROUPS OF 24 PER PAGE
BEGIN HEADING
PRINT 1 DOUBLE LINE WITH PAGE.V AS FOLLOWS

          PAGE   *
PRINT 1 LINE AS FOLLOWS
                              DEPOT TO BASE SHIPMENTS
SKIP 1 OUTPUT LINE
PRINT 1 DOUBLE LINE WITH A GROUP OF DEPOT FIELDS SUPPRESSING FROM COLUMN 91 THUS
  DEPOT ** ** ** ** ** ** ** ** ** ** ** ** ** ** ** ** ** ** ** ** ** ** ** **
        TOTAL
PRINT 1 LINE AS FOLLOWS
 BASE
END ''HEADING
FOR BASE=1 TO 120, PRINT 1 DOUBLE LINE WITH BASE, A GROUP OF SHIP(BASE,DEPOT)
                   FIELDS, TOT(BASE) SUPPRESSING FROM COLUMN 92 AS FOLLOWS
   **      *  *  *  *  *  *  *  *  *  *  *  *  *  *  *  *  *  *  *  *  *  *  *
          ***
SKIP 1 OUTPUT LINE
PRINT 1 DOUBLE LINE WITH A GROUP OF SUM(DEPOT) FIELDS, GRAND SUPPRESSING FROM
        COLUMN 92 AS FOLLOWS
  TOTAL ** ** ** ** ** ** ** ** ** ** ** ** ** ** ** ** ** ** ** ** ** ** ** **
          ***
END
```

Fig. 3-7 -- A report generator program

Chapter 4

SIMSCRIPT II: LEVEL 4

4-00 INTRODUCTION

Thus far we have dealt with an algebraic language. While having features that are clearly noncomputational, such as ALPHA mode, the majority of the statements have had a computational or input/output flavor. This section adds a new dimension to SIMSCRIPT II by providing language statements that are (1) oriented to problem definition and modeling, and that (2) manipulate data structures more complex than simple variables and arrays.

The section is roughly organized into three parts: definition, organization, and manipulation. First, definitions are provided for the three constituents of the SIMSCRIPT II world view: entities, attributes, and sets. Next, the relationships between these constituents are discussed, with special mention made of how they are organized. Finally, statements that use these constituents to perform particularly useful functions are presented.

4-01 ENTITIES AND ATTRIBUTES

While subscripted and unsubscripted variables are adequate for most procedural programming problems, e.g., algebraic calculations for scientific and business applications, variables are inadequate as basic language constructs for a large class of modeling problems. The inadequacy stems from two sources: (1) the need for more organizational structure than simple arrays afford, and (2) the lack of clarity of programs written within the descriptive limits of variable name and subscript expression conventions. While the first limitation is certainly the stronger, insofar as inadequate structure imposes conceptual limitations, the benefits of descriptive notation cannot be minimized. SIMSCRIPT II provides needed structure and narrative clarity through statements that define and manipulate entities, attributes, and sets.

An *entity* is a program element, much like a variable, that exists in a modeled system. It is like a subscripted variable in that it has values, called *attributes*, associated with it that, when assigned specific values, define a particular configuration or *state* of the entity. Unlike subscripted variables, entities have their attributes named, not numbered, enhancing model description. For example, in Levels 1-3 a collection of ten men having the attributes of age, number of dependents, and social security number may be described by a two-dimensional array defined as follows:

RESERVE MAN AS 3 BY 10

with the understanding that MAN(1,4) represents the age of the fourth man, MAN(3,6) the social security number of the sixth man, etc., according to the layout:

		1	2	3	4	5	6	7	8	9	10
AGE	1										
DEPENDENTS	2										
SOC.SEC	3										

Level 4, however, permits the entity MAN to be defined by the statement

EVERY MAN HAS AN AGE, A NUMBER.OF.DEPENDENTS
AND A SOCIAL.SECURITY.NUMBER

and a particular man's attributes to be accessed by references such as AGE(MAN) and SOCIAL.SECURITY.NUMBER(MAN). A particular man is specified by the value of the variable MAN. Thus, the EVERY statement defines a *class of objects*, each called MAN, having similar properties. Every MAN, of which there may be many, has the same attributes.

Entities and their attributes are declared in a program preamble
by statements of the general form

EVERY *entity name* HAS AN *attribute name list*

Entity and attribute names follow the same naming convention as variables and routines and each variable, entity, attribute, and routine
name must be unique. To assist in the creation of readable programs,
the words A, THE, and SOME can be used in place of AN, as in

EVERY MAN HAS AN AGE, SOME DEPENDENTS AND A
SOCIAL.SECURITY.NUMBER

Entity declarations implicitly state that attributes occupy specific
locations in *entity records*. The above declaration states that the
value of AGE is to be found in word 1 of a MAN record, the value of
DEPENDENTS in word 2, etc. Each MAN record can be pictured as

MAN

value of AGE
value of DEPENDENTS
value of SOCIAL.SECURITY.NUMBER

and the form AGE(MAN) can be translated into "the value found in the
first word of the record indexed by the value MAN." Since attribute
names specify *relative locations* of values in entity records, no two
entities can have an attribute with the same name placed in different
words within the two entity records. The statements

EVERY MAN HAS AN AGE
EVERY WOMAN HAS AN AGE

specify a *common attribute*, AGE, correctly; the statements

EVERY MAN HAS AN AGE
EVERY WOMAN HAS SOME DEPENDENTS AND AN AGE

do not. Sections *4-03* and *4-04* discuss entity types and entity declarations more fully, and clarify the notion of an "entity index" referred
to above.

4-02 SETS

If attributes were the only modeling feature offered, it is doubtful whether this level would make a major contribution to modeling. While they provide considerable descriptive power through the *attribute name (entity name)* notation, the use of attribute values to relate entities to one another is probably their overriding contribution.

Consider the following situation: Over the years, a group of men living in one community join various clubs and lodges. As men are born, grow up, remain in or move out of the community, and die, the lodge and club memberships change. To model the relationships that exist between the men of the community, both over time and at particular instants of time, we require some way of grouping the individual lodge and club members together. Such a grouping is defined by the statements:

```
        EVERY COMMUNITY OWNS A MASONS,AN ELKS AND A
            BOY.SCOUTS
        EVERY MAN MAY BELONG TO THE MASONS,THE ELKS
            AND THE BOY.SCOUTS
```

The first statement declares that each entity of the class COMMUNITY *owns* a set called MASONS, a set called ELKS, and a set called BOY.SCOUTS. Each of these sets corresponds to a logical grouping of men in the community. This statement does not specify which men belong to the particular sets; rather, it establishes a system of *set pointers* and *set attributes* for the *owner entities* that enable *set memberships* to be constructed. Each COMMUNITY is given a logical entity record[†] with the following attributes automatically defined:

[†]Since particular SIMSCRIPT II implementations may store entity data differently and there are actually two different types of entities, the logical rather than physical aspects of entity-attribute associations are stressed.

COMMUNITY

F.MASONS
L.MASONS
F.ELKS
L.ELKS
F.BOY.SCOUTS
L.BOY.SCOUTS

The attributes starting with F. are set pointers that point to the
first member of the respective sets. The attributes starting with L.
are set pointers that point to the *last* member of the respective sets.
The *set members*, as we shall see, point to one another, defining their
interrelationships and making the connection between the set owner and
the set members complete.

The second statement declares that each entity of the class MAN
may belong to sets called MASONS, ELKS and BOY.SCOUTS. It is important to note that membership is declared as possible in this statement
and not made mandatory. As might be expected, this statement automatically defines set attributes for member entities:

MAN

P.MASONS
S.MASONS
P.ELKS
S.ELKS
P.BOY.SCOUTS
S.BOY.SCOUTS

The attributes starting with P. are set pointers pointing to the
predecessor entity in the indicated set; the attributes starting with
S. are set pointers pointing to the *successor entity* in the indicated
set. The concepts of predecessor and successor, as well as first and
last, can be best explained by an illustration. In Fig. 4-1 the

entity COMMUNITY owns one set called MASONS. The members of the set are entities of the class MAN. The entity-set relationships are defined by the statements:

EVERY COMMUNITY OWNS SOME MASONS
EVERY MAN MAY BELONG TO THE MASONS

The entity records shown contain the automatically generated ownership and membership pointers F.MASONS, L.MASONS, P.MASONS and S.MASONS.

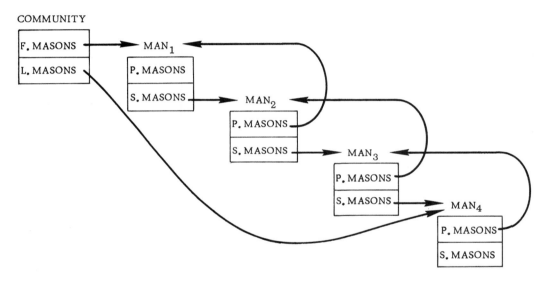

Fig. 4-1 -- Owner-member set relationships

The set owner, the entity named COMMUNITY, has two attributes that point to the member entities that are *logically* first and last in the set MASONS. The member entities, here called MAN_1, MAN_2, MAN_3, and MAN_4, have two attributes that point to the members of the set that *logically* precede and succeed them. Thus, F.MASONS in COMMUNITY points to the entity record of MAN_1, indicating that it is the first entity (logically) in the set MASONS. The pointer P.MASONS of MAN_1, points nowhere (has a zero value), as MAN_1 has no predecessor in MASONS. The S.MASONS pointer, however, points to MAN_2, which logically follows it in MASONS; as shown, P.MASONS of MAN_2 points back to its predecessor, MAN_1. The same is true of MAN_3. MAN_4, as the last member of MASONS, differs somewhat. It has no successor, and is pointed to directly by L.MASONS, the last-in-set pointer of COMMUNITY.

The items to note from this example are:

(1) A set is made up of entities that point to one another, thereby expressing their member relationships.

(2) First and last-in-set pointers join a set's owner and its member entities.

(3) A specific entity can own or belong to any number of sets so long as it has the required pointer attributes. For example, the entity MAN might own the set CHILDREN whose members are also entities MAN. These relationships might be defined by the statement:

EVERY MAN MAY BELONG TO THE MASONS,OWN
SOME CHILDREN AND BELONG TO THE CHILDREN

Figure 4-2 illustrates a collection of MAN entities having one possible relationship to each other.

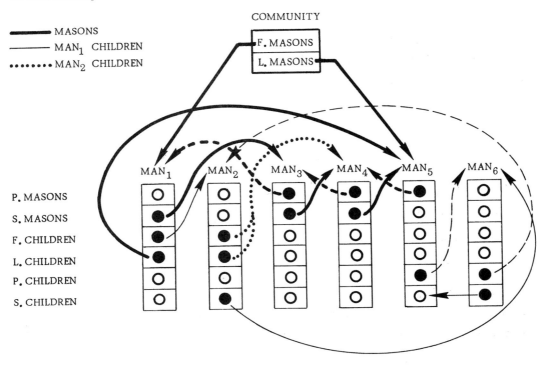

Fig. 4-2 -- Set relationships

The relationships expressed in Fig. 4-2 are:

(a) COMMUNITY owns the set MASONS whose members are MAN_1, MAN_3, MAN_4, and MAN_5.

(b) MAN_1 owns a set CHILDREN whose members are MAN_2, MAN_6, and MAN_5.

(c) MAN_2 owns a set CHILDREN whose single member is MAN_4.

These relationships are depicted in Fig. 4-3.

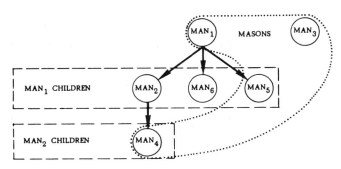

Fig. 4-3 -- Set relationships

An entity's attributes and set relationships can be declared in one or more EVERY statements using *attribute name clauses, set ownership clauses,* and *set membership clauses.* The clauses have the form

attribute clause	or	HAS *attribute name list* HAVE *attribute name list*
set ownership clause	or	OWNS *set name list* OWN *set name list*
set membership clause	or	BELONGS TO *set name list* BELONG TO *set name list*

When more than one clause is used in an EVERY statement, adjacent clauses are separated by commas. If desired, a clause can be preceded by the words MAY or CAN. Some examples are:

```
EVERY MAN HAS list,OWNS list AND MAY BELONG TO list
EVERY CITY OWNS list AND HAS list
EVERY CAR HAS list,AND MAY OWN list
```

The items in an attribute name or set name list must be separated by both a comma *and* one of tne words A, AN, THE or SOME. Some examples are:

```
EVERY MAN HAS A NAME,AND AN ADDRESS,OWNS SOME
    CHILDREN AND MAY BELONG TO THE MASONS,A CHURCH,
    A FAMILY AND AN ALUMNI.CLUB
EVERY X HAS A P,A Q,A Z AND AN A
EVERY PROGRAM HAS AN ENTRY,OWNS SOME LABELS,
    BELONGS TO A PREAMBLE AND HAS A LENGTH
```

Set names follow the same naming conventions as entities and attributes and, like them, must be unique.

EVERY statements define data structures. The next several sections explain how these data structures are created and used and the items in them given further definition.

4-03 *TEMPORARY ENTITIES*

An EVERY statement defines the structure of a class of entities. Entity classes can be of two types — temporary or permanent. This section discusses temporary entities; Sec. *4-04* discusses permanent entities.

When the statement

TEMPORARY ENTITIES

appears before a collection of EVERY statements in a preamble, it declares that all following entities are temporary. This means that storage is allocated to entities individually as they are *created* during the course of program execution. Individual entity records are provided for each temporary entity when a CREATE statement is encountered. This statement is of the form

CREATE *entity name* CALLED *variable*

When executed, a CREATE statement finds a contiguous number of words in memory for the attributes and set pointers of the entity class designated, and assigns a pointer to these words to the indicated variable. Each entity so created is a unique and distinct individual that is identified by its pointer word. From here on, we shall refer

to this pointer word as the *identification number* of the entity. As
long as variables into which identification numbers are placed are
distinct, the identity of individual entities is preserved. For example:

Entity definition in a preamble:

```
TEMPORARY ENTITIES
    EVERY SHIP HAS A NAME AND A TONNAGE
```

CREATE statements in a program:

```
CREATE SHIP CALLED VESSEL
CREATE SHIP CALLED V(I)
```

These two CREATE statements assign different entity records to the
variables VESSEL and V(I). VESSEL points to a block of words in core,
while V(I) points to a different block of words.

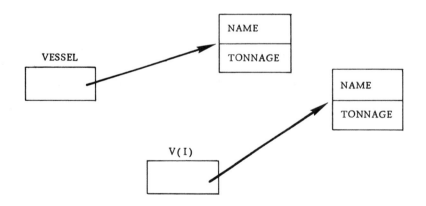

If desired, the words A or AN can be used after CREATE to improve
readability, as in

```
CREATE A SHIP CALLED QUEEN.MARY
CREATE AN EVENT CALLED BIRTH
```

If no variable is specified in a CALLED clause, the entity identification number is assigned to a global variable with the same name as the
entity class, e.g., the statement CREATE A SHIP finds two available
consecutive words in memory and puts a pointer to them in a global
variable named SHIP that the system automatically provides. The

convention that assigns a global variable to each entity class, e.g., SHIP to SHIP, will be usefully employed in later sections. The global declaration is done automatically by the SIMSCRIPT II system — just as though the programmer had written the statement

DEFINE *entity name* AS AN INTEGER VARIABLE

To refer to the attributes of a temporary entity, one uses the form *attribute (identification number)* as in NAME(VESSEL) and TONNAGE (QUEEN.MARY). Since attributes are words in memory, like variables, they can be used the same way variables are used, in input/output, decision, and computation statements. The following program illustrates this:

```
          PREAMBLE
          NORMALLY,MODE IS INTEGER
          TEMPORARY ENTITIES
              EVERY SHIP HAS AN AGE AND A TONNAGE
          DEFINE V AS 1-DIMENSIONAL ARRAY
          END


          MAIN
          READ N   RESERVE V AS N
          FOR I=1 TO N,DO
              CREATE A SHIP CALLED V(I)
              READ AGE(V(I)) AND TONNAGE (V(I))
          LOOP
  'READ'  READ OLD
          FOR I=1 TO N,WITH AGE(V(I)) < OLD,
              ADD TONNAGE(V(I)) TO SUM.TONS
          PRINT 1 LINE WITH OLD,SUM.TONS THUS
              TOTAL TONNAGE OF SHIPS LESS THAN ** YEARS OLD=******
          LET SUM.TONS=0
          IF DATA IS ENDED,STOP
          ELSE GO TO READ
          END
```

In this program N temporary entities of the class SHIP are created and their identification numbers stored in the subscripted variables V(1),V(2),...,V(N). The attributes of these entities are accessed in READ, WITH, and ADD statements.

As temporary entities are created, entity records are fetched from a pool of unused memory words. The assignment of entity records to entities is similar to the assignment of pointer and data words to

arrays as they are reserved. Like arrays, entities can be released
when they are no longer needed. To do this, the statement

DESTROY *entity name* CALLED *variable*

uses the identification number of the entity stored in the indicated
variable to point to a block of memory words that are to be released.
When destroyed (released), the words are returned to the pool of unused memory words for later use. The words THE or THIS can be used
before the entity name, if desired, as in:

DESTROY THE SHIP CALLED VESSEL
and DESTROY THIS SHIP CALLED V(I)

A short form of this statement using only an entity name

DESTROY *entity name*

is treated as

DESTROY *entity name* CALLED *entity name*

The statement

DESTROY THE SHIP

is interpreted as

DESTROY THE SHIP CALLED SHIP

4-04 PERMANENT ENTITIES

Permanent entities are defined in a similar manner as temporary
entities, by preceding the EVERY statements declaring them by the
statement

PERMANENT ENTITIES

Entities declared as permanent are stored collectively rather than in
individually identifiable records. A group of permanent entities is
created by a single statement; the attributes of the entities in the
group are stored as indexable arrays. The number of entities in a
group is specified by a variable N.*entity*. Attribute arrays are
allocated by a CREATE statement of a different form from that used
for temporary entities. Given the preamble declaration

PERMANENT ENTITIES
EVERY HOME HAS AN ADDRESS AND AN AREA

and the assignment of a value to N.HOME by a READ or LET statement,
the statement

CREATE EACH HOME

allocates arrays for the attributes of the N.HOME entities of the
class HOME by executing the statement RESERVE ADDRESS AND AREA AS
N.HOME. That is, the attributes of permanent entities are stored in
arrays and are reserved together when a CREATE statement is encountered.
In such statements, the words EVERY and ALL can be used in place of
EACH. Several permanent entities can be created together by naming
a list of entity names, as in

CREATE EVERY HOME,HOTEL AND RESTAURANT

which is of the general form

CREATE *permanent entity name list*

If the value of N.*entity* has not been specified, an arithmetic
expression can be used in the CREATE statement to indicate the size
of the attribute arrays. For example, the following statements are
equivalent:

    (1)   LET N.HOME = 5
            CREATE EVERY HOME
    (2)   CREATE EVERY HOME(5)

When the second form is used, N.*entity* is set to the value of the
parenthesized expression.

     Entities so created are referred to, not by an identification
number that is a computer location, but by an index. Thus we speak
of the attributes of each HOME as ADDRESS(1),ADDRESS(2),...,ADDRESS(5),
AREA(1),AREA(2),...,AREA(5). The layout of these attributes is shown
in Fig. 4-4.

```
ADDRESS                    AREA
1                         1
2                         2
3                         3
4                         4
5                         5
```

Fig. 4-4 -- Attribute storage of
permanent entities

The program of Sec. *4-03* is repeated here, using permanent rather
than temporary entities to illustrate the difference in how they are
defined and used.

```
        PREAMBLE
        NORMALLY,MODE IS INTEGER
        PERMANENT ENTITIES
            EVERY SHIP HAS AN AGE AND A TONNAGE
        END


        MAIN
        READ N.SHIP    CREATE EVERY SHIP
        FOR I=1 TO N.SHIP,
            READ AGE(I),TONNAGE(I)
 'READ'READ OLD
        FOR I=1 TO N.SHIP,WITH AGE(I) < OLD,
            ADD TONNAGE(I) TO SUM.TONS
        PRINT 1 LINE WITH OLD,SUM.TONS THUS
            TOTAL TONNAGE OF SHIPS LESS THAN ** YEARS OLD=******
        LET SUM.TONS=0
        IF DATA IS ENDED,STOP
        ELSE GO TO READ
        END
```

Unlike temporary entities, permanent entities cannot be destroyed
individually; they can be destroyed collectively by releasing all
their attributes in RELEASE statements, as in

RELEASE AGE AND TONNAGE

All attributes of permanent entities must be released at the same time.

Like temporary entities, permanent entities have global variables
defined for them. Each statement of the form

EVERY *entity name* HAS...

prompts the automatic generation of a statement

DEFINE *entity name* AS AN INTEGER VARIABLE

4-05 *SYSTEM ATTRIBUTES*

For reasons that will become clear in succeeding sections, it is often desirable to use system attributes rather than global variables. The statement

THE SYSTEM HAS *attribute name list*

declares that the listed names are attributes of the program as a whole — what we call the "system." For most purposes the statements

       (a) THE SYSTEM HAS AN X AND A Y

and   (b) DEFINE X AND Y AS VARIABLES

are equivalent. Since there is only one system, references to system attributes need not be indexed, as do references to attributes of permanent and temporary entities. A value of 1 is assigned to the variable X by the statement LET X=1, whether X is defined by (a) or (b) above. System attributes will be subscripted if the background dimensionality condition at the time of their declaration is greater than zero. X is declared to be a 2-dimensional system attribute by the statements

NORMALLY, DIMENSION IS 2
THE SYSTEM HAS AN X

The importance of system attributes lies not so much in their use as global variables, but as pointers that enable a program as a whole to own sets. The statement

THE SYSTEM OWNS A QUEUE

specifies that a program contains two INTEGER system attributes named F.QUEUE and L.QUEUE that point to the first and last entities belonging to a set named QUEUE. Several system-owned sets can be defined at one time by the statement

THE SYSTEM OWNS *set name list*

The following preamble illustrates some typical set declarations.

```
PREAMBLE
NORMALLY,MODE IS INTEGER
THE SYSTEM OWNS A SCHOOL
PERMANENT ENTITIES
    EVERY STREET HAS A SIGN AND OWNS HOUSES
    EVERY HOUSE HAS A NUMBER, OWNS A FAMILY AND
        BELONGS TO SOME HOUSES
TEMPORARY ENTITIES
    EVERY PERSON HAS A NAME,AN AGE,A SEX,BELONGS
    TO A FAMILY AND MAY BELONG TO A SCHOOL
    EVERY FAMILY OWNS SOME PERSON
END
```

Subscripted system-owned sets are defined by setting a dimensionality
background condition that makes the set pointers arrays, rather than
unsubscripted variables, as in

```
NORMALLY, DIMENSION = 2
THE SYSTEM OWNS A TABLE AND HAS A MATRIX
```

Subscripted system attributes used as data or as set pointers must be
RESERVED before they can be used. To use the system set TABLE and
the system array MATRIX, a statement such as

```
RESERVE F.TABLE,L.TABLE AND MATRIX EACH N BY M
```

must be executed.

4-06 ATTRIBUTE DEFINITIONS—MODE AND DIMENSIONALITY

Attributes of the system, and of permanent and temporary entities,
can be INTEGER, REAL, or ALPHA valued. As with global and local variables, modes can be declared by default, using NORMALLY statements,
and explicitly, using DEFINE statements. Except for set pointers,
which are automatically defined as INTEGER, all attributes are sus-
ceptible to programmer definition.

Permanent and temporary entity declarations define the dimensionality of their attributes implicitly, making additional definitions unnecessary. The statement

```
EVERY MAN HAS AN AGE
```

declares that AGE has a single subscript, an identification number if

MAN is temporary, or an index if MAN is permanent. The notation AGE(I), read AGE of I, provides for this subscript.

System attributes, on the other hand, must be declared and reserved as explained in Sec. *4-05*.

The rules for assigning modes and dimensionalities to attributes are straightforward:

Mode
$\left\{\begin{array}{l}\end{array}\right.$
(a) The current "background mode" is assigned to all attributes specified in EVERY and THE SYSTEM statements except for automatically generated set pointers that are always INTEGER.

(b) DEFINE statements *following* EVERY and THE SYSTEM statements can redefine attribute modes.

Dimensionality
$\left\{\begin{array}{l}\end{array}\right.$
(a) The current "background dimensionality" is assigned to all attributes and sets specified in THE SYSTEM statements.

(b) EVERY statements specify the dimensionality of the attributes and sets listed in them.

The following preamble illustrates each of these rules:

```
PREAMBLE
NORMALLY DIMENSION IS 2
THE SYSTEM HAS AN EXCESS
DEFINE EXCESS AS AN INTEGER ARRAY
NORMALLY DIMENSION = 0,
MODE IS REAL
THE SYSTEM HAS A VALUE AND
    OWNS A COLLECTION
PERMANENT ENTITIES
    EVERY SAMPLE BELONGS TO THE COLLECTION
        AND HAS A PRICE AND A NAME
TEMPORARY ENTITIES
    EVERY POINT HAS AN IDENTITY AND A
        TIME.OF.COLLECTION
DEFINE NAME AND IDENTITY AS ALPHA VARIABLES
END
```

This preamble defines four system attributes, one of which is REAL valued (VALUE), one of which is a base pointer for a two-dimensional array (EXCESS) whose elements are INTEGER valued, and two of which are INTEGER-valued set pointers (F.COLLECTION,L.COLLECTION). It also

defines a class of permanent entities (SAMPLE) and a class of temporary
entities (POINT). Each entity of type SAMPLE has two INTEGER attributes (P.COLLECTION and S.COLLECTION), a REAL attribute (PRICE), and
an ALPHA attribute (NAME). These attributes are stored as one-dimensional arrays of dimension N.SAMPLE. Each entity of type POINT has
an ALPHA attribute (IDENTITY) and a REAL attribute (TIME.OF.COLLECTION).
These attributes are stored in individual words of temporary entity
records. Figure 4-5 illustrates the storage of the attributes of
N.SAMPLE permanent entities of the class SAMPLE.

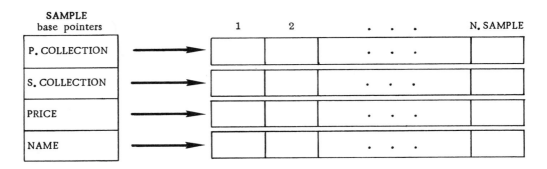

Fig. 4-5 -- Storage of attributes of a permanent entity

Figure 4-6 illustrates the layout of an entity record for a
temporary entity of the class POINT.

| IDENTITY |
| TIME. OF. COLLECTION |

Fig. 4-6 -- Storage of attributes
of a temporary entity

Figure 4-7 illustrates the arrangement in memory of the system
attributes VALUE, EXCESS, F.COLLECTION, and L.COLLECTION.

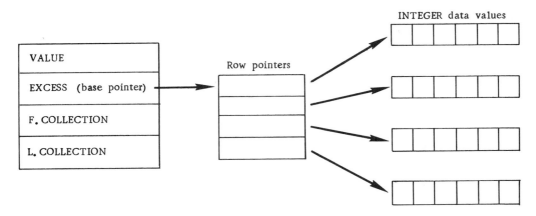

Fig. 4-7 -- Storage of system attributes and set pointers

4-07 ATTRIBUTE DEFINITIONS—PACKING AND EQUIVALENCE

Thus far, all discussions of data have assumed that data values
are stored individually in separate and distinct computer words.
While this is by far the most usual form of data storage, situations
exist whereby more than one data value must be placed in a single
computer word. The most commonly encountered reason for doing this
is to "squeeze" programs with large data requirements into limited
memory space.

When more than one data value is placed in a computer word, the
values are said to be *packed* in the word. When a data value is given
different names the names are said to be *equivalent*. SIMSCRIPT II
offers facilities for packing INTEGER and ALPHA and equivalencing
INTEGER, ALPHA, and REAL attribute values. Subscripted system attributes, and attributes of temporary and permanent entities, can be
packed and equivalenced. Unsubscripted system attributes can only
be equivalenced. This is one reason for defining certain values as
system attributes, rather than as global variables, which can be
neither packed nor equivalenced.

Attribute packing is specified by attaching a *packing factor*
enclosed in parentheses to an attribute name. Three types of packing

are available: field, bit, and intra. Field and bit packing apply
to all subscripted attributes; intrapacking applies only to subscripted
system attributes and to attributes of permanent entities.

The SIMSCRIPT II system uses programmer-specified packing factors
to store and retrieve data values. The fact that data are packed is
reflected in a program's preamble but not in its executable statements. A programmer operates at all times on a logical level, e.g.,
AGE(MAN); the SIMSCRIPT II system determines where AGE(MAN) is physically located.

Using *field and bit packing*, data fields can be laid out within
computer words. The field packing notation (1/2) specifies that the
attribute value to which it is attached is to be put in the first
half of a computer word. The bit packing notation (1-16) specifies
that bits[†] 1 through 16 are to be used to store an attribute value.
Since computers differ in word size and in instructions available to
access parts of words, it is impossible to specify all the possible
field and bit packing factors available in different SIMSCRIPT II
implementations. Table 4-1 shows the packing factors available in
an IBM 360 implementation; readers using other implementations will
have to consult their implementation manuals for the packing factors
available to them.

Attribute names are processed as they appear in EVERY statements,
and are assigned their indicated positions within successive computer
words. *Attribute equivalence* is specified by placing parentheses
around a list of attributes. All attributes within parentheses are
assigned to the same computer word; if two attributes have the same
packing factors, their names are synonyms. Overlapping packing factors can be specified. Attributes enclosed in equivalencing parentheses appear in a list, without the words A, AN, or THE before them.
The parenthesized list must, however, be preceded by one of these
words. The following examples illustrate the use of field and bit
packing factors for attributes of temporary entities:

[†]Or bytes, or digits, depending on the computer implementation.

Table 4-1

FIELD AND BIT PACKING FACTORS FOR IBM 360

Field Packing Factor	Attribute Value Placement
1/2	first half of computer word
2/2	second half of computer word
1/4	first quarter of computer word
2/4	second quarter of computer word
3/4	third quarter of computer word
4/4	fourth quarter of computer word

Bit Packing Factor	Attribute Value Placement
n - m	bits n through m inclusive
	$1 \leq n \leq 32$
	$1 \leq m \leq 32$
	$n \leq m$

TEMPORARY ENTITIES

(a) Declaration:

EVERY MAN HAS AN AGE AND A NAME

Entity record:

```
word 1    | AGE  |
word 2    | NAME |
```

(b) Declaration:

EVERY MAN HAS AN (AGE(1/2) AND NAME(2/2))

Entity record:

```
word 1    | AGE | NAME |
```

(c) Declaration:

EVERY MAN HAS AN AGE(1/4), A NAME AND A SEX(1/4)

Entity record:

word 1	AGE	
word 2	NAME	
word 3	SEX	

(d) Declaration:

EVERY MAN HAS AN (AGE(1-8) AND NAME(9-32))

Entity record:

	1	9	32
word 1	AGE	NAME	

(e) Declaration:

EVERY PART HAS A (RIGHT.VALUE(2/2),LEFT.VALUE(1/2),TOTAL.VALUE)

Entity record:

	TOTAL.VALUE	
word 1	LEFT.VALUE	RIGHT.VALUE

(f) Declaration:

EVERY MAN HAS AN (AGE(1/4),NAME(2/4),WEIGHT(17-32))
AND OWNS A FAMILY

Entity record:

word 1	AGE	NAME	WEIGHT
word 2	F.FAMILY		
word 3	L.FAMILY		

(g) Declaration:

EVERY MAN HAS AN AGE(1/4),OWNS A FAMILY,HAS A (NAME(2/4)
AND WEIGHT(2/2))

Entity record:

word 1	AGE		
word 2	F.FAMILY		
word 3	L.FAMILY		
word 4		NAME	WEIGHT

Field and bit packing of attributes of permanent entities and subscripted system attributes places two or more attributes in the same array. The declaration

```
PERMANENT ENTITIES
EVERY HOUSE HAS AN (ADDRESS(1/2),AND ZIP(2/2))
```

places similarly indexed values of ADDRESS and ZIP in the same computer word. This declaration, followed by the statement CREATE EVERY HOUSE (5) allocates storage as follows:

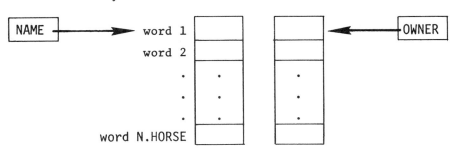

ADDRESS(1)	ZIP(1)	word 1
ADDRESS(2)	ZIP(2)	word 2
ADDRESS(3)	ZIP(3)	word 3
ADDRESS(4)	ZIP(4)	word 4
ADDRESS(5)	ZIP(5)	word 5

Base Pointer of ADDRESS and ZIP

More than one set of attributes, of course, may be packed in a single EVERY statement, e.g.,

```
EVERY SHIP HAS A (TONNAGE(1/2),A CAPACITY(2/2)),A
        (DESTINATION(1/2) AND HOME.PORT(2/2))
```

This statement pairs the attributes TONNAGE and CAPACITY and the attributes DESTINATION and HOME.PORT in adjacent parts of attribute arrays. Some additional examples follow.

PERMANENT ENTITIES

(a) Declaration:

EVERY HORSE HAS A NAME AND AN OWNER

Attribute arrays:

NAME and OWNER are separate arrays.

(b) Declaration:

EVERY HORSE HAS A (NAME,OWNER)

Attribute arrays:

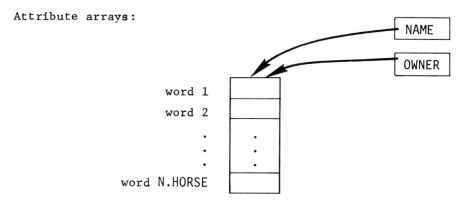

NAME and OWNER refer to the same data array.

(c) Declaration:

EVERY HORSE HAS A (NAME(1/2),OWNER(2/2))

Attribute arrays:

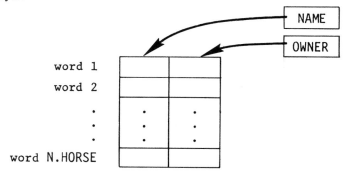

NAME is stored in the left half, and OWNER in the right half of a data array.

SYSTEM ATTRIBUTES

(a) Declaration:

NORMALLY, DIMENSION = 0
THE SYSTEM HAS A HIGH AND A LOW

Attributes:

HIGH	LOW

(b)   Declaration:

NORMALLY, DIMENSION = 1
THE SYSTEM HAS A HIGH AND A LOW

Attributes:

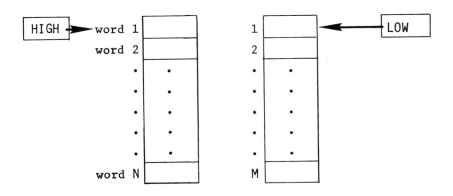

(c)   Declaration:

NORMALLY, DIMENSION = 1
THE SYSTEM HAS A (HIGH,LOW)

Attributes:

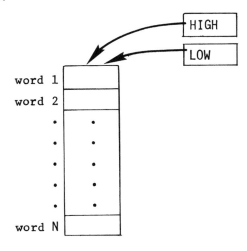

HIGH and LOW are synonyms.

(d) Declaration:

```
NORMALLY, DIMENSION = 1
THE SYSTEM HAS A (HIGH(1/4), LOW(2/2))
```

Attributes:

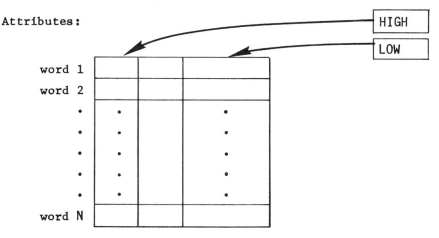

The second quarter of each data word is unused.

Intrapacking is used to compress array storage of subscripted
system attributes and attributes of permanent entities. The intrapacking notation (*/2) specifies that two values are to be packed in
one word, i.e., the array in which they are stored is compressed.
For example, the declarations

```
NORMALLY, DIMENSION = 1
THE SYSTEM HAS A LIST(*/2)
```

and the statement RESERVE LIST(*) AS 10 specifies and allocates storage
to LIST as follows:

LIST(1)	LIST(2)
LIST(3)	LIST(4)
LIST(5)	LIST(6)
LIST(7)	LIST(8)
LIST(9)	LIST(10)

base pointer of LIST → word 1, word 2, word 3, word 4, word 5

When a system attribute is multidimensional, packing takes place
at the data-storage level only; the array pointer words are unpacked.
Thus the statements

```
                NORMALLY, DIMENSION = 2
                THE SYSTEM HAS A LIST(*/2)
       and      RESERVE LIST(*,*) AS 3 BY 4
```

specify and allocate storage to LIST as follows:

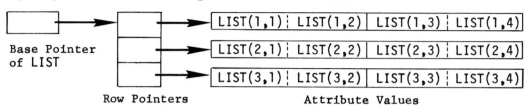

Base Pointer
of LIST

Row Pointers   Attribute Values

As with field and bit packing, intrapacking specifications depend on computer implementation. Table 4-2 shows permissible intrapacking factors for the IBM 360; other implementations have their permissible factors specified in their implementation manuals.

Table 4-2

INTRAPACKING FACTORS FOR IBM 360

Intrapacking Factor	Attribute Value Placement
(*/2)	2 values per word
(*/4)	4 values per word

When necessary, further specification can be made of attribute values to entity arrays or records. Attributes of temporary entities can be assigned to particular words of entity records by following their declaration by the clause IN WORD i, where i is an integer constant, as in examples (a) and (b) below:

(a) Declaration:

   EVERY MAN OWNS A FAMILY,HAS AN AGE IN WORD 1, AND HAS A NAME

   Entity record:

word 1	AGE
word 2	F.FAMILY
word 3	L.FAMILY
word 4	NAME

(b) Declaration:

EVERY MAN HAS AN (AGE(1/4),SEX(2/4),NAME(2/2))
IN WORD 1 AND A DEBT IN WORD 2

Entity record:

AGE	SEX	NAME

word 1 → AGE | SEX | NAME
word 2 → DEBT

word 1	AGE	SEX	NAME
word 2	DEBT		

Specification of the word in a temporary entity record in which an attribute value is located is required for *common attributes*, attributes that are common to more than one entity class. All common attribute values must be in the same relative locations in all entity records, and hence must have the same packing factors and word assignments whenever they appear. For example:

EVERY MAN HAS AN (AGE(1/2),NAME(2/2)) IN
   WORD 1,OWNS A FAMILY AND BELONGS TO
   A LODGE
EVERY WOMAN HAS AN(AGE(1/2),NAME(2/2)) IN
   WORD 1,AND BELONGS TO A FAMILY

Since AGE and NAME are common to both MAN and WOMAN, they have the same packing factors and word specification in both EVERY statements.

When entities belong to *common sets* their set pointers must be explicitly declared and located. In the above example, if both entities of the class MAN and WOMAN belonged to the set FAMILY, the declarations would have to be rewritten as:

EVERY MAN HAS AN(AGE(1/2),NAME(2/2)) IN
   WORD 1,OWNS A FAMILY,BELONGS TO A FAMILY
   AND HAS A P.FAMILY IN WORD 4 AND A S.FAMILY
   IN WORD 5
EVERY WOMAN HAS AN(AGE(1/2),NAME(2/2)) IN
   WORD 1,BELONGS TO A FAMILY AND HAS A
   P.FAMILY IN WORD 4 AND AN S.FAMILY IN WORD 5

Entity records of MAN and WOMAN would look like:

	MAN		WOMAN	
word 1	AGE	NAME	AGE	NAME
word 2	F.FAMILY		unused	
word 3	L.FAMILY		unused	
word 4	P.FAMILY		P.FAMILY	
word 5	S.FAMILY		S.FAMILY	

Putting the set pointers P.FAMILY and S.FAMILY in words 2 and
3 in this example, rather than in 4 and 5, would save two words in
each WOMAN record.

Care must be taken when mentioning set pointers in EVERY statements
that they are not inadvertently defined as something other than INTEGER.
Moreover, every qualified set pointer *must* be listed in any EVERY statement.

Attributes of permanent entities and system attributes are not
assigned to words but to arrays by the clause IN ARRAY i, where i is
an integer constant. This is important in certain implementations,
as it affects the compilation process; specifying an attribute's
array number can often lead to compiler efficiencies.

The results of packing, equivalence, and word and array specification are shown in Table 4-3.

Table 4-3

ATTRIBUTE SPECIFICATIONS

Specification	Assignment
No packing, equivalance, or word or array specification	Attributes assigned to separate words or arrays in the order of their appearance in preamble
Word or array specification	Attributes are assigned to specified words or arrays; remaining attributes assigned as above
Equivalence specification	Specified attributes assigned to the same word or array
Packing specification	Field and bit packing used to place more than one attribute within a computer word Intrapacking used to compress storage for arrays

The EVERY statement thus permits a great deal of specification, or lack of specification, of an entity's attributes. The use of packing factors, equivalence parentheses, and WORD and ARRAY clauses gives a programmer a good deal of control over the allocation of computer storage. Succeeding sections elaborate on entity-attribute-set definitions, introduce statements for using entities, attributes, and sets, and present programming examples.

4-08 ATTRIBUTE DEFINITIONS—FUNCTIONS

When defined by statements of the form

THE SYSTEM HAS AN *attribute name* FUNCTION
EVERY *entity name* HAS AN *attribute name* FUNCTION

a system attribute or an attribute of a permanent or temporary entity is treated as a function and not as a variable. That is, a subprogram having the same name as the declared attribute must be provided. The subprogram must have the same number of arguments as the declared or implied dimensionality of the attribute, i.e., no arguments for an unsubscripted system attribute, one argument for an temporary or permanent entity, two arguments for a 2-dimensional system attribute, etc.

Function attributes, because they are computational procedures, have no storage space allocated to them. Declarations of attributes as functions interspersed between other attribute declarations have no effect, therefore, on storage allocation of attributes to arrays or entity records. The following example illustrates this:

Declaration:

EVERY AUTO HAS A(PASSENGER.LIMIT(1/2),AND
WEIGHT(2/2)),A FUEL FUNCTION,A CONSUMPTION.RATE,OWNS SOME PASSENGERS
AND HAS A FUEL.CAPACITY AND A DEPARTURE.TIME

Entity record:

word 1	PASSENGER.LIMIT	WEIGHT
word 2	CONSUMPTION.RATE	
word 3	F.PASSENGERS	
word 4	L.PASSENGERS	
word 5	FUEL.CAPACITY	
word 6	DEPARTURE.TIME	

Assume the attribute function FUEL is defined by the following
program:

```
ROUTINE FOR FUEL(AUTO)
RETURN WITH FUEL.CAPACITY(AUTO)-(TIME-DEPARTURE.TIME(AUTO))*
    CONSUMPTION.RATE(AUTO)
END
```

The amount of fuel currently in a particular auto, assuming that
the current time is contained in the global variable TIME, can thus
be found by writing LET AMOUNT=FUEL(AUTO). As the variable TIME
changes, the reported value of FUEL changes.

Function attributes have a number of uses: they can be used, as
above, to determine values of continuously changing quantities; to
perform complex calculations; to define optional attributes;[+] and
to perform monitoring, printing, and other input/output operations.
An example follows:

Declaration:

```
EVERY MAN HAS A CREDIT.RATING FUNCTION,A BANK.BALANCE,
    A DEBT.TOTAL,A MORTGAGE.PAYMENT,A NUMBER.OF.DEPENDENTS
    AND A SALARY
```

Function attribute definition:

```
ROUTINE FOR CREDIT.RATING(J)
IF (SALARY(J)-MORTGAGE.PAYMENT(J)) < 100* NUMBER.OF.DEPENDENTS(J)
  OR DEBT.TOTAL(J) > 4*BANK.BALANCE(J),RETURN WITH 0
OTHERWISE RETURN WITH 1
END
```

Program statement:

```
IF CREDIT.RATING(CUSTOMER)=0,GO REFUSE.CREDIT
ELSE CALL ACCEPT.CREDIT
```

4-09   MORE ON SETS: THEIR DECLARATION AND USE

Sets, as we have described them, are collections of entities
organized by systems of pointers. Set owners point to the first and
last members of sets; set members point to one another. Sets are

---

[+]See Sec. 4-14-6.

like arrays in that they are composed of elements that can be identified and manipulated, but are unlike arrays in their method of organization and their dynamic and changeable, rather than static and fixed,
nature.

As described in previous sections, sets are declared in EVERY
statements when their owner and member entities are defined. Every
set must have an owner, either an entity or the system, and can have
either permanent or temporary entities as members. When more than
one type of temporary entity belongs to a set, the predecessor and
successor attributes of the entities must be located in the same
words in the entity records.

Sets named in EVERY statements have the following properties:

(a) Owner entities have *first and last pointers* named F.*set*
     and L.*set*;

(b) Member entities have *predecessor and successor pointers*
     named P.*set* and S.*set*;

(c) Set members are ranked on a first-in, first-out basis when
     they are put in a set. This ranking gives the highest
     priority to the first entity put in a set;

(d) A request to remove an unspecified entity from a set removes
     the entity with the highest current priority;

(e) Each member entity has a *membership attribute* named M.*set*
     that is "yes" if an entity is in the set and "no" if it is not;

(f) Each owner entity has a *counter attribute* named N.*set* whose
     value is the number of member entities currently in the set.

All set owner and member attributes are INTEGER valued and have names
formed by prefixing a letter and a period to the set name.[†]

The declarations

                PERMANENT ENTITIES
                   EVERY CITY OWNS A CLUB
                TEMPORARY ENTITIES
                   EVERY MAN MAY BELONG TO THE CLUB

define three attributes for the owner entity of CLUB and three attributes for its member entities. Since CITY is a permanent entity, its

---

[†]While normally INTEGER, N.*set* and M.*set* attributes can, when
necessary, be defined as REAL.

owner attributes are stored as arrays:

MAN, being a temporary entity, has its member attributes stored in individual entity records:

Every program commences execution with empty sets. As a program proceeds, statements are executed that file entities in sets, examine sets, and remove entities from sets. Set memberships change dynamically when FILE and REMOVE statements alter set pointers, changing relationships that affect set membership and set ranking. The FILE statement has two basic forms:

(a_1) FILE *arithmetic expression* FIRST IN *set*

(a_2) FILE *arithmetic expression* LAST IN *set*

(b_1) FILE *arithmetic expression* BEFORE *arithmetic expression* IN *set*

(b_2) FILE *arithmetic expression* AFTER *arithmetic expression* IN *set*

The words FIRST or LAST are optional. When both are omitted, FILE LAST is implied; the statements

FILE *arithmetic expression* LAST IN *set*

and   FILE *arithmetic expression* IN *set*

are equivalent.

In each of the forms, the words THE or THIS are optional before the expression or the set name, as in

```
FILE THE BIRD IN THE NEST
FILE THIS JOB FIRST IN THIS QUEUE
FILE FIDO AFTER ROVER IN THE KENNEL
```

Used in this context, an arithmetic expression must evaluate to an entity identification number; it must be either the address of a temporary entity record obtained from a previous CREATE statement or an integer number denoting one of N.*entity* permanent entities of a specific type.

In case (a), the indicated item is filed at the head (tail) of the set, and it is given top (bottom) priority. In (b), the position of filing is specified. The actions that take place when a "FILE FIRST" statement is executed are illustrated by two examples. The examples use a set whose owner and member entities are both temporary, but they can as well be both permanent, or one permanent and one temporary. The set and the entities are defined by the statements:

```
TEMPORARY ENTITIES
EVERY FARM OWNS A KENNEL
EVERY DOG HAS A NAME AND BELONGS TO SOME KENNEL
DEFINE NAME AS AN ALPHA VARIABLE
```

The two illustrations are included in the program segment shown below. We first consider the situation before and after the first dog is filed in a kennel; later we examine a subsequent situation. Assume a FARM has been created whose identification number is stored in the global variable FARM. This could have been done by the statement CREATE A FARM.

Program Segment

```
READ NUMBER.OF.DOGS
FOR I=1 TO NUMBER.OF.DOGS,DO
    CREATE A DOG
    READ NAME(DOG)
    FILE DOG FIRST IN KENNEL(FARM)
LOOP
```

The entity record of FARM looks like:

	FARM
word 1	F.KENNEL
word 2	L.KENNEL
word 3	N.KENNEL

After the first dog is created, its entity record looks like:

DOG

NAME
P.KENNEL
S.KENNEL
M.KENNEL

At this point the variables F.KENNEL, L.KENNEL, N.KENNEL, P.KENNEL, S.KENNEL and M.KENNEL are all zero, indicating that KENNEL(FARM) is empty and DOG is not in some KENNEL. We will assume that M.KENNEL is either 0 (no) or 1 (yes).

After the FILE statement is executed, the entity records look like:

FARM

F.KENNEL	●
L.KENNEL	●
N.KENNEL	1

DOG

NAME	ROVER
P.KENNEL	0
S.KENNEL	0
M.KENNEL	1

The owner entity FARM points to the member entity DOG: DOG, being the only entity in KENNEL(FARM), is both first and last. Since DOG is alone in KENNEL(FARM) it has no predecessor or successor entities.

After the second DOG is created and filed, the entity records look like:

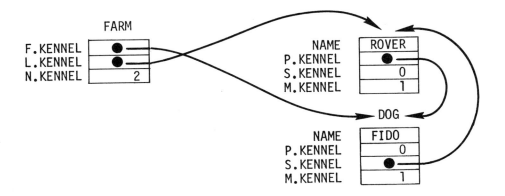

With two members in the set, the first and last pointers lead to different entity records. The first entity, *pointed to* by F.KENNEL(FARM),

points ahead to the second entity with its successor pointer. The
second entity *points back* at the first entity with its predecessor
pointer. Both the predecessor pointer of the first entity and the
successor pointer of the last entity are zero, indicating their respective roles.

An important point to note is that the global variable DOG now
points to the second DOG (the second DOG created, not necessarily the
second in the set). The entity record of the first DOG created can
only be accessed through the pointers to it, L.KENNEL(FARM) and
S.KENNEL(DOG). These pointers illustrate the general form of an
attribute reference.

attribute (entity identification)

Since an entity identification can itself be an attribute, as in the
case of a pointer, *nested* entity references can be made, as in

S.KENNEL(F.KENNEL(FARM))[†]

which has the same value as S.KENNEL(DOG) since F.KENNEL(FARM)=DOG.
Any level of entity nesting is possible as long as all nested expressions evaluate to entity identification numbers.

When a third DOG is created and filed, the entity records look
like:

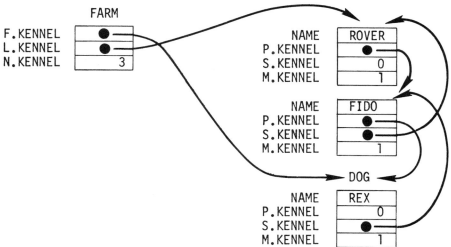

Additional creations and filings are analogous.

[†]This is read as "the successor of the first in KENNEL of FARM."

A "FILE LAST" statement has an effect similar to a "FILE FIRST", but operates on the opposite end of a set. If our example program segment were written with the statement FILE DOG LAST IN KENNEL(FARM), after executing three creates and files the entity records would look like:

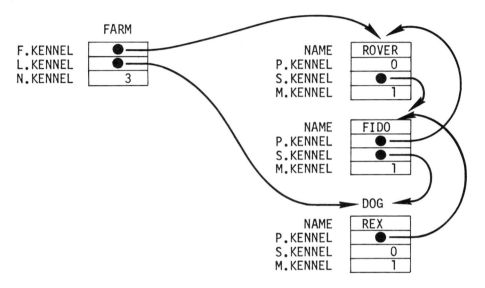

The "FILE BEFORE" and "FILE AFTER" statements are described through a different example.

Assume the entity record organization shown in Fig. 4-8 was created by the following program statements:

```
CREATE A DOG CALLED ROVER
FILE ROVER FIRST IN KENNEL(FARM)
CREATE A DOG CALLED FIDO
FILE FIDO FIRST IN KENNEL(FARM)
```

The statements

```
CREATE A DOG
FILE THE DOG AFTER FIDO IN KENNEL(FARM)
```

insert the entity record for the newly created DOG after the entity record pointed to by the variable FIDO. The resulting entity record organization is shown in Fig. 4-9.

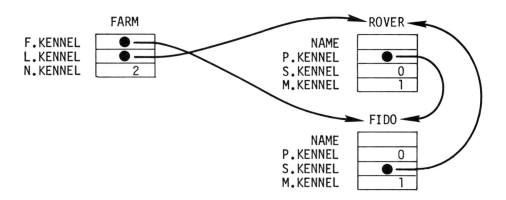

Fig. 4-8 -- A set with two members

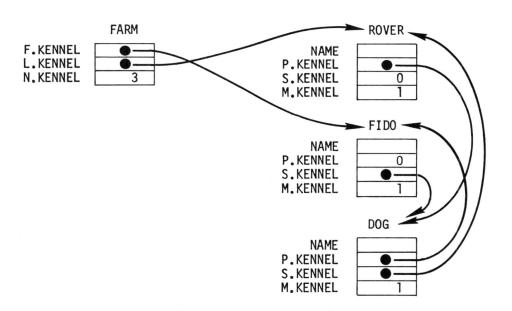

Fig. 4-9 -- A set with three members

Entities are removed from sets by REMOVE statements. Two basic forms of removal are possible; each works analogously to, and accomplishes the reverse tasks of, a FILE statement.

(a$_1$)   REMOVE FIRST *variable* FROM *set*

(a$_2$)   REMOVE LAST *variable* FROM *set*

(b)   REMOVE *arithmetic expression* FROM *set*

The word THE is optional after REMOVE, as is either of the words THE and THIS before the set name. In addition, either of the words THIS or ABOVE can be used before the expression in form (b).

A "REMOVE FIRST" or "REMOVE LAST" statement removes from a set the entity pointed to by the first or last pointer attribute of the set owner. The identification number of the removed entity is assigned to the variable in the REMOVE statement. For instance, in the situation shown in Fig. 4-9, the statement

REMOVE THE FIRST HOUND FROM KENNEL(FARM)

removes the first entity (FIDO) from KENNEL(FARM), makes the second entity first, and puts a pointer to FIDO in HOUND. The attribute values of FIDO, which now can also be called HOUND, are unchanged except for M.KENNEL. Although FIDO is no longer in KENNEL(FARM), its attribute S.KENNEL still points to DOG. In most instances, pointer values are meaningless once an entity is removed from a set. If the name FIDO were replaced by DOG in Fig. 4-8, this figure would show the organization of KENNEL(FARM) after FIDO had been removed from Fig. 4-9.

If an attempt is made to remove the first or last member from an empty set, the program terminates with a message and an error halt.

A "REMOVE specific entity" statement (form (b)) extracts a particular entity from a set; the entity identification number is given by the arithmetic expression. Referring again to Fig. 4-9, the statement

REMOVE THIS DOG FROM KENNEL(FARM)

converts the set shown in that figure to the set shown in Fig. 4-8. If the arithmetic expression is not an identification number of an entity currently in the set (signaled by a "yes" in its membership attribute), the program terminates with a message and an error halt.

The presence of a membership attribute in an entity permits both error checking (cannot file Y after X because X is not in the set; cannot remove X because X is not in the set; cannot destroy X if it is a member of some sets; cannot file X in a set if it is already in it) and questioning about set membership. The logical expressions

arithmetic expression IS IN *set*

and   *arithmetic expression* IS NOT IN *set*

can be used in IF statements and WITH clauses to take actions conditional on set membership. As options, the words THE and THIS can precede the arithmetic expression, and the words A, AN, THE, or SOME the set name. One can write

IF ROVER IS NOT IN SOME KENNEL,

or   WITH THIS DOG IN A KENNEL,

et cetera. In these statements the set name KENNEL *cannot* be subscripted. It is impossible for an entity to belong to more than one set of a given class at a time. A DOG can belong to KENNEL(FARM) or KENNEL(HOUSE), etc., but not to both. A membership attribute signals class, and not specific owner, membership.

Each set's first pointer is used to determine whether or not a specific set has members. The logical expressions

set IS EMPTY

and   *set* IS NOT EMPTY

are available. As with the preceding expressions, the words THE and THIS are allowed before the set name to improve readability. Using the "IS NOT EMPTY" and "IS EMPTY" logical expressions, one can write statements such as

IF KENNEL(FARM) IS NOT EMPTY,
    REMOVE THE FIRST DOG FROM KENNEL(FARM)
ELSE

and

IF SEX(PERSON)="MALE" AND FAMILY(PERSON) IS EMPTY,
    CALL BACHELOR.ACTION GIVEN PERSON
ELSE

All the statements described thus far assume that every set has a full complement of ownership and membership attributes, i.e., that both first and last, predecessor and successor pointers, and counter and membership attributes are defined. To perform all of the available set manipulations, they must all be present. When set needs are more modest, sets with fewer pointers can be designed, with a gain in efficiency in set manipulations at the expense of some manipulative power.

The sets pictured in all preceding illustrations contain all possible pointers. Additionally, they *rank* on a first-in, first-out, priority scheme, i.e., FILE LAST is the default condition. Other rankings are possible. For example, in a set defined by the declarations

```
EVERY COUNTRY OWNS AN ARMY
EVERY MAN HAS A HEIGHT AND A WEIGHT
    AND BELONGS TO AN ARMY
```

we might want the various men in the army sets to be ranked by weight or height, rather than by set entrance time. Furthermore, we might want this ranking to be in ascending or descending order. This can be done by including a *set definition statement* after the EVERY statements that first mention a set, and after any attribute definition statements that might be associated with the EVERY statement. A set definition statement, like an attribute definition statement, begins with DEFINE. The following statements define the set ARMY as being, respectively: (1) ranked in descending order by the HEIGHT attribute of the entities in it; (2) ranked in ascending order by these same attributes; (3) ranked in descending order by the WEIGHT attribute of the entities in it; (4) ranked in descending order by the HEIGHT attributes, and, for those entities whose HEIGHT attributes have equal value, ranked in ascending order by their WEIGHT attributes.

```
(1)  DEFINE ARMY AS A SET RANKED BY HIGH HEIGHT
(2)  DEFINE ARMY AS A SET RANKED BY LOW HEIGHT
(3)  DEFINE ARMY AS A SET RANKED BY WEIGHT
(4)  DEFINE ARMY AS A SET RANKED BY HIGH HEIGHT,
         THEN BY LOW WEIGHT
```

Example (3) shows that omission of the words HIGH or LOW implies HIGH. Example (4) shows how rankings can be cascaded, one after another, by THEN BY clauses to resolve ties when ranking attributes are equal. As many THEN BY clauses can be used as are needed in any given application. A comma must precede each THEN BY clause.

If a set is to be ranked only by entry time of entities into it, a short form can be used. Depending upon whether the ranking gives highest priority to the earliest or latest arrival, the DEFINE statement is written as:

<pre>
        (1) DEFINE ARMY AS A FIFO SET
    or (2) DEFINE ARMY AS A LIFO SET
</pre>

If form (1) is used, entities are put in sets on a *first-in, first-out* basis; they are filed last as they are put in and removed in the order in which they were filed. If form (2) is used, entities are put in sets on a *last-in, first-out* basis.

In some cases, not all of the automatically defined set pointers are needed. This is true in FIFO- and LIFO-defined sets, where entities are never inserted in the middle of a set, but only at the beginning or end. A FIFO set need have only first, last, and successor pointers; a LIFO set need have only first and successor pointers. FIFO and LIFO set organizations are shown in Fig. 4-10.

Since ranked sets are defined with respect to ranking values of their members, it rarely, if ever, makes sense to use FILE BEFORE or FILE AFTER in such sets. Doing so will, in fact, destroy the ranking concept. A clause can be appended to a set declaration statement to delete unused set attributes; any or all of the three owner-entity and three member-entity attributes may be deleted. If the first-in-set attribute is deleted, the "IS EMPTY" logical expression cannot be used; if the membership attribute is deleted, the "IS IN *set*" logical expression cannot be used. Table 4-5 on page 241 defines the statements that cannot be used when certain set attributes are deleted.

The deletion clause is of the form

WITHOUT *attribute list* ATTRIBUTES

Attribute list is a list of one or more of the letters F, L, P, S, N, and M. The presence of a letter indicates that the attribute formed by prefixing it and a period to the set name is not automatically generated. For example, we might write the following statement defining a LIFO set:

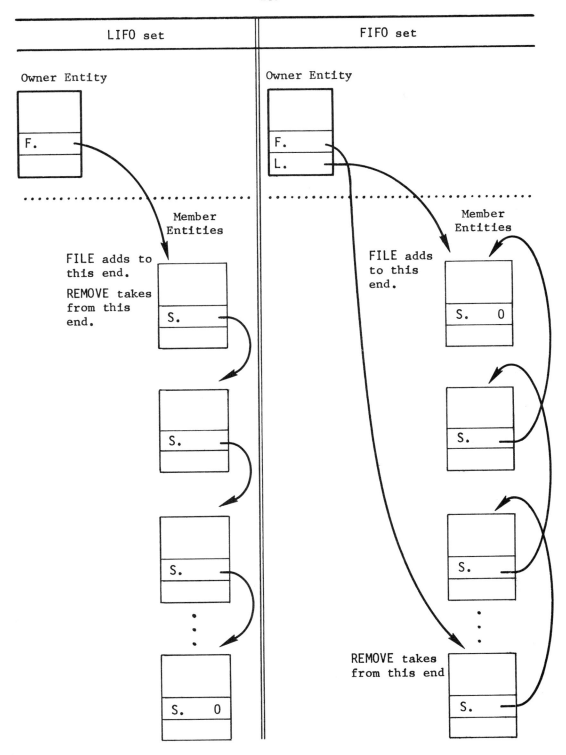

Fig. 4-10 -- LIFO and FIFO set organizations

DEFINE ARRIVALS AS A LIFO SET WITHOUT L,P,N
AND M ATTRIBUTES

The astute reader will note that while it is possible to delete *all*
attributes, doing so completely destroys the concept of a set. The
programmer is cautioned against deleting set attributes without care-
fully considering the consequences (see Table 4-5, page 241).

When required, two or more sets having the same properties can
be declared in the same DEFINE statement. A list of set names can
appear after the word DEFINE, and the word SETS used instead of SET.

4-10 ENTITY CONTROL PHRASES

Two new forms of the FOR statement make it possible to step
through collections of entities, just as the FOR $v = e_1$ TO e_2 BY e_3
statement made it possible to step through successive elements of
arrays. One form deals exclusively with permanent entities and the
other deals with sets.

Permanent entities, having their attributes stored as arrays,
are indexed sequentially. The first entity of the permanent entity
class AUTO has index 1, the second 2, ..., the nth N.AUTO. To step
through a sequence of index numbers from 1 to N.*entity* for a particular
permanent entity class one writes

        (1) FOR EACH *entity*
   or   (2) FOR EACH *entity* CALLED *variable*

Form (1) is equivalent to the statement FOR *entity* = 1 to N.*entity*,
where *entity* is the global variable with the same name as the entity
class. Thus, the statement FOR EACH AUTO is equivalent to the statement FOR AUTO = 1 TO N.AUTO. The words EVERY and ALL may be used in
place of EACH, if desired.

Form (2) is equivalent to the statement FOR *variable* = 1 TO
N.*entity*, where the variable named in the CALLED phrase, instead of
the global variable with the same name as the entity, is used to
receive the sequential index values. This variable can be global or
local. It cannot be subscripted.

"Regular" FOR statements and WITH, UNLESS, WHILE, and UNTIL

statements can be appended to permanent entity control FOR phrases
as required.

The following statements illustrate a typical permanent entity
FOR phrase application:

Program Preamble:

```
        PERMANENT ENTITIES
            EVERY MAN HAS A NAME, AND AN AGE
```

Main Program:

```
        READ N.MAN
        CREATE EVERY MAN

        FOR EVERY MAN, READ NAME(MAN), AGE(MAN)
            .
            .
            .
        FOR EVERY MAN WITH NAME(MAN)="JOHN", DO
            ADD AGE(MAN) TO SUM
            ADD 1 TO N

        LOOP

            .
            .
            .
```

Experience has shown that some people would rather write FOR EACH
JOB, rather than FOR I = 1 TO N.JOB even if JOB has not been defined
as a permanent entity. That is, they prefer not to make up a local
variable name (I in this instance) just to step through a sequence of
values from 1 to N (N.JOB in this instance), but would rather use a
name that is easy to remember and has some meaning. To facilitate
this, the phrase

        INCLUDE *entity name list*

can be appended to a PERMANENT ENTITIES statement, as in

        PERMANENT ENTITIES INCLUDE MAN, COUNTRY AND FISH

This phrase defines the listed names as permanent entities without attributes, but with the associated global variables *entity* and
N.*entity*. The above statement defines the global variables MAN, N.MAN,

COUNTRY, N.COUNTRY, FISH, and N.FISH and permits the statements

```
          FOR EVERY MAN
          FOR EACH COUNTRY
and       FOR ALL FISH
```

to be used. The following short example illustrates why this might be a useful shorthand:

Program Preamble:

```
          PERMANENT ENTITIES INCLUDE ELEMENT
```

Main Program:

```
          READ N.ELEMENT
          RESERVE LIST(*) AS N.ELEMENT
          FOR EACH ELEMENT, LET LIST(ELEMENT)= 1
```

It should be clear that such a statement is impossible for temporary entities. Scattered throughout memory, rather than stored sequentially, temporary entities cannot be indexed by ordinal numbers; they can only be pointed to by set pointers. To process all the temporary entities of a given class, the entities must be stored in a set as they are created, and must be processed by a statement that deals with the set. This statement, which by its nature deals with both permanent and temporary entities, has two basic forms:

(a) FOR EACH *variable* OF *set*
(b1) FOR EACH *variable* FROM *arithmetic expression* OF *set*
(b2) FOR EACH *variable* AFTER *arithmetic expression* OF *set*

Form (a) selects entities that are members of an indicated set in order of their ranking and assigns their identification number to a named variable. If the set is empty, all of the statements controlled by the FOR statement are bypassed. The control variable can be either local or global. It cannot be subscripted.

Form (b1) does the same task as form (a), except that it starts with the set member identified by the indicated expression. Form (b2) is similar to (b1), but starts with the set member that follows the identified member. If the identified member is not in the set (denoted by a "no" in its membership attribute), the program terminates with an error message.

In forms (a) and (b), the words EVERY and ALL can be used instead of EACH, and the words IN, ON, and AT used as synonyms for OF.

To step backward through a set, the phrase

IN REVERSE ORDER

is placed after the set name. Set control can range from simple statements such as

FOR EVERY JOB IN QUEUE

to complicated statements such as

FOR ALL FISH AFTER MINNOW(I) IN POND IN REVERSE ORDER

Since many variations of FOR statements are possible, a few illustrations follow. In these illustrations, we assume that permanent entities with identification numbers 1, 2, 3, 4, 5, and 6 are filed in a set in the order of 1, 3, 2, 4, 6, 5. They may have arrived in this order and be stored as FIFO, or they may have been ranked on some attribute value; the method of ranking is not important in this example. Table 4-4 states different control statements and indicates the identification number sequence of entities that are passed on to the controlled statements by each. The entities are filed in a set named FILE; the local variable J is used within the control loop for the selected identification numbers.

Section 2-07 gave the expansion of the "regular" FOR statement into simpler SIMSCRIPT II statements so that persons wishing to perform atypical operations within the control of a FOR statement will know how the statement works and avoid writing incorrect programs. The following program is a prototype of the code generated for statements of the form

```
FOR EACH V OF set†, DO statement group LOOP

          LET V = F.set
          GO TO L.2
'L.1'     LET V= L.4
'L.2'     IF V= 0 GO TO L.3
          ELSE   LET L.4= S.set(V)
                   •
                   •
                   •
      statement group
                   •
                   •
                   •
          GO TO L.1
'L.3'
```

A comparison of this program with that of Sec. *2-07* reveals that the
two are analogous. The first LET statement picks up the initial item
in the iteration sequence; the statement labeled 'L.2' checks to see

Table 4-4

ILLUSTRATIVE SET CONTROL STATEMENTS

Control Statement	Identification Number Sequence					
FOR EACH J IN FILE	1	3	2	4	6	5
FOR EACH J FROM 4 IN FILE	4	6	5			
FOR EACH J AFTER 4 IN FILE	6	5				
FOR EACH J IN FILE IN REVERSE ORDER	5	6	4	2	3	1
FOR EACH J FROM 4 IN FILE IN REVERSE ORDER	4	2	3	1		
FOR EACH J AFTER 4 IN FILE IN REVERSE ORDER	2	3	1			
FOR EACH J IN FILE UNTIL J=3	1					
FOR EACH J IN FILE IN REVERSE ORDER UNTIL J=3	5	6	4	2		
FOR EACH J FROM 2 IN FILE UNTIL J=6	2	4				
FOR EACH J IN FILE WITH J≠5	1	3	2	4	6	

---

†*set* represents a subscripted or unsubscripted set. If subscripted,
F.*set* must have the same number of subscripts.

if the sequence has ended; and the statement labeled 'L.1' sets the control variable to a new value for the next iteration. Variations of the FOR phrase produce variations in this prototype; for example, writing FOR EACH V FROM W OF *set* changes the first statement to LET V= S.*set*(W). Adding an IN REVERSE ORDER clause changes the LET statement following the ELSE statement to LET L.4 = P.*set*(V), etc. The consequences of particular statements within a FOR phrase control loop can always be determined by constructing the program generated by the specific FOR phrase and analyzing its relation to the statements involved.

Table 4-5 lists the set attributes that are required for the different set operations described.

Table 4-5

REQUIRED SET ATTRIBUTES

Statement	Attributes Required					
	F	L	P	S	M	N
FILE in a ranked set	x			x		
FILE FIRST	x			x		
FILE LAST	x	x		x		
FILE BEFORE	x		x	x		
FILE AFTER	x			x		
REMOVE FIRST	x			x		
REMOVE LAST	x	x	x	x		
REMOVE specific	x		x	x		
IS EMPTY	x					
IS IN set					x	
Automatic checking[†]					x	
FOR EACH V IN set	x			x		
FOR EACH V IN set IN REV.		x	x			
FOR EACH V FROM W IN set				x		
FOR EACH V FROM W IN set IN REV.			x			
FOR EACH V AFTER W IN set				x		
FOR EACH V AFTER W IN set IN REV.			x			

[†]Following sections describe automatic set diagnostics performed only when a membership attribute is included.

4-11 COMPOUND ENTITIES

At times it is convenient for several entities jointly to have attributes and own sets. Such entities are called *compound entities*. Statements such as

```
     PERMANENT ENTITIES
(1)  EVERY MAN AND WOMAN OWNS A FAMILY AND HAS
       A BANK.ACCOUNT
(2)  EVERY CITY,COUNTY,STATE HAS A CENSUS
(3)  EVERY MODEL,COLOR,YEAR,MFG HAS A SALES.VOLUME
```

define compound entities composed of 2, 3, and 4 permanent entities, respectively. The first defines three two-dimensional arrays: F.FAMILY, L.FAMILY, and BANK.ACCOUNT, each dimensioned as N.MAN BY N.WOMAN. The second defines a three-dimensional array CENSUS dimensioned as N.CITY BY N.COUNTRY BY N.STATE. The third defines a four-dimensional array dimensioned in a similar way. Compound entities are defined by statements of the form

EVERY *compound entity name list* HAS *attribute name list* AND OWNS *set name list*.

As in the case of individual entity definitions, HAS and OWNS clauses can appear in the same or different statements. The word HAVE can be used for HAS and OWN for OWNS. Compound entities *cannot* belong to sets. By definition, the individual entities of which compound entities are composed must exist, e.g., if there is a compound entity MAN AND WOMAN there must be an entity MAN and an entity WOMAN.

A *compound entity name list* is a list of entity names that have either been declared previously in EVERY or INCLUDE statements, or, by their presence in a compound entity declaration, are declared as entities of the type specified in the current background condition, i.e., by the last PERMANENT ENTITIES or TEMPORARY ENTITIES statement. Three kinds of compound entities are possible: those composed exclusively of permanent entities; those composed exclusively of temporary entities; and those composed of both permanent and temporary entities.

Members of sets owned by compound entities can be either permanent

or temporary entities. Set membership is declared as usual. Moreover, "compound sets" can have any of their six set attributes deleted
and be defined as FIFO, LIFO or RANKED. The following statements
might appear in a program in conjunction with declaration (1) above:

```
TEMPORARY ENTITIES
  EVERY CHILD BELONGS TO A FAMILY AND HAS AN AGE
DEFINE FAMILY AS A SET RANKED BY AGE WITHOUT N AND M ATTRIBUTES
```

Attributes of compound entities and sets owned by compound entities are subscripted. Subscripting takes place in the order in
which compound entities are defined. Thus, in the statements

```
LET BANK.ACCOUNT(I,J) = 1000
FILE THIS CHILD IN FAMILY (MAN,WOMAN)
```

the variables I and MAN can range from 1 to N.MAN, and the variables
J and WOMAN can range from 1 to N.WOMAN.

Arrays are allocated to "permanent" compound entities when their
individual entities are created. While it is usual, it is not necessary that they be created together. Given the declarations

```
PERMANENT ENTITIES
  EVERY MAN HAS A JOB AND A SALARY
  EVERY WOMAN OWNS SOME JEWELRY
  EVERY MAN AND WOMAN OWNS A FAMILY AND HAS A
    BANK.ACCOUNT
```

the statement

```
CREATE EACH MAN AND WOMAN
```

reserves arrays for the attributes of MAN and WOMAN, and the compound
entity MAN,WOMAN. The CREATE statement is in fact translated into
several RESERVE statements:

```
RESERVE JOB(*) AND SALARY(*) AS N.MAN
RESERVE F.JEWELRY(*), L.JEWELRY(*) AND N.JEWELRY(*)
  AS N.WOMAN
RESERVE F.FAMILY(*,*), L.FAMILY(*,*), N.FAMILY(*,*) AND
  BANK.ACCOUNT(*,*) AS N.MAN BY N.WOMAN
```

Attributes of permanent compound entities can be released by
regular RELEASE statements such as

```
RELEASE BANK.ACCOUNT
```

Compound entities composed exclusively of temporary entities, or of mixtures of permanent and temporary entities, look the same as "permanent" compound entities but function differently. The difference lies in the fact that all attributes of "mixed" or "temporary" compound entities are functions; they have no storage allocated to them. They cannot be created or destroyed, as can (and indeed must) the entities of which they are composed. A routine must be written for each compound attribute (including set pointers) of this type that accepts the attribute indices as arguments and returns a single value— an attribute value or a set pointer. Thus, the declaration

EVERY JOB,MAN HAS AN INFLUENCE FUNCTION

where JOB and MAN are temporary entities, defines INFLUENCE as a function having the background mode. This function can be further defined, as in

DEFINE INFLUENCE AS A REAL FUNCTION

if necessary. When a statement like LET T= TIME*INFLUENCE(JOB,PERSON) is executed, the routine INFLUENCE is called with the arguments JOB and PERSON — two identification numbers of temporary entities. The routine must perform a task such as:

```
ROUTINE INFLUENCE (I,J)
DEFINE I AND J AS INTEGER VARIABLES
IF STATUS(J) > 5M AND PRIORITY(I) > PM
RETURN WITH(STATUS(J)/5M)*(PRIORITY(I)/PM)
ELSE RETURN WITH 1
END
```

4-12 IMPLIED SUBSCRIPTS

Preceding sections described how attributes are defined and touched on their use. Examples showed that attributes look like subscripted variables when they appear in programs; every attribute reference is of the form

attribute name(entity identification)

For attributes of individual entities, the entity identification is either an index or identification number; for attributes of compound entities, the entity identification is a list of index or identification numbers.

The automatic definition of global variables with the same names as declared entities was also discussed. They were used in minimizing the need for local variables in situations like:

```
CREATE A SHIP
READ NAME(SHIP), TONNAGE(SHIP),...,SPEED(SHIP)
```

When used in this manner, attribute subscripts are stated explicitly; identification or index numbers are used to access attribute values. The above statements are functionally equivalent to the statements:

```
CREATE A SHIP CALLED S
READ NAME(S), TONNAGE(S),..., SPEED(S)
```

Since all items indexed by entity names (attributes and sets) are declared in the program preamble, it is possible to declare a default or implied subscript if one is omitted from an attribute or set reference. An *implied subscript* is a global variable having the same name as the entity associated with the attribute or set referenced. In the case of compound entities, subscripts are implied in the order they appear in the defining EVERY statement. For obvious reasons, common attributes cannot have implied subscripts. Some examples of entity definitions and implied subscripts follow:

(1) Declaration:

```
PERMANENT ENTITIES
EVERY MAN HAS AN AGE
```

Use:

```
LET AGE= 1 is equivalent to LET AGE(MAN)= 1
```

Whenever the attribute AGE appears without an entity reference, the global variable MAN is used as an identification number.

(2) Declaration:

```
TEMPORARY ENTITIES
EVERY PROGRAM OWNS SOME LABELS
EVERY LABEL BELONGS TO SOME LABELS
```

Use:

CREATE A PROGRAM
.
.
.
CREATE A LABEL CALLED EXIT
FILE EXIT IN THE LABELS

FILE EXIT IN THE LABELS is equivalent to FILE EXIT IN THE LABELS(PROGRAM).

(3) Declaration:

PERMANENT ENTITIES
EVERY CITY,STATE HAS A POPULATION

Use:

	LET POPULATION = 400000
is equivalent to	LET POPULATION(CITY,STATE) = 400000
	LET POPULATION(NEW.YORK) = 8000000
is equivalent to	LET POPULATION (NEW.YORK,STATE) = 8000000

Implied subscripts cannot be used in free-form READ statements to input attributes of permanent entities, as the form READ *attribute* implies input of the entire attribute array.

4-13 *DISPLAYING ATTRIBUTE VALUES*

Specific attribute values can be output by conventional PRINT and WRITE statements. An attribute reference appearing in an output list calls for the retrieval and display of a single value just as a subscripted variable or function reference does. Some examples of attributes used in PRINT and WRITE statements are:

(1) PRINT 1 LINE WITH POPULATION(STATE) AS FOLLOWS
        POPULATION IS ********
(2) WRITE I, S(X), INDEX(I), NAME(INDEX(I)) AS 3 I 5, A 10
(3) FOR EACH CARROT IN BUNCH, WRITE LENGTH(CARROT) AS I 4

Implied subscripts can be used in PRINT and WRITE statements, as well as in computational statements. Attributes declared by the statement

PERMANENT ENTITIES
    EVERY BOOK HAS A PAGE.COUNT, A SUBJECT AND AN AUTHOR

can be displayed by the statement

FOR EVERY BOOK, WRITE PAGE.COUNT,SUBJECT AND AUTHOR AS I 4, 2 A 10

The LIST statement can be used to display all the attributes of an entity without writing all their names. Three forms are available:

(1) LIST ATTRIBUTES OF *entity* CALLED *arithmetic expression*

displays the attributes of the particular entity referenced. The statement can be used for both permanent and temporary entities. The format used is that employed for displaying values of expressions or unsubscripted variables. A short form

LIST ATTRIBUTES OF *entity*

displays the attributes of the entity whose index or identification number is contained in the global variable with the same name as the entity.

(2) LIST ATTRIBUTES OF EACH *entity*

displays the attributes of all the entities in a permanent entity class. The format used is that employed in listing one-dimensional arrays. If only one attribute of a permanent entity class is to be printed, it must be done by referencing the pointer to the array containing the attribute values, e.g., by a statement of the form

LIST *attribute*

(3) LIST ATTRIBUTES OF EACH *entity* IN *set*

displays the attributes of all the entities, permanent or temporary, filed in an indicated set. Since only one heading is printed, the labeled output is only meaningful for sets with one class of entity filed in them. The variable with the entity name is modified by this statement.

LIST statements of type (2) and (3) can be modified by WITH, UNLESS, WHILE and UNTIL phrases.

The use of each of these statement forms is illustrated in the following examples:

Entity and set declaration:

```
            PERMANENT ENTITIES
                EVERY COUNTRY OWNS A FLEET

                EVERY SHIP HAS A NAME , BELONGS TO A FLEET
                    AND OWNS A CREW
            TEMPORARY ENTITIES
                EVERY MAN HAS A SERIAL.NO, A RATING, A SKILL
                    AND BELONGS TO A CREW
```

Use of LIST statements:

```
(a)  REMOVE THE FIRST MAN FROM CREW(VESSEL)
     LIST ATTRIBUTES OF MAN
(b)  FOR EACH MAN IN CREW(SHIP) WITH RATING > 4,
         FIND PERSON = THE FIRST MAN
     LIST ATTRIBUTES OF MAN CALLED PERSON
(c)  READ N.COUNTRY AND N.SHIP
     CREATE EACH COUNTRY AND SHIP
                .
                .
                .
     LIST ATTRIBUTES OF EACH COUNTRY
(d)  LIST ATTRIBUTES OF EACH MAN IN CREW(QUEEN.MARY)
(e)  LIST ATTRIBUTES OF SHIP CALLED 4
(f)  LIST NAME, (VALUE(I) + COST)/RATE,ATTRIBUTES OF SHIP CALLED TITANIC
```

4-14 SOME SAMPLE PROGRAMS

The programs in this section illustrate the concepts and statements described thus far. The reader is urged to follow them closely and identify the features used in each of them. A useful exercise is the reformulation and reprogramming of the examples using different concepts and statements.

4-14-1 An Inventory Control Program

```
     PREAMBLE   NORMALLY MODE IS INTEGER
     PERMANENT ENTITIES
        EVERY ITEM HAS A RP ''REORDER POINT'',
                    AN SCL ''STOCK CONTROL LEVEL'',
                    A STOCK ''AMOUNT ON HAND'',
                    A DUE.IN ''AMOUNT ORDERED, NOT RECEIVED'',
                    A DUE.OUT ''AMOUNT OF BACK ORDERS''
     END
```

```
MAIN  READ N.ITEM   CREATE EACH ITEM
FOR EACH ITEM, READ RP(ITEM),SCL(ITEM),STOCK(ITEM),DUE.IN(ITEM),
   DUE.OUT(ITEM)
'READ' IF DATA IS ENDED, GO TO FINISH  ELSE
   READ TRANSACTION, ITEM, QUANTITY
   IF TRANSACTION= 1 ''PROCESS AN ORDER

      IF STOCK GE QUANTITY, SUBTRACT QUANTITY FROM STOCK
      GO TO REORDER.CHECK
      OTHERWISE ''INSUFFICIENT STOCK'' ADD QUANTITY-STOCK TO DUE.OUT
                        LET STOCK=0
'REORDER.CHECK'
      IF STOCK + DUE.IN- DUE.OUT LE RP,
         LET ORDER= SCL+DUE.OUT-DUE.IN-STOCK
         PRINT 1 LINE WITH ORDER,ITEM THUS
            ORDER *** UNITS OF STOCK NO. ***
         ADD ORDER TO DUE.IN
      REGARDLESS  GO READ
   OTHERWISE ''PROCESS A RECEIPT''
   SUBTRACT QUANTITY FROM DUE.IN
   IF DUE.OUT > QUANTITY, SUBTRACT QUANTITY FROM DUE.OUT
      GO TO READ
   ELSE  ADD QUANTITY-DUE.OUT TO STOCK
   LET DUE.OUT=0  GO TO READ
'FINISH'
   LIST ATTRIBUTES OF EACH ITEM
   STOP
   END
```

Two good exercises for the reader are: (1) identify each customer and generate a shipment notice for each order, and (2) keep track of to whom stock is owed (backorders) and ship it out according to some rational policy.

4-14-2 Two Illustrations of Set Ranking by Function Attributes

As described in Sec. 4-09, sets are normally ranked on either the order in which entities are filed in them (FIFO and LIFO) or on attributes of their member entities. In the latter case, while cascading can be used to resolve ties, only simple single-attribute ranking comparisons can be made. Complex ranking comparisons can be devised using function attributes as ranking variables. The following short program illustrates how a function attribute can be used to define a ranking variable that is the weighted average of several attribute values.

```
        PREAMBLE
        TEMPORARY ENTITIES
          EVERY JOB HAS A LABOR.COST, A MATERIAL.COST,
            AN OVERHEAD, A PROFIT, A RANKING FUNCTION
            AND BELONGS TO A QUEUE
         PERMANENT ENTITIES
           EVERY MACHINE OWNS A QUEUE
        DEFINE QUEUE AS A SET RANKED BY HIGH RANKING
        END

            MAIN
            READ N.MACHINE      CREATE EVERY MACHINE
'NEW.JOB'   CREATE A JOB
            READ LABOR.COST, MATERIAL.COST, OVERHEAD
             AND PROFIT ''INITIAL VALUES''
            READ MACHINE ''TO DO THIS JOB
            FILE JOB IN QUEUE (MACHINE)
                 .
                 .
                 .
            REMOVE JOB FROM QUEUE (MACHINE)
                 .
                 .
                 .
            GO TO NEW.JOB
                 .
                 .
                 .
            END



            ROUTINE FOR RANKING GIVEN JOB
            DEFINE JOB AS AN INTEGER VARIABLE
            RETURN WITH (LABOR.COST * 2 + MATERIAL.COST * 3
                + OVERHEAD + PROFIT * 4) / 10
            END
```

The preamble defines RANKING as a function attribute of JOB and as the attribute by which jobs are ranked when they are filed in a set QUEUE(M). The routine RANKING provides a procedure for computing a ranking value; the routine is invoked each time a JOB is filed. It is used to compute a ranking value for the JOB being filed, and for all the jobs against which this job's ranking value must be compared in order to insert it properly.

A somewhat different use of function attribute is found in the following program, which uses an attribute of the first member of a set owned by an entity as the ranking value for that entity's filing in another set.

```
PREAMBLE
TEMPORARY ENTITIES
   EVERY JOB OWNS A ROUTING, BELONGS TO A QUEUE AND HAS A VALUE
   EVERY PATH HAS AN ORIGIN, A DESTINATION, A RANKING FUNCTION
      AND A DISTANCE AND BELONGS TO A ROUTING
PERMANENT ENTITIES
   EVERY MACHINE OWNS A QUEUE
DEFINE QUEUE AS A SET RANKED BY HIGH RANKING
DEFINE ROUTING AS A SET RANKED BY LOW DISTANCE
DEFINE RANKING AS AN INTEGER FUNCTION
END


ROUTINE FOR RANKING(J)
DEFINE J AS AN INTEGER VARIABLE
RETURN WITH ORIGIN(F.ROUTING(J))
END
```

4-14-3 A Data Analysis Application

```
PREAMBLE
PERMANENT ENTITIES
EVERY COUNTY HAS A NAME AND A STATE
EVERY YEAR HAS A NATIONAL.GNP, A RC.PRICE.RC
EVERY COUNTY, YEAR HAS A POPULATION, A LOCAL.GNP, AND
       A LOCAL.GNP.PERCAPITA
EVERY YEAR, CAR HAS A NATIONAL.SALES, A PRICE
       AND A SALES.GNP.RC
EVERY COUNTY,YEAR,CAR HAS A LOCAL.SALES,AND A
       LOCAL.SALES.PERCAPITA
DEFINE NAME AND STATE AS ALPHA VARIABLES
DEFINE LOCAL.GNP.PERCAPITA AND LOCAL.SALES.PERCAPITA
       AS REAL VARIABLES
END


MAIN READ N.COUNTY, N.YEAR, N.CAR
CREATE EVERY COUNTY, YEAR AND CAR
FOR EVERY COUNTY, DO READ NAME(COUNTY) AND STATE(COUNTY)
ALSO FOR EVERY YEAR,
   READ POPULATION(COUNTY,YEAR), LOCAL.GNP
LOOP
FOR EVERY YEAR, DO READ NATIONAL.GNP(YEAR)
ALSO FOR EVERY CAR,
   READ NATIONAL.SALES(YEAR,CAR) AND PRICE(YEAR,CAR)
LOOP
```

```
FOR EVERY COUNTY, FOR EVERY YEAR, FOR EVERY CAR,
   READ LOCAL.SALES(COUNTY,YEAR,CAR)
            ''COMPUTATIONS''
FOR EVERY COUNTY, FOR EVERY YEAR, DO
   LET LOCAL.GNP.PERCAPITA= LOCAL.GNP/POPULATION
   FOR EVERY CAR,
   LET LOCAL.SALES.PERCAPITA= LOCAL.SALES/POPULATION
LOOP
FOR EVERY CAR, FOR EVERY YEAR, DO
   FOR EVERY COUNTY, DO
      COMPUTE A= SUM, B= SUM.OF.SQUARES OF LOCAL.GNP.PERCAPITA
      COMPUTE C= SUM OF LOCAL.SALES.PERCAPITA
      COMPUTE D= SUM OF LOCAL.GNP.PERCAPITA * LOCAL.SALES.PERCAPITA
   LOOP
LET SALES.GNP.RC = (N.COUNTY*D-A*C) / (N.COUNTY*B-A**2)
LOOP

FOR EVERY YEAR, DO
   FOR EVERY CAR DO COMPUTE A=SUM,B=SSQ OF PRICE
                    COMPUTE C=SUM OF SALES.GNP.RC
                    COMPUTE D=SUM OF PRICE*SALES.GNP.RC
   LOOP
   LET RC.PRICE.RC= (N.CAR*D-A*C)/(N.CAR*B=A**2)
LOOP
LIST SALES.GNP.RC, RC.PRICE.RC AND NATIONAL.GNP


STOP
END
```

This program reads data on auto sales and prices for different
population units, and computes regression coefficients that allow the
following graphs to be drawn:

for a given year and car

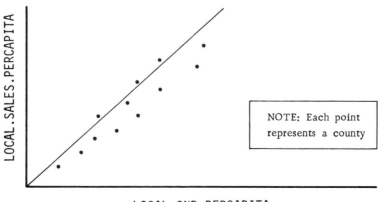

NOTE: Each point
represents a county

for a given year

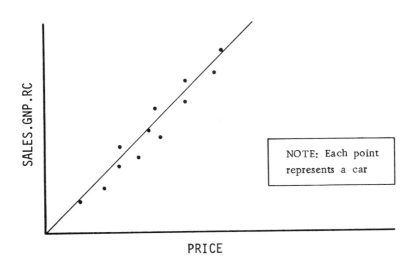

PRICE

NOTE: Each point represents a car

The reader should (1) ensure that he understands the computations the program performs and the reason why the individual loops are written as they are, and (2) rewrite the program where he can to make it more efficient.

4-14-4 *An Analysis of Prime Numbers*

```
PREAMBLE  NORMALLY MODE IS INTEGER
THE SYSTEM OWNS SOME PRIMES
TEMPORARY ENTITIES
    EVERY PRIME HAS A VALUE AND BELONGS TO SOME PRIMES
END

MAIN READ N
FOR I= 2 TO N, DO ''CREATE PRIME NUMBERS''
    FOR EACH PRIME IN PRIMES WITH MOD.F(I,VALUE) = 0,
        FIND THE FIRST CASE
    IF NONE, CREATE A PRIME  LET VALUE = I
            FILE PRIME IN PRIMES
    REGARDLESS
LOOP
FOR EACH I OF PRIMES WITH S.PRIMES(I) NE 0,
COMPUTE MAX= THE MAX(I) OF VALUE(S.PRIMES(I))-VALUE(I)
PRINT 2 LINES WITH N.PRIMES,VALUE(MAX),VALUE(S.PRIMES(MAX)) THUS
    MAXIMUM GAP AMONG THE FIRST **** PRIMES
    OCCURS BETWEEN **** AND ****
STOP
END
```

4-14-5 Dynamic Definition and Use of Array Attributes

The following statements illustrate how to create, use, and destroy array attributes:

Declaration:

```
PREAMBLE
TEMPORARY ENTITIES
   EVERY ENTITY HAS AN ARRAY
DEFINE ARRAY AS AN INTEGER VARIABLE
DEFINE DUMMY AS A 2-DIMENSIONAL ARRAY
END
```

Creation:

```
CREATE AN ENTITY
RESERVE DUMMY(*,*) AS 3 BY N
LET ARRAY(ENTITY) = DUMMY(*,*)
LET DUMMY(*,*) = 0
```

Use:

```
FILE ENTITY IN SET
            .
            .
            .
REMOVE THE LAST ENTITY FROM THE SET
LET DUMMY(*,*) = ARRAY(ENTITY)
FOR J = 1 TO DIM.F(DUMMY(I,*)), READ DUMMY(I,J)
```

Destruction:

```
REMOVE ENTITY FROM SET
LET DUMMY(*,*) = ARRAY(ENTITY)
RELEASE DUMMY
DESTROY ENTITY
```

4-14-6 Using "Optional" Attributes

In certain situations, especially ones involving data processing, entities are defined that have a large number of attributes, many of which are constants. For example, in census records the code n/a (not applicable) appears in many places. When, in such situations, it is necessary to conserve the amount of space allocated to individual entity records, function attributes can be used to define "optional attributes." These are actually entities stored in a special set only

if their values differ from specified default values. Thus, if the
optional attribute RAPID.TRANSIT is other than 0 for a particular
city, a record for it will appear in that city's optional attribute
set. Otherwise, the value of RAPID.TRANSIT would be found in the
default list (DEFAULT(1)=0).

The following declarations and programs show how to set up and
use optional attributes.

Declarations:

```
PREAMBLE
TEMPORARY ENTITIES
    EVERY CITY OWNS SOME OPTIONS, HAS A NAME,
        A POPULATION, A STATE AND AN OPTIONAL
        FUNCTION
    EVERY OPTION HAS A VALUE AND A CODE AND
        BELONGS TO SOME OPTIONS
    DEFINE NAME AND STATE AS ALPHA VARIABLES
    DEFINE WHICH AS A ''GLOBAL'' VARIABLE
    DEFINE DEFAULT AS A 1-DIMENSIONAL ARRAY
        •
        •
        •

END
```

Function attribute definition:

```
ROUTINE OPTIONAL (J)
DEFINE I AND J AS INTEGER VARIABLES
FOR EACH I IN OPTIONS(J),
    WITH CODE(I) = WHICH,
    FIND THE FIRST CASE
IF FOUND, RETURN WITH VALUE(I)
ELSE RETURN WITH DEFAULT(WHICH)
END
```

Program initialization to set up optional attribute structure:

```
MAIN
    •
    •
    •
READ N RESERVE DEFAULT(*) AS N
READ DEFAULT ''LIST OF DEFAULT VALUES''
    •
    •
    •
```

```
         .
         .
         .
CREATE A CITY
UNTIL MODE IS ALPHA,DO
     CREATE AN OPTION
     READ CODE AND VALUE
     FILE OPTION IN OPTIONS
LOOP
     .
     .
     .
END
```

Program statements that employ optional attributes:

```
LET WHICH = 1  ''INDICATING THE FIRST
               ''OPTIONAL ATTRIBUTE

LET X = OPTIONAL(CITY)
     if an entity CITY has an entity filed in
     its OPTIONS set with CODE = 1, X is set
     to the VALUE of the entity

     if an entity CITY has no such entity filed
     in OPTIONS, X is set to DEFAULT(1)
```

The program can be made even more straightforward if functions are used to define the optional attributes themselves. If RAPID.TRANSIT is an optional attribute of CITY, it can be defined and used by the following statements:

```
DEFINE RAPID.TRANSIT AS AN INTEGER FUNCTION
ROUTINE RAPID.TRANSIT(CITY)
DEFINE CITY AS AN INTEGER VARIABLE
LET WHICH = 1
RETURN WITH OPTIONAL(CITY)
END
```

The following diagram shows the record structure for a temporary entity of type CITY that has several "normal attributes" and several "optional attributes":

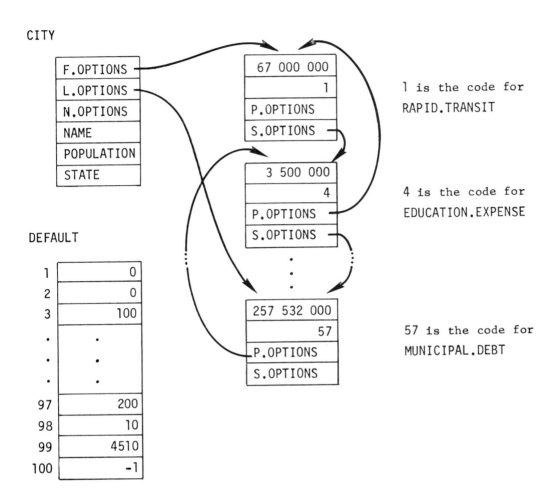

CITY

F.OPTIONS
L.OPTIONS
N.OPTIONS
NAME
POPULATION
STATE

67 000 000
1
P.OPTIONS
S.OPTIONS

1 is the code for
RAPID.TRANSIT

3 500 000
4
P.OPTIONS
S.OPTIONS

4 is the code for
EDUCATION.EXPENSE

DEFAULT

1	0
2	0
3	100
.	.
.	.
.	.
97	200
98	10
99	4510
100	-1

257 532 000
57
P.OPTIONS
S.OPTIONS

57 is the code for
MUNICIPAL.DEBT

4-15 DELETION OF SET ROUTINES

Certain routines are automatically generated for each defined
set during the processing of a program preamble. Sets declared as
FIFO (explicitly or implicitly), LIFO, or RANKED require different
routines to perform their operations. Each generated routine is
tailored to individual program specifications reflecting such things
as set attribute deletions and cascaded set rankings.

The most generally defined set, an unranked one declared as
either FIFO or LIFO, has seven routines generated for it. Four are
for filing and three for removing. The routines are named, and their
functions stated in Table 4-6.

Table 4-6

SET MANIPULATION ROUTINES

Routine	Generated Name	Function
File first	A.set	Files an entity first or ranked
File last	B.set	Files an entity last
File before	C.set	Files an entity before a specified entity
File after	D.set	Files an entity after a specified entity
Remove first	X.set	Removes the first entity
Remove last	Y.set	Removes the last entity
Remove specific	Z.set	Removes a specified entity

A set declared by the statement

DEFINE QUEUE AS A FIFO SET

thus has seven routines, A.QUEUE, B.QUEUE, ..., Z.QUEUE generated for it.

Ranked sets, by their definition, do not permit filing first, last, or before or after a specific entity without attention to the specified set ranking. Hence, ranked sets generate four routines, there being only one file routine.

In addition, certain set operations are impossible if specific set attributes are not present. For instance, filing before is impossible in a LIFO set if the predecessor attribute has been deleted.

Table 4-7 shows the set attributes that must be present for the indicated set operations to be performed.

Since all set attributes are not required for all set operations, Table 4-7 can be used to determine which attributes to delete in order to save memory space. For example, if a program only files and removes first, the set attributes L and P can be deleted without penalty. If they are not deleted, the generated programs keep track of and update them anyway.

Specific set routines can also be deleted to conserve memory space when their associated operations are not used in a program.

Table 4-7

SET OPERATION-SET ATTRIBUTE RELATIONSHIPS

Set Operation Mnemonic	Set Name Prefix	Required Set Attribute
FF	A.	F,S
FL	B.	F,L,S
FB	C.	F,S,P
FA	D.	F,S
RF	X.	F,S
RL	Y.	F,L,S,P
RS	Z.	F,S,P

To do so, a list of the set operation codes shown in Table 4-7 is attached to a DEFINE SET statement in the following form:

,WITHOUT *set operation code list* ROUTINES

The comma is optional. A typical program might contain the statement

DEFINE QUEUE AS A FIFO SET WITHOUT P AND N
ATTRIBUTES AND WITHOUT FB, FA AND RS ROUTINES

In sophisticated programs wherein a programmer wants to use set statements but wants to provide his own set operation routines, all seven routines can be deleted. The codes F and R delete the four file and three remove routines, respectively. A complete range of set specifications is thus possible. Mere mention of a set name in EVERY statements calls for all three set attributes for the owner and member entities, and all seven set routines. Additional definition in a DEFINE SET statement can selectively delete set attributes and set routines. The extreme statement

DEFINE *set* AS A SET WITHOUT F,L,P,S,M AND N
ATTRIBUTES WITHOUT F AND R ROUTINES

removes all mechanisms that make set operations possible.

* 4-16   LEFT-HANDED FUNCTIONS

Functions are normally thought of as "right-handed," in the sense that they appear on the right-hand side of the equal sign in assignment statements. They are used for computing values, rather than for storing them.

One example of a right-handed SIMSCRIPT II function is OUT.F, which is used to access characters in the current output buffer (see Sec. 3-11). The statement LET A = OUT.F(1), where A is an ALPHA variable, extracts the first character from the current output buffer and assigns its value to A. The single character is left-adjusted within A and followed by blanks.

Defining a function as "left-handed" indicates that it receives values, rather than that it computes them. SIMSCRIPT II allows the function OUT.F to be used in both a right-handed and left-handed manner. LET OUT.F(1)=A takes the leftmost character from the ALPHA variable A and stores it in the first position in the current output buffer.

Any function can be defined to be used in both a right- and left-handed manner, i.e., to compute a value, the right-handed version of the routine is called; when a reference is made in a left-handed manner, i.e., to store a value, the left-handed version is called.

No new concepts or statements are involved in the definition of right-handed routines, for all the functions dealt with thus far have been right-handed. All of the by now familiar declarative forms

```
ROUTINE name
ROUTINE name GIVEN argument
ROUTINE name (argument list)
```

indicate that the statements that follow, up to the statement END, define a computational process, hence, a right-handed function. In programs that use both right- and left-handed functions, the word RIGHT may be put before ROUTINE, but this is optional.

A left-handed function is headed by one of the forms of the ROUTINE statement shown above, preceded by the word LEFT, as in

```
    LEFT ROUTINE ACCESS GIVEN I AND J
and LEFT ROUTINE ALLOCATE
```

In addition to the usual mechanism for transmitting input argument values to a function when it is called, a left-handed function must have a way of receiving a right-hand-side value. A statement of the form

ENTER WITH *variable*

must be the first executable statement in every left-handed routine.
It specifies that the value "computed on the right" is to be stored
in the named variable, which can be local or global, unsubscripted,
subscripted, or an attribute, for use within the routine. From there
on, a left-handed routine functions exactly like any other program;
it can store the value, perform computations with it, execute input-
output statements, etc. The following example illustrates the definition and use of right- and left-handed routines:

> The computational section of this program (MAIN) seems to deal
> with simple subscripted variables. Actually, the surrounding
> routines and the preamble define the data structure dealt with.
> In this sense, the program is independent of the structure used
> for storing and analyzing its data.

```
        PREAMBLE
        THE SYSTEM OWNS SOME DATA
        TEMPORARY ENTITIES
            EVERY SAMPLE HAS A VALUE AND BELONGS TO SOME DATA
        DEFINE X AS A REAL FUNCTION
        DEFINE VALUE AS A REAL VARIABLE
        END

        MAIN
        READ N   FOR I=1 TO N, READ X(I)
        FOR I= 1 TO N-1, WITH X(I) < 2*X(I+1)
            COMPUTE M= AVG, V= VARIANCE, K= NUMBER OF X(I)**2
        LIST K,M,V
        STOP
        END
- - - - - - - - - - - - - - - - - - - - - - - - - - - - - - - - -
        RIGHT ROUTINE X(I)
        DEFINE I,J,S AS INTEGER VARIABLES
        IF I > N.DATA,
        PRINT 1 LINE WITH I THUS
            MEMBER *** OF COLLECTION X DOES NOT EXIST
        STOP
        ELSE
        IF I=1, RETURN WITH VALUE(F.DATA)
        ELSE  LET S=S.DATA(F.DATA)
        FOR J= 1 TO I-2, LET S=S.DATA(S)
        RETURN WITH VALUE(S)
        END
```

```
          LEFT ROUTINE X(I)
          DEFINE I,J,S AS INTEGER VARIABLES
          DEFINE A AS A REAL VARIABLE
          ENTER WITH A
          IF N.DATA=I-1,CREATE A SAMPLE CALLED S
                    FILE S LAST IN DATA
                    GO PLACE
          ELSE IF N.DATA < I-1, PRINT 2 LINES WITH I,N.DATA THUS
             TRYING TO CHANGE THE ***TH VALUE IN A COLLECTION
                WITH ONLY *** MEMBERS
                STOP
          ELSE   IF I=1, GO TO PLACE  ELSE  LET S=F.DATA
          FOR J= 1  TO I-2, LET S= S.DATA(S)
   'PLACE' LET VALUE(S)= A
          RETURN END
```

* 4-17 MONITORED ATTRIBUTES AND VARIABLES

Thus far, program names representing data values have had either memory locations or programs associated with them. Names defined as variables referred to values stored in computer words; names defined as functions referred to values computed or stored by associated programs.

A new data type, a *monitored variable*, has *both* a storage location and a program associated with it. The statements required to define and use monitored variables parallel the statements required to define variables and functions and to implement left-handed functions.

A variable (or array or attribute) is defined as monitored by a statement of the form:

    (a) DEFINE *name* AS A VARIABLE MONITORED ON THE LEFT

or   (b) DEFINE *name* AS A VARIABLE MONITORED ON THE RIGHT

or   (c) DEFINE *name* AS A VARIABLE MONITORED ON THE RIGHT
              AND THE LEFT

The word THE before RIGHT and LEFT is optional.

Since monitored variables have data values as well as programs associated with them, mode and dimensionality declarations can also be included, as in

        DEFINE X AS A REAL, 2-DIMENSIONAL ARRAY MONITORED
           ON LEFT AND RIGHT

Monitoring on the right and on the left is obtained through programs

similar to right- and left-handed functions. If a variable is declared
as monitored on the right (or left), a right-handed (or left-handed)
monitoring routine must be provided. A routine is able to perform a
monitoring function by the inclusion of one executable statement.
The statement differs, depending upon whether the routine is right-
or left-handed.

The task of a right-handed routine is to return a data value to
a calling program. A typical right-handed routine (*not* performing a
monitoring task) looks like:

```
ROUTINE EXAMPLE(I,J)
        .
        .
        .
    statements using I and J
        .
        .
RETURN WITH expression
END
```

The routine name (EXAMPLE) represents a program name, the argument
list transmits initial values for I and J from a calling program to
EXAMPLE, and the RETURN WITH statement returns a computed value to a
calling program.

Used for monitoring, a routine name represents both data and
program. EXAMPLE(K,5) is both a legitimate subscripted variable and
a call on a routine with arguments K and 5. The additional statement
needed to convert a "regular" right-handed routine to a right-handed
monitoring routine fetches a data value associated with a variable
and makes it accessible to a routine. The statement is

```
MOVE TO variable
```

The program

```
ROUTINE EXAMPLE(I,J)
MOVE TO Q
        .
        .
        .
    statements using I, J, and Q
        .
        .
RETURN WITH expression
END
```

starts out by assigning the value of EXAMPLE(I,J) to Q, which then
can be used freely in the routine. The MOVE statement variable can
be local or global, unsubscripted or subscripted, an attribute, or
even a left-handed function.

Except for defining EXAMPLE as being monitored, no other change
is made in the rest of the program. EXAMPLE is reserved and used
regularly; all data references are to EXAMPLE(I,J), as though it were
a simple subscripted variable.

Used for left-handed monitoring, the MOVE statement must assign
a value to the data cell associated with a monitored variable. The
statement that does this is of the form

MOVE FROM *arithmetic expression*

The value of the arithmetic expression is stored in the variable
referenced by the routine name and its arguments, if any, e.g.,
EXAMPLE(I,J). The form of a typical left-hand monitoring routine is

```
LEFT ROUTINE EXAMPLE(I,J)
ENTER WITH Q
        .
        .
        .
    statements using I,J,Q
        .
        .
        .
MOVE FROM expression
RETURN
END
```

A value is transmitted to the routine by the ENTER statement, computations are performed, and a value is assigned to the monitored variable by the MOVE statement.

The following short programs use monitored variables in several
different ways.

(1) Monitored variables used for data editing, where the monitored
variable feature provides two important benefits: (a) it keeps the
operational program clear of data checking and message printing statements, making it easier to understand, and (b) conversion of the program to remove the editing feature can be accomplished by changing

only one preamble card and throwing away two routines; the operational program is unchanged. However, the program must be recompiled.

```
          PREAMBLE
          DEFINE DATA AS A REAL,2-DIMENSIONAL ARRAY
            MONITORED ON THE RIGHT AND THE LEFT
          NORMALLY,MODE IS INTEGER
          DEFINE M AND N AS VARIABLES
          END

          MAIN
          READ N,M RESERVE DATA AS N BY M
          UNTIL MODE IS ALPHA,
             READ I,J, DATA(I,J)
          FOR I=1 TO N, FOR J=1 TO M, DO
             IF DATA(I,J)=0
                  IF J > I, LET DATA (I,J) = 1
                           GO TO L
                  ELSE LET DATA(I,J) = -1
             ELSE
    'L'   LOOP
          SKIP 1 FIELD ''THE ALPHA FLAG''
          UNTIL MODE IS ALPHA, DO
             READ I,J
             PRINT 1 LINE WITH I,J, DATA(I,J) LIKE THIS
                THE VALUE OF DATA(**,**) IS ****.**
          LOOP
          STOP
          END
- - - - - - - - - - - - - - - - - - - - - - - - - - - - - - - - -
          ROUTINE FOR DATA(L,K)
          DEFINE VALUE AS A REAL VARIABLE
           ''THE FETCHING OF DATA(L,K) IS
           ''INHIBITED UNTIL THE SUBSCRIPTS ARE
           ''VERIFIED
          IF L ≤ 0 OR L > N OR K ≤ 0 OR K > M, STOP
          OTHERWISE...
          MOVE TO VALUE    ''THE VALUE OF DATA(L,K) IS FETCHED
          RETURN WITH VALUE
          END

          LEFT ROUTINE FOR DATA(L,K)
          DEFINE VALUE AS A REAL VARIABLE
          ENTER WITH VALUE
          IF L ≤ 0 OR L > N OR K ≤ 0 OR K > M,
               RETURN  ''DON'T CHANGE THE VALUE
                       ''OF DATA(L,K) IF SUBSCRIPTS
                       ''ARE OUT OF BOUNDS
          OTHERWISE...
          MOVE FROM VALUE    ''TO DATA(L,K)
          RETURN
          END
```

(2) Monitored variables used for data transformations.

```
PREAMBLE
TEMPORARY ENTITIES
  EVERY SAMPLE HAS AN XVAL AND A YVAL AND
    BELONGS TO A GRAPH
PERMANENT ENTITIES
  EVERY SERIES OWNS A GRAPH
DEFINE XVAL AND YVAL AS REAL VARIABLES
  MONITORED ON THE RIGHT
DEFINE GRAPH AS A SET RANKED BY HIGH YVAL WITHOUT
  M ATTRIBUTE, WITHOUT FB,FA,FL AND RS ROUTINES
NORMALLY, MODE IS INTEGER
END

MAIN
READ N.SERIES   CREATE EVERY SERIES
FOR EACH SERIES, DO
    READ N
ALSO FOR I= 1 TO N,DO
        CREATE A SAMPLE
        READ XVAL AND YVAL
        FILE SAMPLE IN GRAPH
LOOP
FOR EACH SERIES, NOW PLOT.GRAPH
STOP
END

ROUTINE TO PLOT.GRAPH
''ASSUME XVAL BETWEEN 0 AND 132
''ASSUME YVAL BETWEEN 0 AND LINES.V-4
START NEW PAGE
PRINT 1 LINE WITH SERIES AS FOLLOWS
        PLOT OF SERIES NUMBER **
FOR EACH I IN GRAPH, COMPUTE X AS THE MAXIMUM OF XVAL(I)
PRINT 2 LINES WITH X,YVAL(F.GRAPH) THUS
        X RANGE IS 0 TO ***.*
        Y RANGE IS 0 TO **.*
SKIP 1 OUTPUT LINE
FOR EACH I IN GRAPH, DO
    IF I = F.GRAPH, GO TO 'W' ELSE
    SKIP TRUNC.F(YVAL(I)) - TRUNC.F(YVAL(P.GRAPH(I))) OUTPUT LINES
'W' WRITE AS B TRUNC.F(XVAL(I)) + 1, "*"
LOOP
RETURN
END
```

```
'' MONITOR ROUTINES CONVERT DATA VALUES
'' BEFORE THEY ARE PLOTTED.CONVERSION IS
'' OUTSIDE THE PLOTTING ROUTINE
ROUTINE FOR XVAL(I)
DEFINE V AS A REAL VARIABLE
MOVE TO V
RETURN WITH LOG.E.F.(V)    '' FOR EXAMPLE
END

ROUTINE FOR YVAL(I)
DEFINE V AS A REAL VARIABLE
MOVE TO V
RETURN WITH V**2           '' FOR EXAMPLE
END
```

The monitoring routines deliver transformed values of attributes to the plotting routine without changing their values in memory. As there are no left-handed monitoring routines, XVAL and YVAL are stored as they are read. To change the transformations, one need only change the monitoring routines; MAIN and PLOT.GRAPH stay the same.

* 4-18 SUBPROGRAM—A NEW VARIABLE TYPE

A variable declared as SUBPROGRAM by a statement of the form

DEFINE *variable list* AS A SUBPROGRAM VARIABLE

has as its value the address of a routine. An assignment such as

LET X = 'SIN.F'

where X is a SUBPROGRAM variable, stores the computer address of a routine (SIN.F in this case) in a variable. The computer address can be thought of as the name of the routine. SUBPROGRAM variables serve the purpose of allowing routines to be called indirectly, rather than explicitly.

A *subprogram literal* of the form *'name'* is formed by enclosing in single quotes the name of any routine used as a procedure or right-handed function, either present in the SIMSCRIPT II library[†] or defined within a program. A subprogram literal can be used to assign a routine name to a SUBPROGRAM variable in an assignment statement or through

---

[†]Except for in-line functions (see Table 2-4).

an argument list, or can be used as a test constant in a logical expression. Examples (a), (b), and (c) illustrate each of these uses.

DEFINE RTN AS A SUBPROGRAM VARIABLE

(a)   LET RTN = 'DATA.TRANSFORM'

(b)   CALL PROGRAM ('DATA.TRANSFORM')
      ROUTINE PROGRAM (RTN)
      DEFINE RTN AS A SUBPROGRAM VARIABLE
         .
         .
         .
      CALL RTN(Y) YIELDING X
         .
         .
      RETURN WITH X**3
      END

(c)   IF RTN = 'DATA.TRANSFORM', GO TO L1 ELSE

SUBPROGRAM variables can be used rather than actual routine names in procedure calls. When a SUBPROGRAM variable appears in a call statement, the routine name stored in the variable is used in the routine call.

One must be careful to distinguish between the direct and indirect use of a SUBPROGRAM variable, however. If X is defined as a SUBPROGRAM array in a statement such as:

DEFINE X AS A 1-DIMENSIONAL, SUBPROGRAM ARRAY

the statement

(a)   RESERVE X(*) AS 10

allocates 10 data words to X itself; the statement

(b)   RELEASE X

releases the space allocated to X; but the statement

(c)   RELEASE X(7)

releases the routine whose name is stored in X(7). When all the elements of X are referred to, as in (a) and (b), X itself is the object of a statement. When a particular element of X is mentioned, as in (c), an indirect routine reference is implied.

If X is a right-hand monitored, 2-dimensional array, two steps
are needed to release both the array and its monitoring routine.

RELEASE X   releases the array X(*,*)
LET Y= 'X'   stores the "name" of the monitoring routine for X
                in the SUBPROGRAM variable Y
RELEASE Y   releases the routine named X

It is not possible to release a left-handed routine.

SUBPROGRAM variables can be global or local, SAVED or RECURSIVE,
subscripted or unsubscripted. They are initialized to zero when a
program begins execution or routines containing them (as RECURSIVE
variables) are called. Routines called indirectly through SUBPROGRAM
variables do not have their arguments checked during compilation —
the clauses

GIVING i ARGUMENTS

and   YIELDING i VALUES

cannot be used to ensure that argument conventions are being obeyed.

SUBPROGRAM variables can also be used to call functions indirectly. To do this, the following is required:

(1) The SUBPROGRAM variable must be declared to be INTEGER, REAL
or ALPHA mode in a statement of the form

DEFINE *variable list* AS A *mode* SUBPROGRAM VARIABLE

All functions called indirectly through this variable must be of
the declared mode. If no mode is declared the current background mode
is assumed.

(2) An indirect function call is indicated by putting a dollar
sign ($) before a SUBPROGRAM variable name. If F is a SUBPROGRAM
variable, LET X = F assigns the name of a routine to the variable X,
while LET X = $F computes a value by calling on a function whose name
is stored in F and stores it in X.

As with routines used as procedures, when a subscript list follows
a SUBPROGRAM variable it applies to the function called indirectly,
and not to the SUBPROGRAM variable itself. SUBPROGRAM arrays can be
defined and routine names can be stored in them but they cannot be
used to call upon routines.

Several examples illustrate the definition and use of SUBPROGRAM
variables:

(1) Use of SUBPROGRAM variables as right-handed functions.

```
            PREAMBLE
            DEFINE FUNCTION AS A REAL, SUBPROGRAM VARIABLE
            DEFINE N AS AN INTEGER VARIABLE
            DEFINE X AS A 1-DIMENSIONAL ARRAY
            END
            MAIN
            READ N    RESERVE X(*) AS N
            READ X
            LET FUNCTION = 'EXP.F'
  'COMPUTE' FOR I= 1 TO N, COMPUTE S AS THE SUM,
            M AS THE MEAN AND V AS THE VARIANCE
            OF $FUNCTION(X(I))
            PRINT 2 LINES WITH S, M AND V THUS
                SUM= **.* MEAN= *.*
                    VARIANCE= *.**
            IF FUNCTION=  'EXP.F',
                LET FUNCTION= 'SQRT.F'
                GO COMPUTE
            ELSE
            IF FUNCTION= 'SQRT.F',
                LET FUNCTION= 'LOG.10.F'
                GO COMPUTE
            ELSE
            STOP   END
```

(2) A different version of (1).

```
            PREAMBLE
            DEFINE FUNCTION AS A REAL, SUBPROGRAM VARIABLE
            DEFINE N AS AN INTEGER VARIABLE
            DEFINE X AS A 1-DIMENSIONAL ARRAY
            END

            MAIN
            READ N   RESERVE X(*) AS N
            READ X
            CALL PROCESS.DATA GIVEN 'EXP.F'
            CALL PROCESS.DATA GIVEN 'SQRT.F'
            CALL PROCESS.DATA GIVEN 'LOG.10.F'
            STOP
            END
```

```
        ROUTINE TO PROCESS.DATA(J)
        DEFINE J AS A SUBPROGRAM VARIABLE
        DEFINE I AS AN INTEGER VARIABLE
        FOR I = 1 TO N, COMPUTE S AS THE SUM,
        M AS THE MEAN AND V AS THE VARIANCE
        OF $J(X(I))
        PRINT 2 LINES WITH S, M AND V THUS
            SUM= **.*   MEAN= *.*
                  VARIANCE= *.*
        RETURN
        END
```

(3) SUBPROGRAM variable used for program control.

```
        PREAMBLE
        DEFINE ROUTER AS A SUBPROGRAM VARIABLE
        DEFINE DATA AS A REAL, 1-DIMENSIONAL ARRAY
        DEFINE STOCK AND BORROW.BIN AS VARIABLES
        END

        MAIN
        RESERVE DATA(*) AS 3
        LET ROUTER= 'INPUT'
'A'     CALL ROUTER
        LIST DATA, STOCK, BORROW.BIN
        IF ROUTER = 0, STOP
        ELSE GO TO A
        END

        ROUTINE INPUT
        READ DATA
        IF DATA(1) = 0  LET ROUTER= 'RECEIPT'
        ELSE LET ROUTER= 'SHIPMENT'
        RETURN
        END

        ROUTINE RECEIPT
        ADD DATA(2)-1 TO STOCK
        ADD 1 TO BORROW.BIN
        LET ROUTER= 'INPUT'
        RETURN
        END

        ROUTINE SHIPMENT
        IF DATA(2) ≤ STOCK,
            SUBTRACT DATA(2) FROM STOCK
            PERFORM SHIPPING.NOTICE
            LET ROUTER= 'INPUT'
            RETURN
        ELSE LET ROUTER= 'BORROW'
            RETURN
        END
```

```
ROUTINE SHIPPING.NOTICE
PRINT 1 LINE WITH DATA(2), DATA(3) THUS
   SHIP *** UNITS TO CUSTOMER *****
RETURN
END

ROUTINE TO BORROW
LET DIFF = DATA(2) - STOCK
IF DIFF ≤ BORROW.BIN,
   ADD DIFF TO STOCK
   SUBTRACT DIFF FROM BORROW.BIN
   LET ROUTER= 'SHIPMENT'
   RETURN
ELSE PRINT 1 LINE WITH DATA(3) THUS
   CAN NOT FILL ORDER FOR CUSTOMER *****
IF DATA(3) > 100,
   LET ROUTER= 0
   RETURN
OTHERWISE
   LET ROUTER= 'INPUT'
   RETURN
END
```

4-19 TEXT—A NEW MODE

The TEXT mode is declared for either attributes, variables, or functions by the usual statements

> NORMALLY, MODE IS TEXT
>
> or   DEFINE *name* AS A TEXT VARIABLE

TEXT variables store character strings of arbitrary length through a dictionary (symbol table) mechanism. Character strings are stored in sets, the "value" of a TEXT variable being a pointer to a particular string. Several TEXT variables with the same value, i.e., with the same character string assigned to them, have the same pointer value. A character string is only stored once. Once stored, subsequent attempts to store identical strings only retrieve existing pointer values.

A character string can be entered into a program in four ways: The statement

> READ *variable list*

where *variable* has been declared as TEXT, reads a *word* (defined in
the footnote on p. 120) in free-form. If X and Y are TEXT, the statement READ X AND Y when reading the following data card

```
column number
00000000011111111112222222222333
12345678901234567890123456789012
ANTIDISESTABLISHMENTARIANISM IS
```

assigns the string ANTIDISESTABLISHMENTARIANISM to X and the string
IS to Y.

The statement

READ *variable* AS T e

illustrates a format for inputting TEXT data. The arithmetic expression associated with a TEXT variable must, of course, be positive.
If, in performing a formatted TEXT read, the end of a data card is
encountered before e characters have been read, a new card is read
and reading of the character string continues. The statement

READ TEXT.VAR AS B 1, T 400

defines an input character string of 400 characters. All characters
encountered in a formatted TEXT read are considered part of the text.

The statement

INPUT *text list*

uses a special delimiting character to mark off successive TEXT variables in a free-form style statement. The delimiting character is
stored in the ALPHA global variable MARK.V, which has a default value
of "*". MARK.V may be changed when necessary. A *text list* is a list
of TEXT variable names and /, B, and S formats. The statement

INPUT X,/,Y,S 10, Z

starts reading at whatever column the current input pointer is positioned; reads all the characters up to the first asterisk as the character string value of X; skips to a new card; reads all the characters
up to the first asterisk as the character string value of Y; skips
over the next 10 columns and reads all the characters up to the next

asterisk as the character string value of Z. The delimiting character, * in this case, does not become part of the input character string.

A character string can also be entered into the dictionary as a TEXT literal, specified as |*character string*|. Within a TEXT literal a parallel (|) is represented by an underscore (_).

TEXT variables can be used in several ways: they can be concatenated (linked together), compared, erased, or displayed.

The system function CONCAT.F(A,B) adds the character string pointed to by the TEXT variable B to the character string pointed to by the TEXT variable A. A new character string is formed; A and B remain. For example, if A= |SIMSCRIPT_| and B= |II|, the statement LET C= CONCAT.F(A,B) sets C= |SIMSCRIPT_II|.

Comparisons are made possible by considering all arithmetical and relational operations performed with TEXT variables and functions as INTEGER mode. Thus, if V1 and V2 are TEXT mode variables or functions, the logical expressions V1 = V2, V1 NE V2, V2 = |*character string*|, etc., are true or false depending upon whether the variables (functions) have the same pointer values. For example, if V1 = |SPORTS_CAR| and V2 = |SPORTS_| the logical expression V1 = V2 is false. The logical expression V1 = CONCAT.F(V1, |CAR|), however, is true. The comparison V1 > V2 is meaningless, as it expresses an algebraic relation between two pointer values.

Statements of the form

LET *text variable* = |character string|

do either of two things: if the indicated character string is not already in the dictionary, it is placed in it and a pointer to the string stored in the text variable; if the literal string is already in the dictionary, the existing pointer is used.

Character strings pointed to by TEXT variables are destroyed by statements of the form

ERASE *pointer list*

The entire dictionary can be erased by the statement

FOR EACH V IN THE DICTIONARY, ERASE V

Since more than one TEXT variable can point to the same text data, the ERASE statement must be used with care. The following few statements show why care is necessary.

```
DEFINE NAME AND LABEL AS TEXT VARIABLES
READ NAME AS /,T 50
LET LABEL = NAME
        .
        .
        .
ERASE NAME
```

The text pointed to by LABEL no longer exists. The FOR phrase

FOR EACH *variable* IN THE DICTIONARY,

can be used like any other FOR phrase to control a program's operations.

Each TEXT variable has an INTEGER attribute whose value is the number of characters contained in the variable. Each declaration

DEFINE *name* AS A TEXT VARIABLE

defines an attribute LENGTH.A(*name*). To illustrate: LET NAME= |JOHN_SMITH| sets the TEXT variable NAME "equal to" the character string |JOHN_SMITH|. After execution of the LET statement, LENGTH.A (NAME) equals 10.

TEXT values can be output by three different statements. Statements of the form

WRITE *variable* AS T e

write output on the current output unit, starting at the column pointed to by the current output pointer. More than one line is printed if the expression e requires it.

Statements of the form

OUTPUT *text list*

commence writing at the current output pointer column, and continue until the TEXT data stored in one or more variables are exhausted. The formats B,S,/, and * can be used in the *text list* for editing.

And the statement

LIST *variable*

displays the first 14 characters of a TEXT variable in the standard
LIST format. If a TEXT variable contains fewer than 14 characters,
the characters displayed are left-adjusted.

The INPUT, OUTPUT, READ, and WRITE statements can be followed
up by a USING clause when necessary.

Conversion between TEXT and other modes is provided by three
functions:

TTOA.F(pointer)   converts the first four[†] characters of the
                    TEXT value pointed at to ALPHA.

ATOT.F(variable)   converts the four[†] characters of the indi-
                    cated ALPHA variable to TEXT, storing them
                    in the dictionary, if necessary.

ITOA.F(expression) converts the first four[†] digits of an
                    INTEGER expression to ALPHA.

Table 4-8 shows the functions provided by SIMSCRIPT II for converting from one data mode to another.

Table 4-8

MODE CONVERSION FUNCTIONS

	INTEGER	REAL	ALPHA	TEXT
INTEGER	----	Automatic or REAL.F	ITOA.F	----
REAL	INT.F or TRUNC.F	----	----	----
ALPHA	----	----	----	ATOT.F
TEXT	----	----	TTOA.F	----

The features of the TEXT mode are illustrated in the following
examples:

(1) This program reads a number of sentences, orders them according to their length, and prints them out:

[†]Assuming an ALPHA variable can hold four characters.

```
            PREAMBLE NORMALLY, MODE IS INTEGER
            DEFINE SENTENCE AS A 1-DIMENSIONAL,
                TEXT ARRAY
            END

            MAIN
            READ N RESERVE SENTENCE(*) AS N
      LET   LET MARK.V= "."
            FOR I= 1 TO N, INPUT SENTENCE(I)
 'ANOTHER'  FOR EACH I IN THE DICTIONARY,
            COMPUTE MAX= THE MAXIMUM(I) OF LENGTH.A(I)
            IF MAX= 0,STOP
            OTHERWISE
            OUTPUT SENTENCE (MAX)
            ERASE SENTENCE (MAX)
            GO TO ANOTHER
            END
```

(2) This program reads a deck of name cards, in which names are
punched in the form *first name blank last name*, and counts the number
of occurrences of different names:

```
            PREAMBLE
            DEFINE FIRST AND LAST AS TEXT VARIABLES
            NORMALLY,MODE IS INTEGER
            END

            MAIN
  'READ'    IF DATA IS ENDED,
                PRINT 1 LINE WITH JOHN,GREG,SMITH,HH THUS
                    COUNTS ARE *** *** *** **
            STOP ELSE
            READ FIRST AND LAST
            IF FIRST EQUALS |JOHN|, ADD 1 TO JOHN
            ELSE
            IF FIRST EQUALS | GREGORY|, ADD 1 TO GREG
            ELSE
            IF LAST EQUALS |SMITH|, ADD 1 TO SMITH
            ELSE
            IF CONCAT.F(FIRST,LAST)= | HORATIOHORNBLOWER|
                ADD 1 TO HH
            ELSE GO READ
            END
```

(3) These program segments are part of a large simulation program:

```
            PREAMBLE
            TEMPORARY ENTITIES
                EVERY JOB HAS A DESCRIPTION, A PRIORITY, A
                DUE.DATE AND MAY BELONG TO A QUEUE
```

```
                    .
                    .
                    .
        DEFINE PRIORITY AS AN INTEGER VARIABLE
        DEFINE DESCRIPTION AS A TEXT VARIABLE
        DEFINE DUE.DATE AS A REAL VARIABLE
                    .
                    .
                    .
    END

    MAIN
            .
            .
            .
    ''READ DATA FOR JOBS''
    CREATE A JOB    START NEW INPUT CARD
    READ DESCRIPTION,PRIORITY,DUE.DATE
        AS T 50, I 10, D(10,2)
                .
                .
    REMOVE THE FIRST JOB FROM QUEUE(5)
    LIST ATTRIBUTES OF JOB
            .
            .
    END
```

(4) Three ways to do INTEGER to TEXT conversion:

> I is an INTEGER variable
>
> T is a TEXT variable

(a) WRITE I AS /, I 10, "*" USING THE BUFFER   includes all
      INPUT T USING THE BUFFER   leading blanks

(b) WRITE I AS /, I 10 USING THE BUFFER   starts reading
      READ T USING THE BUFFER   at the first non-
                                           blank character

(c) LET T = ATOT.F(ITOA.F(I))

(5) Use of TEXT for output messages.

Routine definition:

```
        ROUTINE ERROR GIVEN T
        DEFINE T AS A TEXT VARIABLE
        WRITE T AS /, B 10, "THE ERROR IS", T 25
        END
```

Routine use:

```
        IF VALUE > LIMIT, CALL ERROR(| FATAL,VALUE TOO HIGH|)
                        STOP
        ELSE IF VALUE = LIMIT,CALL ERROR(| RECOVERABLE,CONTINUING|)
                        PERFORM RECOVERY

            REGARDLESS
```

(6) Creating, using, and destroying an entity having a TEXT
attribute:

```
        PREAMBLE
        TEMPORARY ENTITIES
            EVERY MAN HAS A NAME,AN AGE AND A SALARY AND BELONGS
                         TO A GROUP
        DEFINE NAME AND N AS TEXT VARIABLES
        THE SYSTEM OWNS A GROUP
        END


        MAIN
        LET MARK.V = "."
 'BACK' READ N
        IF N NE | DATA GROUP ENDED |,
            CREATE A MAN
            LET NAME = N
            READ AGE AND SALARY
            FILE THIS MAN IN GROUP
            GO BACK
        ELSE
            START NEW PAGE
            PRINT 2 LINES WITH N.GROUP AS FOLLOWS
               THIS GROUP CONTAINS *** PEOPLE
               NAME            AGE        SALARY
            FOR EACH MAN IN GROUP,DO
               REMOVE THE MAN FROM THE GROUP
               WRITE NAME,AGE AND SALARY AS B 15, T 25, 2 I 10
               ERASE NAME
               DESTROY MAN
            LOOP
        IF DATA IS ENDED, STOP
        ELSE GO BACK
        END
```

4-20 ASSIGNMENT WITHOUT CONVERSION

At times it is necessary to store REAL numbers in INTEGER
variables, and INTEGER, ALPHA, TEXT, or SUBPROGRAM values in REAL
variables. When this is done, it is generally for some purpose outside the facilities of SIMSCRIPT II, e.g., communication with a

machine-language subprogram or performance of a rather exotic algorithm. The STORE statement permits any computable value to be
assigned without conversion. The form

STORE *arithmetic expression* IN *variable*

expresses a command to compute or retrieve a value and to assign it
to a stated location.

Table 4-9 reviews the forms a STORE statement can take.

Table 4-9

STORE STATEMENT COMPONENTS

Arithmetic Expression	Variable
INTEGER expression data value array pointer identification number	Variable Attribute Left-handed function Monitored variable
INTEGER constant	
REAL expression	
REAL constant	
ALPHA variable	
"ALPHA literal"	
TEXT variable	
|TEXT literal|	
SUBPROGRAM variable	
·SUBPROGRAM literal'	

Chapter 5

SIMSCRIPT II: LEVEL 5

5-00 INTRODUCTION

Unlike Levels 1 through 4, which present a rather general programming language, Level 5 provides concepts and programming features for a specific applications area, discrete-event simulation. Readers unfamiliar with this subject are advised to read any one of a number of current texts or P. J. Kiviat, *Digital Computer Simulation: Modeling Concepts*, The RAND Corporation, RM-5378-PR, August 1967. While some methodological comments are made in this section, it is not intended as a text, and will most likely prove unsatisfactory to persons unfamiliar with the subject. Readers who have done simulations, and particularly those who have used a simulation programming language, should have no difficulty following the section without additional preparation.

Simulation as we deal with it is the use of a numerical model of a system to study its behavior as it operates over time. Discrete-event simulation deals with models whose entities interact with one another at discrete points in time, rather than continuously. This section presents concepts and statements designed to aid in modeling systems and in programming them so that they can be simulated. Its organization reflects subject areas that are important to this task:

Sec. *5-01*, *DESCRIBING SYSTEM DYNAMICS*

Sec. *5-02*, *CONTROLLING SYSTEM DYNAMICS*

Sec. *5-03*, *MODELING STATISTICAL PHENOMENA*

Sec. *5-04*, *MODEL DEBUGGING AND ANALYSIS*

5-01 DESCRIBING SYSTEM DYNAMICS

The basic unit of action in a SIMSCRIPT II simulation is an
activity. In a simulation of supermarket operations, we might find
such activities as: customer selecting merchandise, customer walking
to checkout counter, and customer checking out, among others that deal
with different aspects of supermarket operations. Two important facts
about activities are (1) that they take time, and (2) that they
(potentially) change the state of a system.

When one constructs a simulation model he must provide a characterization of system activities that enables the model, when operating,
to reproduce the time-dependent behavior of the system being simulated.
That is, he must construct the activities in such a way that, when
each occurs, the system state changes in the proper way. This imposes
requirements for (1) correctly modeling the things that activities
do, and for (2) sequencing the execution of subprograms that represent
activities, so that the order of performance of activities within a
model corresponds to the order in which the same activities occur in
the real system.

The concepts embodied in Levels 1 through 4 are the stuff that
activity descriptions are made of. Systems are described (modeled)
in the language of entities, attributes, and sets.

Keeping track of simulated time and organizing subprograms that
represent system activities are the primary tasks of Level 5. The
central concept employed is that of an *event*. An event is an instant
in time at which an activity starts or stops. Usually, an activity
is bounded by two events, as shown below:

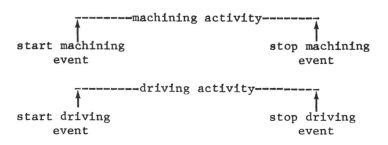

Typical activities

The time between events that represents the duration of an
activity is always modeled as a time-delay factor. Changes in a
system that take place when an activity starts or stops, in the
instant of time when an activity begins or ends, are associated with
events rather than activities. This is the crucial difference between
discrete-event and continuous-time simulators. In discrete-event
simulation languages such as SIMSCRIPT II, state-changes take place
only at specified points in time at which interactions between system
entities occur. In continuous-time simulation languages, interactions
and state-changes take place continuously. To model continuous
changes, either analog computers or numerical integration procedures
must be employed.

Some activities have no duration and are modeled as single events.
These are activities such as the preparation of a report or a plan
that is issued periodically. Activities can be modeled as consuming
zero time if no system interactions occur during the activity time,
and the activity time is short.

To model an activity that takes some time to perform, one specifies two events. In the first event, the necessary tests and state-
changes are made to put the activity into operation and an instruction
is given to the SIMSCRIPT II system to schedule a second event to
occur after the passage of some units of simulated time. When this
time passes and the second event is called, it does what testing and
state-changing it must to terminate the activity. It may trigger one
or more subsequent events. The keys to understanding how the passage
of time is simulated are to understand (1) that events take place
instantaneously, (2) that events are modeled as SIMSCRIPT II subprograms that are executed in zero simulated time, and (3) that the
SIMSCRIPT II system contains a special routine, called a *timing routine*,
that accepts requests for the execution of events at specified future
times and organizes them so that the event routines are called in the
order of their time scheduling, and hence in the order in which they
should occur temporally. The timing routine also keeps track of simulated system time with an artificial system clock.

In this section we limit ourselves to the definition of important
simulation concepts, such as:

activity
event
timing routine
simulation clock
event scheduling in simulated time
instantaneous changes of system state

and the presentation of statements that allow these concepts to be
defined within a SIMSCRIPT II program. Section *5-02* goes further
into how the timing routine works and how events are scheduled and
executed.

While it has not been pointed out explicitly why the normal main-
program-subprogram structure is not adequate for the simulation task,
it is not difficult to reason out why this is so. Consider the following situation: a simulation model has one kind of entity, call it a
MAN, that performs one kind of activity, call it a JOB. Let the job
activity be delimited by the two events START.JOB and END.JOB. Let
two men somehow appear and be given jobs to perform, i.e., the simulation must execute the routine START.JOB for each MAN. If the men
arrive at the same time these programs must be executed simultaneously,
i.e., in parallel. On a sequential computer this is impossible, of
course. It is possible, however, to execute them sequentially without
advancing the simulation clock after the first event has occurred.[†]
If two events occur when the simulation clock has the same time, we
can think of them as happening simultaneously.

Now, within the event START.JOB the event END.JOB will be scheduled
to occur after some job performance delay time. When the event END.JOB
occurs for the first MAN, the simulation clock will be advanced to
some higher value, i.e., it will indicate that simulated time has
passed. Therefore, when the first START.JOB has occurred it cannot
CALL its respective END.JOB and advance the simulation clock because
the second START.JOB has not yet been executed. Some statement other
than CALL is required to instruct the SIMSCRIPT II system that END.JOB
is to be called after all events that have lower clock times associated
with them have been called.

[†]Section *5-06* discusses techniques for handling complex time
interactions.

In Fig. 5-1 two jobs are started and ended at different times
to illustrate the concepts of *event occurrence* and *event scheduling*.

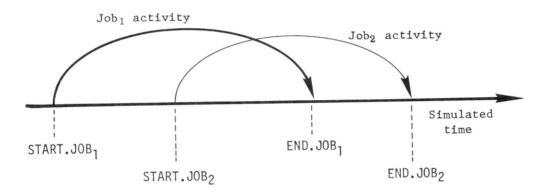

Fig. 5-1a -- Two overlapping activities

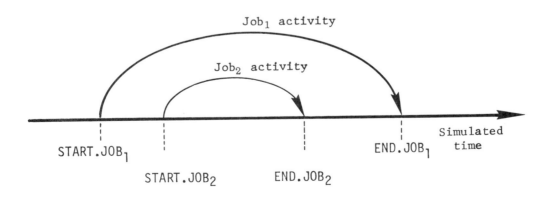

Fig. 5-1b -- Two nested activities

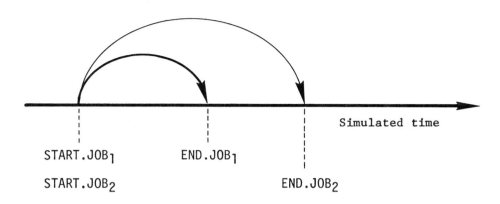

Fig. 5-1c -- Two activities with a common event time

Table 5-1 lists the order in which subprograms representing the START.JOB and END.JOB events of Fig. 5-1 have to be executed.

Table 5-1

FIGURE 5-1 EVENT ORDER

	Fig. 5-1a	Fig. 5-1b	Fig. 5-1c
Time	START.JOB$_1$	START.JOB$_1$	$\begin{pmatrix} \text{START.JOB}_1 \\ \text{START.JOB}_2 \end{pmatrix}$ in parallel
	START.JOB$_2$	START.JOB$_2$	
	END.JOB$_1$	END.JOB$_2$	END.JOB$_1$
	END.JOB$_2$	END.JOB$_1$	END.JOB$_2$

Two classes of events are possible in any simulation model: events generated within the model and events fed to the model from the outside world. The former are called INTERNAL or ENDOGENOUS events, the latter EXTERNAL or EXOGENOUS events. Each has a routine associated with it that describes actions the simulated system takes when the event occurs. The difference between the types is that INTERNAL events are caused by the explicit reaction of a model to its operations — the

model generates or "makes up" INTERNAL events as it progresses —
while EXTERNAL events are fed to a model from a data source (a magnetic tape or disk, or punched cards). Generally, EXTERNAL events
provide stimuli to a model and INTERNAL events react to them.

Event Declaration

A routine is declared to be an event rather than a callable subprogram by use of the word EVENT or UPON rather than ROUTINE in its
first statement. Typical event declaration statements are:

```
EVENT ARRIVAL GIVEN LOCATION AND ALTITUDE
UPON DEPARTING(DESTINATION)
UPON LEAVING THIS PLACE
EVENT ALLOCATION(SUM, PERSON1, PERSON2)
```

These statements show that event declarations are similar to routine
declarations in that they can have input arguments and can use the
different input argument forms described in Sec. 2-19. Events cannot
have yielding arguments for the simple reason that they are not called
directly from subprograms and have no place to return output values.

The general form of an event declaration statement is:

> EVENT *name optional input argument list*
>
> or   UPON *name optional input argument list*

Events can be triggered either internally or externally. If they
are triggered internally it is by something called an *event notice*
(discussed in the following subsection); if they are triggered externally it is by an *external event data card* (discussed in Sec. 5-02).
Since an event subprogram can occur in either of two ways, and each
of these ways provides a different source of data for the event, a
logical expression is provided for use within an event in determining
how an event occurrence was triggered. The expression compares the
keyword EVENT with either of the property words INTERNAL or EXTERNAL
and yields a true or false result. The form of the expression is

> EVENT IS *property*   or   EVENT IS NOT *property*

as in the statements

```
           IF EVENT IS INTERNAL, GO TO INTERNAL.PROCESS ELSE
  and      IF EVENT IS EXTERNAL AND DATA IS ENDED, STOP OTHERWISE
```

Succeeding subsections contain examples that make it clear why this statement is necessary and how it is used.

Internal Events

When an event is generated within a program, a message, called an *event notice*, is used to carry information about the event from the generating routine to the SIMSCRIPT II timing routine, and from it to the event when its turn for execution comes about. An event notice is very much like a temporary entity; in fact, it is a temporary entity that has five special attributes. The first of these contains the simulated time at which the event represented by the event notice is to occur; the second contains an event type code that tells whether an event occurred internally or externally; the third, fourth, and fifth are attributes for the set the timing routine uses to keep track of scheduled events. These attributes are called TIME.A, EUNIT.A, P.EV.S, S.EV.S, and M.EV.S, respectively. The timing set is sub-scripted and named EV.S.

Event notices can have attributes that are either variables or functions, and can own and belong to sets. EVERY statements are used to declare them.

The statement

EVENT NOTICES

placed before a group of EVERY statements notifies the compiler that event notices rather than temporary or permanent entity declarations follow. The compiler places the special attributes in the first five words of each event notice record; the programmer does not have to name them. He must be careful not to place attributes of his own in these first five words.

Often, event notices only have the special attributes and no additional attributes or set pointers. They are used to trigger events, not to carry information to them. When this is the case, the phrase

INCLUDE *event notice name list*

is added to the EVENT NOTICES statement to notify the compiler that
these event notices exist and five-word event notice records have to
be defined for them. A typical simulation program preamble might
start off like this:

```
        PREAMBLE
        EVENT NOTICES INCLUDE ARRIVAL, WEEKLY.REPORT AND END.SIM
        EVERY JOB.OVER HAS A NEXT.JOB AND OWNS SOME RESOURCES
```

When created, records for these event notices look like

	ARRIVAL	WEEKLY.REPORT	END.SIM	JOB.OVER
word 1	TIME.A	TIME.A	TIME.A	TIME.A
word 2	EUNIT.A	EUNIT.A	EUNIT.A	EUNIT.A
word 3	P.EV.S	P.EV.S	P.EV.S	P.EV.S
word 4	S.EV.S	S.EV.S	S.EV.S	S.EV.S
word 5	M.EV.S	M.EV.S	M.EV.S	M.EV.S
				NEXT.JOB
				F.RESOURCES
				L.RESOURCES
				N.RESOURCES

Section *5-02* describes how event notices are created and used.
It is sufficient at this point that the reader understand that they
are created and destroyed like temporary entities, and used by the
SIMSCRIPT II timing routine to organize the execution of events in
proper time sequence.

The reader should also understand at this point that it is possible to have many events of the same kind scheduled to occur at the
same or different times in the future. For example, a machine-shop
simulation having an event END.JOB that signals the completion of a
machining operation and changes the state of the simulated system
when a job is completed, can have many END.JOB events scheduled and
held in abeyance by the timing routine. These events are usually
scheduled to take place at different times, and the timing routine

is able to organize them, by ranking them on their scheduled occurrence times so that the events with the earliest (smallest) event time are selected first. If two events of the same kind happen to have the same event time, the timing routine uses a first-scheduled, first-occurs rule to "break the tie." The order in which events are executed is determined by the order in which they are scheduled. While several events can take place at the same instant in simulated time (the simulation clock has the same value during each event) there are often good reasons for wanting to give priority to one event notice or other. The BREAK TIES statement accomplishes this.

A statement of the form

BREAK <i>event name</i> TIES BY HIGH <i>attribute name</i>
or   BREAK <i>event name</i> TIES BY LOW <i>attribute name</i>

gives priority to the event with the high (low) attribute value when two or more event notices of the same type have the same event time. The attributes are, of course, ones that have been defined in EVERY statements for the event named. In cases where more than one set of tie-breaking attributes are needed, clauses of the form

, THEN BY HIGH <i>attribute name</i>
or   , THEN BY LOW <i>attribute name</i>

can be added to the BREAK TIES statement. As many may be added as are necessary.

Events defined by the statements

EVENT NOTICES
EVERY ARRIVAL HAS A VALUE, A DUE.DATE AND A PRIORITY

can have ties resolved among competing event notices by statements such as

(a)   BREAK ARRIVAL TIES BY HIGH PRIORITY
(b)   BREAK ARRIVAL TIES BY HIGH PRIORITY, THEN BY LOW DUE.DATE
(c)   BREAK ARRIVAL TIES BY HIGH VALUE, THEN BY LOW PRIORITY,
       THEN BY HIGH DUE.DATE

In (a), among ARRIVAL event notices scheduled to occur at the same simulated time, the event notice with the largest PRIORITY attribute will occur first. In (b), among event notices scheduled to occur at the same simulated time and having identical PRIORITY values, the notice with the smallest DUE.DATE will occur first. And similarly for (c) and other variations.

Conflicts between different kinds of events are of similar importance. It often happens that several different events are scheduled for the same time, as for example, the arrival of a job, the completion of a task, and the preparation of a management report. Resolving these conflicts is important in situations where events compete for the same resources or have some effect upon one another. A statement of the form

PRIORITY ORDER IS *event name list*

places an ordering upon the events named so that in cases where event notices of different kinds have the same event time, the event notice of the higher-priority event type is selected first. Priority in this case corresponds to position in the PRIORITY statement; the first event named is given the highest priority. If no PRIORITY statement appears in a program, events are given priority in the order in which they appear in the preamble, in either INCLUDE or EVERY statements. If only a subset of the events of a program are listed in a PRIORITY statement, the remaining events are given lower priority than the ones listed, and are ranked among themselves in the order in which they appear.

The following preamble illustrates the use of BREAK TIES and PRIORITY statements in a typical simulation program:

```
PREAMBLE
EVENT NOTICES INCLUDE END.OF.JOB AND SHIFT.CHANGES
   EVERY CAR.ARRIVAL HAS A VALUE AND AN IDENTITY
   EVERY TRUCK.ARRIVAL HAS A LOAD.WEIGHT AND A DENSITY
   EVERY START.JOB HAS A VEHICLE AND A CREWSIZE
BREAK CAR.ARRIVAL TIES BY HIGH VALUE
BREAK TRUCK.ARRIVAL TIES BY LOW DENSITY, THEN BY HIGH LOAD.WEIGHT
BREAK START.JOB TIES BY LOW CREWSIZE
PRIORITY ORDER IS TRUCK.ARRIVAL, CAR.ARRIVAL, START.JOB, END.OF.JOB,
   SHIFT.CHANGES
DEFINE IDENTITY, LOAD.WEIGHT, AND CREWSIZE AS INTEGER VARIABLES
DEFINE VEHICLE AS AN ALPHA VARIABLE
END
```

External Events

Events can be triggered from outside a simulation model by declaring them to be EXTERNAL EVENTS. Some events are triggered only externally. Other events are triggered only internally; for them, only EVENT NOTICES declarations are used. Some events are triggered in both ways. We have described how event notices are defined and left the discussion of how they are used to the next section; we do the same for external events, describing now how they are defined and leaving the discussion of how they are used to Sec. *5-02*.

An event is defined as having an external trigger by using its name in a statement of the form:

EXTERNAL EVENTS ARE *event name list*

When an event name appears in an EXTERNAL EVENT statement and is not declared as an event notice, provision is made to create a five-attribute event notice, named *event*, each time a data card containing the event name appears on an *external event unit*. The event notice is of the form:

word 1	TIME.A
word 2	EUNIT.A
word 3	P.EV.S
word 4	S.EV.S
word 5	M.EV.S

The first, third, fourth, and fifth attributes have the same meaning as in the preceding subsection; the second attribute contains the number of the input unit on which information about the event is contained. External event input units are defined in a statement of the form:

EXTERNAL EVENT UNITS ARE *device name list*

In this statement, device names can be given as integer constants or as variables. If variables are used, they must be initialized to device name values before the start of simulation. If no EXTERNAL EVENT UNITS statement appears, the *standard input unit* is assumed to

be a source of external event data. If several input devices are
used, the standard input unit must be listed with them if it is to
be a source of external events.

A simulation program having the events ARRIVAL and REPORT might
contain the following statements in its preamble:

        EXTERNAL EVENTS ARE ARRIVAL AND REPORT
        EXTERNAL EVENT UNITS ARE DAILY.ARRIVALS, WEEKLY.ARRIVALS,
        AND 5

These statements indicate that the SIMSCRIPT II system must be prepared
to execute the events ARRIVAL and REPORT as external events, and that
three input devices are to be used to input external event triggers.
The programmer indicates mnemonically that he intends to put information about arrivals that occur daily on one input device and information about arrivals that occur weekly on another. The SIMSCRIPT II
system attaches no significance to the names; it merely knows that
three input devices are to be used.

Events that are only triggered externally can be given tie-breaking
priority over other external events and over internally generated events
by putting their names in a PRIORITY statement. Using the above statements as an example, the statement

                PRIORITY ORDER IS REPORT AND ARRIVAL

states that if simultaneous events come up on the multiple event units,
REPORT events are to be executed before ARRIVAL events. It is not
possible to attach priorities to external event units, e.g., service
DAILY.ARRIVALS before WEEKLY.ARRIVALS. Only events may be given
priorities.

Events that occur both internally and externally can be given
priority over other kinds of events but cannot be ranked among themselves by a BREAK TIES statement. As only the internally generated
event notices have ranking attributes, the externally triggered event
notices compete with them on a first-come, first-served basis.

5-02 *CONTROLLING SYSTEM DYNAMICS*

Three things must be understood about system dynamics: how the

SIMSCRIPT II timing routine organizes events so that they are executed properly in simulated time; how internal events are scheduled; and how external event data are prepared and input. The first three parts of this section address these issues.

The Timing Routine

Every simulation program contains the statement

START SIMULATION

which instructs the SIMSCRIPT II operating system to start taking instructions from the simulation timing mechanism. For there to be something to do at the start of simulation, a programmer must initialize the system state and provide initializing events that set the system in motion. A typical simulation main program is organized as:

```
MAIN
        local declarations
        initialization of entities, attributes and sets
        initialization of events
        specification of external event units
START SIMULATION
        control statements
END
```

When the timing mechanism finds nothing to do, i.e., no events are scheduled, control passes to the statement after START SIMULATION. As long as events are being executed, the timing routine, represented in the main program by the START SIMULATION statement, is in control. One way to end a simulation is to cease scheduling future events and let the timing mechanism automatically branch beyond the START SIMULATION statement when all currently scheduled events are completed.

The heart of the timing routine is a singly subscripted set in which event notices are filed. Each subscript value denotes a different event class; in a simulation with six different event classes there are six different sets. The global variable EVENTS.V has as its value the number of event classes. The timing routine set is named EV.S, which stands for "events set"; it has the attributes F, P, S, and M and the routines FF, RS and RF are defined. Internal

events with BREAK TIES conditions are put into their proper sets by
routines named C.*event*; internal events not named in BREAK TIES statements, and external events, are put into their sets by a routine named
A.EV.S, which is the standard FILE routine for the set EV.S.

Each event has a global variable I.*event* associated with it that
denotes the subscript value of the event class in the subscripted
events set. In a program without a PRIORITY statement, values are
assigned to these variables in ascending order as event names appear.
When a PRIORITY statement is used, values are assigned in the order
in which events appear in the statement. An example illustrates these
points:

Preamble:

```
PREAMBLE NORMALLY MODE IS INTEGER
EXTERNAL EVENTS ARE ARRIVAL AND STOP.SIMULATION
EVENT NOTICES INCLUDE ARRIVAL, END.OF.JOB AND SHIFT.CHANGE
   EVERY START.JOB HAS A VALUE, A DUE.DATE AND A
      PROCESS.TIME AND BELONGS TO A ROUTING.SET
PERMANENT ENTITIES....
   EVERY MACHINE HAS A CAPACITY AND A RATE AND OWNS A
      WAITING.LINE
TEMPORARY ENTITIES....
   EVERY JOB HAS A TIME.WANTED, OWNS A ROUTING.SET AND
      BELONGS TO A WAITING.LINE
PRIORITY ORDER IS STOP.SIMULATION, SHIFT.CHANGE, END.OF.JOB,
   START.JOB AND ARRIVAL
BREAK START.JOB TIES BY LOW DUE.DATE, THEN BY HIGH VALUE
END
```

Five events are defined: ARRIVAL, STOP.SIMULATION, END.OF.JOB,
SHIFT.CHANGE, and START.JOB: EVENTS.V=5. The subscripted set EV.S
therefore has five subscript values. These values are specified by
the order of the events in the PRIORITY statement and are:
I.STOP.SIMULATION=1, I.SHIFT.CHANGE=2, I.END.OF.JOB=3, I.START.JOB=4,
and I.ARRIVAL=5.

The subscripted variable F.EV.S has five elements, one for each
event class. Each event notice has five attributes, TIME.A, EUNIT.A,
P.EV.S, S.EV.S and M.EV.S; START.JOB has six additional attributes.

The routines A.EV.S, X.EV.S, and Z.EV.S are generated to file
events not mentioned in BREAK TIES statements in their proper sets

and remove the first event or a specific event from a set. The routine C.START.JOB is generated to file event notices in EV.S (I.START.JOB) according to the rankings specified in the BREAK TIES statement.

Simulation event control is maintained in the following way:

(a) Every time an internal or external event is scheduled it is filed in its proper set. Events are filed in their sets in the order in which they are to be executed, i.e., the event with the smallest event time is filed first.

(b) When control returns to the timing mechanism from an event, or from the main program, the next event to be performed is selected by taking the event with the smallest event time from its set. This is done by searching the event sets in the order specified by their I.*event* variables, and keeping the identification of the event notice with the smallest event time. By doing this, two events of the same class will have their tie resolved by the ranking within the set, and two events of different classes with the same event time will have their tie resolved by keeping the identification of the first one found.

Figure 5-2 pictures the way the events of the above preamble are organized. Normally, a programmer does not deal with the set EV.S directly, or with the variables F.EV.S, P.EV.S, S.EV.S, M.EV.S, TIME.A, and EUNIT.A. He inserts events into the event sets with special statements and data inputs, and has them removed from the sets automatically. When an event is removed, its event time TIME.A is transferred to the simulation clock TIME.V, becoming the updated simulation time, and control is transferred to the event routine.

Scheduling Internal Events

We have shown how an event notice is taken from its event set by the timing routine and used to initiate the execution of an event. The details of how an event is executed once its notice is received are discussed a little later in this section. Here we discuss how an event notice for an internal event is filed in its appropriate event set.

The statement

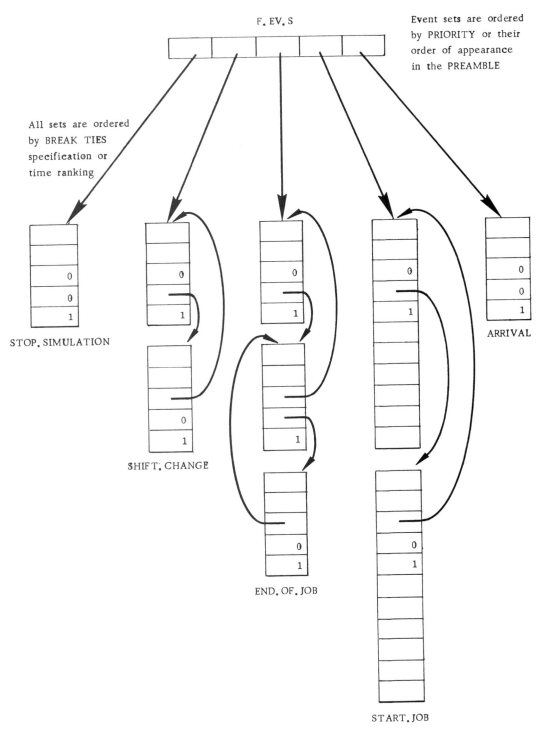

Fig. 5-2 -- Timing set organization

SCHEDULE AN *event* AT *time expression*

creates an event notice of class *event*, sets its TIME.A attribute to
the value of the *time expression*, and files the event notice in the
proper set for that event class. The words CAUSE and RESCHEDULE are
synonyms for SCHEDULE. Situations often exist where they are more
expressive of the task being performed. The event notice is actually
a temporary entity. The statement specifies that a temporary entity
of a certain size be created, with its identification number stored
in a global variable with the same name as the entity, and be used for
scheduling the future occurrence of an event of that class. The
statement is equivalent to a statement of the form:

SCHEDULE AN *event* CALLED *event* AT *time expression*

where *event* is the global variable associated with the entity class.
One can just as easily write a SCHEDULE statement with a different
variable name, as in

SCHEDULE AN ARRIVAL CALLED RUSH.ORDER AT *time expression*

If an event notice already exists (it may have been created previously), one can specify that it be used in a SCHEDULE statement by
using the word THIS rather than AN, as in

SCHEDULE THIS ARRIVAL AT *time expression*

This inhibits creation of a new entity. The identification number
of the event notice that is to be used is assumed to be stored in the
global variable ARRIVAL. The statement form

SCHEDULE THIS *entity* CALLED *variable* AT *time expression*

says that an identification number of an event notice of the class
entity is stored in *variable* and is to be used in a scheduling statement.

Several variations of these statement forms are permitted. The
words A and AN are synonyms, as are the words THIS, THE, and THE ABOVE.
Thus one can say:

(a) SCHEDULE AN ARRIVAL AT *time expression*
(b) SCHEDULE THE ABOVE ARRIVAL CALLED RUSH AT *time expression*
(c) CAUSE THIS ARRIVAL AT *time expression*

Statement (a) creates an event notice before scheduling; statements (b) and (c) use event notices of type ARRIVAL, whose identification numbers are stored in RUSH and ARRIVAL, respectively.

If an event notice has attributes, as in START.JOB defined on p. 295, values can be assigned to them in two ways: through standard *attribute (entity)* references in LET statements and through the SCHEDULE statement itself. Recall that the event START.JOB was defined by the statement

```
EVENT NOTICES....
    EVERY START.JOB HAS A VALUE, A DUE.DATE AND A PROCESS.TIME
    AND BELONGS TO A ROUTING.SET
```

This means that every START.JOB entity record looks like:

word 1	TIME.A
word 2	EUNIT.A
word 3	P.EV.S
word 4	S.EV.S
word 5	M.EV.S
word 6	VALUE
word 7	DUE.DATE
word 8	PROCESS.TIME
word 9	P.ROUTING.SET
word 10	S.ROUTING.SET
word 11	M.ROUTING.SET

The first five attributes of every event notice cannot be used by a programmer. He cannot pack, equivalence, or delete them. He can do anything he wishes with attributes he defines.

A statement of the form

SCHEDULE AN *event* GIVEN *expression list* AT *time expression*

(1) Uses the time expression to set TIME.A(*event*).

(2) Sets EUNIT.A(*event*) to zero, indicating that the event is being scheduled internally.[†]

[†]See discussion on p. 304.

(3) Files the event notice in EV.S(I.*event*) thereby setting the pointers P.EV.S and S.EV.S and the membership attribute M.EV.S.

(4) Assigns the values given in the *expression list* to the successive attributes of the event notice, starting with the attribute following M.EV.S. If fewer expressions are listed than there are attributes, the remaining attributes are set to zero. If no expression list appears and an event notice has attributes defined, they are all set to zero.

Thus the statement

```
SCHEDULE A START.JOB GIVEN COST+LABOR, DATE.REQUESTED+1
        AND STANDARD.TIME*SAFETY.FACTOR AT time expression
```

assigns the values of COST+LABOR, DATE.REQUESTED+1, and STANDARD.TIME* SAFETY.FACTOR to the attributes VALUE, DUE.DATE, and PROCESS.TIME, respectively, and sets the membership attributes of ROUTING.SET to zero.

In conformance with the conventions followed in CALL statements, the following input argument forms are equivalent in a SCHEDULE statement:

> GIVEN *expression list*
> GIVING *expression list*
> (*expression list*)

So far the discussion has relied on an intuitive understanding of how time is represented within a simulation program. We now clarify this issue.

Time is represented in SIMSCRIPT II by a REAL global variable named TIME.V. At the start of simulation, TIME.V is zero; from then on, TIME.V is increased to simulate the passage of real time. Each time an event is selected from the event sets, the value of the time attribute of the selected event, TIME.A, is used to update TIME.V. Occasionally, the value of TIME.V will be the same before and after the updating. When this is so, the events that occur during this time are considered to happen simultaneously.

The phrase

> AT *time expression*

at the end of a SCHEDULE statement states when in the future a specified event is to occur. The expression is REAL valued and can be thought of as a dimensionless, decimal-valued quantity. It is this time that is stored in the TIME.A attribute of the event notice, that is compared against other event times during next event selection, and that becomes TIME.V when the event occurs. An *absolute time* is always specified in an AT phrase. The phrase

AT 0.00

is usually used to initialize events that start off a simulation.

AT TIME.V + 1.5

illustrates an incremental form of the phrase. It states that the event being scheduled is to occur at the current simulation time plus 1.5 time units. If the basic time unit is interpreted as hours, the phrase is read, "in one and one-half hours from now"; if the basic time unit is interpreted as microseconds, the phrase is read as, "in one and one-half microseconds from now."

In most simulations, simulated time corresponds to real time, and the time units employed are minutes, hours, and days. SIMSCRIPT II assumes that the units of TIME.V are days (e.g., 1.47 is one and forty-seven one-hundredths days) and permits events to be scheduled with a *relative time* specification. The phrases

IN *arithmetic expression* DAYS
IN *arithmetic expression* MINUTES
IN *arithmetic expression* HOURS

schedule the indicated event at TIME.V plus the specified number of days, hours, or minutes. The word UNITS can be used instead of DAYS, and the word AFTER substituted for IN. Conversions are made possible by assuming that the units of TIME.V are days and having two standard conversion variables. HOURS.V and MINUTES.V are initialized by the SIMSCRIPT II system to 24 and 60, respectively, for this purpose. They can be changed by a programmer if need be. Their mode is REAL.

If time is kept in units of days, hours, and minutes, one often wants to know, not what absolute time it is, i.e., the value of TIME.V, but what day of the week, hour of the current simulated day, or minute of the current simulated hour it is. Three system functions described in Table 5-2 provide this capability.

Table 5-2

TIME CONVERSION FUNCTIONS

Name	Argument	Function Mode	Function Values	Examples
WEEKDAY.F	REAL time expression	INTEGER	1 - 7 day of current week	WEEKDAY.F(5.32) = 6
HOUR.F	REAL time expression	INTEGER	0 - 23 hour of current day	HOUR.F(5.32) = 7
MINUTE.F	REAL time expression	INTEGER	0 - 59 minute of current hour	MINUTE.F(5.32) = 40

These functions are useful for converting cumulative event times to calendar-type times during program checkout, and for making decisions based on day, hour, and minute restrictions within a program. Some examples illustrate these uses:

(1) A check to allow arrival events to occur only on weekdays or Saturday:

```
IF WEEKDAY.F(TIME.V)≤6, PERFORM START.PROCESS
                  GO AROUND
OTHERWISE RESCHEDULE THIS ARRIVAL AT TRUNC.F(TIME.V)+1.
```

(2) An event trace statement put at the head of an event routine:

```
WRITE WEEKDAY.F(TIME.V), HOUR.F(TIME.V) AND MINUTE.F(TIME.V)
   AS "EVENT ARRIVAL OCCURRED DURING DAY", I 2, "AT TIME",
   I 2, ":", I 2, /.
```

or equivalently:

```
PRINT 1 LINE WITH WEEKDAY.F(TIME.V), HOUR.F(TIME.V),
   MINUTE.F(TIME.V) AS FOLLOWS
EVENT ARRIVAL OCCURRED DURING DAY ** AT TIME **:**
```

(3) Used with a TEXT array of names as in (2):

In the preamble:

```
DEFINE WEEKDAY AS A 1-DIMENSIONAL, TEXT ARRAY
```

During initialization:

```
RESERVE WEEKDAY(*) AS 7
READ WEEKDAY
```

Data card:

```
MONDAY  TUESDAY  WEDNESDAY  THURSDAY  FRIDAY  SATURDAY
   SUNDAY
```

At the head of an event routine:

```
WRITE AS "EVENT ARRIVAL OCCURRED ON"
OUTPUT WEEKDAY(WEEKDAY.F(TIME.V))
WRITE HOUR.V(TIME.V), MINUTE.F(TIME.V) AS
" AT TIME", I 2, ":", I 2, /.
```

A third kind of event scheduling uses the words

$$\text{NOW} \qquad \text{or} \qquad \text{NEXT}$$

in statements such as

```
SCHEDULE AN ARRIVAL NOW
CAUSE A REPLAY(SITUATION, SEGMENT) NEXT
```

and   `RESCHEDULE  THIS REPAIR NEXT`

Events scheduled NOW within an event occur as soon as the event returns
control to the timing routine. They precede events having the same
event time that may have been scheduled earlier by AT or IN clauses.
If two or more events are scheduled to occur NOW, they are ranked on
their PRIORITY if they are of different classes, on their BREAK TIES
attributes if these are specified, or on a first-in, first-out basis
if no BREAK TIES attributes have been specified.

It is difficult to describe the operations of these different
SCHEDULE statements by examples that are not imbedded in a simulation
model. The reader should review this section to make sure he understands the concepts of:

> *creating an event notice*
> *scheduling an event*
> *assigning attributes to an event notice*
> *scheduling by* AT, IN *and* NOW *phrases,*

and turn to the example in Sec. *5-05* for instances of how the SCHEDULE
statement is used in simulation programs.

A twin of the SCHEDULE statement is the CANCEL statement, which
removes a specified event from its event set. It is of the form:

CANCEL THIS *event*
and   CANCEL THIS *event* CALLED *variable*

As usual, if the first form is used it is interpreted as CANCEL THIS *event* CALLED *event*. The words THE or THE ABOVE can be substituted for THIS when necessary. The event notice removed is not automatically destroyed. An attempt to CANCEL an event that has not been scheduled terminates a program with an error message.

Triggering Events Externally

Events are triggered externally by *event data cards* that are read in chronological order from external event input devices. An event card contains the name of an event, the time at which it is to occur, and optional data, which can be continued on subsequent cards. The cards are read one at a time, their information recognized and deciphered, and event notices created for the events they represent. This section deals with two issues: the operations performed by SIMSCRIPT II when external event cards are read, and the format of external event data cards.

When a START SIMULATION statement is recognized, one of the first tasks performed is reading information about the first event named on each external event device. The system schedules the first event on each device and initializes the reading mechanism for subsequent external event triggers. When an external event data card is read, the event class is recognized and the event time computed from data on the card. An event notice named *event* is created, and the event time and number of the unit from which the event card was read are stored in the TIME.A and EUNIT.A attributes of the notice.

If the event is of a class that can only be triggered externally, the event notice contains the five standard event attributes. If it can also be triggered internally, the notice conforms to the preamble declaration for the event class, i.e., it might have five words, or six, or eleven.

After TIME.A and EUNIT.A are specified, the event notice is filed in the set that corresponds to the event class. Internally and

externally generated event notices are filed together. They are distinguished by the coding of EUNIT.A. If EUNIT.A has a special code
value, usually zero, an event notice represents an internally generated
event. Otherwise it represents an externally triggered event and
EUNIT.A is the number of the device from which the external event card
was read.

The format of an external event card is:

1) event name, e.g., ARRIVAL
2) one or more blank columns
3) event time in any of three formats
4) data for the event (optional)
5) MARK.V character (normally *)

The event name and event times are read in free-form by the SIM-
SCRIPT II system. Event data are punched in whatever format a programmer finds convenient. The MARK.V symbol is used by the system to
advance properly from one set of external event data to another. As
data for an event can be on many cards, and a program can leave some
data unread, the SIMSCRIPT II system must have a way of advancing to
the start of a new set of event data when it receives a signal to
read in the next external event trigger.

The three formats in which event time can be stated are:

Decimal time units format

In this format, time is specified as a REAL valued decimal number
such as 0.0, 15.56 or 20.0. The number is interpreted as the absolute
time at which the event triggered by the event card is to occur.

Day-Hour-Minute format

In this format, three INTEGER numbers specify the day, hour of
the day, and minute of the hour at which the event triggered by the
event card is to occur. All three numbers must be present. Typical
event times in this format are: 0 0 0; 0 12 30; 2 15 37; representing
the start of simulation, 12:30 in the afternoon of the first day, and
3:37 in the afternoon of the third day, respectively. Hours are numbered from 0 to 24 and minutes from 0 to 60.

Calendar time format

In this format the day in which the event is to occur is expressed as a calendar day, and the hour and minute of the hour as INTEGER numbers. For example, the entry 1/15/69 4 30 represents 4:30 in the morning on 15 January 1969. When using the calendar date format the year can be expressed as 1969 or as 69; if the form XX is used, 19XX is assumed. Years after 1999 and before 1900 must therefore be expressed completely. Some sample external event data cards are:

```
ARRIVAL 1/15/69 05 35 *
ARRIVAL 14 05 35 *
ARRIVAL 476.2 *
ARRIVAL 4/17/1960 00 00 *
END.OF.SIMULATION 1000.0 *
SALE 5/10/66 12 00 YOYO 15 2.3 1 1 2 *
SALE 5/11/66 12 30 TOP 22 19.6 2 2 4 *
PURCHASE 500.00 MAGNETIC SOLENOID* 22.50 *
PURCHASE 750.00 RESISTOR* 1.50 *
PURCHASE 750.00 CATHODE RAY TUBE DISPLAY DEVICE* 600.00 *
```

Before the calendar format can be used, the calendar date of the start of simulation must be set to provide an origin against which calendar time specifications can be compared. This must be done before the START SIMULATION statement is executed. The origin is set by executing a statement of the form

```
CALL ORIGIN.R(INTEGER month expression,INTEGER day expression,
     INTEGER year expression)
```

as in the statements:

```
        CALL ORIGIN.R(4,22,68)
        CALL ORIGIN.R(6,2,69)
   and  CALL ORIGIN.R(FIRST.MONTH,FIRST.DAY,FIRST.YEAR)
```

Since simulation time is stored in TIME.V and in the TIME.A attribute of all event notices as a REAL number, conversions must be made between calendar specifications and the SIMSCRIPT II internal representation. The algorithm that performs this conversion assumes the origin date is a Monday, and that simulation starts at the beginning of that day (0000 hours). TIME.V is always set to zero at the start of simulation.

Four functions are provided to convert year, month, and day expressions into cumulative simulation times and vice versa. These functions are described in Table 5-3. As they all depend on a simulation time origin, ORIGIN.R must be called before they can be used.

Table 5-3

TIME CONVERSION FUNCTIONS

Name	Arguments	Function Mode	Function Values	Example
DATE.F	3 INTEGER expressions month,day,year	INTEGER	current simulation day	DATE.F(7,15,68) = 14
YEAR.F	REAL time expression	INTEGER	current year	YEAR.F(476.2) = 1969
MONTH.F	REAL time expression	INTEGER	1 - 12 current month	MONTH.F(476.2) = 10
DAY.F	REAL time expression	INTEGER	1 - 31 day of current month	DAY.F(476.2) = 21

NOTE: Time origin set by CALL ORIGIN.R(7,1,68).

DATE.F can be used as a "calendar-type" time format in statements such as SCHEDULE AN ARRIVAL AT DATE.F(MONTH,DAY,YEAR) + SERVICE. YEAR.F, MONTH.F, and DAY.F are also useful in decision and output statements.

An event notice for the next (first) event on each external event device is always filed in the event set that the data card specifies. When an externally triggered event becomes the current event, the number of the unit containing the event data is put in READ.V and control is passed to the event routine. In this routine, free-form or formatted READ statements can be used to read the data. The current input pointer, RCOLUMN.V, is positioned to read the first column after the event time. A short example illustrates this:

```
          EVENT ARRIVAL
          DEFINE X AND Y AS INTEGER VARIABLES
          READ X AND Y AS B 20, 2 I 5
               .
               .
               .
          RETURN
          END
```

External event data card:

```
00000000011111111112222222222333333333344444444445
12345678901234567890123456789012345678901234567890
ARRIVAL 525.30     1234512345
        ↑          └───┘└───┘
                        2 data fields read by ARRIVAL

        position of RCOLUMN.V when timing routine
        transfers to event ARRIVAL
```

A RETURN statement in an event routine means something different from a RETURN statement in a routine that is used as a procedure or function. For one thing, it returns to the timing routine. This corresponds to the notion that the timing routine is the main or executive program of a simulation and calls on all events. Second, if an event is called externally, before returning to the event selection mechanism the next event data card is read from the READ.V unit and scheduled according to its event time. If the first character encountered upon reading the event data is not an asterisk signaling the end of data for the previous event, data fields are skipped until an asterisk is found. A programmer is thereby guarded against inadvertently reading too little data within an event and throwing all subsequent event cards out of sequence. Normally, each event reads all the data provided to it; in no cases should it try to read more, i.e., pass into the next set of event data. When an event reads less data than is provided, the programmer can pass over it by moving to the next asterisk, or leave this task to the SIMSCRIPT II system itself.

The asterisk can also be used to preposition an external event file before the start of simulation. This is often useful when several groups of data are contained in one file, or when simulations are continued from previous runs. The following main program passes over a section of one of its external event units before starting simulation.

```
        PREAMBLE
        EXTERNAL EVENTS ARE ARRIVAL AND COMPLETION
        EXTERNAL EVENT UNITS ARE 5 AND 7
        DEFINE X AS AN ALPHA VARIABLE
           •
           •
           •
        END

        MAIN
        READ N '' THE NUMBER OF EXTERNAL EVENTS TO SKIP
        FOR I=1 TO N, DO UNTIL X="*", READ X USING 5     LOOP
        START SIMULATION
        END
```

External event data are normally input through cards or through
tapes produced by WRITE statements. Rarely are external event data
read or written with a BINARY read or write statement. The standard
SIMSCRIPT II external event mechanism reflects this state of affairs
by reading only data in printable form; a programmer with a definite
need for binary external event data must find another way of reading
such data into a SIMSCRIPT II simulation program. The following prototype program illustrates one way of doing this. It uses a routine
that reads a binary tape and schedules the events found on it internally.

```
        PREAMBLE
        EVENT NOTICES INCLUDE A1, A2,..., AN
        END
- - - - - - - - - - - - - - - - - - - - - - - - - - - - - - - -
        MAIN
        USE UNIT 6 FOR INPUT
        CALL EXTERNAL
        START SIMULATION
        STOP
        END
- - - - - - - - - - - - - - - - - - - - - - - - - - - - - - - -
        ROUTINE EXTERNAL
        DEFINE V AS AN INTEGER VARIABLE
        UNTIL V="*", READ V AS BINARY
        READ EVENT.CODE AND TIME AS BINARY
        GO TO L(EVENT.CODE)
'L(1)'  CAUSE AN A1 AT TIME
        RETURN
'L(2)'  CAUSE AN A2 AT TIME
        RETURN
           •
           •
           •
'L(N)'  CAUSE AN AN AT TIME
        RETURN
        END
```

```
- - - - - - - - - - - - - - - - - - - - - - - - - - - - - - - - - - - - - - - - -
          EVENT A1
          READ event data list AS BINARY
            •
            •
            •
          CALL EXTERNAL
          RETURN
          END
```

Within an Event Subprogram

When an event occurs, control passes from the SIMSCRIPT II timing routine to it. Before the transfer, TIME.V is set to the time for which the event had been scheduled, and a global variable with the same name as the event is set to the identification number of the event notice that triggered the event; the notice is removed from the event set.

If the event is triggered externally, READ.V is set to the number of the unit from which the triggering event card was read. This enables the event routine to read data automatically from the same unit. The following short routine demonstrates a typical externally triggered event.

```
          EVENT ARRIVAL
          CREATE A PERSON
          READ NAME(PERSON) AND DESTINATION(PERSON)
          LET ARRIVAL.TIME(PERSON) = TIME.V
          FILE PERSON IN INTRANSIT(DESTINATION(PERSON))
          RETURN
          END
```

The important things to remember about an externally triggered event are:

(1) TIME.V is set to the event time.

(2) READ.V is set to the number of the unit on which data for the event are stored.

(3) RCOLUMN.V is positioned to read the first column after the time data.

(4) When the RETURN statement is executed, data on the current external event unit are read until an * is found, and the data following the * used to schedule the next external event for that input unit. Control is then passed to the timing routine to select the next event.

If the event has been triggered internally, the event notice
that triggered the event takes on importance, as the additionally
defined attributes of the event notice, if any, are transferred to the
arguments of the event routine. The event notice is destroyed unless
a contrary instruction is given. This is done by appending the phrase
SAVING THE EVENT NOTICE to the EVENT statement, as in

EVENT ARRIVAL GIVEN NAME AND DESTINATION SAVING THE EVENT NOTICE

It is common practice to give event notices of internal events
many attributes and save them for use within an event routine and
afterward. Also, event notices can be reused. The following short
routines demonstrate these two points:

(a) Event notice used as an entity

```
EVENT ARRIVAL(NAME,DESTINATION) SAVING THE EVENT NOTICE
LET ARRIVAL.TIME(ARRIVAL)=TIME.V
FILE ARRIVAL IN LIST.OF.ARRIVALS
SCHEDULE AN ARRIVAL("WALDO",CODE3) AT TIME.V ÷ 10.40
RETURN
END
```

(b) Event notice reused to schedule another event

```
EVENT ARRIVAL(N,D) SAVING THE EVENT NOTICE
DEFINE N AS AN ALPHA VARIABLE
DEFINE D AS AN INTEGER VARIABLE
CREATE A JOB
LET IDENT(JOB)=N
LET PLACE(JOB)=D
FILE JOB IN LIST.OF.JOBS
CAUSE THIS ARRIVAL("WALDO",CODE3) AT TIME.V + 10.5
RETURN
END
```

The important things to remember about an internally triggered
event are:

(1) TIME.V is set to the event time.

(2) A global variable with the name as the event is set to the
identification number of the event notice that triggered
the event. The attributes of the event notice are available
through this variable.

(3) The event notice that triggered the event is destroyed unless
a SAVING phrase is used.

(4) When the RETURN statement is executed, control passes to
the timing routine to select the next event.

If an event is triggered both internally and externally, and has
arguments, the arguments can only be set if the event is scheduled
internally. The following routine illustrates the basic form of an
event that can occur both ways:

```
           EVENT ARRIVAL(NAME,DESTINATION)
           DEFINE NAME AND DESTINATION AS INTEGER VARIABLES
           IF EVENT IS INTERNAL, GO AROUND
           OTHERWISE READ NAME AND DESTINATION AS B 20, 2 I 10
'AROUND'   rest of event program
           RETURN
           END
```

5-03 MODELING STATISTICAL PHENOMENA

As simulation is essentially a tool for drawing statistical infer-
ences about the operations of stochastic systems, it is essential that
SIMSCRIPT II provide facilities for modeling statistical phenomena.

The heart of the SIMSCRIPT II statistical sampling package is
the function RANDOM.F,[+] which generates a stream of pseudorandom numbers between 0 and 1. Starting from an initial value, RANDOM.F generates successive REAL numbers that can be used in decisionmaking statements or as data in other statistical calculations. The numbers generated by RANDOM.F are statistically independent of one another.

RANDOM.F has one argument, an index number that picks one of
several random number streams. RANDOM.F(1) samples from random number
stream 1, RANDOM.F(5) from random number stream 5, etc. All SIMSCRIPT
II programs are initialized with 10 random number streams. The starting numbers for these streams are contained in the INTEGER system array SEED.V; traditionally, the first number in a pseudorandom number
sequence is called the seed of the sequence. As pseudorandom numbers
are generated new values are assigned to SEED.V so that it contains
the current number expressed in INTEGER form.

Should more streams be needed, a programmer can override the default condition by releasing SEED.V and specifying his own array size,
as in:

[+]The algorithm used in this function is implementation dependent.

```
MAIN
RELEASE SEED.V(*)
READ N   RESERVE SEED.V(*) AS N
READ SEED.V
START SIMULATION
END
```

RANDOM.F can be used in IF and WITH statements for decisionmaking, as in these examples:

(a)   IF RANDOM.F(1) $\leq$ TRANSITION.PROBABILITY, GO BACK
      OTHERWISE

(b)   FOR EACH CONTESTANT, DO
         IF RANDOM.F(CONTESTANT) > FINISH,
            FILE CONTESTANT IN POSSIBLE.WINNER
         ELSE
            ADD 1 TO STEPS(CONTESTANT)
      LOOP

RANDOM.F can be viewed in two ways, as generating uniformly distributed pseudorandom variables between 0 and 1, or as generating probabilities. The above examples illustrate the use of the function in the probability sense.

When one considers statistical distributions rather than probabilities, as is typical in simulation models, he is interested in a variety of them. SIMSCRIPT II provides eleven functions for generating independent, pseudorandom samples from commonly encountered statistical distributions. Each of these functions has as its arguments the parameters that describe the distribution, and a pseudorandom number stream index. Each time one of the functions is invoked, a pseudorandom number is generated from the indicated stream and an appropriate transformation made to convert the number to the correct sampling distribution. The functions, the arguments, and their properties are described in Table 5-4.

If the stream number i is negative in any of these functions, 1-RANDOM.F(ABS.F(i)), a quantity called an *antithetic variate*, is generated. Antithetic variates are used in simulation experiments to reduce the variance of estimates of simulation-generated data. Discussions of their use can be found in most good simulation texts.

These statistical functions are often used within simulation models to generate activity times. Some examples illustrate their use:

Table 5-4

STATISTICAL DISTRIBUTION FUNCTIONS

Name	Arguments	Function Mode	Function Value
BETA.F	e_1, e_2, i REAL,REAL,INTEGER	REAL	Generates a beta distributed REAL number with e_1 = power of x, e_2 = power of (1 - x) using stream i
BINOMIAL.F	i_1, e, i_2 INTEGER,REAL,INTEGER	INTEGER	Generates the INTEGER number of successes in i_1 independent trials, each having probability of success e using stream i_2
ERLANG.F	e, i_1, i_2 REAL,INTEGER,INTEGER	REAL	Generates an Erlang distributed REAL number with mean= e and k=i_1 using stream i_2
EXPONENTIAL.F	e, i REAL, INTEGER	REAL	Generates an exponentially distributed REAL number with mean=e using stream i
GAMMA.F	e_1, e_2, i REAL,REAL,INTEGER	REAL	Generates a Gamma distributed REAL number with mean=e_1 and k=e_2 using stream i
LOG.NORMAL.F	e_1, e_2, i REAL,REAL,INTEGER	REAL	Generates a lognormally distributed REAL number with mean=e_1 and standard deviation=e_2 using stream i
NORMAL.F	e_1, e_2, i REAL,REAL,INTEGER	REAL	Generates a normally distributed REAL number with mean= e_1 and standard deviation= e_2 using stream i
POISSON.F	e, i REAL,INTEGER	INTEGER	Generates a Poisson distributed INTEGER number with mean=e using stream i
RANDI.F	i_1, i_2, i_3 INTEGER,INTEGER,INTEGER	INTEGER	Generates an INTEGER number uniformly distributed between i_1 and i_2 inclusive using stream i_3
UNIFORM.F	e_1, e_2, i REAL,REAL,INTEGER	REAL	Generates a uniformly distributed REAL number between e_1 and e_2 using stream i
WEIBULL.F	e_1, e_2, i REAL,REAL,INTEGER	REAL	Generates a Weibull distributed REAL number with shape parameter=e_1 and scale parameter=e_2 using stream i

(a)   An arrival event schedules subsequent arrivals, assuming that the time between arrivals is an exponentially distributed quantity with mean of MEAN time units.

```
EVENT ARRIVAL
    statements to process an arrival
SCHEDULE AN ARRIVAL AT TIME.V + EXPONENTIAL.F(MEAN,1)
RETURN
END
```

(b)   Same as (a) but the number of units that arrive is assumed to have a Poisson distribution with mean 5.

```
EVENT ARRIVAL SAVING THE EVENT NOTICE
LET NUMBER = POISSON.F(5.0,1)
    statements to process the arrivals
SCHEDULE THIS ARRIVAL AT TIME.V + EXPONENTIAL.F(MEAN,1)
RETURN     END
```

(c)   Evaluation of π.

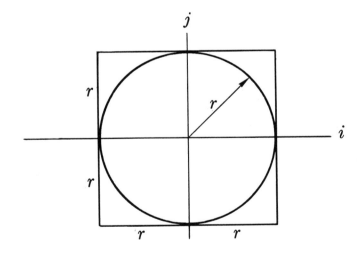

In a rectangular coordinate system the equation of a circle is $i^2 + j^2 = r^2$; that is, any point (i,j) with $i \leq r$ and $j \leq r$ and $i^2 + j^2 \leq r^2$ lies inside a circle of radius r. The area of the circle is πr^2.

A square of side 2r has an area $= 4r^2$. The ratio of the area of the circle to the area of the square is $\pi r^2 / 4r^2 = \pi/4$.

If we generate N points (i,j) within the square in a random
fashion, then some of them will fall within the circle, and some will
not. In fact, the proportion of those falling within the circle will
be approximately $\pi/4$ of all the points. If M is the total number of
those that fall within the circle, then M/N is approximately equal to
$\pi/4$. We can estimate the value of π as 4M/N. The accuracy of this
estimate improves as N increases, and is proportional to $\sqrt{N}$.

This program uses the function UNIFORM.F to generate points (i,j)
that are randomly distributed within a square of side R. It does this
by generating random numbers between 0 and R and assigning them to
i and j. The point (i,j) is somewhere inside the square.

If $i^2 + j^2 \leq r^2$ then the point also lies within the circle and 1
is added to M to tabulate this fact. This procedure is repeated N
times. Each time, a different i and j are generated and used to
determine if the point (i,j) lies within the circle.

At the end of N point generations, the approximation to π is
printed.

```
MAIN DEFINE M,K AND N AS INTEGER VARIABLES
NORMALLY, MODE IS REAL
READ R LET C=R**2
FOR K=1 TO N, DO
    LET I=UNIFORM.F(0.0,R,1)
    LET J=UNIFORM.F(0.0,R,1)
IF I**2 + J**2 ≤ C, ADD 1 TO M REGARDLESS
LOOP
PRINT 1 LINE WITH N, (4*M)/N THUS
   THE ESTIMATED VALUE OF PI AFTER *** SAMPLES IS *.*****
STOP
END
```

When sampling distributions cannot be characterized by one of the
statistical sampling functions, declarations can be given that define
table look-up sampling variables. A table look-up sampling variable
has a list of possible numerical values and their associated probabilities attached to it. It selects a sample value by generating a
random number and matching it against the possible probability values.
Table look-up variables, hereafter called RANDOM variables, are declared
in statements of the form:

DEFINE *name* AS A *mode*, RANDOM STEP VARIABLE

or   DEFINE *name* AS A RANDOM LINEAR VARIABLE

for attributes and global variables.

The first form states that sampling is done from a REAL or INTEGER valued sampling distribution in a step-like manner; the second states that sampling is performed with linear interpolation done between REAL sample values. The following illustrations describe how this is done:

Assume that a RANDOM variable, or attribute, has the following sampling distribution associated with it:

Cumulative Probability	Sample Value
0.10	1.0
0.20	2.5
0.25	3.0
0.38	9.0
0.45	11.8
0.60	20.9
0.77	30.0
0.90	33.3
0.99	50.0
1.00	66.7

Note that the cumulative probabilities in the left-hand column range from 0.0 to 1.0. Sampling is performed by generating a probability value using RANDOM.F(1), matching it with a value in column 1, and selecting an appropriate value from column 2. Since samples from RANDOM.F are always between 0.0 and 1.0, and are uniformly distributed between these extremes, the samples drawn from column 2 will be chosen randomly.

If the sampling variable is defined by the statement

DEFINE SAMPLE AS A REAL, RANDOM STEP VARIABLE

sampling is done as follows in the statement, LET X=SAMPLE:

(1) A random number is drawn from RANDOM.F(1).

(2) This random number is compared with successive cumulative probability values until a value is found that equals or exceeds it.

(3) The column 2 value associated with this cumulative probability value is returned as the value of the sample.

Examples:

(a) If the random number drawn is 0.20, SAMPLE=2.5
(b) If the random number drawn is 0.45, SAMPLE=11.8
(c) If the random number drawn is 0.65, SAMPLE=30.0
(d) If the random number drawn is 0.95, SAMPLE=50.0

RANDOM variables defined as STEP can be either INTEGER or REAL valued.

If the sampling variable is defined by the statement:

DEFINE SAMPLE AS A RANDOM LINEAR VARIABLE

sampling is done as follows:

(1) A random number is drawn from RANDOM.F(1).

(2) This random number is compared with successive cumulative probability values until a value is found that equals or exceeds it.

(3) Interpolation is done between the column 2 value associated with the stopping cumulative probability value and the column 2 value preceding it. If i represents the index of the stopping probability, $C(i)$ the probability, and $V(i)$ the sample value, the interpolation formula is

$$\text{sample} = V(i-1) + \frac{\text{RANDOM.F} - C(i-1)}{C(i) - C(i-1)} \quad [V(i) - V(i-1)]$$

That is, the percentage by which the random sample exceeds $C(i-1)$ times the difference between $V(i)$ and $V(i-1)$ is added to $V(i-1)$.

Examples:

(a) If the random number drawn is 0.20, SAMPLE=2.5
(b) If the random number drawn is 0.45, SAMPLE=11.8
(c) If the random number drawn is 0.65, SAMPLE=23.6
(d) If the random number drawn is 0.95, SAMPLE=42.6

RANDOM values defined as LINEAR can only be REAL valued. Interpolations are done in REAL arithmetic and are accurate to as many decimal places as the computer carries; rounding is done in the above examples for illustration only.

Whenever a RANDOM variable appears in a "get" sense, i.e., on the right-hand side of an equals sign, a routine that performs the above sampling procedure is executed. SIMSCRIPT II generates such routines using random number stream 1. If the programmer wants to use some other stream he does the following:

(1)   Signals the compiler not to generate a sampling routine by omitting the words STEP or LINEAR from a DEFINE statement, e.g.,

```
DEFINE SAMPLE AS A REAL, RANDOM VARIABLE
```

(2)   Writes a routine of the following format:

```
ROUTINE name(index)
RETURN WITH function(F.name(index), stream number)
END
```

function is one of three system sampling routines:

Function	Sampling Desired
RSTEP.F	REAL, RANDOM STEP
ISTEP.F	INTEGER, RANDOM STEP
LIN.F	RANDOM LINEAR

F.*name* is the first pointer of the set that contains the sampling data (see below).

index is an optional subscript or identification number.

Example:

Define SAMPLE as a RANDOM attribute of an entity JOB. The values of SAMPLE are REAL; sampling is done using LINEAR interpolation and random number stream 6.

```
TEMPORARY ENTITIES.....
  EVERY JOB HAS A SAMPLE
DEFINE SAMPLE AS A REAL, RANDOM VARIABLE
- - - - - - - - - - - - - - - - - - - - - - - - -
ROUTINE SAMPLE(JOB)
DEFINE JOB AS AN INTEGER VARIABLE
RETURN WITH LIN.F(F.SAMPLE(JOB),6)
END
```

RANDOM variables can only be read and sampled; assignments cannot be made to them.

Sampling is always done automatically; from a programmer's point of view a RANDOM variable acts like a right-handed function.

Because of the special storage assigned to RANDOM variable sample

values and probabilities, special input treatment is necessary. When
a variable defined as RANDOM appears in a free-form READ statement,
the following occurs:

(1) Pairs of free-form data values are read until a MARK.V
character appears.

(2) The first of each pair is assumed to be a probability. The
second is assumed to be a sample value.

(3) A system-defined, three-word entity, RANDOM.E, is created
for each pair. The probability value is assigned to its
first attribute, PROB.A; the sample value is assigned to
its second attribute, IVALUE.A if the variable is INTEGER,
or RVALUE.A if the variable is REAL.

(4) The entities are filed in a set having the same name as the
RANDOM variable. The third attribute in each RANDOM.E
record is a pointer named S.*variable*.

(5) F.*variable* occupies the space declared for the RANDOM variable or attribute.

Input probabilities can be cumulative or individual. If cumulative,
the last probability must be 1.0; if individual, they must sum to 1.0.
All RANDOM variables have their probabilities stored cumulatively.
If individual probability values are read, the SIMSCRIPT II system
accumulates them.[†]

The following examples illustrate how RANDOM variables are defined
and used:

(A) Definition:

DEFINE WORDS AS AN INTEGER, RANDOM STEP VARIABLE

Input statement:

READ WORDS

Input data:

0.1 10 0.2 25 0.35 40 0.55 100 0.8 150 1.0 200 *

[†]If any probability is less than 0 or greater than 1, a program
terminates with an error message. If the last probability is 1, the
probabilities are assumed to be cumulative. If the last probability
is not 1, the probabilities are summed so that they are stored cumulatively. The last probability is set to 1.

Storage of WORDS sample values:

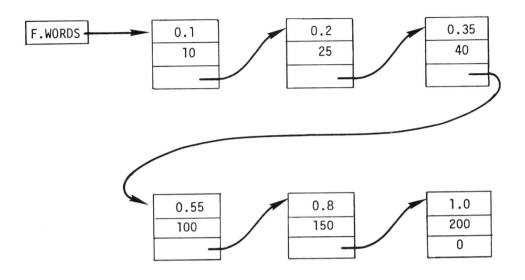

Use of WORDS:

    (a)   LET SENTENCE=WORDS

    (b)   IF WORDS GREATER THAN LIMIT, GO OUT ELSE....

In this example WORDS is a global variable. Sampling probabilities are expressed cumulatively in six pairs of sampling values; the pairs are stored in six entities in a set named WORDS.

(B)   Definition:

            DEFINE WORDS AS AN INTEGER, RANDOM STEP VARIABLE

   Input statement:

            READ WORDS

   Input data:

            0.1 10 0.1 25 0.15 40 0.2 100 0.25 150 0.2 200 *

   Storage of WORDS sample values:

            Same as in (A); individual probability values are accumulated as the data are read.

RANDOM variables cannot appear in any other form of READ statement, since input of a RANDOM variable "value" obviously means something special.

If WORDS is an array or an attribute, one can say READ WORDS(I) but not READ WORDS, if the latter statement is interpreted as a free-form array read statement. Only a single RANDOM variable data list can be read at one time. If WORDS is an attribute, READ WORDS is interpreted as READ WORDS(*entity*), using implied subscripting.

It is possible for a program to construct RANDOM variable sampling sets as well as read them. To construct a set of sampling probabilities and values for a RANDOM variable called SAMPLE, one writes:

```
FOR I=1 TO N,                    or something similar
    CREATE A RANDOM.E
    LET PROB.A=expression        or perhaps READ PROB.A
    LET RVALUE.A=expression      or perhaps READ RVALUE.A
    FILE RANDOM.E IN SAMPLE
LOOP
```

5-04 MODEL DEBUGGING AND ANALYSIS

Debugging

The most difficult task in programming, next to deciding on the architecture of a program, is debugging. This can be especially difficult in a high-level programming language like SIMSCRIPT II, where many statements are often generated for each one a programmer writes. Additional debugging difficulties are caused by dynamic storage allocation mechanisms that, by their flexibility, allow a programmer to work himself into unanticipated situations.

Much of SIMSCRIPT II that has already been described was designed with debugging in mind. The LIST statement, monitored variables, and the membership attribute all have this orientation.

Two new definitional statements, BEFORE and AFTER, make it possible for a programmer to monitor six of the more complex SIMSCRIPT II statements in an easy way. Table 5-5 names the arguments automatically

GIVEN to routines called through BEFORE and AFTER declarations.

Table 5-5

BEFORE AND *AFTER* ARGUMENTS

	BEFORE	AFTER
CREATING AN *entity*	-----[†]	Entity identifier
DESTROYING AN *entity*	Entity identifier	-----[†]
SCHEDULING AN *event*	Entity identifier, time	Entity identifier, time
CANCELING AN *event*	Entity identifier	Entity identifier
FILING IN A *set*[††]	Entity identifier, set subscripts	Entity identifier, set subscripts
REMOVING FROM A *set*[†††]	Entity identifier, set subscripts	Entity identifier, set subscripts

[†]Not allowed.

[††]In FILE BEFORE and FILE AFTER statements, the second entity identification number is not GIVEN.

[†††]By definition, the entity identification GIVEN for a REMOVE FIRST or REMOVE LAST is zero.

To use BEFORE or AFTER tracing, a programmer writes a routine having the same number of input arguments as are transmitted for the operation being monitored. Suppose it is necessary to check the subscripts for FILE and REMOVE operations in a certain doubly subscripted set. The statements to this might look like:

Preamble:

BEFORE FILING AND REMOVING FROM QUEUE, CALL CHECK

Routine:

```
ROUTINE CHECK GIVEN ENTITY, SUB1 AND SUB2
DEFINE ENTITY, SUB1 AND SUB2 AS INTEGER VARIABLES
IF 0 < SUB1 ≤ M AND 0 < SUB2 ≤ N, RETURN
OTHERWISE...
   PRINT 2 LINES WITH SUB1 AND SUB2 THUS
      INCORRECT DIMENSIONS IN SET QUEUE
         SUB1 = ****        SUB2 = ****
CALL DUMP
STOP
END
```

As shown, the routine must be written with the number of subscripts of the set being traced in mind.

The program in Sec. *5-05* illustrates various ways in which BEFORE
and AFTER statements can be used.

Analysis

The principal outputs of simulation experiments are statistical
measurements. Such quantities as the average length of a waiting
line and the percentage idle time of a machine are typical. Normally,
statements must be scattered throughout a program to collect this
information, and special summarization statements written to print it
out at the end. Aside from being tedious and time-consuming, writing
data-collection and analysis statements is a task to be avoided,
because it clutters up the operating logic of a program with statements whose only function is the collection of output information.

Two new statements, ACCUMULATE and TALLY, completely eliminate
this kind of programming. They are preamble statements that instruct
the compiler to generate automatic data collection and analysis statements at appropriate places in a program. All operating programs are
left clear of data collection and data reduction statements.

A statement of the form:

TALLY *compute list* OF *name*

performs the same computations as the COMPUTE statement[†] described
in Sec. *3-07*, but in a global rather than local manner. Each time

---

[†]Except for MAXIMUM(e) and MINIMUM(e).

name changes value, appropriate accumulations are made to collect the
statistics requested in the compute list. *Name* is the name of a
global variable or system attribute, subscripted or unsubscripted,
or an attribute of a temporary or permanent entity. If *name* is a
global variable, system attribute, or attribute of a permanent entity,
as many variables are reserved to store the statistical counters as
there are elements of *name*. If *name* is an attribute of a temporary
entity, each entity record is given statistical accumulation attributes. *Name* cannot be a function attribute, a variable monitored on
the left, or a RANDOM variable.

The preamble generates attributes and routines for each TALLY
statement. A left-hand routine that does data accumulation is always
generated for each tallied variable. The number of generated attributes and other routines varies with the statistical quantities specified. Table 5-6 states the cases in which additional routines and
attributes are generated.

Table 5-6

TALLY ACTIONS

Statistical Quantity	TALLY Action
NUMBER	Attribute generated if MEAN, VARIANCE, STD.DEV, MEAN.SQUARE, MINIMUM or MAXIMUM requested and NUMBER not requested
SUM	Attribute generated if MEAN, VARIANCE or STD.DEV requested and SUM not requested
MEAN	FUNCTION with name in TALLY list generated
SUM.OF.SQUARES	Attribute generated if MEAN.SQUARE, VARIANCE or STD.DEV requested and SUM.OF.SQUARES not requested
MEAN.SQUARE	Function with name in TALLY list generated
VARIANCE	Function with name in TALLY list generated
STD.DEV	Function with name in TALLY list generated
MAXIMUM	Uses name in TALLY list
MINIMUM	Uses name in TALLY list

Some examples illustrate the use of the TALLY statement and the attributes and functions generated by it:

(a) Use of TALLY with an unsubscripted global variable.

Preamble:

```
PREAMBLE
DEFINE X AS A REAL VARIABLE
TALLY M AS THE MEAN AND V AS THE VARIANCE OF X
END
```

Preamble generates:

(1) A left-handed monitoring routine named X, which is called whenever an assignment is made to X anywhere in the program. The function counts the number of times X changes value and accumulates the sum and sum of squares of X.

(2) Global variables A.1, A.2, A.3 to accumulate the NUMBER, SUM, and SUM.OF.SQUARES of X for the computations of MEAN and VARIANCE.

(3) Functions M and V that compute MEAN and VARIANCE from A.1, A.2, and A.3 whenever they are referenced.

Programmer uses TALLY variables in statements such as:

```
PRINT 1 LINE WITH M AND V AS FOLLOWS
  MEAN = **.***    VARIANCE = ***.***
IF V/M > SMALL.ENOUGH, GO AHEAD
OTHERWISE LIST M AND V STOP
```

(b) Use of TALLY with an attribute of a permanent entity.

Preamble:

```
PREAMBLE
PERMANENT ENTITIES....
  EVERY MAN HAS SOME CASH.IN.POCKET AND OWNS A FAMILY
     .
     .
     .
  TALLY AVERAGE.CASH AS THE MEAN AND MAX.CASH AS THE
    MAXIMUM OF CASH.IN.POCKET
     .
     .
     .
END
```

Preamble generates:

(1) A left-handed monitoring routine named CASH.IN.POCKET with one argument, the index number of the referenced entity.

(2) Attributes A.1 and A.2 to accumulate the SUM and NUMBER for each entity. A.1 and A.2 are both arrays with N.MAN elements.

(3) A function AVERAGE.CASH to compute MEAN from A.1 and A.2.

Programmer uses TALLY variables in statements such as:

```
FOR EACH MAN, LIST AVERAGE.CASH(MAN) AND MAX.CASH(MAN)
FOR EACH MAN, COMPUTE M AS THE MEAN OF AVERAGE.CASH(MAN)
```

(c) Use of TALLY with an attribute of a temporary entity.

Preamble:

```
PREAMBLE
TEMPORARY ENTITIES
  EVERY JOB HAS A NUMBER.OF.OPERATIONS
       .
       .
       .

TALLY TOTAL AS THE SUM OF NUMBER.OF.OPERATIONS
       .
       .
       .
END
```

In program —

Preamble generates:

(1) A left-handed monitoring routine named NUMBER.OF.OPERATIONS with one argument, the identification number of the referenced entity.

(2) An attribute named TOTAL for the temporary entity JOB.

Programmer uses TALLY variables in statements such as:

```
FOR EACH JOB IN QUEUE(MACHINE), DO
    IF TOTAL(JOB) > MAX.ALLOWED, GO LOOP
    OTHERWISE... REMOVE THE JOB FROM QUEUE(MACHINE)
                 PERFORM NEXT.JOB GIVEN JOB
  'LOOP'LOOP
```

From these examples one sees that certain counters, defined as variables or as attributes, are required for the statistical computations. These counters are listed in Table 5-7.

Table 5-7

COUNTERS REQUIRED FOR *TALLY* STATISTICS

Statistic	Counters
NUMBER	N, the number of samples
SUM	$\sum x_i$, the sum of the sample values
SUM.OF.SQUARES	$\sum x_i^2$, the sum of squares of the sample values
MEAN	$\sum x_i$, N
MEAN.SQUARE	$\sum x_i^2$, N
VARIANCE	$\sum x_i$, $\sum x_i^2$, N
STD.DEV	$\sum x_i$, $\sum x_i^2$, N
MAXIMUM	M, the value of the largest sample and N
MINIMUM	m, the value of the smallest sample and N

Statistical computations of a different sort are made when the word ACCUMULATE replaces TALLY. These calculations introduce time into the average, variance, and standard deviation calculations, weighting the collected observations by the length of time they have had their values. Table 5-8 compares the TALLY and ACCUMULATE computations. To do this concisely, some additional notation must be defined:

Symbol	Meaning
T_L	The simulated time an ACCUMULATED variable was set to its current value
T_0	The simulated time at which ACCUMULATION starts

ACCUMULATE and TALLY statements cannot be declared for the same variable. A programmer must decide whether a variable is time-dependent or not, normally a simple task, and specify one or the other. An example of the use of the ACCUMULATE statement is given in the following example:

Table 5-8

TALLY AND *ACCUMULATE* COMPUTATIONS

	TALLY	ACCUMULATE
NUMBER	N	N
SUM	$\sum x$	$\sum x*(TIME.V - T_L)$
SUM.OF.SQUARES	$\sum x^2$	$\sum x^2*(TIME.V - T_L)$
MEAN	SUM/NUMBER	SUM/(TIME.V - T_0)
MEAN.SQUARE	SUM.OF.SQUARES/ NUMBER	SUM.OF.SQUARES/(TIME.V - T_0)
VARIANCE	MEAN.SQUARE - MEAN	MEAN.SQUARE - MEAN
STD.DEV	SQRT.F(VARIANCE)	SQRT.F(VARIANCE)
MAXIMUM	Largest X	Largest X
MINIMUM	Smallest X	Smallest X

```
PREAMBLE
PERMANENT ENTITIES....
    EVERY MACHINE HAS A STATUS, A PROCESSING.SPEED
      AND OWNS A QUEUE
TEMPORARY ENTITIES....
    EVERY JOB HAS A VALUE AND BELONGS TO A QUEUE
ACCUMULATE AVG.QUEUE AS THE MEAN AND MAX.QUEUE AS
    THE MAXIMUM OF N.QUEUE
ACCUMULATE MACHINE.STATE AS THE MEAN OF STATUS
END
```

Let **Fig. 5-3** represent the changes in value of N.QUEUE(1) over part of a simulation run. As there are N.MACHINE queues, this is but one of several similar plots.

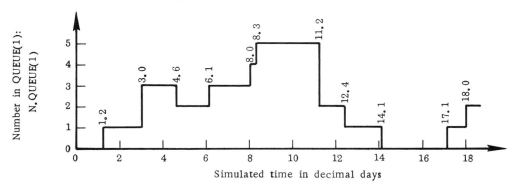

Fig. 5-3 -- A sample time-series

The following sums are maintained for the computation of AVG.QUEUE(1) (see Table 5-9).

Table 5-9

ACCUMULATE COMPUTATIONS

N.QUEUE(1) (1)	Time value began (2)	Time value ended (3)	Increment (4)=(3)-(2)	Area (5)=(1)*(4)	Sum Σ(5)
0	0	1.2	1.2	0	0
1	1.2	3.0	1.8	1.8	1.8
3	3.0	4.6	1.6	4.8	6.6
2	4.6	6.1	1.5	3.0	9.6
3	6.1	8.0	1.9	5.7	15.3
4	8.0	8.3	0.3	1.2	16.5
5	8.3	11.2	2.9	14.5	31.0
2	11.2	12.4	1.2	2.4	33.4
1	12.4	14.1	1.7	1.7	35.1
0	14.1	17.1	3.0	0	35.1
1	17.1	18.0	0.9	0.9	40.0

If, at simulated time 11.2 (TIME.V=11.2), AVG.QUEUE(1) appears in a statement such as LIST AVG.QUEUE(1), it is computed from Table 5-9 data as 31.0/11.2=2.77. That is, the average number of jobs in QUEUE(1) from TIME.V=0 to TIME.V=11.2 is 2.98. If at some time between changes in N.QUEUE(1), say at TIME.V=10, a value for AVG.QUEUE(1) is requested, it is computed as $[16.5 + 5 (10 - 8.3)]/10 = 2.5$ by the function AVG.QUEUE.

More complete information on the values attained by tallied global variables, system attributes, and attributes of permanent entities can be obtained by requesting a frequency count of the number of times a variable takes on specified ranges of values. Statements of the form:

TALLY $name_1$ (r_1 TO r_2 BY r_3) AS THE HISTOGRAM OF $name_2$

define an array $name_1$ with $(r_2 - r_1)/r_3 + 1$ elements, for each element of $name_2$. The interval between r_2 and r_1 is divided into classes r_3 units wide; if a sample value falls between r_1 and $r_1 + r_3$, a 1 is added to $name_1(1)$, if it falls between $r_1 + r_3$ and $r_1 + 2r_3$, a 1 is added to $name_2(2)$, etc. To get the average value of a variable over the life of a program and the distribution of values it has at different times, one writes:

```
PREAMBLE
DEFINE VAL AS A REAL VARIABLE
TALLY AVERAGE AS THE MEAN AND FREQ(0 TO 100 BY 5) AS THE HISTOGRAM OF VAL
END
```

Whenever VAL changes, observations are summed to provide data for computing AVERAGE, and counts are made in 21 interval counters that indicate the number of times VAL is between 0 and 5^-, 5 and 10^-, 10 and 15^-, etc. If a value is less than r_1 it is counted in the first cell; if equal to or greater than r_2 it is counted in the last cell.

Compilation of histograms for global variables, system attributes, and attributes of permanent entities generate histogram arrays of one more dimension than the variables themselves. This dimension is for the histogram array, which is reserved by the system automatically in the following places:

Sampled variable type	Place of reservation
Unsubscripted global variable or system attribute	MAIN routine
Subscripted global variable or system attribute	When it is RESERVED
Attribute of permanent entity	When it is CREATED

Histograms cannot be compiled for attributes of temporary entities.

Histograms are defined differently for variables that appear in ACCUMULATE statements. For them, what is of interest is not how many times values within a given range appear, but the total time spent in the different ranges during a simulation run. This allows the calculation of state probabilities.

Consider the following example:

```
PREAMBLE
PERMANENT ENTITIES....
EVERY MACHINE HAS A PROCESSING.SPEED AND A STATUS AND
  OWNS A QUEUE
TEMPORARY ENTITIES....
  EVERY JOB HAS A VALUE AND BELONGS TO A QUEUE
ACCUMULATE MEANQ AS THE MEAN OF N.QUEUE
ACCUMULATE STATE.PROBS(0 TO 2 BY 1) AS THE HISTOGRAM OF
  STATUS
  ''POSSIBLE VALUES OF STATUS ARE''
    ''STATUS=0  MACHINE IDLE''
    ''STATUS=1  MACHINE IDLE BUT COMMITTED''
    ''STATUS=2  MACHINE ENGAGED''
END
```

As simulation proceeds, the value of STATUS changes for the different machines. Each time STATUS changes, the length of time the machine was in that particular state is added to the proper element of the array STATE.PROBS. Since MACHINE is a permanent entity, and STATUS therefore a one-dimensional array, STATE.PROBS is a two-dimensional array. The first dimension is N.MACHINE, the second is $3 = ((2-0)/1 + 1)$.

The percentage time, and therefore the state probabilities, spent in each state by each machine can be obtained by:

```
FOR EACH MACHINE,
  PRINT 1 LINE WITH STATE.PROBS(MACHINE, 1)/TIME.V, STATE.PROBS
    (MACHINE, 2)/TIME.V, STATE.PROBS(MACHINE, 3)/TIME.V AS FOLLOWS
  PROBABILITIES OF BEING IN STATES 0,1 AND 2 ARE *.**, *.**, *.**
```

and adaptive decisions can be made within a model by statements like:

```
IF STATE.PROBS(1,1)/TIME.V < STATE.PROBS(2,1)/TIME.V, CALL PERFORM(1)
  GO TO L
ELSE CALL PERFORM(2)  GO TO L
```

Each TALLY or ACCUMULATE statement generates a routine for initializing the counters used in calculating its statistical quantities, some of which are not initially zero. These routines are named R.*name*, where *name* is the variable or attribute being tallied or accumulated. These routines can be invoked at any time by statements of the form:

RESET THE TOTALS OF *variable list*

Thus, the declarations of the preamble on p. 332 make the following statements possible:

```
RESET TOTALS OF N.QUEUE(MACHINE)
RESET TOTALS OF STATUS(5)
RESET TOTALS OF N.QUEUE(5) AND STATUS(5)
FOR EACH MACHINE, RESET TOTALS OF N.QUEUE
```

The RESET statement makes possible the preparation of reports on a cumulative or periodic basis.

In cases where both periodic and cumulative statistics are required, the TALLY, ACCUMULATE, and RESET statements can be qualified so that multiple statistical counters are used. The statement forms to do this are:

TALLY *variable* AS THE $name_1$ *statistic* OF $name_2$

TALLY *variable*(n TO n BY n) AS THE $name_1$ HISTOGRAM OF $name_2$

ACCUMULATE *variable* AS THE $name_1$ *statistic* OF $name_2$

ACCUMULATE *variable*(n TO n BY n) AS THE $name_1$ HISTOGRAM OF $name_2$

RESET $name_1$ TOTAL OF $name_2$

To generate daily, weekly, and cumulative statistics for N.QUEUE in the above preamble one would write:

```
ACCUMULATE DMEANQ AS THE DAILY MEAN, WMEANQ AS THE WEEKLY
   MEAN, MEANQ AS THE GRAND MEAN OF N.QUEUE
```

Periodic events would then print the relevant statistics daily and weekly, and reset the appropriate counters by the statements:

```
        RESET THE DAILY TOTALS OF N.QUEUE
        RESET THE WEEKLY TOTALS OF N.QUEUE
   or   RESET THE DAILY AND WEEKLY TOTALS OF N.QUEUE
```

The example of Sec. *5-05* illustrates these statements in the context of a real simulation model.

Since certain ACCUMULATE counters are nonzero, RESET must be called before dynamically allocated variables that are initialized to zero are used. A recommended procedure is to RESET immediately after every CREATE or RESERVE for a variable that is accumulated. Going back to the above preamble, the following pair of statements should appear in that part of the simulation program that allocates storage to MACHINE:

```
          CREATE EACH MACHINE
          FOR EACH MACHINE, RESET TOTALS OF N.QUEUE(MACHINE)
```

If a RESET statement does not use a *name* to qualify TOTALS, *all* counters associated with the relevant variable are initialized.

Places in a program where variables cannot be monitored for TALLY or ACCUMULATE are where array pointers are passed as array arguments. Consider the following preamble, routine, and calling statement:

```
          PREAMBLE
          DEFINE VAR AS A REAL, 1-DIMENSIONAL ARRAY
          TALLY M AS THE MEAN OF VAR
          END
- - - - - - - - - - - - - - - - - - - - - - - - - - - - - -
          MAIN
          READ N    RESERVE VAR(*) AS N
          FOR I=1 TO N, RESET TOTALS OF VAR(I)
          READ VAR
          CALL MANIPULATE GIVING VAR
          LIST VAR,M
          STOP
          END
- - - - - - - - - - - - - - - - - - - - - - - - - - - - - -
          ROUTINE TO MANIPULATE GIVEN ARRAY
          DEFINE ARRAY AS A REAL, 1-DIMENSIONAL ARRAY
          DEFINE I AS AN INTEGER VARIABLE
          FOR I=1 TO DIM.F(ARRAY(*)), WITH ARRAY(I)¬=0,
            LET ARRAY(I) = ARRAY(I)**2
          RETURN
          END
```

The values of VAR are changed within MANIPULATE but under the name ARRAY. Tallying cannot take place.

A final note on analysis has to do with minimizing storage requirements for computations of statistical quantities. The reasons for wanting to do so are brought out in the following example:

```
          PREAMBLE
          PERMANENT ENTITIES....
            EVERY MACHINE OWNS A QUEUE
          TEMPORARY ENTITIES....
            EVERY JOB BELONGS TO SOME QUEUE, AND HAS A VALUE,
              A DUE.DATE AND A LATENESS
          EVENT NOTICES INCLUDE ARRIVAL AND STOP.SIMULATION
            EVERY END.JOB HAS A JOB AND A NEXT.JOB
          TALLY AVG.LATE AS THE MEAN OF LATENESS
```

```
          END
              .
              .
              .
          EVENT END.JOB(JOB,NEXT.JOB)SAVING THE EVENT NOTICE
          DEFINE JOB AND NEXT.JOB AS INTEGER VARIABLES
          LET LATENESS=DUE.DATE(JOB)-TIME.V
          IF NEXT.JOB EQUALS 0, DESTROY THIS JOB
                               DESTROY THIS END.JOB
                               RETURN
          ELSE RESCHEDULE THIS END.JOB(NEXT.JOB,UNIFORM.F(MIN,MAX,1))
                 AT TIME.V + EXPONENTIAL.F(REAL.F(NEXT.JOB),1)
          RETURN    END
```

In this example, each temporary entity JOB has eight attributes:
P.QUEUE, S.QUEUE, M.QUEUE, VALUE, DUE.DATE, LATENESS, A.1, and A.2.
The first six names are defined in the preamble. The last two are
generated by the SIMSCRIPT II system as statistical counters for the
attribute LATENESS.

If the logic of the program does not require that the value of
LATENESS be accessible, it is possible to perform TALLY computations
on it without its being stored. One wishes to do this when he wants
the convenience of TALLY and ACCUMULATE specifications, but does not
want to waste computer words in storing unnecessary information.

Declaration of a variable as DUMMY allows it to be used in TALLY
or ACCUMULATE statements without having its value stored. Statements
such as

(a) EVERY JOB BELONGS TO SOME QUEUE,AND HAS A VALUE,
     A DUE.DATE AND A LATENESS DUMMY
(b) DEFINE GLOBAL AS A REAL, DUMMY VARIABLE

specify that variables (or attributes) are to be treated as REAL or
INTEGER numbers in all computations, but are not to be given storage
locations. If the statement (a) above were included in the sample
program on the preceding page, only seven words would be needed for
each JOB. Savings from DUMMY specifications can be significant in
programs that have large numbers of statistical variables. These
savings can be important, e.g., they might allow 8000 rather than
7000 JOB records to be processed simultaneously.

All preamble-defined variables and attributes can be declared

as DUMMY. A DUMMY variable must appear in a TALLY or ACCUMULATE statement. DUMMY attributes are declared in EVERY or THE SYSTEM statements.
DUMMY global variables are declared in DEFINE statements.

5-05   A SIMULATION EXAMPLE

The example described in this section is designed to illustrate
as much of SIMSCRIPT II as is possible in a natural problem setting.
While it contains most of the language's features, and all of the
ones important to simulation studies, it does not contain them all.
Those features not expressed are described in detail in their respective sections.

Despite the fact that the features illustrated are not exhaustive,
the example may still seem forced and artificial. This is not sur-
prising, for it is a rare program that requires the full facilities
of a rich and complex programming language. The particular example
used is an extension of the job shop model of Chapter 3 of the SIMSCRIPT
report.[†]

The plan of this section is as follows: the first subsection
describes the system that is modeled in general terms, presents the
problems the model has been designed to study, and places the rest of
the section in perspective. The next subsection contains a listing
of the complete simulation program followed by a set of data cards.
The last subsection works through the program section by section —
and occasionally, where it is warranted, statement by statement —
explaining the syntax and semantics of the statements, permitting
variations where it seems interesting, and background mechanisms
where it seems worthwhile.

The System

The system under study is shown abstractly in Fig. 5-4. It is
a shop containing N production centers, each containing M_i identical

---

[†] H. M. Markowitz, B. Hausner, and H. W. Karr, *SIMSCRIPT: A
Simulation Programming Language*, Prentice-Hall, Inc., Englewood Cliffs,
N.J., 1963.

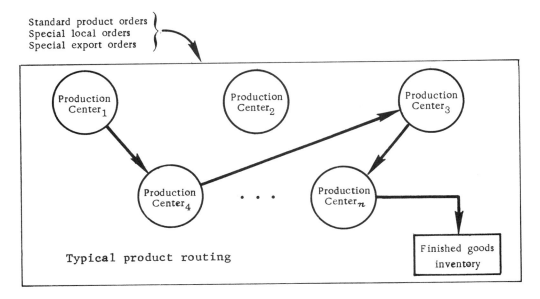

Standard product orders
Special local orders
Special export orders

Production Center$_1$

Production Center$_2$

Production Center$_3$

Production Center$_4$

· · ·

Production Center$_n$

Finished goods inventory

Typical product routing

Fig. 5-4 -- System under investigation

machines, and a finished goods inventory storage area. The shop produces P standard products for local sale and distribution, and variations of the standard products for local and export distributors. Each
product ordered goes through the shop, undergoing processing at production centers according to standard routings, production times, and product expediting procedures.

Each production center has an in-process inventory area where products in process are stored if they cannot be processed when they arrive
at the center. The production rules of the shop, in order to minimize
the value of in-process inventory, always remove partially completed
products from production center queues according to their value.

Table 5-10 shows the entity-attribute-set model of the shop and
its product line.

Aside from the attributes required to accumulate system performance
data, Table 5-10 shows the entities, attributes, and sets needed to describe the static structure of the shop. Permanent entities are used
for production centers and product descriptions, which are fixed in number. Temporary entities are used for jobs and for job processing specifications, which are variable in number. Before going on, the reader
should make sure he understands this characterization of the system.

Table 5-10

ENTITIES, ATTRIBUTES, AND SETS OF THE SHOP MODEL

Entity	Set or Attribute	Comment
PRODUCTION.CENTER	NUMBER.IDLE	The number of idle machines in a production center
	QUEUE	Each production center has a collection of in-process products, called jobs
PRODUCT	SALES.FREQUENCY	Characterizes the frequency with which orders for standard products arrive at the shop
	NAME	Identifies the product
	STRUCTURE	Each product has a list of standard operations that have to be performed
JOB		Each order is called a job
	VALUE	The dollar value of each job
	DUE.DATE	The time a job is promised to a customer
	ARRIVAL.TIME	The time at which a particular job is ordered
	EXPEDITE.FACTOR	The degree to which a job's processing can be speeded up at a production center
	ROUTING	A list of production centers through which a job has to be processed
	FINISHED.GOODS.INVENTORY	Jobs can be placed in finished goods inventory awaiting shipment
THE SYSTEM	FINISHED.GOODS.INVENTORY	Jobs are placed in finished goods inventory if finished before their due date
OPERATION	MACHINE.DESTINED	The production center at which a job has to be processed
	CODE	A number representing a particular processing operation
	PROCESS.TIME	The length of time it takes to perform a processing task
	STRUCTURE	The standard production list on which different production centers appear
	ROUTING	The processing operations required for a particular job

The shop operates roughly as follows. When orders for standard
products come into the shop, a standard production sequence is copied
from an order book onto a job's production routing tag. The job is
sent to the first production center, where it is worked on if a machine
is free. If no machines are available to process the job, it is put
in a work-in-process queue until a machine becomes available. When
a job finishes processing on a machine, its routing tag is examined,
and the job is sent on either to another processing center or to
finished goods inventory.

The preamble declarations for the temporary and permanent entities specify the items of information that are needed to model the
shop. These are: relevant processing center and job characteristics,
and waiting line disciplines.

The dynamic structure of the shop is captured in the two events,
SALE and END.OF.PROCESS. Two other events, WEEKLY.REPORT and
END.OF.SIMULATION, serve only to print system performance data and
stop the simulation. The event SALE is set up to happen both internally and externally. When triggered internally, SALE represents
either a local or export sale of a standard product. Two external event
data tapes are provided to supply special order information. In SALE,
jobs are assigned to machines and the system state is changed to
reflect such assignments. Whenever a job is assigned to a machine
an event END.OF.PROCESS is scheduled to terminate the processing,
make the machine available for another job, and pass the job on for
further processing or shipment.

BREAK TIES and PRIORITY statements are used in the preamble to
ensure that system events occur in the correct order when simulation
time ties occur.

At the end of the preamble, BEFORE, TALLY, ACCUMULATE, and
DEFINE statements finish off the program specification. The BEFORE
statements, and the routines associated with them, are used in one
instance to catch programming errors. The DEFINE statements make
declarations that are necessary, but were not made before. The TALLY
and ACCUMULATE statements collect information on the performance of
the simulated system.

The simulation is being run to determine how many machines are needed at each production center to provide "adequate" customer service. To study the effects of varying the number of machines in each center, a TALLY statement looks at the length of time jobs spend in the shop, and an ACCUMULATE statement looks at the waiting lines that build up at the various production centers. Some number of machines will be chosen that balances the cost of degraded customer service with the costs of additional machines.

The program listing that follows has been written and annotated to make it as readable as possible. Those statements that are not clear from the program itself are clarified in the section following the listing.

```
..          SAMPLE SIMSCRIPT II SIMULATION PROGRAM
..               A JOB SHOP SIMULATION


PREAMBLE
NORMALLY MODE IS INTEGER AND DIMENSION IS 0

PERMANENT ENTITIES.....
     EVERY PRODUCT HAS A SALES.FREQUENCY AND A NAME AND OWNS A STRUCTURE
          DEFINE SALES.FREQUENCY AS A REAL RANDOM LINEAR VARIABLE
          DEFINE NAME AS AN ALPHA VARIABLE
     EVERY PRODUCT,PRODUCT HAS A PRODUCT.SALES(*/2)
     EVERY PRODUCTION.CENTER HAS A (MAX.IN.QUEUE(1/2),MAX.QUEUE(2/2)) IN ARRAY 1,
        A (WNUM(1/2), MNUM(2/2)) IN ARRAY 2, A WSUM, A MSUM, A NUMBER.IDLE
        AND OWNS A QUEUE
          DEFINE NUMBER.IDLE AS A VARIABLE MONITORED ON THE LEFT

TEMPORARY ENTITIES.....
     EVERY JOB HAS A VALUE IN WORD 2, A DUE.DATE, AN ARRIVAL.TIME,
        AN EXPEDITE.FACTOR FUNCTION, MAY BELONG TO A QUEUE, OWNS A ROUTING
        AND MAY BELONG TO THE WAITING.SET
          DEFINE EXPEDITE.FACTOR AS A REAL FUNCTION
          DEFINE VALUE, DUE.DATE AND ARRIVAL.TIME AS REAL VARIABLES
          DEFINE ROUTING AS A FIFO SET WITHOUT P AND N ATTRIBUTES
          DEFINE QUEUE AS A SET RANKED BY HIGH VALUE
     EVERY OPERATION HAS A ( CODE(1/2) AND MACHINE.DESTINED(2/2) ) IN WORD 1
        AND A PROCESS.TIME AND BELONGS TO A STRUCTURE AND A ROUTING
          DEFINE STRUCTURE AS A SET RANKED BY LOW CODE WITHOUT M ATTRIBUTE
                   AND WITHOUT R ROUTINES
          DEFINE PROCESS.TIME AS A REAL VARIABLE


EVENT NOTICES INCLUDE WEEKLY.REPORT
     EVERY SALE HAS A PRODUCT.TYPE, A PRICE AND A PRIORITY
          DEFINE PRICE AS A REAL VARIABLE
     EVERY END.OF.PROCESS HAS AN ITEM AND A PRODUCER

BREAK SALE TIES BY HIGH PRICE THEN BY LOW PRIORITY
EXTERNAL EVENTS ARE END.OF.SIMULATION AND SALE
EXTERNAL EVENT UNITS ARE LOCAL.SALES AND EXPORT.SALES
PRIORITY ORDER IS END.OF.PROCESS, SALE, WEEKLY.REPORT AND END.OF.SIMULATION

BEFORE FILING AND REMOVING FROM QUEUE CALL QUEUE.CHECK
BEFORE DESTROYING JOB, CALL STAY.TIME


               DEFINE STAY AS A REAL DUMMY VARIABLE
TALLY AVG.STAY AS THE WEEKLY MEAN, VAR.STAY AS THE WEEKLY VARIANCE, SUM.STAY AS
          THE WEEKLY SUM, SUM.SQUARES.STAY AS THE WEEKLY SUM.OF.SQUARES, AND
          NUM.STAY AS THE WEEKLY NUMBER OF STAY
ACCUMULATE WSUM AS THE WEEKLY SUM, WNUM AS THE WEEKLY NUMBER, AVG.QUEUE AS THE
          WEEKLY MEAN, MAX.QUEUE AS THE WEEKLY MAXIMUM AND FREQ(0 TO 25 BY 1)
          AS THE WEEKLY HISTOGRAM OF N.QUEUE
ACCUMULATE MSUM AS THE MONTHLY SUM, MNUM AS THE MONTHLY NUMBER, AVG.IN.QUEUE AS
          THE MONTHLY MEAN, MAX.IN.QUEUE AS THE MONTHLY MAXIMUM OF N.QUEUE


THE SYSTEM OWNS A FINISHED.GOODS.INVENTORY
DEFINE FINISHED.GOODS.INVENTORY AS A SET RANKED BY DUE.DATE
DEFINE LOCAL TO MEAN DEFINE I,J,K,L,M AND N AS SAVED INTEGER VARIABLES
DEFINE WEEK TO MEAN *HOURS.V*7 HOURS
DEFINE PRIORITY.FREQUENCY AS A 2-DIMENSIONAL ARRAY
DEFINE TITLE AS A TEXT VARIABLE
DEFINE WEEK.COUNTER AND TAPE.FLAG AS INTEGER VARIABLES
DEFINE AVERAGE AS A REAL FUNCTION WITH 1 ARGUMENT
END
```

```
MAIN
'INITIALIZE'  PERFORM INITIALIZATION
LET BETWEEN.V='TRACE'     START SIMULATION


'' PERFORM NEXT EXPERIMENT ''
FOR EACH JOB IN FINISHED.GOODS.INVENTORY, DO
      REMOVE THE JOB FROM FINISHED.GOODS.INVENTORY
      DESTROY THE JOB
LOOP

FOR EACH PRODUCTION.CENTER,
FOR EACH JOB IN QUEUE, DO
      FOR EACH OPERATION IN ROUTING, DO
            REMOVE THE OPERATION FROM ROUTING
            DESTROY THE OPERATION
      LOOP
      REMOVE THE JOB FROM QUEUE
      DESTROY THE JOB
LOOP

FOR EACH PRODUCT, DO
      FOR EACH OPERATION IN STRUCTURE, DO
            REMOVE THE OPERATION FROM THE STRUCTURE
            DESTROY THE OPERATION
      LOOP
ALSO FOR EACH RANDOM.E IN SALES.FREQUENCY, DO
            REMOVE THE RANDOM.E FROM SALES.FREQUENCY
            DESTROY THE RANDOM.E
LOOP

RELEASE NAME, F.STRUCTURE,L.STRUCTURE, N.STRUCTURE, F.SALES.FREQUENCY,
    PRODUCT.SALES, NUMBER.IDLE, F.QUEUE, L.QUEUE, N.QUEUE, MAX.IN.QUEUE,
    MAX.QUEUE, WSUM, MSUM, WNUM, MNUM
RELEASE PRIORITY.FREQUENCY
ERASE TITLE

RESET TOTALS OF STAY
FOR EACH PRODUCTION.CENTER, RESET TOTALS OF N.QUEUE

LET WEEK.COUNTER=0
WRITE AS "*****",/
LET TAPE.FLAG=0

'' REUSE EXTERNAL EVENTS IN NEXT EXPERIMENT
REWIND LOCAL.SALES AND EXPORT.SALES

GO INITIALIZE
STOP   END
```

```
ROUTINE FOR INITIALIZATION
LOCAL
DEFINE PF TO MEAN PRIORITY.FREQUENCY
DEFINE SF TO MEAN SALES.FREQUENCY
DEFINE CHECK AS AN ALPHA VARIABLE
LET EOF.V=1
INPUT TITLE
IF EOF.V=2, PRINT 1 LINE AS FOLLOWS
            END OF DATA HIT
            STOP
ELSE
```

```
READ N.PRODUCTION.CENTER
    CREATE EVERY PRODUCTION.CENTER
    FOR EACH PRODUCTION.CENTER, READ NUMBER.IDLE(PRODUCTION.CENTER)

READ N.PRODUCT
    CREATE EVERY PRODUCT
    RESERVE PRIORITY.FREQUENCY(*,*) AS N.PRODUCT BY *
    FOR EACH PRODUCT, DO
            READ NAME(PRODUCT)
            READ SALES.FREQUENCY(PRODUCT)
            RESERVE PRIORITY.FREQUENCY(PRODUCT,*) AS PRODUCT
            FOR I=1 TO PRODUCT, READ PRIORITY.FREQUENCY(PRODUCT,I)
            UNTIL MODE IS ALPHA, DO THIS.....
                    CREATE AN OPERATION
                    FILE THE OPERATION IN STRUCTURE
                    READ CODE, MACHINE.DESTINED AND PROCESS.TIME
            LOOP
            SKIP 2 FIELD
            CAUSE A SALE IN SF HOURS
            LET PRODUCT.TYPE=PRODUCT
            LET PRICE=PRODUCT*RANDOM.F(1)
            LET PRIORITY=PF(PRODUCT, TRUNC.F(PRICE)+1)
    LOOP

READ LOCAL.SALES, EXPORT.SALES AND SAVE.TAPE

READ MONTH, DAY AND YEAR    CALL ORIGIN.R(MONTH,DAY AND YEAR)

READ CHECK   IF CHECK EQUALS "OK", CALL REPORT   RETURN
             OTHERWISE  PRINT 1 LINE AS FOLLOWS
    EITHER TOO MUCH DATA OR DATA HAS BEEN READ INCORRECTLY
STOP   END




EVENT SALE(PRODUCT,PRICE,PRIORITY) SAVING THE EVENT NOTICE
DEFINE SF TO MEAN SALES.FREQUENCY
LOCAL
IF SALE IS EXTERNAL, READ PRODUCT, PRICE AND PRIORITY AS B 30,I 5, D(10,3), I 5
REGARDLESS  ADD 1 TO PRODUCT.SALES(PRODUCT, TRUNC.F(PRICE)+1))
CREATE A JOB
    LET VALUE=PRICE
    LET DUE.DATE=TIME.V + PRICE + PRIORITY
    LET ARRIVAL.TIME=TIME.V
IF SALE IS INTERNAL,
    FOR EACH PIECE OF STRUCTURE, FILE PIECE IN ROUTING  GO TO JOB
'' PROCESS SPECIAL ORDERS
OTHERWISE UNTIL MODE IS ALPHA, DO THE FOLLOWING...
                READ N
                FOR EACH  PIECE IN STRUCTURE WITH  CODE(PIECE) = N,
                FIND THE FIRST CASE, IF NONE GO TO LOOP
                FILE PIECE IN ROUTING
    'LOOP'  LOOP
'JOB'  NOW ATTEND.TO.JOB
IF SALE IS EXTERNAL, DESTROY THE SALE   RETURN
OTHERWISE.....
    SCHEDULE THE SALE(PRODUCT, PRODUCT*RANDOM.F(1), PRIORITY.FREQUENCY(PRODUCT,
             TRUNC.F(PRICE)+1) IN SF HOURS
RETURN   END




ROUTINE TO ATTEND.TO.JOB
LET PRODUCTION.CENTER=MACHINE.DESTINED(F.ROUTING(JOB))
IF NUMBER.IDLE IS POSITIVE,
    SUBTRACT 1 FROM NUMBER.IDLE    PERFORM ALLOCATION
    RETURN
OTHERWISE   FILE JOB IN QUEUE   RETURN
END




ROUTINE FOR ALLOCATION
REMOVE THE FIRST OPERATION FROM THIS ROUTING
SCHEDULE AN END.OF.PROCESS GIVEN JOB AND PRODUCTION.CENTER IN
    PROCESS.TIME*EXPEDITE.FACTOR HOURS
RETURN   END
```

```
ROUTINE EXPEDITE.FACTOR
IF TIME.V IS GREATER THAN DUE.DATE RETURN WITH 0.5  ELSE
RETURN WITH MIN.F((DUE.DATE-TIME.V)/PROCESS.TIME,1)
END



UPON END.OF.PROCESS GIVEN JOB AND PRODUCTION.CENTER
IF ROUTING IS EMPTY, IF DUE.DATE <= TIME.V,
                        DESTROY THIS JOB   GO TO PC
                    ELSE FILE THIS JOB IN FINISHED.GOODS.INVENTORY  GO TO PC
OTHERWISE  CALL ATTEND.TO.JOB
'PC'
IF QUEUE IS EMPTY,
    ADD 1 TO NUMBER.IDLE   RETURN
ELSE  REMOVE THE FIRST JOB FROM QUEUE
PERFORM ALLOCATION  RETURN
END



EVENT FOR WEEKLY.REPORT SAVING THE EVENT NOTICE
RESCHEDULE THIS WEEKLY.REPORT IN 1 WEEK
ADD 1 TO WEEK.COUNTER
NOW REPORT
RESET WEEKLY TOTALS OF STAY
FOR EACH PRODUCTION.CENTER, RESET WEEKLY TOTALS OF N.QUEUE
IF MOD.F(WEEK.COUNTER,4)=0, FOR EACH PRODUCTION.CENTER, RESET MONTHLY TOTALS
    OF N.QUEUE   ELSE
RETURN   END



EVENT FOR END.OF.SIMULATION
FOR I=1 TO EVENTS.V, FOR EACH NOTICE IN EV.S(I), DO
    REMOVE THE NOTICE FROM EV.S(I)
    DESTROY THE NOTICE
LOOP
NOW REPORT
LIST PRODUCT.SALES
RETURN   END



ROUTINE FOR QUEUE.CHECK GIVEN ENTITY AND I
LOCAL
IF 1 LE I LE N.PRODUCTION.CENTER, RETURN
OTHERWISE... PRINT 1 LINE WITH I AS FOLLOWS
    STOPPED TRYING TO REFERENCE QUEUE(     *)
TRACE  STOP  END



ROUTINE FOR STAY.TIME GIVEN JOB
LET STAY=TIME.V - ARRIVAL.TIME(JOB)
RETURN   END



ROUTINE TO TRACE
LOCAL
IF FINISHED.GOODS.INVENTORY IS EMPTY, GO AROUND
ELSE  FOR EACH JOB IN FINISHED.GOODS.INVENTORY UNTIL DUE.DATE > TIME.V, DO
        REMOVE THE JOB FROM FINISHED.GOODS.INVENTORY  DESTROY THE JOB
        LOOP
'AROUND'
GO TO END.OF.PROCESS, SALE, WEEKLY.REPORT AND END.OF.SIMULATION PER EVENT.V
'END.OF.PROCESS'  WRITE ITEM, PRODUCER, TIME.V AS "ITEM", I 5, "STOPPED",
                    "PROCESSING ON MACHINE", I 5, " AT TIME=",D(10,3), /
                    RETURN
'SALE'  WRITE TIME.V, PRODUCT.TYPE, PRICE AND PRIORITY AS "SALE OF TYPE", I 3, "
            " PRODUCT AT TIME=", D(10,3), " FOR $", D(6 2), " PRIORITY=", I 3,
            /    RETURN
'WEEKLY.REPORT'
'END.OF.SIMULATION'
RETURN
END
```

```
LEFT ROUTINE NUMBER.IDLE(M)
DEFINE J AS A SAVED, 2-DIMENSIONAL ARRAY
DEFINE K AS A SAVED, 1-DIMENSIONAL ARRAY
ENTER WITH N
IF TAPE.FLAG=0,   LET TAPE.FLAG=1
                  RELEASE J AND K
                  RESERVE K(*) AS N.PRODUCTION.CENTER
                  RESERVE J(*,*) AS 100 BY N.PRODUCTION.CENTER
REGARDLESS  ADD 1 TO K(M)
LET J(K(M),M)=N
IF K(M)=100, WRITE M AS I 3 USING SAVE.TAPE
             FOR I=1 TO 100, WRITE J(I,M) AS I 3 USING SAVE.TAPE
             WRITE AS / USING SAVE.TAPE
REGARDLESS   MOVE FROM N
RETURN  END



ROUTINE TO REPORT
LOCAL
IF TIME.V=0,
   START NEW PAGE  ''AND''  OUTPUT TITLE
   SKIP 2 OUTPUT LINES
   PRINT 3 LINES AS FOLLOWS
                  P R O D U C T    D A T A
        NAME          SALES FREQUENCY        PRODUCTION SEQUENCE
                        PROB.    VALUE    CODE  CNTR   TIME
   FOR EACH PRODUCT, DO
      LET I=F.SALES.FREQUENCY
      LET J=F.STRUCTURE
      PRINT 1 LINE WITH NAME, PROB.A(I), RVALUE.A(I), CODE(J),
                    MACHINE.DESTINED(J) AND PROCESS.TIME(J) THUS
         ****            *.**    *.**      **    **    *.**
      IF I¬=0, LET I=S.SALES.FREQUENCY(I)  ELSE
      IF J¬=0, LET J=S.STRUCTURE(J)  ELSE
      IF I=0 AND J=0, GO TO 'LOOP'  ELSE
      IF I¬=0 AND J=0, PRINT 1 LINE WITH PROB.A(I) AND RVALUE.A(I) THUS
                               *.**    *.**
      ELSE IF I=0 AND J¬=0, PRINT 1 LINE WITH CODE(J), MACHINE.DESTINED(J),
                                       AND PROCESS.TIME(J) THUS
                               **      **    *.**
      ELSE IF I¬=0¬=J, PRINT 1 LINE WITH PROB.A(I), RVALUE.A(I), CODE(J),
                               MACHINE.DESTINED(J) AND PROCESS.TIME(J) THUS
                         *.**      *.**       **    **    *.**
   'LOOP' LOOP
   SKIP 2 OUTPUT LINES
   PRINT 2 LINES AS FOLLOWS
                P R O D U C T I O N   C E N T E R   D A T A
                   CENTER      NUMBER OF MACHINES
   FOR EACH PRODUCTION.CENTER, PRINT 1 LINE WITH PRODUCTION.CENTER AND
                            NUMBER.IDLE THUS
             **                   **
   SKIP 2 OUTPUT LINES
   PRINT 2 LINES AS FOLLOWS
                   I N I T I A L    E V E N T S
                     EVENT TYPE       TIME
      FOR I=1 TO EVENTS.V, FOR EACH J IN EV.S(I),
      PRINT 1 LINE WITH I AND TIME.A(I) THUS
                       *             **.**
REGARDLESS.....
START NEW PAGE
PRINT 1 LINE AS FOLLOWS
PRINT 3 LINES LIKE THIS.....
              W E E K L Y   R E P O R T


PRINT 2 LINES WITH AVG.STAY AND VAR.STAY AS FOLLOWS
   JOB STAY STATISTICS ARE:  AVERAGE STAY= *.**
                            VARIANCE    = *.**
SKIP 3 OUTPUT LINES
BEGIN REPORT
BEGIN HEADING
PRINT 2 LINES AS FOLLOWS
     PRODUCTION CENTER QUEUEING REPORT
       CNTR     AVG. QUEUE    MAX. QUEUE
END  ''HEADING
FOR EACH PRODUCTION.CENTER, PRINT 1 LINE WITH PRODUCTION.CENTER,
                         AVG.QUEUE AND MAX.QUEUE THUS
        **            *.**            *
END  '' REPORT
```

```
PRINT 1 LINE WITH AVERAGE(AVG.QUEUE(*)) LIKE THIS
    OVERALL AVERAGE QUEUE LENGTH OF ALL QUEUES IS  *.**
SKIP 3 OUTPUT LINES
FOR EACH PRODUCTION.CENTER, DO
    BEGIN REPORT PRINTING FOR I=1 TO 25 IN GROUPS OF 5
    BEGIN HEADING
      PRINT 1 LINE WITH PRODUCTION.CENTER LIKE THIS
    HISTOGRAM OF QUEUE LENGTH FOR PRODUCTION CENTER  **
    END '' HEADING
      PRINT 1 LINE WITH A GROUP OF FREQ(PRODUCTION.CENTER,2) FIELDS THUS
        *     *     *     *     *
    END '' REPORT
LOOP
IF MOD.F(WEEK.COUNTER,4)¬=0, RETURN
OTHERWISE...  START NEW PAGE
PRINT 1 LINE AS FOLLOWS
        M O N T H L Y   R E P O R T
SKIP 2 OUTPUT LINES
SKIP 3 OUTPUT LINES
BEGIN REPORT
BEGIN HEADING
PRINT 2 LINES AS FOLLOWS
      PRODUCTION CENTER QUEUEING REPORT
        CNTR      AVG. QUEUE     MAX. QUEUE
END  ''HEADING
FOR EACH PRODUCTION.CENTER, PRINT 1 LINE WITH PRODUCTION.CENTER,
                         AVG.IN.QUEUE AND MAX.IN.QUEUE THUS
        **          *.**          *
END  '' REPORT
PRINT 1 LINE WITH AVERAGE(AVG.IN.QUEUE(*)) LIKE THIS
    OVERALL AVERAGE QUEUE LENGTH OF ALL QUEUES IS  *.**
RETURN
END



ROUTINE FOR AVERAGE GIVEN ARRAY
LOCAL
DEFINE ARRAY AS A 1-DIMENSIONAL ARRAY
FOR J=1 TO DIM.F(ARRAY(*)), COMPUTE M AS THE MEAN OF ARRAY(J)
RETURN WITH M
END
```

SAMPLE DATA FOR SEVERAL JOB SHOP EXPERIMENTS USING THE LEVEL 5, SECTION 5.05
JOB SHOP SIMULATION PROGRAM.....TITLES, AS SHOWN, CAN EXTEND OVER SEVERAL CARDS
AND ARE ENDED BY A MARK.V CHARACTER   *
5   10 10 5 5 3
3
TOP   0.25 10.0   0.50 15.0   0.75 20.0   1.00 25.0
1   1 1 0.2   2 2 0.5   3 4 0.3*
YOYO   0.10 3.7   0.28 5.6   0.39 7.2   0.60 9.2   0.81 10.6   0.95 15.2
          1.00 20.0*
1 2   15 1 1.2   16 3 0.8   17 5 0.2   18 2 1.5*
DOLL   0.1 1.0   0.2 2.0   0.2 3.0   0.4 4.0   0.1 5.0
1 2 3   20 5 4.2   21 4 5.6   22 1 3.2   23 5 2.00*

1   2   3
7 1 1968
OK
THIS IS A TITLE CARD FOR THE SECOND SIMULATION EXPERIMENT OF THE SERIES
DATA CARDS FOR THIS EXPERIMENT WILL HAVE THE SAME FORMAT AS THOSE OF THE
PREVIOUS EXPERIMENT AND WILL END WITH AN "OK" CARD   *

THE FOLLOWING CARDS ARE SAMPLES OF THE DATA CARDS PUNCHED FOR ONE OF THE TWO
EXTERNAL EVENTS TAPES   .... THIS IS JUST A SAMPLE FROM THE TAPE

SALE 7/2/68   12 00   2 1.98 1   15 17 18 *
SALE 7/2/68   13 25   1 0.97 1   1 2 3 *
SALE 7/3/68   01 30   2 1.50 2   16 17 18 *
SALE 7/3/68   07 00   3 2.50 1   20 22 23 *
END.OF.SIMULATION 9/1/69   12 00 *

Comments on the Simulation Program

The program is arranged functionally and is discussed as it appears. The order of the program is: preamble, main routine, initialization, events and routines of the simulation model, routines for monitoring, debugging, and analysis.

PREAMBLE

The preamble is divided into seven sections: permanent entities, temporary entities, event notices, event control, debugging, analysis, and miscellaneous declarations. Most simulation programs are organized this way.

One compound and two simple permanent entities are declared. The special features of each are:

- PRODUCT has a RANDOM attribute and an ALPHA attribute, each of which requires definition in a DEFINE statement.
- PRODUCT.SALES, the single attribute of the compound entity PRODUCT,PRODUCT is intrapacked to conserve storage space.
- PRODUCTION.CENTER has two pairs of attributes that are packed in the same array, and one attribute that is monitored. The packed attributes use field-packing, equivalence, and array specification. The monitored attribute requires an additional DEFINE statement.

PRODUCT.SALES could just as easily have been defined as a global array or as a two-dimensional system attribute. As a global array, however, it could not have been packed. As a system attribute, it would not be eligible for implied subscripting.

Two temporary entities are declared. The special features of each are:

- JOB has one attribute placed in a specific word in its entity record, and has a function attribute. The function attribute requires a DEFINE statement to declare its mode.
- Two sets in which a JOB participates have their implied properties modified by DEFINE statements.
- Two attributes of OPERATION are packed in the first word of the entity record.
- A set to which an OPERATION belongs has its removal routines deleted by a DEFINE statement.

Three event notices are declared. The special features of each are:

- WEEKLY.REPORT has no attributes and neither owns nor belongs to sets other than the standard one defined for all event notices.

- One event, SALE, breaks ties among competing event notices through a BREAK TIES declaration. The other internal events break ties, if they occur, on a first-come, first-served basis.

Two external event types, END.OF.SIMULATION and SALE, are declared. Two input devices are declared as suppliers of external event triggers. The priority order of the four event types is declared in a PRIORITY statement.

Two BEFORE statements are used. Each states that a certain routine is to be called before a specified action takes place. The arguments to these routines are not stated, but implied. (See Table 5-5.)

One TALLY and two ACCUMULATE statements are used. The special features of each are:

- The TALLY statement compiles statistics for a DUMMY variable. This variable is declared in a separate DEFINE statement.

- All of the statistical counters used in the TALLY and ACCUMULATE statements are defined so they can be released. If they were not named, they would be given local names such as A.1 and A.2.

- FREQ is a two-dimensional array. The first dimension is an entity index. The variable for which it accumulates a histogram is an attribute of PRODUCTION.CENTER. The second dimension is the histogram index and is an integer between 1 and 26.

The remaining statements are self-explanatory. They

- Declare a system-owned set.

- Use DEFINE TO MEAN statements to create shorthand notation.

- Declare four global variables: a two-dimensional array, two INTEGER variables and a TEXT variable.

- Declare a function and specify the number of arguments it must always have.

MAIN PROGRAM

The main routine has three functions: it initializes the model so simulation can start, it transfers control to the timing routine when initialization is complete, and it resets the entire system to an "empty" condition at the end of a simulation run so another experiment can begin.

Initialization takes place in the routine INITIALIZATION, which is called by MAIN. After initialization, the SUBPROGRAM system variable BETWEEN.V is set to the routine name 'TRACE', indicating that this routine is to be called before each event of the simulation.[†] Simulation is then begun by the START SIMULATION statement that removes the first event from the sets EV.S ( ) and transfers to it. Simulation proceeds until an END.OF.SIMULATION event occurs. This event, aside from its obvious task of reporting the results of the simulation experiment, empties the events sets, EV.S ( ). When END.OF.SIMULATION returns control to the timing routine, the lack of scheduled events causes control to pass to the statement after START SIMULATION. In many simulations this will be STOP. In this example, it is the first of many statements that release and destroy all permanent and temporary entities for the reinitialization of a new experiment. After these statements have been executed, all the memory structures set up by the previous experiment have been erased.

In performing this erasure, the system set FINISHED.GOODS.INVENTORY, and the sets owned by all the permanent and temporary entities, are emptied and their members destroyed. Finally, all attributes of permanent entities are released. Special features to notice are:

- The PRODUCTION.CENTER loop, in which operations owned by jobs that are owned by production centers are successively removed and destroyed.

- The RANDOM variable SALES.FREQUENCY is treated as a set when it is emptied.

- All permanent entity attributes, including set pointers and statistical accumulators, are released.

In many programs, so extensive a reinitialization process will not be necessary. For example, it is usually sufficient to zero out all attribute values and empty all sets. This example has been written to illustrate what seems to be the worst case.

[†]See Sec. 5-06.

In situations where single simulation runs are made and no re-initialization is necessary, the initialization routine can be released and its space regained for array and entity storage. The following routine shows how this is done.

Add to preamble:

    DEFINE INITIALIZATION AS A RELEASABLE ROUTINE

Use this routine:

    MAIN
    PERFORM INITIALIZATION
    RELEASE INITIALIZATION
    START SIMULATION
    STOP   END

PROGRAM INITIALIZATION

INITIALIZATION starts with some declarations. The first takes advantage of the DEFINE TO MEAN statement of the preamble to define some local INTEGER variables I, J, K, L, M, and N. The next two statements are local DEFINE TO MEAN declarations that create a shorthand notation for two lengthy variable names. The last declaration declares a local ALPHA variable that is used to verify that all input data have been read.

Since a mistake may have been made in setting up a simulation run, EOF.V is set to 1 to give the program control over the actions taken when the end of the input data file is reached. If, when reading TITLE, an end-of-file is encountered, EOF.V is set to 2 and this fact is picked up in the following IF statement.

A sequence of simulation experiments can also be stopped this way. When all the data for a sequence of runs are exhausted, these statements will stop the program.

The INPUT statement reads characters from the current input unit READ.V until an asterisk, the MARK.V default symbol, is reached. A typical simulation TITLE card might be:

    SIMULATION RUN NO. 1 JOB SHOP WITH 10 CENTERS   *

If some symbol other than * is to be used as a TEXT terminator, a statement such as LET MARK.V="?" is put at the head of INITIALIZATION.

A value that is the number of production centers is then read, and used to reserve the arrays that hold the attributes of PRODUCTION. CENTER. This value is also used to read in the number of machines in each production center, which are all idle at the start of simulation.

A similar process then takes place for PRODUCT. It is more complex in that a richer variety of data structures is associated with PRODUCT than with PRODUCTION.CENTER. The data structures are:

- PRIORITY.FREQUENCY, which is a "ragged table" as described in Sec. *2-08*
- SALES.FREQUENCY, which is RANDOM variable
- STRUCTURE, which is a set with OPERATIONS as members

Also, an initial local SALE for a standard product is scheduled for each product type. In scheduling these sales, the PRICE of each SALE is a random variable between 0 and the product type, e.g., a type 3 product can be sold for between $0 and $3, and the PRIORITY assigned to a sale is determined by a random draw from the PRIORITY. FREQUENCY table.

At the end of initialization, the numbers of the input devices for the LOCAL.SALES and EXPORT.SALES external event units are read. This allows devices to be changed between simulation runs. Finally, the ORIGIN.R routine is invoked to set the simulation calendar so that calendar dates can be used on the external event tapes.

If the last data field read is not the character string OK, the run terminates with an error message.

EVENTS AND ROUTINES OF THE SIMULATION MODEL

The event SALE is written to react properly to both internal and external event triggers. The event creates a job, determines its routing through the shop, and starts it in its processing sequence. If the sale is internal, a new order is scheduled for the same product some time in the future.

The EVENT statement defines SALE as an event routine with three input arguments. It also declares that when a SALE event notice is

items of information about each event type. The program could as
easily be written to take actions on the event types, such as turning
off the trace by setting BETWEEN.V=0 when TIME.V reaches a certain
value or a special kind of event occurs.

Routine NUMBER.IDLE is a left-handed routine that implements the
monitoring of the attribute NUMBER.IDLE. It has several unusual
features. One reason for defining NUMBER.IDLE as a left-hand monitored
variable is to enable the programmer to save values of the number of
machines idle over time for later processing, without putting the code
to do this in the simulation routines. If at some later date the
programmer wants to remove this feature from the program, he need only
remove the preamble card that states that NUMBER.IDLE is monitored
and the routine NUMBER.IDLE, and recompile the program. No changes
need be made to any other routines.

The program uses two SAVED local arrays to collect and write on
tape successive values of NUMBER.IDLE for each of the production centers. A global variable TAPE.FLAG is used to tell the routine when
initialization of the SAVED local variables is required; TAPE.FLAG
is set to zero at the start of every simulation experiment. The program puts successive files of arrays on tape. Each file contains
data for a different experiment. The routine demonstrates SAVED
variables, local arrays, a left-handed function, subscripted subscripts, and monitored variables.

The last routines deal with reports of system activity during
a simulation experiment. They print out the parameters of the experiment and the measurements made during the experiment. They illustrate
the report-generating facilities of SIMSCRIPT II as well as the
COMPUTE statement.

5-06 MISCELLANEOUS SIMULATION TOPICS

Event Tracing and Monitoring

Statistics obtained through TALLY and ACCUMULATE statements
reveal aggregate properties of a model, but say little about the way
it responds in particular situations. When checking out a model, it

is important that all aspects of system dynamics be verified; given
a situation, what events are generated to resolve it; given a system
state, what events are executed in passing from it to another state.

Unless output statements are incorporated into every event routine, it is impossible to trace system dynamics completely. BEFORE
and AFTER statements are useful but inadequate as a sole source of
tracing ability. What is wanted is an entry to the timing routine
that allows selected information to be output before each event is
executed.

The SUBPROGRAM system variable BETWEEN.V is provided for this
purpose. The timing routine contains the statements

          IF BETWEEN.V IS NOT ZERO, CALL BETWEEN.V
          REGARDLESS....

immediately before the statements that branch to the selected "next"
event routines. After a next event selection has been made, and
before the event routine is called, BETWEEN.V is examined to see if
tracing is to be done. At the start of every simulation the system
sets BETWEEN.V to zero; unless the programmer assigns a routine name
to it, events are executed one after another without interruption.

A global variable named EVENT.V makes selective tracing possible.
After the timing mechanism selects an event notice and sets TIME.V
to its TIME.A attribute, EVENT.V is set to a code number representing
the class of event that has been chosen. These codes are integers
from 1 to EVENTS.V; they are assigned in two ways: (1) events appearing in a PRIORITY statement are numbered 1,2,...,N in the order in
which they are listed, and (2) events not appearing in a PRIORITY
statement are numbered in the order in which they appear in a preamble.
If some events appear in a PRIORITY statement and some do not, numbering starts with those events in the PRIORITY statement and continues
with the remaining events. The code assigned to a particular event
is stored in the global variable I.*event*.

EVENT.V is most conveniently used in a computed GO TO statement,
directing control to statements that are relevant to the event type
just selected. The following example illustrates how a tracing routine
is written:

```
         PREAMBLE
         EVENT NOTICES.... INCLUDE ARRIVAL AND SALE
            EVERY END.OF.PROCESS HAS A TIME AND A WHO.COMPLETED
            EVERY SHIFT.CHANGE HAS A PERIOD.NUMBER
         PRIORITY ORDER IS SALE, SHIFT.CHANGE AND ARRIVAL
                      .
                      .
                      .
                  etc.
                      .
                      .
                      .
         END


             MAIN
             NOW INITIALIZE
             LET BETWEEN.V='TRACE'
             START SIMULATION
             STOP END
- - - - - - - - - - - - - - - - - - - - - - - - - - - - - - - - - - - -
             ROUTINE TO TRACE
             GO TO SALE, SHIFT.CHANGE, ARRIVAL OR END.OF.PROCESS
                 PER EVENT.V
    'SALE'  WRITE TIME.V AS "SALE OCCURRED AT ",D(10,4),/
             RETURN
 'SHIFT.CHANGE' WRITE TIME.V, PERIOD.NUMBER AS "SHIFT CHANGE OCCURRED",
                 "AT ",D(10,4)," FOR PERIOD ", I 4,/
             RETURN
 'ARRIVAL' WRITE TIME.V AS "ARRIVAL OCCURRED AT ",D(10,4),/
             RETURN
 'END.OF.PROCESS' WRITE TIME.V, TIME AND WHO.COMPLETED AS "END OF",
                     "PROCESS OCCURRED AT ",D(10,4),"JOB TOOK ",D(5,1),
                     "TIME UNITS AND WAS COMPLETED BY MAN NO. ",I 4,/
             RETURN
             END
```

The key items to notice about this program are:

- EVENT.V is an INTEGER variable that the timing routine sets to a code representing the type of event about to be executed.

- TIME.V is a REAL variable that is the simulated time the event about to be executed is to occur.

- A global variable having the same name as the event type selected contains the identification number of the selected event notice. This permits implied subscripts to be used in the trace routine.

A programmer can check for a particular event by using the I.*event* variables, as in:

```
ROUTINE TO TRACE
IF EVENT.V = I.ARRIVAL,
   WRITE TIME.V AS "ARRIVAL AT ",D(10,4),/
ELSE
RETURN END
```

BETWEEN.V can also be used to turn BEFORE and AFTER traces on
and off. Either programmed conditions or events can be used. The
following program illustrates this.

```
PREAMBLE
TEMPORARY ENTITIES...
   EVERY DOG BELONGS TO SOME KENNEL
PERMANENT ENTITIES...
   EVERY FARM OWNS A KENNEL
EVENT NOTICES...
   EVERY SALE HAS A PRICE AND A DOG.NUMBER
EXTERNAL EVENTS ARE SIGNAL AND END.OF.SIMULATION
DEFINE PROGRAM AS A SUBPROGRAM VARIABLE
BEFORE FILING IN KENNEL, CALL PROGRAM
END
```
- -
```
MAIN
LET PROGRAM = 'FILE.TRACE'
CALL INITIALIZATION
START SIMULATION
END
```
- -
```
EVENT SIGNAL
READ CODE IF CODE = 1, LET PROGRAM = 0   RETURN ELSE
IF BETWEEN.V = 0, LET BETWEEN.V = 'TRACE'
                   RETURN
ELSE LET BETWEEN.V = 0    RETURN
END
```
- -
```
ROUTINE TO TRACE
PRINT 1 LINE WITH EVENT.V AND TIME.V THUS
   EVENT TYPE ** EXECUTED AT TIME ****.**
RETURN
END
```
- -
```
ROUTINE FOR FILE.TRACE GIVEN ENTITY AND SUB
DEFINE ENTITY AND SUB AS INTEGER VARIABLES
WRITE SUB AS "DOG PUT IN KENNEL(",I 2,")",/
RETURN    END
```

The system provides another kind of trace facility through a
TRACE statement. When used, this statement displays the memory location the statement was executed from, and the locations of all higher-
level routine calls currently in effect. The TRACE statement thus

provides a dynamic map of the function and procedure calls that are in effect when it is executed. The output of TRACE looks like:

```
AT LOCATION ******
CALLED FROM ******
CALLED FROM ******
          .
          .
          .
CALLED FROM ******
```

The AT LOCATION line displays the memory location of the object program statement that called TRACE. The first CALLED FROM line displays the memory location of the object program statement that called the routine that called TRACE. And so on. If TRACE is executed in a main routine, no CALLED FROM lines appear.

A programmer can identify the source program statements that correspond to displayed memory locations from the memory map and assembly listings that are part of the normal SIMSCRIPT II compiler output. Since computer systems generate maps and listings in different formats, it is impossible to discuss how one does this here. The following program uses symbolic names rather than memory locations to illustrate TRACE; SIMSCRIPT II implementation manuals give more explicit information.

Example of the use of TRACE:

```
        PREAMBLE
        NORMALLY MODE IS REAL
        DEFINE COMPUTE AS A REAL FUNCTION
        END


        MAIN
        READ X, Y AND Z AS 3 D(10,3) USING UNIT 6
 π₁     CALL CALCULATE GIVING X, Y AND Z YIELDING Q
        LIST X, Y, Z AND Q
        STOP    END
- - - - - - - - - - - - - - - - - - - - - - - - - - - -
        ROUTINE TO CALCULATE GIVEN A, B, AND C YIELDING D
        IF A > B+C, LET D=A RETURN ELSE
        IF A > B, LET D=A-B RETURN ELSE
        IF A > C, LET D=A-C RETURN ELSE
 π₂     LET D=COMPUTE(A, B, C)
        RETURN    END
- - - - - - - - - - - - - - - - - - - - - - - - - - - -
```

```
          ROUTINE TO COMPUTE(E, F, G)
          IF G IS NEGATIVE,
    π₃        TRACE
              WRITE E, F, G AS /, B 10, "AN ERROR WAS FOUND, THE",
                "DATA IS", 3 D(5,1).
              STOP
          ELSE RETURN WITH SQRT.F(E**2+F**2+G**2)
          END
```
- -

Given as data the numbers -10, 10, and -5, this program produces
the display

```
          AT LOCATION π₃
          CALLED FROM π₂
          CALLED FROM π₁
          AN ERROR WAS FOUND, THE DATA IS -10.0  10.0  -5.0
```

By tracing through the memory locations, a programmer can see
that the error was found at π_3 — in routine COMPUTE, called from π_2 —
in routine CALCULATE, called from π_1 — in the main routine. Each of
the π_i can be traced to a source program statement. The flow of the
program can be reconstructed and the source of the error exposed.
The reader should go through the examples in previous sections and
attempt to use TRACE wherever he feels it is applicable.

TRACE is also used by the SIMSCRIPT II system when a system error
is found, such as an attempt to read a decimal number into an INTEGER
variable. The information produced by the trace display enables a
programmer to locate errors in his source program, although both he
and the system may have gone through several levels of calls before
the error was found and flagged.

TRACE uses the current output unit. If a program finds an error
while a tape, disk, or drum is current, a printer should be specified
before TRACE is called. Assume that unit 3 is the standard output
unit, a printer. A safe statement for using TRACE is:

TRACE USING 3

When the system calls TRACE, it automatically sets the standard output device as the current output unit and restores the unit that was
current when the trace is completed.

Synchronous Variables

Certain simulations can suffer from what is called "parallel interaction," two events happening at the same time that affect one another. A simple example of this can be seen in the situation where two events examine and possibly modify the same variable. Since the events are executed serially, though with the same TIME.V, the event that occurs first can modify the variable so that the value seen by the second event is not the one it should be seeing. The problem is one of synchronization, of getting variables to change value, not necessarily when assignments are made, but when simulated time increases.

In programs where it is necessary to account for parallel interactions, it is possible to do so by using a left-hand monitored array and the BETWEEN.V mechanism. The following example illustrates how "synchronous variables" can be defined and used:

```
PREAMBLE
THE SYSTEM OWNS A SYNCH.SET AND HAS AN (X,Y) IN ARRAY 1
TEMPORARY ENTITIES...
   EVERY MEMO HAS A VALUE AND A SUB AND BELONGS
      TO THE SYNCH.SET
DEFINE SUB AS AN INTEGER VARIABLE
DEFINE X AS A REAL, 1-DIMENSIONAL ARRAY MONITORED
   ON THE LEFT
DEFINE Y AS A REAL, 1-DIMENSIONAL ARRAY
END
- - - - - - - - - - - - - - - - - - - - - - - - - - - - - - - - -
MAIN
LET BETWEEN.V='SYNCH'
START SIMULATION
STOP    END
- - - - - - - - - - - - - - - - - - - - - - - - - - - - - - - - -
ROUTINE SYNCH
DEFINE T AS A REAL, SAVED VARIABLE
IF T = TIME.V, RETURN
OTHERWISE
LET T = TIME.V
FOR EACH MEMO IN SYNCH.SET, DO
   REMOVE MEMO FROM SYNCH.SET
   LET Y(SUB) = VALUE
   DESTROY MEMO
LOOP
RETURN    END
- - - - - - - - - - - - - - - - - - - - - - - - - - - - - - - - -
```

```
LEFT ROUTINE X(J)
DEFINE J AS AN INTEGER VARIABLE
ENTER WITH A
CREATE A MEMO
FILE MEMO IN SYNCH.SET
  LET SUB=J
  LET VALUE=A
RETURN    END
```

In a program containing these definitions and routines, the value of an element of X is changed only when simulated time advances. A statement such as LET X(5) = X(5) + 1 within an event does not change the value of X(5) until simulated time advances.

The routine for X can be used as a prototype for all synchronous variables. Only the number of subscripts and mode need be changed for other situations. The SYNCH routine can be used as is, or incorporated into a more extensive "BETWEEN.V" routine.

Activity Scanning

Event scheduling is one of several methods of controlling system dynamics. Other computer simulation languages, such as GSP, CSL, and SIMULA, are based on *activity scanning* and *process control*.

The concept of activity scanning is easily incorporated in a SIMSCRIPT II simulation through the BETWEEN.V mechanism. The following program shows how this can be done. Since implementation is up to the programmer, any degree of sophistication required is available. It is possible to program a simulation using pure event sequencing, pure activity scanning, or a mixture of both.

Consider a shop in which a man and a machine must work together to produce some products, the man can work alone to produce others, and the machine can work alone to produce others. The basic element of interest is the multiresource nature of the problem and how it is handled by activity scanning. To emphasize this aspect, all other facets of the problem are simplified.

```
        PREAMBLE
        PERMANENT ENTITIES....
            EVERY MACHINE HAS A STATUS, A CLOCK AND A PROCESSING.TIME
            EVERY MAN HAS A CONDITION, A WATCH AND A WORK.TIME
        THE SYSTEM OWNS A QUEUE
        EVENT NOTICES INCLUDE STATE.CHANGE
            EVERY SALE HAS A CODE AND MAY BELONG TO THE QUEUE
        DEFINE CODE, STATUS AND CONDITION, AS INTEGER VARIABLES
        PRIORITY ORDER IS STATE.CHANGE AND SALE
        END
- - - - - - - - - - - - - - - - - - - - - - - - - - - - - - - - - -
        MAIN
        READ N.MACHINE AND N.MAN
        CREATE EVERY MACHINE AND MAN ''INITIAL CONDITIONS ALL ZERO
        SCHEDULE A SALE AT 0.0
        LET CODE = UNIFORM.F(1.0,3.0,1)
        LET BETWEEN.V='ACTIVITY.SCAN'
        START SIMULATION
        STOP    END
- - - - - - - - - - - - - - - - - - - - - - - - - - - - - - - - - -
        EVENT SALE GIVEN CODE SAVING THE EVENT NOTICE
        DEFINE CODE AS AN INTEGER VARIABLE
        FILE THIS SALE IN THE QUEUE
        SCHEDULE A SALE AT TIME.V+0.5
        LET CODE = UNIFORM.F(0.0,3.0,1)
        RETURN    END
- - - - - - - - - - - - - - - - - - - - - - - - - - - - - - - - - -
        EVENT STATE.CHANGE
        RETURN    END
- - - - - - - - - - - - - - - - - - - - - - - - - - - - - - - - - -
        ROUTINE FOR ACTIVITY.SCAN
        DEFINE MAN.CODE, MACHINE.CODE AND BOTH.CODE AS INTEGER VARIABLES
        FOR EACH MAN, WITH WATCH=TIME.V, DO LET CONDITION=0
                                            LET WATCH=RINF.C
                                    LOOP
        FOR EACH MACHINE, WITH CLOCK=TIME.V, DO LET STATUS=0
                                            LET CLOCK=RINF.C
                                    LOOP
        UNTIL QUEUE IS EMPTY OR (MAN.CODE=1 AND MACHINE.CODE=1 AND
          BOTH.CODE=1), DO
         REMOVE THE FIRST SALE FROM THE QUEUE
        GO TO MAN OR MACHINE OR BOTH PER CODE
'MAN'       FOR EACH MAN WITH CONDITION=0, FIND THE FIRST CASE
        IF NONE
'FAILURE'     LET MAN.CODE=1  FILE THE SALE IN THE QUEUE  GO TO LOOP
        ELSE LET CONDITION=1 LET WATCH=TIME.V+WORK.TIME
'DONE'      DESTROY THE SALE     GO TO LOOP
'MACHINE'   FOR EACH MACHINE WITH STATUS=0, FIND THE FIRST CASE
        IF NONE,
          LET MACHINE.CODE=1  GO TO FAILURE
        ELSE LET STATUS=1 LET CLOCK=TIME.V+PROCESSING.TIME
                                GO TO DONE
```

```
'BOTH'       FOR EACH MAN WITH CONDITION=0, FIND THE FIRST CASE
             IF NONE,
               GO AHEAD
             ELSE FOR EACH MACHINE WITH STATUS=0, FIND THE FIRST CASE
             IF NONE,
'AHEAD'        LET BOTH.CODE=1  GO TO FAILURE
             ELSE LET CONDITION=1 LET STATUS=1
             LET T=MAX.F(PROCESSING.TIME, WORK.TIME)
             LET CLOCK=T LET WATCH=T GO TO DONE
'LOOP'       LOOP
             FOR EACH MAN, COMPUTE T AS THE MINIMUM OF WATCH
             FOR EACH MACHINE, COMPUTE S AS THE MINIMUM OF CLOCK
             SCHEDULE A STATE.CHANGE AT MIN.F(T,S)
             RETURN
             END
```

The reader will notice that this program has no output statements and no data collection statements and is unrealistic in other ways. One exercise a reader might undertake is conversion of the program to a complete and meaningful simulation model.

In addition to its incompleteness, the program makes no attempts at execute-time efficiency. A second exercise is alteration of the program, perhaps adding events or other mechanisms, to make it execute more efficiently.

5-07 RECAP

Many of the statements in Levels 1 through 5 are definitional. Of the 65 different statements in these levels, 20 are definitional; 14 can only be used in the preamble. This section recaps these statements and restates the most important rules about their use.

Table 5-11 lists the statements that can appear in a preamble and states their rules of precedence.

Table 5-11

PREAMBLE STATEMENTS

Statement Type	Statement	Rules
1a	NORMALLY	Can appear anywhere in preamble.
1b	DEFINE TO MEAN	
1c	SUBSTITUTE	
1d	SUPPRESS SUBST.	
1e	RESUME SUBST.	
1f	LAST COLUMN	
2a	TEMPORARY ENTITIES	A preamble may contain many Type 2a, 2b, and 2c statements. Each may be followed by a group of Type 3a, 4, and 5 statements.
2b	PERMANENT ENTITIES	
2c	EVENT NOTICES	
3a	EVERY	Many can follow a Type 2 statement. An entity or event notice name can appear in more than one EVERY statement.
3b	THE SYSTEM	
4	DEFINE *variable*	No precedence relation if it defines a global variable. Must follow all Type 3a statements if it defines an attribute named in them. A variable, attribute, or function name can only appear in one DEFINE statement.
5	DEFINE *set*	Must follow Type 4 statements in a Type 2 statement group.

No Type 6-9 statements can precede any Type 2-3 statements.

6a	BREAK TIES	One statement allowed for each event notice.
6b	EXTERNAL EVENTS	
6c	EXTERNAL UNITS	
7	PRIORITY	Must follow all Type 2c and Type 6b statements.
8a	BEFORE	Allowed for each temporary entity, set and event notice.
8b	AFTER	
9a	TALLY	One statement allowed for each global variable or attribute.
9b	ACCUMULATE	

Of these statements, only Types 1 and 4 can be used in routines to declare local background conditions, variables, and substitutions.

Appendix

SIMSCRIPT II SYSTEM NAMES

ATTRIBUTES:

EUNIT.A	PROB.A
F.EV.S	P.EV.S
IVALUE.A	RVALUE.A
LENGTH.A	S.EV.S
M.EV.S	TIME.A

CONSTANTS:

EXP.C	RADIAN.C
INF.C	RINF.C
PI.C	

ENTITIES:

RANDOM.E

FUNCTIONS:

ABS.F	FRAC.F	POISSON.F
ARCCOS.F	GAMMA.F	RANDI.F
ARCSIN.F	HOUR.F	RANDOM.F
ARCTAN.F	INT.F	REAL.F
ATOT.F	ISTEP.F	RSTEP.F
BETA.F	ITOA.F	SFIELD.F
BINOMIAL.F	LIN.F	SIGN.F
CONCAT.F	LOG.E.F	SIN.F
COS.F	LOG.NORMAL.F	SQRT.F
DATE.F	LOG.10.F	TAN.F
DAY.F	MAX.F	TRUNC.F
DIM.F	MIN.F	TTOA.F
DIV.F	MINUTE.F	UNIFORM.F
EFIELD.F	MOD.F	WEEKDAY.F
ERLANG.F	MONTH.F	WEIBULL.F
EXP.F	NORMAL.F	YEAR.F
EXPONENTIAL.F	OUT.F	

ROUTINES:

ORIGIN.R	TIME.R

SETS:

EV.S

VARIABLES:

BETWEEN.V	LINE.V	READ.V
BUFFER.V	LINES.V	SEED.V
EOF.V	MARK.V	TIME.V
EVENT.V	MINUTES.V	WCOLUMN.V
EVENTS.V	PAGE.V	WRITE.V
HOURS.V	RCOLUMN.V	

INDEX

NOTE: The letter 'n' following a page
reference indicates a footnote.

The letter 't' following a page reference indicates tabular material.

Imbedded periods have been ignored for
alphabetizing purposes.

SELECTED RAND BOOKS

McKinsey, J. C. C. *Introduction to the Theory of Games*. McGraw-Hill
Book Company, Inc., New York. November 1952.

Williams, J. D. *The Compleat Strategyst: Being a Primer on the Theory
of Games of Strategy*. McGraw-Hill Book Company, Inc., New York.
June 1954.

The RAND Corporation. *A Million Random Digits With 100,000 Normal
Deviates*. The Free Press, Glencoe, Illinois. March 1955.

Hastings, Cecil, Jr. *Approximations for Digital Computers*.
Princeton University Press, Princeton, New Jersey. June 1955.

Bellman, Richard. *Dynamic Programming*. Princeton University Press,
Princeton, New Jersey. November 1957.

Dorfman, Robert, Paul A. Samuelson, and Robert M. Solow. *Linear
Programming and Economic Analysis*. McGraw-Hill Book Company,
Inc., New York. February 1958.

Arrow, Kenneth J. and Marvin Hoffenberg. *A Time Series Analysis of
Interindustry Demands*. North-Holland Publishing Company,
Amsterdam, Holland. July 1959.

Baker, C. L. and F. J. Gruenberger. *The First Six Million Prime
Numbers*. The Microcard Foundation, Madison, Wisconsin.
July 1959.

Buchheim, Robert W. and the Staff of The RAND Corporation. *Space
Handbook: Astronautics and its Applications*. Random House,
Inc., New York. August 1959.

Bellman, Richard. *Introduction to Matrix Analysis*. McGraw-Hill
Book Company, Inc., New York. January 1960

Gale, David. *The Theory of Linear Economic Models*. McGraw-Hill
Book Company, Inc., New York. June 1960.

Bellman, R. E. *Adaptive Control Processes: A Guided Tour*.
Princeton University Press, Princeton, New Jersey. January
1961.

Dresher, Melvin. *Games of Strategy: Theory and Applications*.
Prentice-Hall Inc., Englewood Cliffs, New Jersey. June 1961.

Newell, Allen (ed.). *Information Processing Language-V Manual*.
Prentice-Hall, Inc., Englewood Cliffs, New Jersey.
October 1961.